THE BRUTAL DYNA[...] [...]
MARRIAGE—AND A MURDER . . .
"COMPELLING!"   —*New York* magazine

Diane Pikul's worst nightmare was that Joe
would kill her and get away with it. And
then he would get the children. Joseph Pikul
was a wealthy Wall Street star who liked to
come across as a loving, doting father. But
he was also a closet homosexual, a cross-
dresser, a drug abuser, and a physically violent man who carried the AIDS virus.

Why would an attractive, well-educated
woman like Diane marry such a threatening man, and bear him children? This rivet-
ing true-crime story draws on hundreds of
interviews and exclusive access to Diane's
private papers to probe the strange chem-
istry that bonded them and made the nightmare come true.

MARRYING
THE HANGMAN

"A uniquely urban tragedy, told
brilliantly. . . . The portrait is so finely
drawn that one can almost hear Diane as
she relates to friends the indignities she
has suffered from her spouse. . . . DON'T
MISS THIS ONE!"   —*Publishers Weekly*

"Macabre . . . compelling."   —*Glamour*

MARRYING
THE HANGMAN

Sheila Weller

AN ONYX BOOK

For John and Jonathan

ONYX
Published by the Penguin Group
Penguin Books USA Inc., 375 Hudson Street,
New York, New York 10014, U.S.A.
Penguin Books Ltd, 27 Wrights Lane,
London W8 5TZ, England
Penguin Books Australia Ltd, Ringwood,
Victoria, Australia
Penguin Books Canada Ltd, 10 Alcorn Avenue,
Toronto, Ontario, Canada M4V 3B2
Penguin Books (N.Z.) Ltd, 182–190 Wairau Road,
Auckland 10, New Zealand

Penguin Books Ltd, Registered Offices:
Harmondsworth, Middlesex, England

Published by Onyx, an imprint of New American Library,
a division of Penguin Books USA Inc. This is an authorized reprint of a
hardcover edition published by Random House, Inc.

First Onyx Printing, June, 1993
10 9 8 7 6 5 4 3 2 1

A portion of this work was originally published in *Cosmopolitan*.

Grateful acknowledgment is made to Houghton Mifflin Company, Oxford University Press Canada, and Phoebe Larmore for permission to reprint seven lines from "Marrying the Hangman," from: in the United States, *Two-Headed Poems: Poems Selected and New 1976–1986* by Margaret Atwood, as published by Houghton Mifflin Company. Copyright © 1987 by Margaret Atwood; and, in Canada, from *Selected Poems 1966–1984,* as published by Oxford University Press Canada. Copyright © 1990 by Margaret Atwood. Rights throughout the rest of the world, excluding the United States and Canada, are controlled by the author's agent, Phoebe Larmore. Reprinted by permission.

My friends, who are . . . women, tell me their stories, which cannot be believed and which are true. They are horror stories and they have not happened to me, they have not yet happened to me. . . .

Such things cannot happen to us, it is afternoon and these things do not happen in the afternoon.

—Margaret Atwood,
"Marrying the Hangman"

Prologue

On Friday, October 23, 1987, at ten P.M., Diane Whitmore Pikul drove her Buick station wagon out of the Travelers Garage onto Tenth Street near Seventh Avenue in Greenwich Village. She turned left onto Sixth Avenue and drove past a small nineteenth century building that housed the duplex apartment she shared with her husband, Joseph, a successful Wall Street stock analyst, and their two young children, Claudia and Blake. Diane may have glanced up at the apartment's six windows overlooking the street, making sure they were shuttered and curtained for the weekend. She'd been the last to leave the apartment. Joe and the children were probably at the family's Amagansett house by now, having left in the Mazda three hours before. Her fraught ambivalence about making the trip this particular weekend had unsettled her. She'd become strangely absentminded—even at her job at *Harper's* magazine, where she was assistant to the publisher.

But if Diane felt out of control, she did not look it. Her plaid Ralph Lauren shirt, dark dirndl skirt and black tights constituted the classic off-to-the-country outfit for a woman of means. Like many Manhattan families of privilege, the Pikuls spent the summer on the east end of Long Island, and as many weekends in the fall and spring as weather permitted. There, amid the potato fields, sand dunes and brushy woods, they gave their lives over to a wholesome simplicity. After a week of work, social engagements, restaurant meals, extracurricular classes for the children (each of whom attended a different private school) and, as often as not, Joseph Pikul's arrival from Scandinavia, where he did business, they needed the rest.

Joseph Pikul was settling himself and his two children into the one-story house at Windmill Lane as Diane pushed through traffic. He carried a sleeping Blake, four, into the children's bedroom, while Claudia, eight, watched a video in the baby-sitter's room. Soon after, she, too, fell asleep, and her father put her to bed across from her sleeping brother.

Most likely, Joe—in chinos, polo shirt and crewneck sweater—then sat in the kitchen, eating the cheesecake he had bought at the country store. He often ate compulsively when he was agitated.

Next, he called the Travelers Garage to find out exactly what time his wife had left with the station wagon.

Then Joseph Pikul waited.

Hampered by traffic on the Long Island Expressway and the Montauk Highway, Diane did not get to Windmill Lane until somewhere between 1:15 and 1:30 A.M. She parked in the gravel area fronting the house and, at that hour, must have heard crickets in the woods across the lane and the wind rippling through the trees of the adjacent cemetery.

Joe may have been waiting near the front windows, close enough to have heard her slam the car door. Or he may have been pacing amid the antique and wicker furniture in the peach, lime and cream-colored living room. We will never know exactly where he was when his wife walked in the door, but we do know what came after, and with it this scene of an upscale Manhattan family winding down for a weekend at their country home would go wildly awry.

Did the Pikuls begin to argue because Diane was "late"? The arguing would have been heated and bitter, if it were consistent with previous fights. But if screaming and name-calling occurred, the next-door neighbors did not hear it. And the children either miraculously slept through the din . . . or else what they heard, in deep terror, they suppressed, and have never divulged to anyone.

There is another possibility, which no small amount of evidence suggests: Perhaps there was no arguing at all, and Diane Pikul was ambushed by her husband.

Either with his hand or with a blunt object, Joe Pikul began beating his wife about the head sometime after she walked through the door. He was six feet and husky, she was five three and rail-thin. Trying to ward off his blows, Diane knocked out one of her husband's teeth. But that was the extent of her defense.

The ten or more blows Joe struck to her head would have by themselves killed Diane, but death came more quickly when Joe grasped Diane's neck and began squeezing. In a futile attempt to dislodge his stranglehold, she tried to jam her fingers between her neck and his grip. He squeezed all the harder; deep fingernail scratches in her own skin were all that she got from that effort.

Finally, he took a pink plastic cord and wound it around her neck.

In short order, he would expunge the house of any sign of struggle and, after a brief trip to the beach where he would attempt to bury his wife's body in the sand, he would roll her up in plastic sheets and tarpaulins, tying her neck, wrists and ankles with an array of cords, so that she was packed in the manner of a large army duffel. Soon he would dispose of her body in a way that—he hoped and believed—no one would find it.

We know from her many friends and from the autobiographical writing she left that Diane Pikul had lived her life relishing every new freedom and right won by women over the last three decades. She also suffered from the risks inherent in those freedoms, and those inherent in a character that made seeking danger seem enticing—even perhaps imperative. She had spent most of her twenties and early thirties as an alcoholic, fighting the demons of deep insecurity, low self-esteem and nihilism. Yet, in her new sobriety, she entered a relationship—with Joseph Pikul, another recovered alcoholic—that, for all its apparent hopefulness and privilege, quietly raised the stakes of this battle and moved it from the realm of the bottle to the far more insidious realm of their marriage.

Yet she never thought the risks she took would become

life-threatening, and in this sense, as in so many others, she was typical of her generation of well-brought-up, well-educated American women. Assuming that her firmly middle-class upbringing had granted her a kind of return trip ticket from any emotional or actual brink to which she might wander, Diane Pikul believed that she, and if not she then certainly her children, would always be protected.

She was wrong about this. And the depth of her error, more manifest even in death than in life, is why her story is important.

Diane's body, lifeless and twisted on the sisal-matted floor of the family's weekend retreat, clearly proclaimed how vulnerable she'd actually been. But, as an assault on our assumptions of guaranteed safety and justice, her murder was just the beginning. Further moral shocks would come from the victories Joseph Pikul won afterward. Despite his confession to and indictment for his wife's murder; despite evidence of the brutality of the act, his lack of remorse and his extensive efforts to elude authorities; despite documentation of his unwholesomeness as a parent, his violence and instability, Joseph Pikul received sole custody of his children. Given what we now know of his motivation for killing Diane, he had, to no small extent, tendered a virtual custody bid via homicide—and his action was legally validated.

Joseph Pikul held on to that custody until eight months after he was indicted for the murder of his wife. That the judge who let him keep custody of those children was a woman Diane's age and an active feminist was a particularly pungent irony. Next came Joe's trial for the murder of Diane. As Pikul's lawyers launched their powerful defense in front of a jury of eleven men and one lone woman who had been kept by the judge's pretrial rulings from knowing the defendant's most incriminating actions and statements, it appeared Pikul was headed for a final triumph, and Diane, for another, symbolic, slaying. But the speed and substance of the verdict would prove that appearances aren't everything.

This book is about several things. It is about an American woman's yearnings for bad-girl glamour and emotional risk, and how her fantasies made real were also made fatal. It is about the dark bargains that lived beneath the surface of a seemingly enviable marriage, slowly destroying every good thing the couple fought hard to become and to acquire. It is about how our legal system can put the rights of a murder defendant above the concern for a child's safety and welfare, and how the civil libertarian stand can actually advance this priority. It is also about how justice *does* sometimes triumph in the end: dramatically, unanimously—and briefly.

It is about a woman who tried to re-create herself according to her fantasies and who believed she was indestructible. Whose fate revealed the dangers hidden in her dreams and in whose misplaced faith is found a harrowing lesson in the vulnerability of all women.

PART I

"TOO MANY BABY-SITTERS"

Chapter 1

"Here's my worst nightmare: Joe will kill me. And then he'll get away with it. And then he'll get the children."

Diane Pikul to Maggie Gari, summer 1987

Monday, October 19, 1987

At 9:15 A.M. Diane Whitmore Pikul reached the offices of *Harper's* magazine, where she worked as an assistant to the young publisher, John "Rick" MacArthur. A thin, quick woman who seemed younger than her forty-four years, Diane wore her usual attire: a blousy, smocklike designer dress, big beads, small earrings, a knotted shawl, clunky "little girl" shoes, with both a purse and a canvas tote bag slung over her shoulder. Loose, light brown curls bounced around her fine-featured face, which was partially obscured by oversize sunglasses.

Diane's "look" conveyed a bustling manner and sense of bravado. She gave the impression of being a shrewd, well-exercised woman with perhaps an endearing hint of piquance; a woman who had probably, not long ago, been almost beautiful and who still put great store by her appearance. Her way of dressing was just witty and individual enough not to seem trendy, but a little too worked-at to seem self-assured. She could still turn men's heads, and her female peers frequently called her "great-looking."

But the turmoil in her life entirely betrayed her successfully cultivated image.

Diane was in the process of seeking a divorce from her

husband of ten years, successful Wall Street stock analyst Joseph Pikul. Since he balked at the divorce proceedings, he still lived in their Greenwich Village house, though when he was there he sequestered himself in an attic room above the family's duplex living quarters. He was now in the process of moving his clothes and effects into a second apartment he'd long kept, purportedly for business, on Rector Street near the World Trade Center. A high-strung, unstable man given to genuine, if sporadic, violence, Joe had, early in their marriage, pushed Diane out of a moving car, smashed a full set of dishes on the floor and, just last year, punctured her car tires to keep her from leaving the house.

Lately Joe had been acting more erratic than usual. On a recent business trip to Zurich, he had called Diane from his hotel room six times in the course of one hour, his tone zigzagging from abusive to conciliatory to flauntingly suicidal. Diane believed he was on drugs. She suspected for years that he had a shadowy secret life that included sporadic homosexual alliances. Another part of this life, she had learned fifteen months ago, was his covert habit of dressing up in women's clothes. She also feared that Joe had AIDS. Suddenly, all those veiled idiosyncracies of her husband's, which in the past she had alternately scorned and denied, were seen by her for what they were: signs of a turbulent mind that no amount of therapy could heal, which posed a terrible danger to her children. In the past year, with the help of a therapist, Dr. Shoshona Comet*, Diane had struggled to achieve clarity and control over the inchoate fears and longings that had clouded her judgment and sustained her bad marriage.

But with that clarity and control came risk, the true depth of which only Diane could measure. Joe had always threatened Diane, but over the past two years those threats had accelerated. Now he frequently said: "If you leave me, Diane, I will have you killed. And then I'll have your body dumped where no one will ever find it." In the past, Diane acted as if Joe's threats were a crude bluff. She scoffed at them, her bravado part of their intri-

---

*Citing the sanctity of doctor/patient confidentiality, Dr. Comet refused to be interviewed.

cate dynamic. At heart, however, she believed him and was terrified. Over the years, friends had offered to help her escape or to take her in. She had even made plans to flee with the children. But she never partook of any of these options, immobilized by the fear that Joe would track her down and kill her.

Yet, despite her terror, Diane spoke freely of Joe's threats and bizarre habits to her wide circle of women friends and colleagues. Often she spoke in panic, but other times with a deadpan understatement or a jaunty ruefulness, as if, as her old friend Eleanor Keenan Lamperti once remarked, "Joe's odd behavior, their fights, and the general sense of perversity in her marriage was something she was almost proud of." If, after years of therapy, she had begun to find the wherewithal to leave Joe, nonetheless a part of her still craved this danger; it represented a triumph over her mordantly wholesome Midwestern childhood and constituted the last sinful fillip in a lifestyle made laudably virtuous. She and her best friend, actress and lyricist Maggie Gari, both recovering alcoholics, often ordered rich desserts when they met at restaurants. "If we couldn't have liquor," Maggie explains, "at least we could have chocolate." Perhaps the frisson afforded by her tensions with Joe was, for Diane, a similar substitute.

Diane had been financially dependent on Joe for ten years, ever since the birth of their first child, Claudia, who was now eight and a half. Their son, Blake, was almost five. Joe had not wanted Diane to work, and for a long time she hadn't minded this. After being a hardworking single woman for years, she loved her role as a rich man's wife: decorating both the duplex at Sixth Avenue and Tenth Street and their weekend house in Amagansett; taking the children to ballet, gymnastics and music lessons; going to exercise class, appointments, lunch dates with girlfriends.

Still, living with her husband had become untenable, and these luxuries were no longer worth the danger Joe's escalating instability posed to the children. For a year and a half, she'd labored to gain enough financial independence and vocational potential to be able to leave Joe. She had been working at *Harper's* since April, and her job, despite its meager salary of $22,500, was a key part of her game plan. Her new avocation as a fiction writer, after two decades of procrastination, formed a secondary part. Although Manhattan brimmed with English majors from Seven Sisters colleges who were now preempting midlife crises by taking NYU and New School writing courses, Diane (Mt. Holyoke '65) had surprised even her skeptical friends: the half-dozen autobiographical short stories she'd written over the last year in those very classes had gained her entrance into a select workshop called the Writers Community. Three weeks ago, the director, Allan Gurganus, called to say he had chosen her as one of twelve out of a field of two hundred applicants to join the group.

Gurganus, on his own way to becoming a major literary figure, found Diane's work "original and full of enormous potential." She was, he felt, "just beginning to scrape away the 'writing' and trust her natural voice." Her friends had never seen her so gratified, and not merely by the validation of her talent. After years of seeing herself as a thin-skinned poseur, she had completed her stories, had exposed them to criticism and was starting to trust her own character. She was, as she'd written in one of them, "harvesting lilacs out of the dead land her marriage had become . . . starting all over again at 44." The risk involved in extricating herself from Joe, however, darkened the flowery metaphor.

Raoul Felder, considered the toughest divorce lawyer in New York, represented Diane. She had given him highly embarrassing pictures and videotapes of Joe crossdressing, which she had found in Joe's private room in the duplex's attic. She and Felder had resolved that this evidence would only be offered to a court if it was absolutely necessary in order to keep Joe from getting joint custody of the children. Felder did not like the idea that Joe still lived at home; just a week ago—after hearing that Joe had blindfolded the children to keep them from learning (and thus being able to reveal to Diane) the address of the Rector Street apartment, to which they were driving—he had urged Diane to let him get a court order restraining Joe from contact with her and the children. Diane reacted in a way Felder had come to see as characteristic: She refused, out of fear of Joe's anger and retaliation. "Restraining orders," Felder would later admit, "only work against rational men, who can be deterred by the prospect of going to jail. No one would ever call Joe Pikul 'rational.' " Still, Felder was duty-bound to offer all available legal protection. Diane, however, knew such an order would more likely inflame than restrain her husband.

Joseph Pikul knew that Felder had the cross-dressing tape and pictures. He called this standard possession of divorce artillery "blackmail" and, during those intervals when he conceded that Diane's plans for divorce were irreversible (other times, he professed to hope that counseling would save the marriage), he threatened to retaliate by hiding his assets from Diane and cutting her and the children off without a penny. He'd even had a tap put on the home phone in early summer in order to eavesdrop on Diane's plans and to find out if she had a lover. (She did not.)

Now the worst had happened: Joe said he planned to sue for full custody of the children. His reason, he said, was that Diane was not the traditional stay-at-home mother he wanted for them. She "hired too many baby-sitters," was how he put it to his lawyer and his confidantes. Apart from the full-time sitter who covered for her hours at *Harper's,* Diane hired additional night sitters when necessary. ("What baby-sitters I do use," she had countered in a memo to her lawyer, "are not for the purpose of carousing, rarely even for socializing, and never to a place where I cannot be reached. I regularly have baby-sitters so I can go to my therapist . . . and to my writing workshop.") Diane adored her son and daughter. Although they had the same blue-eyed, white-blond-haired beauty, they were very different children. Claudia was theatrical, talkative, self-confident; Blake was physically energetic but not talkative. Neither Claudia nor Blake would be served by extensive time alone with their troubled father. If Joe did not drop his plans to sue for custody, Diane would have no choice but to use the cross-dressing evidence against him.

This past weekend was the fifth since Labor Day that Joe had spirited the children off. Sometimes he took them to the Amagansett house; other times—this past weekend was one—he had them at the Rector Street apartment. Usually she did not know where they were or when Joe was bringing them home. Legally helpless to prevent him from taking his own children, Diane termed Joe's erratic arrivals and departures, in a memo to Felder, "excessively cruel behavior toward me and a bad environment for the children's well-being, to say the least." This particular weekend, Joe had promised to have the children back to her on Saturday at one P.M.; he did not bring them home until Sunday. Not knowing his apartment's address or phone number, Diane had spent the weekend waiting and worrying.

Sometimes, on such weekends, Joe would call and argue with her in the middle of the children's stay. Once, alarmed that they had not arrived in Amagansett as planned, Diane had called every police department and highway patrol on the route from New York to see if there had been any fatal accidents. A few weeks ago, Joe had hired a baby-sitter to help him with the children; the woman later told her agency supervisor—who then informed Diane—that his screaming had "terrified" her.

Fear of inciting Joe's violence and a reluctance to lose her financial cushion before she was ready had long caused Diane to approach divorce in a hesitant and scattershot manner, but now that she had resolved to act, she had to decide whether to endure a long and ugly custody fight or just take the children and go into hiding: forfeiting claims to Joe's income, leaving possessions behind her. Throughout the summer she'd suffered a terrible premonition, which she'd shared with Maggie Gari: "Joe will kill me. And then they'll let him out. And then he'll get the children." Maggie says, "With that thought always in the back of her mind, how could any course of action seem like the right one?"

Just how an intelligent, well-educated, attractive, resourceful woman like Diane Pikul had landed in this nightmare was a question begging a complicated answer. The explanation is as long as her life, the life of a typical American girl who was raised in the fifties and who came of age in 1965, two years before the mass bohemianism of the late sixties began. Diane's life choices reflected the vanguard posturings of a swing generation of adven-

turous women, presumably the first to be allowed to in-
definitely postpone "safe," traditional life in order to live
out their fantasies—but still unprepared to protect themselves from the dangers that hid in those freedoms. Many
of these women found, as the decades progressed, that
license and brio do not equal immunity from dependence
on a man, real or feared poverty, poor self-esteem or,
finally, from physical danger.

Over the last few days, like a desperate patient who
simultaneously tries contradictory treatments, Diane found
herself doing two things at once. On the one hand, she
stood her ground, fighting for a decent settlement from
Joe and for full custody of the children. She had spent
Saturday in her office, writing a five-page memo to
Felder, which ended with the plea: "Please help me resolve this horrible situation as soon as possible. It is now
time, I fear, for the World War III you promised we
would have if necessary." At the same time, she had
resolved to take the children and go into hiding. She
would find the right house at the right price, right away—
she would finally summon the courage.

After dropping Claudia and Blake off at their schools,
she stepped onto the eleventh floor of 666 Broadway and
walked, as usual, through *Harper's* reception area. With
its scuffed black walls, black metal desk and
two orange-cushioned metal chairs, the waiting area had
an arty severity that harkened to fifties intellectualism;
Diane joked to friends that when she first came upon the
room, she half-expected to find David Susskind and Mort
Sahl sitting there, talking about the A-bomb. In fact,
however, Diane felt ennobled by the intellectual intensity
of *Harper's;* and, though her job was noneditorial and
mundane, she was proud to be working at the nation's
oldest literary magazine. It was as if the very atmosphere
of the periodical that had once published Hawthorne,
Melville and Mencken, and in whose pages were now
found the latest works of Mario Vargas Llosa, William
Gass, Tom Wolfe and Annie Dillard, could return her to
some long-lost seriousness of purpose. But her seriousness
this morning was of a different sort. Karen Hoffman, the
young Texas native who was the magazine's receptionist, noticed Diane looked tense and preoccupied.

"Has Linda come in yet?" were Diane's first words, referring to Linda McNamera, the magazine's advertising assistant.

Karen said yes, thinking Diane seemed particularly distressed this morning. It was easy for Karen to surmise that this troubled mood had to do with Joe. Diane talked about how violent and dangerous he was to most of the women in the office. Yet whenever Karen told Diane about Joe's repeated calls—his paranoid and arrogant demands to know where she was—Diane would respond with what Karen called a "throaty, knowing chuckle that made her seem so in control of the situation." Diane seemed to like to shock the young women whose friendships she cultivated. When she first came to *Harper's* last April, she casually mentioned that Joe was so angry she'd taken a job, "my friends think he'll blow up the magazine." The young women responded by laughing uneasily. "No," Diane said, "I'm not kidding."

During a family crisis a few months ago, many of the young women in the office saw Diane change from a breezy sophisticate so luxuriantly confident of her own youthfulness that she talked proudly of how she could out-exercise the young actresses in her fitness class to a grave older woman insecure in her job and trying to cope with a personal life full of insuperable pressures. They were beginning to see the full toll Diane's marriage was taking. The crisis involved her son, Blake, whom Diane regularly took to a speech therapist. When an elite nursery school would not admit Blake, Joe had locked him in his bedroom because of his "failure." Joe's cruelty to the child so upset Diane, she could speak of little else for a solid week.

Mostly, though, Diane delighted in turning her life into a series of droll vignettes for others' amusement. She could craft a story artfully from beginning to end and deliver it with a cool élan that now and again let through a tongue-in-cheek Midwestern dumbfoundedness. Many mornings, she could be found by the coffee machine, regaling editor Lewis Lapham's assistant, Ann Stern, with tales of her early mornings as a beleaguered working mother. To Ann, a weekend poet in her late forties with a gentle manner, Diane's narrations "were like delightful oral pieces written for your benefit. Her bemused juxtaposition of all the mundane and chaotic things that can happen in a single five minutes—from running out of twist ties for the sandwich bags to calling out to the housekeeper what to unfreeze for dinner while you're under the bed hunting for a daughter's lost hairbow— would have me looking for Diane when I got to work, and saying, 'Tell me a story!' "

Later, many of Diane's friends would believe that her insistence on seeing herself as the heroine of a black-humored story not only had kept her from sensing Joe's menace until it was too late, but had attracted her to Joe in the first place.

One woman who was perhaps too young and recent a friend to understand this was Linda McNamera. Lithe, with light brown hair that flowed almost to her waist, Linda was Diane's best friend in the office. Their almost twenty-year age difference was irrelevant to both of them. So close had they become that Linda insisted that if Diane ever felt it was time to just take the children and run, Linda would come over at any hour to help her pack her suitcases.

Linda was proofing bills for the December issue's ads when Diane appeared and said: "I think I'm going to take you up on that offer."

"Any time," Linda assured her.

"I can't take it anymore; this whole thing with Joe is going to do me in," Diane was saying as Linda joined her in her office. Rick's imposing office faced Diane's, so that the thirty-one-year-old publisher and former newspaperman whose family had founded the philanthropic MacArthur Foundation could always see his secretary working. This morning, Rick was out at a breakfast meeting Diane had scheduled for him. There were authors' contracts to file, correspondence and memos to type up. In addition, she knew she would soon be approached with extra typing by the magazine's vice president of corporate and public affairs, a woman named Randall Warner. If Diane was going to show Linda the drugs she'd found in Joe's drawers and talk about the weekend she spent waiting for Joe to come back with the children, she had better do so before Rick arrived.

When Joe had returned with the children, Diane recounted, he suggested they all go to the Amagansett house the coming Friday night—"to spend one last weekend as a family"—during which they would also divide up the furniture and prepare the house for selling. This "closing-the-house" weekend had been discussed before.

"You're not going to go, are you?" Linda asked.

Diane didn't know; she had not decided whether Joe's wanting them to go meant he had finally accepted the inevitability of the divorce, and this last weekend represented an "adult," "civilized" closure, or whether his suggestion was "typical manic Joe"—the Joe who would scream an abusive remark at Diane, then show up with flowers for a romantic reunion. She sounded weary of making judgment calls about Joe's state of mind and motives.

If she did not go out to Amagansett this weekend, however, Joe might sell both the house and its furnishings out from under her, keeping the revenue for himself. Half of that house was rightfully hers. She owed it to the children to responsibly supervise its sale, to fight for everything to which the three of them were entitled.

"I want to show you something," Diane said, as she reached into her canvas shoulder bag and pulled out two foil-wrapped squares. "Do you know what these are?" she asked, unwrapping one to reveal loose powder; the other, several different sized capsules of the prescription drug variety. "Cocaine and some kind of amphetamines?" Linda guessed. Diane explained she'd found them in Joe's attic room during a rare interval when it was not locked. She planned to bring them to a pharmacist today to have them analyzed.

Diane intended to use the drug test results to undermine Joe's threat to take custody of the children, and the provocative riskiness of this act unnerved and worried Linda. All these months of their friendship, Diane had been big-sisterly to Linda. When Linda was ambivalent about trying for the promotion she eventually received, Diane had kept urging her to pursue it. "I sabotaged every chance I ever got to be promoted when I was your age," she told Linda. "*Don't you* do that." Now Linda wanted to be big sister. "Diane," she said. "*Please*. Be careful." Linda remembers Diane smiling that cool smile of hers and saying, "I'm *always* careful."

"I wanted to say, 'No, you're not. And you can't be careful enough with a man as crazy as Joe!' " Linda recalls. "But something in her face said: Don't remind me of my vulnerability now, when I need all my strength just to keep my head above water and fight him."

When Linda went back to proof ads in her office, Diane picked up the telephone.

The previous summer Diane had begun questioning Kathryn Crowley, then the magazine's young account representative, about Kathryn's hometown Chappaqua in Westchester County. Verdant, with good schools and close enough to Manhattan to commute, as well as having a major magazine (*Reader's Digest*) quartered there, Chappaqua seemed ideal for Diane's purposes, and she had jotted down the name and phone number of one Helen Richards, Kathryn's mother's friend, who was a Chappaqua realtor. The previous Friday Diane called Kathryn and told her she was ready to call her mother's friend, and could Kathryn put in an introductory phone call to her? Kathryn said she would, and Diane vowed to find a house to rent immediately; hidden in a community where she had no links, Joe would not easily be able to find her. She would take the children and flee. Diane had gone through the motions of house-renting once before; her friend Gloria Archer* had accompanied her on rounds with a realtor in Port Washington, Long Island, two months ago. But her need to leave Joe hadn't yet reached the emergency stage and none of the houses that day were affordable to Diane who, on her $340-a-week take-home salary, had a rental limit of $700 a month.

But now Diane felt she could wait no longer to leave. Using the time she had before Rick came in, Diane called realtor Helen Richards.

Helen Richards remembers being in the kitchen of her large colonial house in Chappaqua, settling down with *The New York Times* at about ten A.M. that Monday morning, October 19. She tended to linger at home on Mondays, reaching her real estate office around eleven. Today, she was eager to read the front page piece on last week's 235-point stock market plunge. Helen's husband was a banker, and many of her friends and clients

---

*Name changed to protect privacy.

were also in the Wall Street community. She was just starting the article when the phone rang.

It was the woman—"Diane Whitmore"—whom Kathy Crowley had said was in a hurry to leave her husband. "Oh yes, I'm glad you called; I might have something for you," Helen remembers saying. She explained that while most of her business was sales, she did have one charming rental, a two-bedroom cottage on the grounds of, but separate from, a larger estate, for $700 a month.

Diane Whitmore said she thought it sounded good, inquired about the length of the train commute to Manhattan and told Helen she would try to come out to look at the house after work that day—she would call after lunch to let Helen know which train she'd be taking. Helen Richards, who had no idea this was the closest Diane had ever come to finding a suitable refuge, thought Diane sounded "not at all nervous; she sounded determined and in control of her situation."

But when Maggie Gari got a call from her good friend Diane about a half hour later, Diane sounded *very* nervous. "I think I'm finally losing it; I'm going out of my mind," Maggie remembers Diane whispering. "Rick just came in and thanked me for making some travel reservations, and I don't remember making them. I don't even know what he's *talking* about!" Diane reiterated her frequent fear that all the stress with Joe was taking its toll and was going to get her fired. She didn't, however, mention the phone call to Helen Richards.

"Easy now. You're handling a lot. One step at a time," Maggie said soothingly. Maggie and Diane had met during their recovery from alcoholism ten years before. Of the many friends Diane had met in that context, Maggie was the one who most resembled her. Both pretty, light-haired, fine-boned Protestant girls from the Midwest, they had lived dissipated lives in their twenties, only to become, in their early forties, sober and earnest PTA mothers. They played with the contrast between their past and present. Both identified with the sensibility of the movie *Blue Velvet*. Both talked of how they had been raised to be controlled and polite, no matter what, and how that "front" of good behavior was so hard to get past. "Your problem is that you want to be a good girl and a bad girl at the same time," Maggie had once told

Diane, with a sigh that implied she was speaking for both of them.

Maggie had just seen the new movie *Barfly,* and told Diane that Faye Dunaway played the very character they'd have turned out to be if they hadn't conquered their drinking. Diane's spirits suddenly picked up at Maggie's mention of the movie. Charles Bukowski, on whose poetry and stories the movie was based, was the writer Allan Gurganus had compared her to when he'd called to accept her into the Writers Community. "Being in that class is the only thing that's good in my life now—that and the children," Diane said. She told Maggie she had just finished reading a new novel, *Love Me Tender,* by a young woman named Catherine Texier. She loved the book; Maggie *had* to read it. It was about decadence and lust in New York's downtown, themes in Diane's own stories and in the mutual past she and Maggie half-shudderingly, half-fondly remembered.

The two women made a date to get together for an early dinner Friday night. Perhaps because she knew Maggie would try to talk her out of it, Diane neglected to mention that she might be going out to Amagansett with Joe afterward. A songwriting project had Maggie so busy that "aside from that night," she told Diane, "until the twenty-sixth you can color me gone."

For some reason, Maggie remembers, Diane picked up and mused upon that last line. "Color me gone . . ." she repeated.

Two and a half miles downtown, and unknown to Diane or to anyone at *Harper's* at the time, a drama was developing on Wall Street. By seven A.M. that morning, the specially opened electronic mailboxes of the New York Stock Exchange had produced four to five times the normal sale orders. By 9:30, a half billion dollars worth of stock—fourteen million shares—was being offered for sale. By ten, there had been calls for the sale of $475 million more. Between ten and eleven A.M., while Diane was talking to Maggie on the phone, a full $1.1 billion more sell orders were logged, and the president of the New York Stock Exchange was locked in an emergency meeting with the chairmen of the largest member firms to determine if the exchange should take the drastic step of closing for the day, to stave off an avalanche of selling. The exchange, it was decided, would stay open so that shareholders could "trade their way out" of the crisis.

This news riveted and worried traders all over Wall Street. One of those traders was Diane's husband. A vice president with Arnhold and S. Bleichroeder, Inc., a venerable, privately owned German firm with principally foreign clients, Joseph Pikul, 52, had long been considered a "good stock-picker" and a "good money-maker" by his peers. He was the firm's Scandinavian investments specialist and arguably one of the top men in that field in the country.

Between salary, commissions and private investments, he'd been making between $600,000 and $800,000 a year during the bear market of the eighties. He had between one and two million dollars held in foreign and domestic banks, securities and stocks. Except for a small and usually empty joint account, Pikul denied his wife access to any of these assets.

A large man, he had a wide-planed Polish face and small eyes that often nervously blinked. His thirty-year career had had severe ups and downs. When he was doing well financially and had his emotional problems in check, he evinced charm, generosity and humor toward colleagues, clients and employees. At other times, he was, as a former boss from the early seventies recalled, "like a time bomb ticking inside a walking Brooks Brothers window."

This was one of those other times. Joseph Pikul was particularly troubled these days, even before Friday's 108-point market plunge presaged the nightmare that was forming around him. He had received a positive AIDS test shortly before Labor Day. Women's clothing, jewelry and undergarments—hung and strewn about his Battery Park City apartment—bespoke a strenuously concealed private habit. A recent purchase of a dozen size 18 and 20 bikinis at an East Hampton boutique had him telling the curious salesgirl they were his contribution to a fundraising bazaar to be held at his child's grammar school. The subterfuge of his secret life could only have added to his stress.

A week ago, Joseph Pikul had spoken to two women friends about his marital situation. Ramona Craniotis, a social psychologist, had known Joe since they'd been neighbors shortly after his first marriage collapsed in the early seventies. He was certain now, he told her, that Diane did not have a lover. He wanted to reunite and could not bear the thought of losing the children. He was, moreover, very angry at Diane's divorce lawyers for pressing him for a large settlement.

The second woman he spoke to was his first wife and former business partner, Sandra Jarvinen, still an intermittent confidante. Since August 27, they had had regular conversations ostensibly regarding the payment of back alimony Joe owed her, dating from their 1974 divorce. He had flown to her home near Hyannis, Massachusetts in August, to begin sorting things out.

Here was a man angrily reluctant to settle a divorce with his current wife, with whom he had children, and yet eager to accommodate the thirteen-year-old alimony claims of a self-supporting first wife with whom he had none. Joe wanted something from Sandra and, as leverage, he was willing to listen to and indulge her demands. Since Labor Day, their phone conversations were frequent and amiable. Last week's phone call ended with the decision for Sandra to fly to New York the next week to sign promissory papers. The papers were to be in her favor, but he was so eager to bring Sandra to New York that he offered to pay not only her airfare, but also her missed working-day's revenue. He even offered to reimburse her for new clothes she might buy for the occasion.

Sandra Jarvinen is a large blond woman in her early fifties who dresses in Laura Ashley–style clothes, speaks in a whispery voice and considers herself "a big softy" in her personal life. In business, though, she evinced the shrewd toughness of a master trader who relishes the gamesmanship involved in negotiation. She had been Joe Pikul's college sweetheart, then his bride, during his years at Northeastern and, briefly, at Harvard. They had gone into business together managing hedge funds, and by 1970 they controlled $80 million worth of assets. Then Joseph Pikul began drinking. The calamitous bull market of the early seventies finished his business, and his escalating violence finished his marriage to Sandra.

Despite some ugly years, they had never lost touch with each other. She was what she called his "safety net"—a person to call in the middle of the night. In turn, she continued to regard him affectionately as "brilliant with money, and able to be the most charming man in the world, but an absolute monster with women." He admired her for marrying a widower and taking over the task of mothering the man's nine children. Now Sandra's second marriage was over, and she lived alone in a comfortable house that doubled as her office in Norwell, Massachusetts.

In all their discussions from Labor Day on, Joe Pikul pressed Sandra for a favor she never agreed to. It was a baffling request, she would later say. She could never figure out why he kept asking it of her: He wanted her to sign a paper stating she would become guardian of his two children in the event of the death of both of their parents.

By the end of the day, the Dow Jones had fallen 508 points, its biggest drop since 1929. The lusty bear market of the eighties, upon which Joseph Pikul rebuilt his fortune after its total collapse thirteen years before, was considered to be resoundingly over.

It is not known whether Diane Pikul talked to her husband that day. She worked at her usual tasks of handling the magazine's rights and permissions and taking down and typing up Rick MacArthur's memos and letters. She did extra work for Randall Warner.

Helen Richards never got a call from Diane that day to confirm or reschedule the appointment to see the charming $700-a-month cottage. But then, Helen was too caught up listening to harrowing accounts of what was now deemed "Black Monday" from her husband, clients and friends, and had momentarily forgotten Diane Pikul's urgent phone call that morning.

Tuesday, October 20

Diane met Gloria Archer for a late lunch at a coffee shop near the *Harper's* office. Gloria, who had encouraged her two months before to leave Joe and rent a house on Long Island, was to Diane a kind of mentor and older sister. Coming home this morning from a business trip with her husband, Gloria had encountered a number of messages from Diane left at her husband's office, so she quickly called her friend at the *Harper's* office. By mid-afternoon Gloria, an elegant woman in her fifties who might have stepped out of the pages of *Town and Country* magazine, was rushing down to lower Broadway, where the sidewalks teemed with NYU students and assorted downtowners wending their way in and out of youthful stores like Unique Clothing and Tower Records.

Though Diane had said she needed to talk to Gloria, she seemed, by the time Gloria met her, pensive and removed, "almost spacey—as if the preoccupation with her problems with Joe had become so burdensome and exhausting, she had to take on a different personality to keep herself together." According to Gloria, Diane was obsessed with the danger Joe posed to the children. She said she feared she'd have to use the videotapes and the pictures. But, as she had with Maggie, Diane brightened when she talked of her writing workshop. It was her turn to present a story for the class's critique in the workshop a week from Thursday; she was trying, despite her worries, to bear down and complete it.

"But you see, *now* you have the perfect excuse for not going with Joe to Amagansett!" Gloria exclaimed, for she had been as distressed as Maggie and Linda when Diane said she might go. "You have to stay home and finish the story!"

But Diane ignored her friend's concern; she seemed glazed and impassive.

"Diane," Gloria went on, mustering enthusiasm she hoped would be infectious, "you've got your job, you've got this class—you're all set. You're moving in the right direction. Don't cave in to Joe now. Diane, you've *got* to get out of this thing before he *kills* you."

Gloria saw so much fatigue and defeat in her friend's face, she felt her words were futile. Much of the reason Diane had never left Joe, Gloria believed, revolved around issues of security. In the past, when Diane had tried to leave, Joe would say to her: "Okay, you're going to be flat on your ass in a fifth-floor walkup with those two kids and no money! How are you going to take care of them?" Diane would become, in Gloria's words, "petrified."

With Gloria's help, Diane began to prove, over these last seven months, that she could take care of herself. But, Gloria worried, the more independent Diane became, the more terrified and desperate Joe became. Now he was wooing Diane to Amagansett with the threat that he would sell the house and furnishings out from under her. He was appealing to Diane's Achilles' heel about financial security and, more pointedly, to her deep insecurity about her own capabilities, which he constantly preyed upon. (Sometimes, Diane reported to Maggie Gari, Joe would wake her up in the middle of the night just to tell her she was worthless.)

Gloria felt Diane and Joe had been locked in this classic battle for years now, the one preying on the other's worst fear: his, of being abandoned; hers, of being left unsupported and unself-sufficient. It made Gloria think of Cassius' line from *Julius Caesar:* "The fault, dear Brutus, is not in our stars, but in ourselves." Diane and Joe were bound in a madness of their own making.

Diane asked Gloria wearily, rhetorically: "What can I do?"

Gloria wanted to say, in no uncertain terms: "Just get those kids of yours right now and come stay at my apartment, all of you!" She had come very close in the past, however, to losing Diane's friendship with such adamance. She had learned from hard experience that you could keep a daughter, or a daughterlike friend, only by letting her go—by respecting her own decisions. So she merely said: "Just promise me you'll think of all the good reasons you have not to go this weekend."

Diane said, "I promise." Then, "Anyway, if I do go, I'll get Carina to come along," referring to Carina Jacobsson, a dress designer who used to be the Pikuls' au pair and who remained a family friend. Diane always relied on her to baby-sit. Joe got along well with Carina, who thus served, on such weekends, as an emotional buffer between Diane and Joe.

The thought of Carina coming along on the weekend appeased some of Gloria's fears. Parting in front of the *Harper's* building, they made plans to get together the following week.

*   *   *

While Diane talked with Gloria, three hundred miles away at T. Dean's Store for the Larger Woman in Hanover, Massachusetts, Sandra Jarvinen was purchasing a $295 black shoulder-padded dress for her trip to New York on Thursday. She carefully saved the sales slip for Joe Pikul's promised reimbursement.

Sandra was looking forward to seeing her ex-husband. They always found a way to laugh together, often about how he could never put anything over on *her,* much as he might try. Once he doesn't own you anymore, Sandra would say, he's fine. She looked forward to his finally signing the document that promised her the back alimony.

In recent conversations Joe had so often told her that he didn't want his wife to get to keep the children when he died because she "hired too many baby-sitters." Joe had begun this "too many baby-sitters" complaint in phone calls he made to her from various hotel rooms in Scandinavia at the end of the summer. Hardest to forget was the comment he'd made in Hyannis on August 27, when he'd first broached the subject of Sandra's becoming his children's guardian. Why the rush to secure guardianship, even if you are AIDS-positive? Sandra had wanted to know. The children's mother is alive and healthy.

Joe had said, "Yes, but if she had an accident . . ."

"Don't be ridiculous," she had said, tossing off his threatening tone as a joke.

Before Diane left her office on Tuesday, October 20, she called Carina Jacobsson and asked her to come to Amagansett with the family over the weekend. Carina, a delicate blond with a Swedish accent, remembers she was draping a new Japanese rayon over her design dummy when the call came in to her cutting room at O. P. Andersson Designs on Seventh Avenue. "We'll go to a movie. We don't even have to be around Joe," Diane was saying. She sounded almost as if she were "selling" the weekend.

Carina was in a sticky situation. She felt she owed the Pikuls a lot—Joe was the primary financial backer of the business she'd started with another young Swedish woman, Inga Davidsson—but Joe's behavior had gotten so bizarre over the last months, and he was so verbally abusive toward her during a miscommunication about baby-sitting last week, that she now felt extremely uncomfortable being around him. And while Carina counted Diane as a friend, she was also getting tired of being in the middle of Diane and Joe's conflict, which seemed to have intensified.

"Can I get back to you by Thursday?" Carina asked.

Diane said, "Sure," then signed off with her characteristically lilting, "G'bye."

Carina realized this might be the first time she would say no to Diane.

Wednesday, October 21

Ann Stern, a tall, striking brunette with deep-set eyes and a proud jawline, though closer in age and circumstance to Diane than any other woman at *Harper's,* was perhaps the only woman at the magazine who didn't know something about Joseph Pikul's violence and threats. Ann simply knew Diane was trying, with difficulty, to divorce him.

Ann and Diane liked one another but had kept some distance. Ann enjoyed their ritual morning storytelling sessions at the coffee machine and admired Diane's breezy confidence and absurdist style. It was a persona, Ann had observed, that sharply contrasted with two other sides to Diane: the "good little girl" that she displayed with Rick, even though he was a full thirteen years her junior; and the "substance, authority and womanliness" that Diane evinced with her children the few times they visited the office. Diane compartmentalizes herself deftly, Ann had thought admiringly.

It was not for lack of admiration or even fondness that the two women remained remote. This, Ann believed, resulted from a delicate and unspoken pact: Ann would keep a distance so that Diane would not have to look at her example too closely. Ann had not, despite her considerable beauty, remarried in the sixteen years since her divorce. Despite a financially comfortable ex-husband, she was raising three children with great financial constraint. Just as Diane wrote fiction, Ann had written poetry all her life, yet had never been published. After five years at *Harper's*, Ann, forty-eight, still worked as the assistant to the editor, just as Diane, forty-four, and half a year at *Harper's*, was assistant to the publisher.

Ann could tell Diane looked at her at times and thought: I'm terrified the life she has is the life I'm walking right into! Which is why, Ann believes, Diane cultivated friendships only with the young women in the office.

This is why Ann Stern was so startled when, at noon on Wednesday, October 21, Diane paused in front of her office, leaned on the doorjamb and looked straight into the eyes of the woman to whom she had never before let down her guard. Instead of speaking, "Diane's whole face disintegrated," Ann recalls. "She let herself go. She just sobbed and sobbed. It was so uncharacteristic."

In her big blousy smock dress and fashionably clunky shoes, this woman who had always emitted such humor and bravado suddenly looked, to Ann, like a frightened child. Ann remembers Diane's exact words: "It's so hard. I'm so tired. I don't know if I can do it." It was as if the sound had suddenly been switched on in the silent conversation they had been having with each other all these months.

"But you *can*," Ann said, from the depths of her experience.

"I just want to be alone with my children, in the country," Diane went on. "That's the only time I feel peaceful."

Ann said she understood. Diane nodded gratefully, a little abashedly. Then she shored herself up and walked on to her boss's office.

That evening, when Carina Jacobsson arrived home to her Long Island City apartment and rewound her answering machine, she heard a message from Joe Pikul asking her, in an urgent, stammering voice, to please help them out with the children in Amagansett this weekend.

Joe's desperate tone unnerved Carina, and his calling on top of Diane's call was curiously unprecedented. In the four and a half years she had known them, Joe had never "seconded" a baby-sitting request of Diane's, and certainly not in such an insistent voice. Carina wondered, uneasily: Why does he want me there so badly? Will I have to referee fights all weekend? Is there some crazy errand my minding the children will allow him to go off and accomplish?

Joe's voice on her answering machine decided it. He was just too crazy: Carina didn't want to be around him anymore, didn't want to be a supporting player in the Pikul family drama. She would call Diane tomorrow and say she couldn't go. Then perhaps, lacking baby-sitting help and buffer, Diane herself would back out; she'd keep the kids in the city—and the whole ill-conceived "last family weekend" would never be consummated.

That night, Diane went to a movie to try to escape her tension and confusion. She asked Maggie Gari to come along, but Maggie was too tired for a ten o'clock show. So Diane went alone to the nearby Greenwich Theater and tried to lose herself in a movie starring Kevin Costner, Sean Young and Gene Hackman. Its title: *No Way Out.*

Thursday, October 22

Early in the afternoon, Sandra Jarvinen took a shuttle from Boston to New York. Joe Pikul's private driver, Jim Burns, in a gray Lincoln Continental, chauffeured her from LaGuardia to Joe's office on Wall Street.

"It's been a very hard week," Joe told Sandra when she arrived.

"I know you," she answered him, supportively. "You've been through market crashes before. You'll bounce back from it." Throughout their lunch at a restaurant in the World Trade Center Joe remained tense. Then Joe and Sandra went to the Rector Street apartment, which held two antique pieces he had won in the divorce settlement, which he now promised to give back to her. After Joe returned to his office, Jim Burns chauffeured Sandra on a shopping trip around the city, with money Joe had given her.

Sandra reflected on life's ironies. Here was her ex-husband: now generous, gallant, easily giving her his trust. Today they could talk and laugh together. Sandra had once been so terrified that Joe would make good on his threat to kill her, she had appealed for protection to the local police.

That was thirteen years and eight months ago: precisely when she had served him with divorce papers.

That afternoon, Diane got a message from Carina: She was sorry but she couldn't see clear to get out of the city this weekend. Plans were set now for Joe to drive the children out to the house after school tomorrow. Diane could not stop Joe from doing so, any more than she could have stopped him from taking them away all those recent weekends. She had a choice: to stay in the city while Claudia and Blake spent another weekend with their father alone, or to drive out Friday night to join them.

By late afternoon on Thursday, the Lincoln Continental bearing Joe and Sandra pulled up to the Pikul duplex. The true reason for Joe's flying Sandra to New York became clear: He was going to have her meet his children.

Sandra was in the backseat with Joe when the children emerged and walked to the car. Blake jumped onto his father's lap. "This is my old business partner, Sandy," is how their father introduced her to them. "I taught her everything she knows." Sandra was as impressed with the children as Joe expected her to be. "They're beautiful," she remembers saying. The foursome were chauffeured to Rumpelmayer's, the classic New York ice cream parlor and restaurant across from Central Park. While Claudia ate a steak and Blake a cheese sandwich, Sandra presented Joe with a $699 bill for her day's expenses which included the dress she was wearing.

Before she left by taxi for LaGuardia, Joe again complained about Diane and asked Sandra if she would agree to become the children's guardian. Again Sandra declined. "Joe, it's a bad idea," she told her ex-husband.

At 8 P.M. that evening, thirteen people sat around a table in a small room at the 63rd Street YMCA for the weekly meeting of the Writers Community. They included an

editor, an illustrator, a tax lawyer, an emergency room
doctor and a number of younger struggling writers who
supported themselves doing temp work. They were waiting for the fourteenth, and oldest, member of the group,
Diane Whitmore, to arrive.

Allan Gurganus, thirty-eight, a rangy man with a mustache and wavy, thinning hair, was holding the class up,
waiting for Diane's arrival. He was certain she'd be
there; otherwise, she would have called. The most enthusiastic member of the class, Diane was not one to be
cavalier about her attendance. Before she had come to
the first meeting, she had gone to the public library
where she looked up and read everything Gurganus had
published. At the second class meeting, she had brought
pastries for everyone.

Gurganus appreciated Diane's determined late start at
writing. He himself had been working obsessively on an
epic-sized first novel, over one thousand manuscript
pages in length, for seven years. The labor was so all-
encompassing that he intended to send his friends birth
announcements once he finished it. Just recently, he had
been informed by his agent that the publishing house
Alfred A. Knopf intended to bring out the work, called
Oldest Living Confederate Widow Tells All, as the literary event of the season, a major work by a major new
writer.

Allan Gurganus had been particularly impressed with
the "tenderness and linguistic integrity" of a story of
Diane's about a woman's friendship with her gay hairdresser, a man who eventually dies of AIDS. The woman
and the hairdresser share a years-long affinity for violent
men. Gurganus was going to suggest to Diane tonight
that she write a series of stories about wealthy women's
often surprisingly intimate relationships with their ser-
vicepeople. He assumed Diane to be one of those
"wealthy women," "a comfortable, probably once beautiful, East Side wife": stylish and smart, but not unconventional or unprotected. A woman with few worries or
risks in her life. Thus he'd been quite taken by her description, in that story, of the feeling of being in constant
and imminent danger. He'd thought it "remarkably
authentic."

The workshop members talked, sipped coffee out of

paper cups, smoked and traded information on writing grants and literary colonies as they waited for Diane. One, Carol Morgan, was waiting to thank Diane, whom she saw as "quick, birdlike, very present," for coming so strongly to the defense of her story when it was attacked by another group member the week before. Diane had said she had cried on the subway reading it, that one of its characters reminded her of her mother. Another member, Amy Godine, was surprised that Diane had written a story in which a female character submitted to pain at the hands of a man; Diane appeared to her to be a strong woman who wouldn't easily identify with feminine submission. A third, Lisa Davis, who thought Diane "extraordinarily talented," was hoping she could join the rest of them for dinner afterward this time, instead of running to catch a cab as she usually did, rushing home to relieve the baby-sitter.

Tonight, though, that baby-sitter had been dismissed by Joseph Pikul when he returned the children to the duplex following the Rumpelmayer's meal. By dismissing the sitter and then leaving the apartment himself, he had effectively prevented Diane from being able to attend class.

At 8:15, without Diane, Allan Gurganus called the class to order.

Friday, October 23

As she had at the beginning of the week, Diane sought out Linda McNamera right after she got to work in the morning. She told Linda that she and Joe had had a terrible fight last night when she'd discovered he'd dismissed the baby-sitter. They had fought in the apartment and then down on the street. "This is the first time I ever let the children hear me screaming at him."

All morning long, Linda remembers, Diane agonized about the weekend: Should she go or shouldn't she? The two had a lunch date scheduled for today; Linda was going to take Diane to the NoHo Star, their favorite restaurant in the area. There, away from files and typewriters and bosses, Linda could perhaps persuade her friend to let the children and Joe go without her.

But Diane received extra work, from Rick and from Randall Warner, and had to cancel lunch with Linda.

Sometime in the early afternoon Diane received a phone call that seemed to change her frame of mind from painful ambivalence to almost defiant certainty. Was the phone call from her lawyer? From Joe? Was the phone call really connected to her change of manner? Linda only remembers that from that moment on, Diane's defenses against those who wished to persuade her to stay kicked into high gear. No one could convince her she risked being any kind of a victim.

Diane had begun to confide in Ann Stern since opening up to her on Thursday. She had described her husband as "volatile and unpredictable," yet when Ann expressed alarm at Diane's going to Amagansett, Diane responded with bravado.

"Did you see the movie *Fatal Attraction*?" she asked Ann.

"Why, yes," Ann said. "Just last week. Why?"

"Because you're thinking of that movie, not me."

How deftly she defends herself, Ann thought, but this time with misgivings. Was Diane using her bravado to obscure real danger?

Diane spoke on the phone at least three other times that afternoon. She called Barbara and Marshall Weingarden, with whom the Pikuls often formed a weekend foursome, to break the couples' long-standing date for that evening. Diane explained to Barbara, "Joe and I are getting along so badly, you won't want to be around us." Barbara was by now used to Diane breaking dates for this reason. The Weingardens were the only people left with whom Joe and Diane even attempted to present themselves as a couple, and both of them wondered why the Pikuls even tried. Diane and Barbara then made a date to take their children to the East Hampton library's story hour after Diane's exercise class the next morning.

Hanging up, Barbara wondered, uncomfortably: If they're getting along *that* badly, why on earth is Diane going out to the house this weekend?

Then Diane left a message on Carina's answering machine: "Hi, it's Diane. Sorry you can't come out this weekend, but there'll be other times. G'bye."

Maggie Gari called Diane shortly before five to ask

Diane where she wanted to go for dinner. It was clear
to Maggie from Diane's response that Diane had forgotten all about the date. She told Maggie that going to the
house to divide the furniture with Joe this weekend was
the right thing to do. Maggie was shocked. Diane's tone
of voice indicated she would brook no argument, though,
so Maggie backed off. The exchange made Maggie un-
easy and reminded her of another conversation she'd had
with Diane when the space shuttle Challenger had blown
up. Maggie had called Diane to share her grief, but
Diane, to Maggie's surprise, had rejoined, "It's not a
tragedy. Those people were doing exactly what they
wanted to do," her tone of voice so resolute that Maggie
had recoiled. It occurred to Maggie that her best friend
had an uncomfortably acerbic acceptance of people risking mayhem and creating their own dire destinies.

At 10:20 P.M., Diane walked the short distance from her
Sixth Avenue duplex to the Travelers Garage, just off
Sheridan Square, where the family kept their two automobiles. Joe had already left with the kids in the gray
Mazda; she was taking the Buick station wagon. It was
late at night to be making so long a trip in relative darkness, yet before going to the garage she had further delayed her leaving by stopping for a solitary dinner at
Tony Roma's, the spareribs restaurant next door to the
duplex. Perhaps she considered calling to tell Joe she
would not come after all.

Shortly after Diane left with the car, Joseph Pikul
called the garage to make sure she had left.

She took the Midtown Tunnel to the Long Island Expressway, turned off an hour and a half later at Exit 70
and connected to Route 27, the Montauk Highway. She
drove that two-lane thoroughfare through the familiar
succession of privileged towns—Southampton, Water
Mill, Bridgehampton, Easthampton—where women just
like her were settling in for the night in bed next to their
husbands, the children asleep in the next room, fresh
basil and corn in their refrigerators. At the big
Easthampton windmill she veered right, heading for
Amagansett. At one A.M. she turned left at Windmill
Lane.

It was very dark as she drove past the Windmill Inn,

over the Long Island Railroad tracks, then finally past the tree-filled cemetery that abutted their gray wood one-story house.

Some deep combination of needs, sown in her childhood and developed in her marriage to Joe, had brought Diane to that moment. She fancied herself sophisticated, but she was dangerously naïve; she had cultivated a tension between the healthy impulse to live well and orchestrate her life according to plan and image—and a stronger impulse to push limits and court destruction. All this was played out over the shifting enticements and lurching self-corrections presented by the last three decades. After tonight, Diane's fate, and the fate of her children, would trumpet the illusoriness of many women's gains, not just in their homes and in their psyches, but also in America's courtrooms.

As Diane made the left into the graveled parking area in front of the house, she probably noticed that a light was on in the living room. Her husband had stayed up to wait for her.

PART II

AMERICAN GIRL, MID-CENTURY

Chapter 2

Born in the midwest in the 1940s, I was an only and
asthmatic child, lonely and enamored of fantasy and
having a great desire to please. I wanted to be Nancy
Drew, then Scarlett O'Hara, and most of all I wanted
to see the world and become sophisticated, even
dissipated.

*Diane Whitmore Pikul, from an autobiography written
for Elizabeth Henley's fiction workshop at New York
University, June 1987*

Diane Jackson Whitmore was the late-in-life and longed-
for only child of two entrenched South Bend Indianans.
Born on May 20, 1943, she was third generation South
Bend on her father Donald Whitmore's side; fourth generation on her mother, Jane Jackson Whitmore's. Three
out of her four sets of great-grandparents were farmers,
as were most of their parents. She was born so deep in
that small industrial city ringed by farms, she would
spend her whole life trying to escape her roots.

A redbrick and limestone boomtown of just over a
hundred thousand residents, South Bend was headquarters to Studebaker, where Donald Whitmore worked as
plant engineer. The company was the power behind the
city—and the Studebaker family an important presence
in three quarters of a century of Donald Whitmore's family's life. South Bend prided itself on such practical, physical men as Whitmore, many of whom were first-
generation off the family farm, now eager foot soldiers
and lieutenants in the thriving American auto industry,
which gave the region its glamour and heart. For women,
South Bend provided a world in which their mothers had

known one another all their lives; a world in which women sewed curtains and sent thank-you notes in neat script and made clove-dotted hams and apple pie for Sunday supper. It was a white Protestant world where most everyone looked and behaved like one another; where engines, perhaps even more than humans, gave life its articulation and thrust. People did not often raise their voices; they spoke in cadences as flat and unsurprising as the land.

In the stories she wrote during the last two years of her life, Diane remembered her midwestern childhood with affectionate nostalgia and also as the legacy against which she relentlessly rebelled. In one story, where she confronted her ambivalent feelings about her past, she created a character named Carrie Indiana, who was a "tabula rasa of bland, wholesome, midwestern good looks." In another, she wrote of trying to "forever lay to rest my image of midwestern cleanliness."

So much of Diane's behavior and many of her riskiest choices were inspired by her desire to vanquish all that was embarrassingly "Indiana"—provincial, wholesome, all-American—in her. Yet it was always that very Indiana girl—organized and meticulous, exuberantly marching toward some romanticized self—who carefully recorded her proud "progress" away from the heartland. Of a drug dealer she took as a lover in New York in her early twenties, Diane wrote, a year before her death: "His was the first of a series of guns I woke up to find on my dresser in the morning, a symbol of hope I would never have to go back to Indiana." Ironically, almost touchingly, the closer her life got to deshabille, the more she stood on its sidelines, cheerleading her own advancement to the abyss.

She appeared, toward the end of her life, to have understood she'd struck a bargain. She would accept, even romanticize, an element of danger within love in exchange for the worldliness she coveted. Her fiction indicated that she saw herself as an adventuress, imagining a life without boundaries.

"Go west, young man" was still an abiding adage at the turn of the century, when Diane's great-grandfather Joseph Eckman, her father Donald Whitmore's maternal grandfather, was in his mid-thirties. The Eckmans were Pennsylvania Dutch. Joseph Eckman's father, Henry, had been born on the family farm in Lancaster, Pennsylvania, and Joseph, like his father, had worked on the farm morning till night. The Studebaker family, the pre-eminent builders of farm wagons in the whole country, had their farm and factory nearby, bringing luster and commerce to the region.

When in 1900 the Studebakers made the radical move of abandoning Lancaster and relocating their farm wagon factory to South Bend, Indiana, Joseph Eckman, like many fellow Lancasterans, moved west to South Bend also. With his wife, Anna Van Buskirk Eckman, and their four young children, Etta, Bessie, William and Arthur, he bought a small farm on the outskirts of town that produced wheat, potatoes and corn and eventually grew to four thousand acres. Life on the farm involved hard work but also episodes of cagey mischief—such as those frequent occasions when William and Arthur Eckman (Donald Whitmore's uncles) would sneak off to the local racetrack in the middle of night with two of their father's fastest farm horses to meet two of the Studebaker boys. There the four boys hitched buckboards to their steeds and raced around the empty track under the moonlight, whipping up dirt and shouting at the top of their lungs. Little Diane loved this favorite piece of family lore about her great-uncles, who were appropriately dutiful and taciturn on the outside but who were secretly rebellious and emotional underneath.

Etta Eckman, the older sister of Arthur and William, was brand-new to the area and just eighteen when she met and married a young South Bend man of English extraction named Charles Whitmore, who'd left *his* father's farm to open a sporting goods store. When Etta and Charles's only son, Donald, reached his teens, he worked at the store, named C. H. Whitmore Sporting Goods, every day after high school, checking the stock on croquet mallets, hunting rifles, fishing lines and poles, while in front of his father's counter the townsmen talked about their farms, the railroads, the Great War, and, mostly, about Studebaker, which had begun manufacturing automobiles right there in town in 1916.

Donald Whitmore was a fair-haired young man with a

narrow, high-browed face and patrician nose. His distinguished appearance contrasted greatly with his amiability. In 1926, he entered Purdue University to develop his talent at engineering. When he graduated four years later, his plans for a rosy future were promptly dashed by the Crash of 1929. The Great Depression's impact was immense on Don Whitmore and, later, on his daughter. It would form the basis of his countless lectures to her about the value of money, the uncertainty of financial fate, and the importance of making sure you nail down every cent you're owed.

Because he had gone to South Bend High School with the Studebaker paymaster's daughter, Don Whitmore was hired for an entry-level job there in 1929, just when hundreds of the company's workers were being laid off. More than a little chastened to enter the factory gates around which hordes of unemployed workers milled, Don Whitmore worked his heart out at the auto factory for the sum of $11.48 a week, "after they took out the fifty-two cents for insurance." The man whose daughter would eventually live in a three-thousand-dollar-a-month apartment was "damn grateful" for that forty-eight-dollar gross monthly salary. While he couldn't save money on it, by living at home he could break even.

Two years later, when he got promoted—to double his previous salary—to a job as layout engineer in the machine and assembly division, Don Whitmore was ready to go courting. He courted "up," setting his sights on the pretty daughter of Claude Jackson, the vice president of the First National Bank of South Bend and one of the most prominent men in town. The Jackson family had come to America from Scotland in 1640; one ancestor, Daniel Jackson, had fought in the Revolutionary War. Claude Jackson had married a young South Bend woman, Mame Bucher, whose parents, of German descent, had a local farm.

Their daughter, Jane Jackson, was a lovely, outgoing blond girl whom Don had known, through her brothers Joseph and Charles, since she was fourteen. She and her family lived only a block away from the Whitmores in the "good" neighborhood, Carter Heights, but she lived far more grandly than he. The Jackson home had been built by Frank Lloyd Wright. It was large and sprawling, with an enclosed sun porch, five bedrooms, a maid's room and a reading room. It stood out among the neighborhood's more modest homes.

It was to this house that Donald Whitmore, rising young man at Studebaker with multiple ties to that family, called on Jane one night in the summer of 1931. She was twenty-one, and had just graduated the local St. Mary's College and begun a new job at a local office equipment store. She loved to cook and sew and to read nickel romance novels. She was more generous-featured than Don Whitmore, with a wide forehead, sensual lips and nose. Scrapbook pictures of her, ten years later, reveal almost inexpressibly wistful eyes.

One of the big bands had come to town and was playing at the local dance hall, the Ballet Royal. Don took Jane dancing there, along with her brothers and their dates. "And we fell in love, almost right away."

From the outset, the Crash of '29 was a third partner in their courtship and in their lives. Jane's father's bank had just been liquidated, and Don and Jane were forced by circumstance into an egalitarian courtship; as he recalls, "We would each take a dollar to spend on Saturday night. We'd go out and entertain ourselves royally on that two dollars: go to the dance hall, where you could dance to the orchestra for free and fill yourself up with home brew for ten cents a bottle." Theirs was a sweet, provincial courtship, like so many others being played out at the same time by thousands of couples in hundreds of cities and towns all over the country.

Don and Jane courted for an unusually long time—six years. He kept waiting for his expected fifty-dollars-a-week salary, finally settling on taking a wife on thirty dollars a week. Jane, with her purchasing agent job, was making thirty dollars, too. After a marriage ceremony at the Westminster Presbyterian Church and a reception at the South Bend Country Club, they moved into a one-bedroom apartment with a Murphy bed in the living room. The Mar Main Arms, a redbrick apartment building on the corner of Marion and South Main streets, was in the heart of town.

But their years of financial caution did not pay off. Exactly a week after the long-postponed wedding, Studebaker went into temporary receivership and Don Whit-

more was laid off. "Three weeks later, I got my job back.
But it was a scary time," he says—so scary that Don and
Jane vowed to put off having a baby until they knew they
were secure, and for the same reason, they made the
decision, then highly unusual, to limit themselves to one
child.

On May 20, 1943—nineteen years after her parents
first met, twelve years after their first date and six years
after their wedding—Diane Jackson Whitmore was born
at South Bend's Epworth Hospital. She weighed just an
ounce over six pounds. She had a wide mouth and deep-
set eyes. Her father picked the name Diane "out of the
air; I can't remember why." At the Mar Main Arms,
Diane's parents had redecorated the bedroom in bright
red and white candy stripes for their baby, avoiding a
last-minute paint job of pale pink or blue, and moved
themselves into the Murphy bed. Jane Jackson Whitmore
quit her job and stayed home to devote herself entirely
to her baby girl while Don Whitmore worked double-
shift at Studebaker and brought home two hundred dollars a month.

Diane's bond to her mother was strong. In her Carrie
Indiana story, she wrote of "the relief [Carrie] had so
often found in maternal confession"—that is, confessing
her problems to her mother. A lifelong practice of col-
lecting women confidantes and of carefully keeping such
friendships up over decades would later result. What
Jane Jackson Whitmore gave her little girl, the child on
whom so many deferred dreams were riding, was a lesson
she would carry with her all her life. "Her mother's message to her seems to have been," as Gloria Archer heard
it from Diane, " 'You can have anything you want: grand
life experience, fine material things. You can marry well,
be educated well. You can leave the Midwest, as I did
not do. *Don't stop where I stopped.*'

"Diane and I talked a lot about the book *My Mother,
My Self,*" Gloria Archer says. "Diane understood, as I
did, that what our mothers tell us is very critical, very
powerful. Especially the things they tell us indirectly,
without words."

Certainly Diane was treated like a little princess.
Scrapbook pictures of her show an unusually confident-
looking and self-possessed blond girl with an expressive

face and a mischievous smile, dressed in frilly-collared, cap-sleeved frocks of taffeta, polished cotton and gingham, many of which her mother made. Other pictures show her quite properly gotten up for Sunday services at the Westminster Presbyterian Church, in tiny double-breasted cloth coat and matching hat, white ankle socks and Mary Janes. Don and Jane Whitmore wanted to give Diane only and all of the good, the secure and the right things in life, and these pictures document their efforts.

They were proud, for appearances mattered greatly in their world—appearances, and the opinions of others. In her short story entitled "In the Afterglow," Diane shows an understanding of how this preoccupation might affect the dynamic of family life. She writes about the mother of her main character, Carrie Indiana, "The inordinate concern with the opinions of others, a frequent affliction among parents at the time, would one day result in her gentle spirit's becoming blurred by an almost constant and secret affinity for beer and scotch." (As for Carrie's father, he "usually showed strong emotion only when drinking to excess or driving a new car." Don Whitmore owned fourteen different Studebakers during his tenure at the company.)

Diane's parents were impeccably civil; they never fought. As Diane grew up, she watched her mother and father living a life of suppressed emotion that could be only indirectly released. Maggie Gari grew up in the same kind of Midwestern small city where "people were always acting as if everything was always fine and normal, even when it was not. When you come from such an environment, you can grow up thinking that *some* reaction, even the most negative, is preferable to that awful lack of affect, and this can lead you to choose some pretty intense relationships later on. Having come from that kind of background, I know: Sometimes you wanted to *scream*."

Young Diane did not scream, but she did often gasp for breath. She was asthmatic; she had inherited from her father what she would later call "the weak Eckman lungs." During severe attacks, she spent whole days confined to her bed. As well as giving her what she would later, in a story, call "a desperate desire for deliverance from the suffocating protections afforded a sick child," this enforced isolation made Diane lonely. "Why can't I have a brother or sister like everyone else?" she would often ask her father as he drove them in his Studebaker Commander to the weekly Saturday morning appointment with the allergy doctor, where they both got shots.

"Well, now, it's simple arithmetic," Don Whitmore would answer. "If you had a brother or sister, I could only do half as much for you as I'm doing now. You could only have half as many toys, half as many dresses, half as many pairs of shoes. So I think you're better off without a brother or sister."

After a silence, Diane would nod her head. "I kind of convinced her it was the best thing," her father says today.

Loving the railroad came with the territory in industrial South Bend, and when Diane was three, her father began to share his passion for trains with his daughter. Sunday mornings, Don would take Diane to a park two miles away from the apartment just before nine A.M., when the New York Central Line's top train, with its state-of-the-art engines, was scheduled to whiz by. Having departed from South Bend station, it was on its way to its first stop at Elkind, Indiana, its ultimate destination Buffalo, New York. Diane and her father would stand together on a grassy ridge in the park waiting and waiting, looking down the train track. "And then way in the distance," as Don Whitmore remembers it, "we'd see the smoke coming out of the three locomotives on the front of the train. We'd lean forward together, then we'd jump back a little just as the train came rumbling through. It shook the air, just rolling and rolling from side to side. I was fascinated by it. But not as fascinated as Diane."

When Diane asked, "How come it goes so fast, Daddy?" her father explained that the train carried what was known as a "premium fare." This meant that if it arrived one minute late in Buffalo, each passenger was paid $5; if it arrived two minutes late, they each got $10. The train company was betting on its own schedule, engaging its own engines in a moneyed dare.

Once again Diane's father telegraphed the power of the dollar. Money was why Diane didn't have a little sister or brother. Money was why her parents had waited so long to marry, and why they were sleeping in the living room on the Murphy bed. Money was even why trains went fast.

Diane learned other lessons from her father, too. Lessons about daring and risk taking. One story in particular enthralled her. In 1944, Studebaker was engaged in building for the U.S. government a lightweight tank that could float. The tank was to be shipped abroad to the Russians to be used in their war effort against the Germans in snowy Leningrad, which is why it was camouflaged by pure-white paint. But the tank, called the Weasel by its Indiana makers, was to be tested for combat-worthiness right in South Bend.

Harold Churchill, Studebaker's vice president of engineering, picked Don Whitmore to test it out with him. "Hey, Don, you want to take a ride in this thing?" Churchill had said, as he walked Whitmore to where the first of the tanks had just rolled off the assembly line.

"Sure, Church," Don Whitmore answered. "Where are we going?"

"Right into the St. Joseph River," Churchill replied. "We're going to see if this thing floats." Don Whitmore was startled. What had he gotten himself into here, a suicide mission? But it was too late to back out without losing face.

So with Churchill at the wheel, they drove the white Weasel through the streets of South Bend. As its cleated track ground noisily on the city pavement, Don Whitmore seriously considered just opening the door and jumping out. But he did not.

At the eight-foot-high banks of the St. Joseph River, Churchill gunned the engine of the Weasel, and over the edge they went. "Were you scared, Daddy? Were you scared?" little Diane would ask. Her father always said, "You bet. I didn't know, for a couple of seconds, if we were going to drown or not."

In a matter of seconds, however, the tank—and the two white-knuckled men inside it—bobbed right up. Water stayed out of the tightly sealed windows. The tank floated like a dream—for all of two hundred feet, and four minutes—over to the other side of the river, where a jubilant Churchill and Whitmore "gunned her up to shore." Don Whitmore felt like he was "on top of the world the whole rest of the day."

Diane loved that story, especially the part where he thought of backing out but overcame his fear enough to take the risk. Did she faintly remember that story, her friends would later wonder, while she was wracked with ambivalence about whether or not to go to Amagansett during the last week of her life?

When Diane was five years old she started kindergarten at the James Madison School. The class was filled with children just like her—sons and daughters of white Protestant Midwesterners, with two or three generations rooted in South Bend. Against this homogeneity, Diane felt what she would later call "the inevitable lure of differentness" and struck a friendship with the only black child in the school. She brought the little girl home to her apartment after her first day of school and asked her mother if they could all go out for ice cream sodas. Diane would later transform this experience to fiction in her short story "In the Afterglow": "This posed a problem for her mother, in that small midwestern city of the forties, but being a tactful, resourceful and kind woman, she convinced the little girls that it would be much more fun to make ice cream sodas at home than to have them in the pharmacy of the Mar Main Arms, where the appearance of such a trio might have created unnecessary consternation in the golden glow of that late September afternoon." Don Whitmore remembers the incident this way: "Jane had to tell Diane afterward that it wasn't a smart thing to bring colored children to the drugstore or to the apartment building. Well now, I guess Diane never did it again."

At some point, very early in her childhood, Diane settled on "writer" as what she wanted to be when she grew up. "All the other little girls would say, 'I want to be a nurse' or 'I want to get married and have babies,' " Don Whitmore recalls. "But Diane just said she wanted to be a writer. And she was always writing and making pictures, with that little pad she carried all around."

Jane Whitmore's sister, Belle, lived nearby with her husband, Joseph James, and their son, Tommy, who was close to Diane's age. Belle worked and Tommy, whose father was Catholic, went to parochial school. On school holidays when Belle had to work, Jane Whitmore gladly took her nephew into her home.

Tommy, as handsome as Diane was pretty and as dark as she was fair, was "well behaved and quiet," Don Whitmore remembers. They watched *Kukla, Fran & Ollie* and *Hopalong Cassidy* on the Whitmore's brand-new television set. They were such *good* children—he, the polite and obedient Catholic schoolboy; she, proudly and precociously ladylike, as if she were already going with her mother to afternoon teas.

Did they sense some clandestine kindred spirit brewing underneath their propriety? Did they know that, years later, they would find each other again?

When Diane was six and Don Whitmore was plant designer at Studebaker, the Whitmores moved to a three-bedroom, two-story redbrick house with a large backyard just down the street from the McKinley School, where Diane would be starting first grade. She became best friends with the little girl across the street, Donna Davidson, whose father also worked for Studebaker. Donna noticed that Diane, as an only child, was treated more indulgently than most children. Her parents took her out to dinner. She talked to them forthrightly. She got toys all to herself.

Off to school every morning, at the dawn of the fifties, in her pert little dress, hairbow and saddle shoes, Diane did, as she wrote later, seem to "hav[e] a great desire to please." She received endless commendations from all authority figures. Her first-grade teacher, Nina Lust, wrote, "Diane Whitmore has made superior progress in all her work throughout the semester. It has been a pleasure to work with her. On the Scott Foresman Basic Reading Test, Diane made a perfect score."

Diane was promoted from primary to junior department at Westminster Presbyterian's Sunday School, and she eagerly joined the Blue Birds, and later, the Camp Fire Girls troop that Donna Davidson's mother led. Diane and her troopmates Donna, Sharla Klahr, Jeannie Switzer, Kathy Delehanty and Ann Price became six-way best friends, and in the others' remembrance of Diane there emerges a sense that she, alone among them, would vault past her roots. "Of the six of us, Diane was the most stylish," recalls Sharla Klahr Hickman, who, like all the others except Diane, married right after college and had children soon after. "And she always said she was going to be a writer and maybe an actress, too."

"She had a theatricality that showed up in the way she carried herself and talked" is how Ann Price Watson, now the mother of seven, puts it. "She seemed to secretly consider herself . . . well, *interesting.*"

Yet Diane was also "very much the perfect middle-class, middle-American girl," remembers Kathy Delehanty Stover, who, as a Florida resident, is the only other member of the group, besides Diane, to have settled outside Indiana. "She was beautiful, with a flawless complexion, confident and so well-read. No one else in our grammar school class was as well-read as she."

Adds Jean Switzer Jackson: "Diane was the only one among us who was an only child, and her parents were older than ours were, and she had that health condition that kept her more sedentary and pampered. She led a more mental life."

That mental life was filled with Nancy Drew, Diane's patron saint, role model and alter ego. "She had every single Nancy Drew book ever published," says Jean. Donna and Ann used to borrow them all the time. Kathy and Diane used to go to buy new books in the series the minute they came out, then, Kathy recalls, they would "race back to her house and see who could finish the book first." Jean remembers that Diane "even made her bedroom into the Nancy Drew Library. She made a check-out card for each book and stamped it with a stamp pad when you 'checked it out.' "

In the character of Nancy Drew, Diane must have seen a heightened version of herself. The spiffy female detective in the cloche hat and the bouncy knee-length skirt was, as Diane wished to be, both of and apart from proper, conventional, feminine life. Nancy Drew had delicious access to high drama and mayhem, got herself into thrilling misadventures and intrigues, but always escaped in the nick of time. Diane wrote of Carrie Indiana, "Most of her expectations of life had come from slowly and astutely reading every Nancy Drew mystery book ever published, often from the confines of her sickbed when stricken with her frequent asthma attacks. With a carefully plotted strategy learned from avid reading, she would learn to turn the tabula rasa of her bland, wholesome and midwestern good looks into an image of appeal which . . . could serve as currency in the corridors of power to which she aspired. While not specifically desiring [Nancy's] dead mother, boyfriend named Ned and blue roadster, nor even a career as a girl detective, she did desire freedom."

But "freedom, when it came," the forty-three-year-old Diane added, "had a higher price than she had anticipated."

Diane got almost straight A's at McKinley. She sang in the chorus of the school's Johnny Appleseed play. She attended mother-daughter afternoon teas with her mother. She received two Camp Fire Girls Wood Gatherer's Certificates. On weekends Diane and her group had slumber parties, complete with pillow fights and hair-setting sessions. About this time, Prince Ranier proposed to Grace Kelly. Donna thought the marriage wouldn't last because "*nobody* ever heard of that country, Monaco." Diane rapturously declared that Grace and her prince would stay married forever.

If Diane was mentally adventurous and emotionally romantic, she was physically constrained by her asthma. When she visited Ann at her family's summer cottage at Diamond Lake, Michigan, she would almost always suffer an immediate attack, and her father would be called to come and drive her home. Still, once she and Donna, vacationing with their families at Lake Huron, mischievously commandeered a canoe and, without life jackets, oared it across the lake. Diane had not yet learned to swim. "When our parents found out what we did, they got furious," Donna remembers. "I was scared and intimidated by their reaction, but Diane wasn't. She wasn't one to back down from something once she decided it was right to do it."

One night in the fall of 1955, Don Whitmore came home with bittersweet news to tell his wife and daughter: The family would be leaving Indiana. The wildfire spread of suburbia and the government's huge interstate highway project had turned automobile building into serious big business. The innocence, traditionalism, and homogeneity of cities like South Bend would soon be a quaint memory. In this sophisticated new automotive age, Studebaker, the local-hero company that had built the farm wagons that had cultivated the entire Midwest, just couldn't compete with the Detroit giants, General Motors and Ford. Labor-management problems had gotten out of hand. Even Studebaker's recent merger with Packard wouldn't give it enough of an edge. With the wars finally and resoundingly over, there weren't enough government contracts to make up the difference anymore.

After attending a corporate meeting in which staggering costs of production were revealed, Don Whitmore figured Studebaker didn't have more than a year left. (Actually, the company struggled on for another ten.) He accepted a new, better-paying job with Anchor Steel and Conveyor Company in Detroit.

It wasn't to Monaco, or even to New York yet, but "Carrie" would be leaving Indiana at last.

Chapter 3

Fortunately my parents moved me to Michigan and then to New Jersey, where eventually my asthma and innocence disappeared and I discovered boys and riding around in convertibles in pre–Bruce Springsteen New Jersey. I spent one year in college in Virginia but felt in danger of becoming a Southern belle, so cajoled my parents to send me to an expensive Eastern school, the better to further my plan of living in New York.

Diane Pikul, NYU fiction writing class autobiography, June 1987

Birmingham, Michigan was a shock to twelve-year-old Diane's system. Easily accepted and effortlessly popular in a snug social milieu that was an extension of her parents' deep-rooted connections in South Bend, Diane, for the first time, was judged without the benefit of those supports and deemed "not good enough" for the elite group at Derby and Barnum Junior High Schools. She continued to make almost all A's, but with the cover of her confident persona blown, the alien environment brought out in her a vulnerability and insecurity that life in South Bend had thus far managed to obscure.

The Birmingham kids were "noted for their snobbishness," she wrote at age sixteen, looking back on those years in a high school paper titled "Cliques." "I was desperately unhappy there and I believed that if I continued to live there I would have grown up maladjusted, for I would have lost all confidence in my own self worth.

"It is almost impossible to be sparkling and gay when

you are miserable inside because you aren't accepted. In all the time that I was one of those miserable people I didn't find a way to solve my problem. My only weapon was Hope. I tried to improve my looks and my personality but of course I tried too hard."

In the summer of 1957 Don Whitmore was offered a new job, for even better money, at Mack Truck in North Plainfield, New Jersey, so their Birmingham ranch house was quickly put up for sale. Jane Whitmore had decorated the house in the newly vogue colors of coral and aqua, but hadn't yet sewn the living room drapes—she'd left them pinned the two years they lived there; now, with prospective buyers coming to scrutinize the house, she whisked the drapes under the sewing machine even as the FOR SALE sign went up on the front lawn.

Diane's prospects at North Plainfield High seemed immediately brighter. As soon as the Whitmores moved into the new ranch house in North Plainfield, and just before starting her first year of high school, Diane became best friends with an extremely pretty girl from the "right" group named Eleanor Keenan. They lived close to each other and hit it off right away. "Diane was funny and bright and vibrant; she always wanted to do things," Eleanor remembers. "Going to Diane's house was always great because Diane was the star there."

Diane, like so many well-brought-up middle-class girls, became enamored of Elvis Presley. She loved his open sexuality, his bad-boy-with-a-sweet-heart persona. The ultimate hood, Elvis represented the delicious forbidden fruit for good, college-bound girls who wore pedal pushers and sleeveless Peter Pan–collared blouses or, in winter, skirts two inches past their knees and matching sweater sets.

Diane loved things theatrical and replaced Nancy Drew with Scarlett O'Hara as her role model. Eleanor was Diane's Melanie. "From the beginning," Eleanor recalls, "Diane was the ambitious sophisticate and I was the more naive, complacent local girl. She got a cashmere sweater before I even knew what cashmere was. Her parents always took her out to dinner. She went to Merle Norman for her makeup once and came home and taught me all about how to 'properly' use an eyebrow pencil. Once in a while, we would take the bus to Manhattan and go shopping at Saks Fifth Avenue. Diane wanted to live in New York so badly."

But the girls mostly wanted to stay where they were, acquire neat boyfriends and remain best friends. In Diane's aqua bedroom in the new house, Jane had, once more, put off sewing a hem on the drapes. The straight pins glinting in the window gave the girls happy reassurance that the Whitmores wouldn't be putting their house up for sale. "Please don't *ever* sew the drapes!" Eleanor and Diane would privately joke.

At North Plainfield High, a large brick school set on a manicured campus, Eleanor and Diane were in the Clique. This group of fifteen or so girls were, as she described them in the aforementioned paper, "the group of kids who attend the best parties, dress the nicest, are the cutest looking and so on." Diane wrote, "I have been on both sides of the fence. Being outside of the clique [at her former school in Michigan] has made me more aware of the social problems surrounding me."

She did not elaborate on those "social problems" except to say, "It is impossible to make every unhappy person a member of the clique, but if someone would tell me what to do [to make these excluded girls less miserable] I would really try." With that kernel of generosity in the midst of such cherished elitism, Diane was the archetypal "popular" teenage girl in an era when being socially successful was still the only female game in town, a game one put one's heart and soul into winning.

How hard it would be, later on, to shed the intense status-hunger and -consciousness that bloomed in those suburban classrooms.

Diane had a weekend job as a waitress at Updykes on Route 22, a restaurant famous for its homemade pies. It was a mark of status for a high school girl to get a job there; the management was choosy about who got to wear the restaurant's trademark white-blouse-and-skirt uniform; and only the girls' parents—never boyfriends—were permitted to drive them to work and pick them up. When she wasn't working, she and Eleanor and the other girls in the Clique spent their weekends cheering on North Plainfield High's football and basketball teams, yelling, "Go, Canucks!" The Clique's arrival at the Canuckateen, the weekly postgame dance, was eagerly awaited.

Those dances and boy-girl parties were Diane's initiation into the world of groped-at, halting, intricately measured fifties teenage lust. Diane describes later, in her story "In the Afterglow," "the intoxication of tiptoeing momentarily over the carefully drawn lines of acceptable behavior." Though Diane wrote the story at forty-three, Eleanor Keenan Lamperti says her friend's description of their parties is "wonderfully accurate." She evokes agonizingly clumsy moments in the lives of otherwise self-possessed teenage girls.

No parents were present, although the close supervision of the latter could be almost palpably felt from the floor above. From time to time the mother of the household would descend to the basement cheerily offering from a platter bowls of pretzels and potato chips . . .

At the most recent of these soirees, Carrie had leaned against the bolsters and had the crushing experience of not being chosen by one of the neophyte heroes but shortly thereafter by someone of second string rank, and she was grateful enough for this. The thought of choosing someone herself was way beyond the edge of her mind at that point in American girlhood.

Eddie Dombowski . . . fell midway in the partner acceptability scale of the group clustered in the musty recreation room. He had probably reached the highest point of intellectual and social achievement destined for him in this life.

The sound of the Platters' "Twilight Time" wafted through the room unstereophonically, and Carrie moved awkwardly in Eddie's arms, trying not to step on his feet, little knowing that, graceful as she might become in a number of activities of importance to adulthood, she would never manage to dance cheek to cheek without stepping on toes.

Seductive music twined through the dancing couples as Eddie steered her toward one of the empty couches. Someone turned off two of the four lamps, the record changed, and Eddie turned to kiss her. Obediently, she turned her head, keeping her lips chastely closed. Eddie's hand, which had gripped her shoulder rather desperately, became emboldened by the third passionless meeting of lips and slipped ever so slowly and inexorably downward. Acutely conscious of rules to be observed to preserve her reputation, crucial to her social standing through the years of high school which stretched before her, Carrie pondered, stiffening slightly. Every eye in the room focused surreptitiously on Eddie's errant hand, which came to an uncertain halt at a point midway on Carrie's breast. Knowing her dignity was at stake . . . Carrie carefully calculated that as long as the boy's fingertips were not within two inches of her nipple, she was probably okay.

Diane's steady boyfriend for most of her years at North Plainfield High was a handsome, sandy-haired varsity wrestler named Dave. In three separate prom pictures, Diane and Dave appear in the de rigueur pose for such occasions: he—muscular, crewcut, amiable—standing behind her, his hand cupping the elbow of her corsaged arm as if they're about to polka off together; she, smiling in her strapless dress with its almost ankle-length organza skirt, appearing, apropos of the era, at once winsome and matronly.

In a paper she wrote called "Why I Am Happy," the sixteen-year-old Diane said of Dave: "Having a boyfriend makes my life complete and this particular boy is especially good for me. I would say we have mutual respect and understanding and a lot of fun together. When things are going wrong I always feel that he is someone who really cares. I don't expect to grow up and marry him, though, but he's perfect for now."

Elsewhere in the "Why I Am Happy" paper, Diane says, "I would say I am happy, and when I hear some of the stories of others, I know I am definitely happy compared to them. I get along with my father and I can talk to my mother about *anything*." She also acknowledges her narcissism, competitiveness and fragile ego: "I guess I am spoiled and selfish. I do miss the companionship of brothers and sisters . . . but by being an only child I have grown up feeling at ease with adults.

"I know that if I suddenly found myself with brothers and sisters I would be very unhappy, for I would constantly feel I had to be as good or better than them in everything. A lot of people can't be satisfied with the feeling that they aren't quite as good as the most popular people, I am one of those people. When I moved here it took me almost a year to regain the feeling that I was as good as other people."

Finally, Diane writes: "One person I love very much is my grandfather [her mother's father, Claude Jackson], for he is one person who loves me without reservation, no matter what I do." But, as it appears on the lined-paper page, that sentence reads: ". . . he is *the* one person who loves me without reservation . . ." (emphasis added), with the word "the" then crossed out.

Even at a time when conformity and school spirit were uncynically pursued by most students, Diane's accomplishments at North Plainfield High stand out as impressive. She made honor roll every semester. She was president of the Spanish Club and treasurer of the Dramatics Society. She was Borough Clerk of North Plainfield, New Jersey, on the school's Government Day. She won first prize in the American Legion Oratorical Contest. She won the Junior Chamber of Commerce essay award. She played the lead in the school play, "See How They Run," and performed under duress: Her beloved grandfather, Claude Jackson, had just died and both her parents went to Indiana for the funeral; but Diane had insisted "the show must go on." Eleanor and some of the other Clique girls brought her a dozen roses after the performance. She won an award for meritorious service from the National Thespian Society. She was one of six students to win the school's Outstanding Citizen Award. She was one of ten from her graduating class to be singled out for "outstanding performance" on the National Merit Scholarship Test. She graduated in the top 10 percent of her class. She was voted Most Sophisticated. (Eleanor was voted Best Looking.) She was Class Valedictorian.

She seemed, clearly, to be the mistress of her many

resources and talents. Constructive. Assertive. "Well-rounded," as the favored praise of the times went. A *doer*. She seemed to be well on her way to the most productive and glowing of lives. In 1960, that glowing and productive life, for an upper-middle-class seventeen-year-old girl, would only result from going to a good college, then marrying almost immediately after graduation a young man on the educational track to business or one of the professions, someone from one's same social class or better.

"That was the life all of us girls in the Clique wanted," remembers Eleanor. "Except Diane. She always said she didn't want to get married so fast, she didn't want to have kids right away. She wanted to be a writer. She wanted to have adventures. She wanted to be somebody, although I'm not sure I knew exactly what she meant by that."

Neither did Diane, apparently. She wasn't, after all, a beatnik or an intellectual. No, Diane was, on the surface at least, a bright, shining Popular Girl. Her confusion about what life to lead—that of an iconoclast or that of a socialite—led her somehow to apply to second-string women's schools that stressed the social arts instead of to serious universities. She chose Mary Washington College (the women's adjunct to the University of Virginia) over Connecticut College for Women, possibly because the former recalled Scarlett O'Hara at Tara.

Shortly before high school graduation, Diane broke up with Dave and started dating a North Plainfield High graduate who was attending American University in Washington and whom she had met at a high school football game. Of Greek heritage, Teddy had a swarthy complexion, thick features and glasses: all quite the opposite of the mostly all-American boys Diane was used to. He was not handsome, but he was arresting-looking—"different looking," Eleanor remembers, "and Diane liked that." Teddy did not treat Diane particularly well, sometimes standing her up, keeping her off-balance, but Diane was crazy about him. The romance with this "college man"—the tensions of long distance, of different ages and cultural backgrounds—provided a drama that Diane seemed to welcome. Another thing Diane found compelling about Teddy, Eleanor recalls, is that "he'd *suffered*." He had a serious chronic kidney condition for which he regularly took medication and occasionally had to go to a hospital. Eventually, years after they broke up, Teddy would die from that condition.

Diane's senior essay, for which she won the Junior Chamber of Commerce Award, was called "My True Security: The American Way." She began, "In today's restless world, security has become the shining goal for which everyone must aim."

Once past her opening platitudes, Diane tried to use the specific, hard lessons of her own seventeen years of life to really say something. Remembering her father's lessons of the Depression, she wrote: "A large income or savings account may *seem* to give security . . . but it must be remembered that an economic system is never static; even millionaires may become paupers overnight." And, recalling her painful experience in junior high in Michigan, she opined, with a startling cynicism, that "humans are selfish and fickle creatures . . . [so] true security cannot be found in dependence on another person." Finally, recalling her now virtually conquered asthma and perhaps, as well, Teddy's illness, she said, "neither can [security] be found in a strong body."

"The only true security," the young Diane Whitmore had deduced, "is the integrity of one's own mind, for nothing can ever change that—not poverty, nor unpopularity, nor pain." Several paragraphs later she concluded: "The American way has given me true security by teaching me that I can do anything with my life that I choose and that I as an individual am important. I am secure in the knowledge that no one can violate the integrity of my soul."

With that same privileged idealism and untested conviction, Diane Jackson Whitmore, wearing a mortar board on her head and a magna cum laude pin on her white gown, stood at the podium of her commencement exercises in 1961 and declared in her speech on "Education and Moral Responsibility": "We must see that each human life is an adventure full of new horizons . . ." Like all the speeches given from the podium that bright day, Diane's was full of the spirit of radiant quest made popular by the new President, John Kennedy.

But had "the American way" really taught her she could do "anything with my life that I choose"? Or did it teach how to survive adventure and achieve status better to its sons than to its daughters?

Mary Washington College had cobbled brick sidewalks and moss-covered Federal and Colonial buildings. Some of the azaleas, dogwoods and rhododendrons that dressed the rolling Virginia hills were still in blossom at the tail end of summer, when Diane arrived to begin her freshman year.

It didn't take Diane long to realize that Mary Washington was not for her. The school was so conservative, girls were not allowed to wear Bermuda shorts on campus. There was a rigid curfew system, and the girls there were, to Diane, trivial and provincial with their constant talk of engagement plans to the boys they were dating. Clearly, being a Southern belle looked better from a distance.

Nonetheless, as she had with Eleanor Kennan, Diane made a best friend right away. Pat Barker, another pretty brunette with a gosh-golly personality, complemented Diane's flair. It was another Scarlett/Melanie, sophisticate/sweet-local-girl match. "The minute we met each other in the dorm—she was two rooms down from me—we liked each other, probably as much for how opposite we were as anything else," Pat remembers. "Diane was funny and gutsy and just a little bit hard. Her laugh was so . . . *throaty*. Like she really knew how the world worked, or was doing a good job pretending. She wasn't swayed by sentiment like I was. She didn't go around believing people meant what they said."

Diane didn't reveal much of herself to Pat; she had a fairly distant nature. But she shared with Pat an earnest if groping attempt to be intellectual. "We were real college freshmen—so immersed in the meaning of life, so full of ourselves. So obnoxious! We used to sit in our rooms or walk around campus for hours, talking philosophy." They regularly left index card communiques in each other's rooms; Pat still has this one from Diane:

Pat:

Hume—Consider 2 things:

     What you are justified in assuming in thought
     What you actually do assume in life, whether
     justified or not

Isn't this tied in with the uncertainty of things, but still different?

Also: Kant—Metaphysics becomes meaningless

See you at lunch.

—Diane

P.S. Am borrowing your blue sweater

Immersed in her romance with Teddy, Diane often visited him at American University. True to the times, she remained a virgin. Pat had heard, from Teddy's fraternity brothers, that he was "strange." But Diane did not seem to mind this. "He wasn't very attentive to her," Pat says. "He didn't pursue her or give her any great sense of security, but maybe that made it more dramatic. Whenever that Ray Charles record 'I Can't Stop Loving You' came on the radio, she said that reminded her of Teddy."

Diane fixed Pat up with a first cousin of hers, Burke Jackson, a Yalie. Going to visit Burke one football weekend—both girls in proper train attire: boxy collarless suits, circle pins, teased and hairsprayed flips topped by pillboxes à la Jackie Kennedy—Diane got a glimpse of what the "right" college life was like. Her sleepy little Southern ladies' school was nothing next to the cool, offhand social and intellectual elitism she saw on the New Haven campus.

Perhaps she realized she had been protecting herself—prolonging her only-child special status—by choosing a college where she knew she would have no trouble shining. Diane decided to try to transfer to a Seven Sisters school, settling on Mt. Holyoke, considered to be the prettiest campus and the easiest of the seven to get into. Her two semesters of honor roll grades at Mary Washington would help.

Meanwhile, Pat had become infatuated with Diane's cousin Burke. The girls were now having as many Burke-and-Teddy talks as they'd had Hume-and-Kant talks. One weekend in the spring of 1962, Pat was to go to American University for a school volunteer project.

"Ooo oo, maybe I'll see Teddy there and say hello to him," Pat teased Diane. "If you do, I'll screw things up with you and Burke," Diane replied. Pat was stunned. Didn't Diane know she was just kidding? Pat saw an edge then, a darkness in her friend she hadn't seen before.

When Diane came home from college that summer, Eleanor Kennan, who had finished her first year at a local nursing school, came over to see her best friend. Diane, in plaid Bermudas, looked a little sad. She pointed to the aqua curtains.

The pins were gone. The hems were sewn. The house was going to be put up for sale. Diane's father had taken another new job, this time at the Bosch Arma Corporation. The family would be moving to Massachusetts.

Mt. Holyoke College, in South Hadley, Massachusetts, had an old New England beauty with "American Gothic" buildings, most dating from just before the turn of the century. A classic white clapboard New England town abutted the campus; a peaceful brook intersected it; and a beautiful wild meadow on Prospect Hill buffeted it.

Here, although English and drama were her majors, Diane stopped talking about "wanting to be a writer." She could get away with that in South Bend, in North Plainfield and at Mary Washington, where she was the sophisticated, smart girl among less ambitious peers. But at a Seven Sisters college, every girl expected to be something. Here her aspiration would sound presumptuous and naive. Here, having to compete on the basis of substance, Diane played her surface attributes to the hilt. It was an impressive performance.

Diane's roommate, Mary Beth Whiton, was a fair-skinned and fair-haired girl and, like Diane, a midwesterner who had just transferred from a smaller, less demanding college (Beloit). Again like Diane, she was struggling to leave her midwesternness behind and to develop her intellect. But there the similarity ended. Mary Beth had a serious college girl's indifference to dressing up. Like most of the girls in the dorm, she wore baggy clothes and no makeup on the all-girl campus. Diane wore makeup all the time, set her hair, and had arrived on campus with her dresses carefully wrapped in tissue paper. Mary Beth was struck by the care Diane always took packing and unpacking.

While most of the other sophomore girls were still insecure around boys and sexually inexperienced, Diane, at mixers, gave the impression of both knowing that men were attracted to her and not really caring. She spoke, at least during the first semester, with the lingering Southern accent she'd picked up in Virginia. Diane's "successful femininity" and that throwaway attitude about suitors fascinated Mary Beth and the other girls.

Diane could somehow make fun of the solemn campus rituals. "She did this wonderful satire of 'Gracious Living Night,' where we all had to dress up for a sit-down dinner," Mary Beth recalls. "*I* was too diligent to ever have thought *not* to take something like that at face value. She seemed so unusually confident and knowing for her age; she was able to have a witty running commentary on her life"—the same kind of running commentary that would, years later, charm Ann Stern at *Harper's*.

Once, when Mary Beth was too deep in study to remember a dorm chore, the housemother snapped at her. Mary Beth was mortified, but Diane eased her pain by mimicking the housemother, elaborately, behind the woman's back. "Her daring and her humor made me feel better. Yet that same wit and satire kept the rest of us in the dorm from feeling that we could get close to her," remembers Mary Beth, who is now a clinical psychologist with a private therapy practice. "She entertained us all, she shined it on—but there was somehow an 'object' quality to Diane. She wasn't interactive.

"It looked, on the surface at the time, as if Diane was ahead of the rest of us; as if she had the confidence and experience to gloss over what we were all still struggling with. But, when I look back on those years from the vantage point I now have professionally, I see that she was probably using all those things—the wit, the clothes, the makeup, the satire—as masks with which to shield herself from her own vulnerability and from her deep fear of taking her intellect seriously." Indeed, what none of her roommates knew, but what Diane would later tell women friends from AA, is that when she received her acceptance to Mt. Holyoke, her father had laughed and said, "What do they want *you* for?"

Diane gave hints to the growing emptiness that was perhaps rooted in such remarks, but her roommates did not yet have the perspective to see them for what they were. "Diane used to play Edith Piaf records a lot," Mary Beth recalls. "I could never quite get past being impressed that she had them to consider how she might be identifying with them. I think she was really depressed and empty for much of the three years we roomed together. But we didn't know it, and she didn't know it, because those masks worked so well for her. It's unusual to find someone who's so successful and so fragile at the same time."

Diane made a special friend at Holyoke named Jamie Kleinberg. The two very different young women were equally distinct on campus; each had an impressive image with which to fascinate the other. Jamie, slight, dark and eccentrically dressed, had "culture" written all over her. She spoke in an almost British accent. She was known on campus as a prodigy. The daughter of a father who was a Princeton professor turned wealthy pharmaceuticals entrepreneur and a mother who was a rare book collector, Jamie could read when she was two, was devouring Shakespeare and other classic literary works in elementary school, had skipped two grades in school, was fluent in four languages. She was only at Mt. Holyoke because Radcliffe refused to admit anyone at sixteen. To Diane, Jamie was that dreamed-of thing: securely brilliant, a sophisticated intellectual.

And Jamie thought Diane was "the most elegant young woman on campus," she recalls now. "She always looked smashing. And the way she walked across a room, the way she gestured: well, it was all so ladylike, so different from the sort of down-at-the-heels, sweatshirt-and-jeans typical Mount Holio. She looked like she didn't belong there."

The two girls took a difficult Shakespeare class together and talked about Shakespeare and the novels they were reading. Diane was doubtless deeply flattered to have her opinions on the greatest writer in the English language listened to by someone who'd been reading him since she was seven. One day Diane "flabbergasted" Jamie by interrupting their scholarly conversation to quite firmly insist that they enroll in a local high school's night typing course together. "Diane had gone ahead and researched everything. Which school had the right class. How much it would cost us. What degree of typing skill we'd have when we finished. Even where and when we'd catch the bus from campus. She said, 'With typing, whatever happens, you can always get a job.' Her attitude was just so . . . astonishingly . . . *practical*. Twenty-year-olds just don't think that way. At any rate, I didn't."

The erudite Princeton prodigy—who is now an artisan bookbinder and a restorer of period houses—had seen the mask slip off the coolly glamorous Diane and had glimpsed the sensible, earnest, solidly middle-class Midwestern girl who'd been nurtured on stories about the Depression.

Most of the time, though, Diane kept that mask securely in place. Mary Beth Whiton remembers that Diane always appeared to write papers at the last minute, often staying up all night to do so. This didn't make sense to Mary Beth, given Diane's otherwise meticulous attention to her work. Eventually, Mary Beth came to see that Diane's last-minute behavior was a cover for her ego, a "way out" in case she did not get a good grade. "She was very vulnerable about her work and her intellect. If some professor commented favorably on her work, you could *see* how much it meant to her. By purposely leaving a paper until the last minute, if she didn't get a good grade she got to say: 'That's what I expected. See, I didn't try hard. I didn't take it seriously.' "

Still the doting, preemptively providing mother, Jane Whitmore sent lovingly wrapped packages of homemade baked goods to the girls all the time. Visiting the Whitmores in their new Longmeadow, Massachusetts, home—another ranch house, again all in shades of aqua, and filled with knicknacks—Mary Beth, whose own mother wasn't nearly as domestic, was amazed at how all Diane's needs and desires were maternally anticipated. "Mrs. Whitmore would greet us with hugs. She had prepared whatever we requested for dinner. And the schnauzer, Gretel, was almost as pampered as Diane was. *I* wanted a mother as all-encompassingly there for my needs as

Diane's seemed to be for hers. Of course, I didn't think then of the negative things that can come from that."

Sometimes Diane's father, who had an easygoing, buddy-buddy style with the girls, would take Diane and her roommate out drinking. This, too, amazed Mary Beth; her own father would never do that. Mary Beth felt tipsy after two martinis, but Diane was noticeably good at holding her liquor. She must have practiced at her family's daily "cocktail hour," which Diane had mentioned she enjoyed. Between the closeness to her father it provided and the example of her mother's use of it to blur painful emotion, alcohol had attained a significance in Diane's life.

At a Yale mixer in the winter of her junior year, a handsome young man in his early twenties asked Diane to dance. His name was Doug Johnston, and he was clearly a "catch" by conventional standards. Tall, dark and handsome, from a socially well-placed family, he had grown up in the exclusive community of Oyster Bay, Long Island. He had gone to good schools and was now in Yale Medical School. He was a straight-arrow type: there wasn't an unconventional bone in his body. He hadn't suffered. He liked ladylike women who dressed well, and he expected the girl he married to become a housewife.

Diane started dating Doug Johnston, going down to Yale almost every weekend, dressing up for dinners with him at nice restaurants or making chicken-in-wine dishes with him in his off-campus apartment. He fell deeply in love with her. "She had a spark, a vivacity that I had never encountered before. And she was brutally honest, which was also new for me," recalled Doug, who until his recent death in a plane crash was a plastic surgeon in Florida. "She was always talking about how much she loved New York—the movement, the fast pace, the people. But she presented herself, at first anyway, as a girl who didn't want to do more than settle down with a husband and raise a family. Which was definitely what I wanted."

Doug was the first man Diane made love to, which made the relationship even more special to him and which, in 1964, still signaled among honorable young men a tacit engagement. That summer, Doug interned in Cincinnati while Diane took a waitressing job on Cape Cod. On the day she came to Cincinnati to visit him, he spent hours going from store to store looking for the perfect engagement ring. When he gave her the diamond she "responded enthusiastically."

Back in New Jersey, Eleanor Keenan, now married to a local boy and expecting their first child, learned of Diane's engagement to the "handsome, glamorous young doctor" Diane had brought to Eleanor's wedding. An official announcement appeared with a photo of Diane, in stately profile, in the North Plainfield paper. Good for her, Eleanor thought. She always wanted a sort of "upper crust" fiancé. Now she had one.

But when Eleanor and her husband, Dick Lamperti, visited Diane at college one weekend, Diane surprised them both by pelleting Dick with questions about how he treated Eleanor. Her tone intimated dissatisfaction with Doug. It was almost as if Diane were searching for a reason to break up with him.

Meanwhile, Doug himself noticed that Diane had become detached from her studies—and, possibly, from him as well. He would give her jock-styled reprimands when she let a paper go unwritten until the last minute, telling her she was a "short-ball hitter" who wasn't "putting out the effort." He would get angry at how she seemed to coast, sitting on the sidelines of her potential, nursing some secret and unnamed malaise that she would not or could not share with him.

Perhaps Diane was feeling what many college senior girls, caught between conventionality and something else still undefined, felt at the time: that it would be death to marry a "catch" of a young man and let the saga of her life end there. That she could not turn her back on all the glamorous scenarios she'd been creating. Perhaps she recognized that her longing to end the relationship with Doug was, by some standards, destructive. She wasn't really ending it *for* anything, except some vague idea of adventure and Life Experience, which, for a girl, were still, at best, unlikely notions. Though her mother eagerly busied herself with wedding arrangements, her message to Diane all these years had been *Don't stop where I stopped*.

Diane told Jamie Kleinberg that she was breaking up with Doug because "she just didn't love him." When Diane told Doug, on the phone, that she was going to give him back the diamond ring, that she'd changed her mind about settling down and really wanted a life as a single woman in New York City, he was "absolutely devastated." He even briefly considered walking out on his internship program to be near her and try to win her back again.

Although he stayed in medical school, his attempts to win her back would go on for years. Ironically, she wouldn't be ready to say yes until after he'd finally rescinded the offer.

Shortly before she broke up with Doug in the spring of 1965, and without his ever knowing this, Diane came home to the dorm after a weekend in Cincinnati and told Mary Beth she thought she was pregnant. "Aren't you on any birth control pills?" Mary Beth asked, startled. Diane said no. Mary Beth was astonished at what her roommate had, all this time, been risking. It was less than two months before graduation. Diane had a sound B average. Abortions were illegal, hard to find, expensive and dangerous. "Well, at least you're with a medical student; he can help you," Mary Beth said. But Diane had said, "No, that could ruin his career. I'm not even going to tell him."

For the week that Diane's pregnancy fear lasted, before she finally got her period, Mary Beth was horrified by her roommate's dilemma, panicked at the prospect of Diane losing everything in life she'd worked for.

As for Diane's reaction, Mary Beth recalls: "It was almost as if this was her great drama, a short story she was a character in, a soap opera she was watching.

"She seemed to come so *alive* with that crisis."

Chapter 4

I came to New York in the mid-sixties, living first with roommates on the Upper East Side, then in a tenement on Charles Street, where I began a pattern of abuse of various substances that was to last for many years. Wrote in my journal and became involved with strange men. Glamour was all, and I relentlessly sabotaged every career opportunity in pursuit of bright light and fine restaurants.

Diane Pikul, NYU fiction class autobiography, June 1987

Diane's long-prepared-for postcollege odyssey started out as a classic scenario. Popular literature is full of Seven Sisters graduates coming to the Village "to Live" before going home again. New York is perfect for such catharsis and experimentation; in that myth-laden American capital of sophistication these former cheerleaders and valedictorians, these girlfriends of varsity team captains and medical students can attempt a sweeping self-transformation.

Girls who graduated college in 1965 were on the cusp between the fading conservative ethos of the fifties and the brave new world to come. In that twilight, Diane succeeded at making good on her dreams, then got caught in the undertow of that "success." For while sixties headwinds made it possible for a well-brought-up girl to live alone in a tenement and to take all kinds of un-all-American lovers, there was not yet the feminist consciousness that could shore up such experimentation with ambition, emotional protection and self-respect.

The idea of a young woman taking her career and her

self-sufficiency seriously—seeing these as collateral to cash in at the end of her wild and footloose journey—hadn't yet emerged. The culture hadn't yet provided a woman with the motivation to "do something with herself"; she had to find it within herself. When Diane Whitmore left college, she finally got a chance to play on the high wire, but she had to supply her own safety net.

After spending the summer of 1965 working at a bank in San Francisco, Diane at last came to New York. She lived in an Upper East Side apartment with three other girls she met through a roommate service. Because her grades were good and her Mount Holyoke professors recommended her ("literate, imaginative and attractive," her English teacher had written; "she stands out for her combination of fluency and inventiveness," wrote the director of the college news bureau, where Diane worked as a reporter), she had no trouble getting what was in effect a dream job, secretary to Eleanor Graves, the Modern Living editor at *Life* magazine.

This was a plum opportunity: to work at Time-Life, the most powerful and prestigious magazine corporation in the country, and to have available as mentor one of the most successful women editors in the business. Eleanor Graves did not want this ideal chance lost on her young assistant, whom she remembers as "this little thing with a cloud of blond hair, a piquant face, great intelligence and an impression of self-assurance that may not have been felt very deeply.

"I'd say, '*Life* magazine is open to women—I'm living proof.' I was always encouraging Diane to get more serious about her work. But she didn't want to," Eleanor Graves, now retired, says. "There was some ambivalence about her which was puzzling. She wasn't typical of the entry level girls at Time-Life. She played harder. She seemed to be living for night life. She was definitely not the kind who wanted to settle in New Jersey and have three kids, nor was she the kind who wanted to knock herself out to be an editor. And if a girl had neither of those motivations, well, there could be danger."

In a short story called "The Fantasist and the Star," Diane presents those as days of willed metamorphosis. "Still a rather mousy schoolgirl, I spent long quiet afternoons at my desk, reading the magazines of style to which my boss subscribed, applying research techniques to forge an image that would make me a star in the tabloids and restaurants of Manhattan." It was the season of the discotheque and the Carnaby Street look. Fashionable women wore teased hair behind headbands, great amounts of eye makeup and pale lipstick, and miniskirts to clubs like Arthur. Diane partook of the look, describing herself later as having been "a hip and glossy Alice in Wonderland."

At a downtown loft party, she met artist Red Grooms, whom she dated briefly. And through Time-Life she met journalist Tommy Thompson. She went out several times with this man whose fame would later come from his books about murders within well-heeled families, the very kind of crime of which the ingenue editorial assistant he was dating would later be a victim. But the most significant association Diane formed at Time-Life was with Nancy Kirkland, who was director of picture sales and services for *Sports Illustrated*. The stunning, ladylike woman, whose daughter was the ballet dancer Gelsey Kirkland, saw in Diane a younger version of herself, and their chance meeting at an office party would lead to a deep, mentoring friendship that would last Diane's lifetime.*

Those people who had been close to her in college saw that she was now after something concertedly anticollegiate. Mary Beth Whiton, who was then a graduate student living with roommates on the Upper West Side, took Diane to parties where there were a lot of handsome, confident Columbia law students. Not stuffy or stiff, these were liberal boys, many modeling themselves after Bobby Kennedy and John Lindsay. They were on the brink of high-profile careers and they knew it. "Diane would come to those parties," Mary Beth recalls, "and all those boys—several of whom now are known in politics and law—were interested in her. But she didn't want any of them."

Doug Johnston, who was doing his residency at the Manhattan Veterans Administration Hospital, tried to woo her back. He felt uncomfortable accompanying her

*Nancy Kirkland has declined to be interviewed.

"to those glitzy East Side parties," and watching her "hang around with pseudosophisticates. She was dressed to the hilt, and she was impressed with people who had money. She had had a good start at Time-Life but she wasn't producing any more than the minimum required. It made me mad, seeing someone with her great capacity so grossly underachieving, just floating along, immersed in the social atmosphere and looking for some kind of excitement."

The next year, 1967, Diane moved to Charles Street in the Village. She was going to places like the Dom, and later the Electric Circus upstairs. These were the new discotheques on St. Marks Place in the just-renamed East Village; with their twirling mirrored balls, strobe lights and light shows, they catered to people who imbibed psychedelic drugs instead of liquor. She was reading Anaïs Nin, shopping in the East Village for embroidered peasant dresses, listening to the records of Edith Piaf and Marlene Dietrich. Later she would write that she was content with "her job at a publishing company, her dates, her tenement apartment and unwillingness to settle, her obsession with an odyssey she wanted to take around the globe."

At first uncomfortable, Doug Johnston was now dismayed. His former fiancée, the ladylike girl who would fit right in on Oyster Bay, was living in a broken-down building, dressing like a hippie, hanging out with dope smokers! It was a classic scenario echoed that year throughout downtown Manhattan, as well as in other cities, where college couples would fracture from the *girl* seeking freedom and adventure.

Whenever they came together, things were, according to Doug, "very strongly romantic for a few days. Then Diane would end it. Sometimes she just broke down crying. I'd ask her why and she'd say she couldn't explain it. A feeling of emptiness, of depression, would just creep over her. That's the note we would break up on."

Diane's old friend from Mary Washington, Pat Barker, visited her in late 1967. She was now Pat Jaudon, married to a Navy man, still playing the southern naïf to Diane's wild urbanite. Pat couldn't believe that Diane was living in a *tenement* and that she had spent vacations traveling with guys she'd met through advertisements for rides in

The Village Voice. And that she'd have *sex* with these
. . . strangers. "I sat there, feeling like her father, angry
at some unknown man for 'taking advantage of' my
friend, whereas she had enjoyed the whole experience."

Pat remembers that Diane was reading Truman Ca-
pote's *In Cold Blood* at the time. "When something
crashed outside in the middle of the night, she woke up
frightened, as if she were in the middle of the book's
murder."

Years later, Diane's fiction would reflect the kind of men
she was drawn to. They were the emotional heirs to
Teddy, not Doug, a mixed group of urban cads and exot-
ics, par for the course for downtown life in the late sixties. There was something withheld, off-center, or
dangerous in each of them. She would catalogue them a
year before her death. They included: "George, the
caped and armed drug dealer, who permanently borrowed one of [Diane's] televisions and hi-fis after one of
her departures from which she never expected to return,
but always did; Phil, the tantalizing aloof executive
whose remoteness turned out to be a simple case of im-
potency; Raoul, the Hispanic gang leader turned mayoral
aide whose love of baseball precluded any possibility of
romantic commitment beyond the most urgent; . . . Edu-
ardo, available in his cluttered 14th St. apartment, smoking his pipe and practicing t'ai chi . . . and Johnny, the
overnight success on Wall Street who nearly drove her
crazy with his inability to divest himself of his wife of ten
years."

Diane was very typical in assuming that holding her
own with this assortment of sometimes brutal and re-
jecting men was a proud mark of picaresquery. At the
time, adopting the stance of a moll or "old lady" to
faintly dangerous men was as close as many young
women could get to adventure. It would take the seventies' earnest preachments on self-esteem to divest such
relationships of their glamour.

To Diane, however, abusive relationships never lost
their allure. She wrote to Pat Jaudon of her bouts of
"hysteria" with these sometimes "beautiful and very sick
men," of how "exciting" it was that "all the men in my
life are flamboyant and slightly crazy." In her later sto-

ries about those years, she mentioned, not without pride, mysterious blood stains, alluding to physical violence she apparently felt was linked to her need for "full freedom of expression." She wrote of sleeping with men "to provide the only comfort she could find" where "for a while the pain would abate and be replaced by a physical security." She also wrote that her increasing intake of liquor did two things: It both "center[ed] her in her romantic quest for adventure" and it "led her back to her childish terror."

What pain needed abating? What childhood terror did she mean? Two professionals, one a specialist in alcoholism, the other a psychotherapist, have offered a limited analysis of Diane, based on her fiction and autobiographical writing. Two distinct problems, it would seem, plagued her: first, her desire for romanticized personality transformation through drinking and, secondly, the emotionally anemic childhood that made her transformation feel so necessary.

As to the former: "A lot of well-raised, 'respectable' women who also have the biological predisposition to drink become alcoholics precisely because they are looking for that personality transformation," says Dr. Ann Geller, director of Smithers, one of the country's foremost alcohol treatment centers. "There's a wonderful Eartha Kitt song, 'I Want To Be Evil,' that embodies such a frequent sentiment of alcoholic women of Diane's social class that I've memorized the lyrics. 'I want to wake up in the morning with that dark brown taste, I want to see the signs of dissipation on my face.' " Dr. Geller noted in Diane's writings a similar pride in and idealization of alcoholic dissipation.

"With intoxication," she continues, "this well-brought-up girl is free to become her fantasy self. She's at the mercy of basic instinctual drives, and she's goaded into crazy scenes. That's why it's so hard for her to give up drinking—it makes life so exciting."

Yet eventually Diane *would* give up drinking—so thoroughly and successfully that she inspired others. (Ironically, she was all set to chair an AA meeting in the Hamptons the very weekend she was murdered.) But she never lost the need for excitement and danger, which she would count ten years into her sobriety. Why was her need for drama so deep?

Sydney H. Goldenberg has had considerable experience treating women who seek a sense of palpable risk, often through self-mutilation, in order to overcome a lack of tactile sensation that plagued their childhoods. "Often such a woman will take a nail and scratch herself, usually where no one can see the wound, just to feel the missed sensation," she says. "In looking over the stories Diane wrote and the statements her friends reported her having made, I think she may have felt the emotional counterpart to that tactile loss.

"Diane's mother seems to have felt dead in some way; and certainly when her mother drank, Diane disappeared from her line of vision. She writes, in one story, of her mother's 'gentle spirit becoming blurred.' Children who experience this lack of mirroring and lack of emotional sensation grow up looking for situations in which they can be jolted and can jolt back in order to stimulate and maintain their tenuous sense of aliveness. They want to see how hard they can push before there is danger. They're often drawn to the forbidden."

At some point in the late sixties, Diane's cousin Tommy, the quiet Catholic schoolboy with whom she'd spent so many afternoons in South Bend watching *Kukla, Fran & Ollie,* reappeared. He was a pop star now, the lead singer with his band, Tommy James and the Shondells. His sound was more suburban blue-eyed soul than rock, and in the summer of 1969 he had the number-one hit record in the country, a beautiful, elegiac anthem to "peace" and "love" and "brotherhood" with the appropriately inscrutable title "Crystal Blue Persuasion." Diane went along on one leg of her first cousin's concert tour. She would tell many people later, and proudly, that they had an affair. Diane's relationship with the only man in her life who knew in his bones the background she was rebelling against eventually returned to the more conventionally familial and they kept up with one another's lives until shortly before her murder.

The "on the road" wanderlust that had formerly been claimed by, with few exceptions, men alone had suddenly infected women, too. Alone or in twos, they vagabonded across America or traveled to Europe and Asia in pursuit of "truth," adventure, bonhomie and a way to support oneself without a "straight job." The next generation of young women would spend these same years of their lives—their early- to mid-twenties—in graduate or professional schools and then in entry-level positions of serious careers; but from 1969 to 1971, the very notion of practical foresight was anathema to the prevalent insouciant, seat-of-the-pants mode.

During those years, from the age of 25 to 27, Diane embodied the times. In Vail, Colorado, she was a ski bunny and secretary to a resort hotel executive before spinning off on an increasingly frenetic odyssey described in several letters to Pat Jaudon.

March 12, 1969

Dear Pat:

It was great to get your letter and great also every time I reread it in preparation to writing back. Unfortunately that's as far as I got, so this time I'm just going to barge ahead even though the time and mood are not perfect. . . . You might say that disorganization is one of the keynotes of my current existence. . . . I'm still searching and have no desire to commit myself to a job or to marriage now, though I want to eventually because I'm sure that's where the real satisfaction lies. This is still my fairly selfish educational period.

. . . Left Vail the end of April last year with great plans with Leslie, the friend from California I'd written you about. First drove with another friend through the Southwest to Tucson, a trip I adored after being confined to my mountain village all winter. Flew from there to Los Angeles to meet Leslie (unfortunately never saw San Diego) and we drove to Lake Tahoe with glamorous visions of getting rich as lady dealers. It was a huge disappointment and the entire scene seemed very seedy.

With renewed hope we hotfooted it to San Francisco to be interviewed as stewardesses for the Flying Tigers, which is entirely charter, mostly Asian routes. That too was a disappointment since our only layovers were to be Okinawa, Anchorage and a military base outside of Saigon.

Thoroughly depressed, we retired to Leslie's family's luxurious estate in Palm Springs where we sunned by the pool for a week. Whereupon I accepted a much-repeated job offer from———, a man I'd met at a party in NY the previous fall, at a time when I happened to have read some books he was interested in which convinced him I was a genius. . . .

The job offer Diane accepts is to assist in the creation of an East Coast institute modeled after Esalen. Diane met one of the Esalen founders, who, she writes,

. . . is the closest thing to a messiah personality I've ever encountered—almost physically radiates a sense of having been somewhere you haven't but where you'd like to go. Esalen has workshops in everything fascinating—all forms of psychotherapy, sensory awareness, mysticism, hypnosis, massage, drugs—and to my present way of thinking represents the most revolutionary movement there is, helping people realize their potential on a personal basis, not through an external system of religion or government. . . . I'm going to a 5-day workshop there at the end of April to find out for myself.

Her dream of creating an East Coast Esalen, however, falls through. Diane reports she

spent a delightful couple of weeks not working—you can't imagine how dehumanizing a 9 to 5 routine can be. Had a disastrous short love affair . . . and I ended it in about one hour of hysterics. . . . Sublet an apartment located on the border between the East Village and the Bowery. It had the best library and music collection, stained glass windows and a bed reached by a ladder in a room filled with colored lights and music. The building was occupied by assorted artists and nonconformists, who dropped in at all hours.

Eventually the money ran out and I had to get a job, took the first one that sounded pleasant since I considered it temporary.

Diane's new job was assistant to Allen Funt, producer of TV's venerable *Candid Camera*. Diane describes the job's atmosphere as "never dull but also very nervous-making.

> I became a chain smoker and drank every night . . . [though] I thought the field of film and television much more vital than journalism and if/when I return to a straight job, it might be in that field. A sidelight was three months of once a week therapy which I entered partly from curiosity, partly from hysteria. It was a fascinating experience.

Diane returned to Vail, a waitress, and "fell in love, as much as you can in two months," with a "lovable, entertaining" man "from a miserable disruptive background." In her next letter to Pat she planned to go to "San Francisco, Esalen, L.A., possibly Mexico, definitely Europe sometime next summer."

Instead, however, Diane broke her leg badly while skiing and went home to her parents' house in Longmeadow, Massachusetts, for a long recuperation, during which, she wrote in a letter on April 16, 1970,

> . . . the tensions started to arise from my position as an adult child in my parents' house and from what you would have to call the generation gap. They can't understand why I don't settle down, get married, get a good job, use my education, why I want to travel, etc. At one point my father suggested that I, along with Charles Manson, should have cement poured in my ear (vivid imagery, no?) or go get shot in Biafra. I dissolved in tears and went to New York for two weeks, where I discovered that all my old friends were diverging from the older generation in the same ways as I. The most vital and alive people are unemployed whenever possible (but doing things by way of writing or music or group therapy-sensitivity training things or travel) and were for the most part living in sin or putting off marriage. The people who were still at *Life* magazine (which my parents constantly berate me for leaving) seemed to have lost their spirit, beaten down, sold out, etc.

In her next letter to Pat—dated February 16, 1971—
Diane reported that, after "taking occasional trips with
my rock and roll star cousin and generally sleeping till
noon," she "got down to $4.00 and began eating pasta
and looking for a job, only to discover that the job market was tight and employment agency types were very
wary of my 'instability.' " She had spent the summer as
a Kelly Girl temp and as a secretary for the Rockefeller
brothers. She was

> . . . living in a tenement in Hell's Kitchen, subletting
> an artsy little apartment that belonged to one of Ru-
> dolph Nureyev's friends who was a friend of a friend.
> [Diane's connection was Gelsey Kirkland.] Every-
> where I looked, Nureyev was staring back. Shortly
> after I moved into this place, whose tenant had sworn
> they hadn't seen any trouble in 20 years, strange acro-
> batic people were seen breaking into my apartment
> . . . Afraid to go to sleep at night, I moved into the
> apartment upstairs with a 21-year-old college boy. We
> cooked downstairs and slept upstairs and considered
> it our duplex. The rest of the time we waged war on
> the roaches and when we broke up in mid-August I
> began hopping around to any apartments of friends I
> could find—I moved ten times until I had enough
> money for bribing my way into my own apartment.
> By which time I was exhausted.

The twenty-one-year-old college boy was a blond preppy
with an entry-level job at *The New York Times*. Now an
investment banker, Doug Thompson (not to be confused
with her ex-fiancé Doug Johnston) remembers their tene-
ment-bound, unair-conditioned summer romance as hot
and sweaty—"if you sat in a hard-backed chair in that
apartment long enough, the varnish would melt and your
shirt would stick to the back of the chair." He was a
romantic young prep school boy steeping himself in Real
Life In The Naked City, with an "older woman" of twen-
ty-seven who was reassuringly *of* his type and class and
yet who had turned an experiential and emotional corner
he found intriguing, if impossible to follow.

"We'd sit on the fire escape on Friday afternoons, listening to Simon and Garfunkel on the radio and watching

the New Jersey commuters go into the whorehouse on the corner. When we got fed up with the tenement, we'd walk across town to our friend Nancy Kirkland's Upper West Side apartment to use her shower. Diane and I molded ourselves after the image of Scott and Zelda. Our relationship was all about drinking and filled with drinking: beer and Gordon's gin and tonic. We were probably both alcoholics at the time, but I was a sport alcoholic, doing it for effect, while Diane was a real one.

"Diane would make life dramatic. She liked to argue— about books, politics, anything. We argued a lot about the Vietnam War. She was more liberal than I was. We would get thrown out of restaurants a lot for getting into arguments dead-drunk. Then we'd wander back to a divey bar called the Triple Inn, which was two blocks from our apartment and run by a *Times* printer. We'd have another couple of drinks and, in different states of inebriation, cry over one of her cousin Tommy's songs on the jukebox. Then we'd make up and be very passionate and romantic and wander back home.

"I was aware that she was attracted to violence and that I was one of the most normal guys she'd been with, that she was probably looking for stability with me. I could tell she was vulnerable, and that there was a great deal of loneliness inside her, though she tried to hide it. She wanted to get married. She didn't want to spend the rest of her life working as an office temp and living in a $42.50 tenement apartment on Fifty-fourth Street and Ninth Avenue, where the junkies would escort her back home from the liquor store.

"If I were more responsible, I would have married her. But I was young, and I wanted to see the world. And, I guess, I felt our drinking bouts didn't exactly guarantee future happiness. But Diane was a caring and generous person with more gumption and intellectual energy and fun and humor than almost anyone I'd ever met, before or since. For example, on my twenty-first birthday, she gave me a coming-of-age cocktail party in our fourth-floor walkup. It was a howl—a collection of people, none of whom should have been in the same room together, all climbing up those endless stairs in the ninety-five degree heat. She gave me an assortment of presents from the sublime to the ridiculous: serious poetry and history books on the one hand and, on the other, some hysterical pornography and a collection of condoms you wouldn't believe. Then we all went out to an X-rated movie. Only Diane would think of a celebration like that.

"The picture of her that most stays in my mind is from the day we moved out of that apartment to go our separate ways. We had been carrying things downstairs for hours, between drinks. I was by the U-Haul with the television set and she was walking down the stairs with a lampshade in one hand and an elegant cocktail glass in the other. It was a toss-up as to whether she was going to make it down the last few steps without falling on her face.

"But she looked perfectly controlled and composed and unapologetic as she set the lampshade down on the dirty concrete stoop and, spreading her skirt out under her—she was the best-dressed girl on Fifty-fourth Street between Ninth and Tenth Avenue, I'll tell you that—sat down and slowly finished what was left in her longstemmed glass, as if she was at some Montmartre cafe at the turn of the century . . . or across town at Lutèce."

Diane settled into a small apartment on Twelfth Street between Sixth and Seventh avenues. She continued to indulge in many affairs "with strange men" and in early 1971 took a job with the New York Parks Department, as administrative assistant to the commissioner.

The job, impressive on paper and a potential steppingstone to better things for someone who had ambition, would last seven years. As would her ambivalence toward it. In a letter to Pat Jaudon she said:

When I started the job seemed fairly appealing—lots of days off, work in the field, an office in the middle of Central Park's zoo and a relaxed atmosphere where you can come to work barefoot if you like, which is handy for a person with no money and a closet full of ski clothes. However, I must tell you that this, like all my work experiences, has been disenchanting. I despise the drudgery of sacrificing five of my days to somebody else's work, climbing out of bed at the crack of dawn and getting home too tired to clean myself and my apartment, cook and drink my beloved martinis.

Diane's increased drinking never showed at work; the "good front" she'd been bred to keep up didn't falter during nine to five. Her immediate boss for most of her tenure at that job, Joe Davidson, the New York Commissioner of Parks between 1973 and 1977, "would never have guessed she had a drinking problem. She was discreet and subdued, an excellent typist and assistant, though, unlike a lot of others, she was clearly not ambitious to go further. My wife, who got to know her, remembers her as an unusually kind and lovely person."

Diane was starting to see the career hole she'd dug herself into, yet the way she proposed to solve it was by denying, rather than recognizing and channeling, her considerable intelligence and energy. As she wrote to Pat:

I have reached a point where I would undoubtedly prefer all out domesticity, but I also think I copped out early in my working days when I chose jobs according to social and travel benefits rather than what I was doing. Consequently I am now a glorified secretary and completely unsuited temperamentally. It now appears that I shall have to consider and train myself for something else, possibly wifehood and motherhood. This will probably sound strange to an old married lady like you, but I am just beginning to feel ready to get married, and I think it will take some time longer to be ready for children.

The man she chose for this next stage of her life was Ralph Schnackenberg, a photojournalist she had met several years earlier. Though she would later describe him to friends as a dashing, mysterious character who claimed to be a secret operative for the CIA, Schnackenberg was in fact a short, somewhat portly man five years older than she, who hid his ordinary looks behind the slightly sinister guise of dark glasses, dark muttonchop sideburns and a thick, downturned mustache. His personality, at least today, could be far more accurately described as low-key and thoughtful rather than dark and charismatic.

But, since today he is using a different first name and is living a rural life that is consciously reformed and bucolic, he may well have been a different person during the ten years that he knew Diane. They had met on a train during Diane's *Life* magazine days. Diane was returning to New York from a visit to her parents' house in Massachusetts; Ralph boarded the train in Connecticut. He was charmed and amused by her "elegant, white-gloves air. When I asked her if I could call her in New York, she said, 'That would be grand.' I didn't know people still said 'grand.' " They were friends for a year before becoming lovers, Schnackenberg playing the worldly Villager "talking existentialist crap, which she ate up; taking her to the Cedar Tavern and the White Horse." During Sunday brunches at Daly's Dandelion, Diane drank Ralph and his friends under the table.

Married, going through an ugly separation and divorce, out of the country often on assignment, Ralph had an elusiveness that gave the romance a suitable edge for Diane. Both Mary Beth Whiton and Eleanor Lamperti met Ralph, and both women were surprised by his unprepossessing appearance and demeanor. What did Diane see in this man? By 1971, Diane was proclaiming her passionate love for him, writing to Pat Jaudon that "I feel rather sophomoric rhapsodizing, but he is the most wonderful person according to every standard I have developed over the years and he adores me and we are very happy." They lived together, off and on, in her West Twelfth Street apartment.

They had some good times: having "moveable feast" dinner parties between their apartment and those of their neighbors, and visiting the Caribbean. At about this time, Diane's old college friend Jamie Kleinberg reentered her life. Jamie, married at the time to a chemist and living a wealthy and cultured life in New Jersey, gave elegant parties for which Diane and Ralph would be picked up by limousine. "It was all very Gatsby-esque," Ralph recalls. "Diane was impressed by that life and wanted it for herself, badly."

The professed happiness between Diane and Ralph quickly turned to melodrama. "Our relationship was a Zelda and Scott type thing," Schnackenberg says today, repeating Doug Thompson's phrase but with somewhat darker meaning. "There was a lot of running down the street after one another in nightgowns and banging on taxi doors."

When Avianca Airlines, for whom he was shooting a brochure, gave Ralph a free trip to South America, he brought Diane along. By Jeep and Land Rover, they roamed the continent, seeking out adventure. In Bogota, life was "grand." They were treated to a driver, an interpreter and a bodyguard, all of whom would assemble each day in the hotel lobby to await their VIP clients. "Diane would float down the stairs to her entourage, who would all stand up at once and bow, saying, 'Buenos días, señora,' while the desk clerk whispered to me, 'Is she in the cinema?' Oh, did she *love that.* We were both playing that game to the hilt, but to Diane, that was the way life should be." Things soon grew notably less pampered. In a little mud village called Tabatinga, at the intersection of Peru and Bolivia, Ralph shot a photo essay on the cocaine trade.

"It was strictly frontier justice there. If they thought you were from the drug administration—and any gringo was suspected of that—it was deep trouble. Diane was shaken. 'This is reality, not a game,' I told her. 'You can't get a little drunk and play coquette here.' I had photographed an Indian boy who'd been brought up virtually as a slave, and the strong-arms didn't like my taking pictures of the kid. The Indian boy ran us down a pier to a waiting paddleboat with the warning: 'They're coming after you to kill you—jump on the boat!' There was about a three-foot distance to jump. The Indian kid and some other onlookers were yelling, 'Jump! Jump!' and I tried to pull Diane on, but she just stood there, frozen, as if she was tempting fate—or as if she expected to suddenly wake up from that bad Indiana Jones movie we'd found ourselves in." Then, like Nancy Drew in the impassioned last pages of a tale, she jumped.

The rest of the trip, however, had a distinctly non-Nancy Drew flavor. On the edge of the Amazon jungle in Colombia, Diane and Ralph stayed in "a little rat-hole of a pension owned by a German woman, probably a Nazi, where lizards dropped from the ceiling when you turned the fan on," Ralph recalls. There, "Diane and I had a fight. I can't remember what it was about, but booze would intensify all her reactions, and she just started wailing and shrieking and screaming. She went tearing out of the place in her nightgown, barefoot. The desk clerk informed me, very matter-of-factly: 'Señor, your wife is walking into the jungle.'

"The town's generator had shut off for the night so it was pitch-dark, Diane obviously couldn't see where she was going, but she kept going anyway. She stepped on some metal and cut her foot and we heard her wailing like an animal. Eventually, she came back. They threw us out of the place the next day. To get thrown out of a rat-hole pension—what an achievement!

"We dragged our bags through the dirt street to this dump of a coffee shop, which was the only restaurant in town. Every eye in the place was on us; all these native men had heard what had happened the night before. They were staring at us, waiting for us to continue our fight. Diane whispered to me, 'Let's play Liz and Dick, the morning after. *That'll* get them crazy.' " So just like the passionate, battling Burtons who were then always confounding the public, Ralph and Diane acted as if their fight had never happened. "The men sipping their coffee just stared, not knowing what to think of us."

Diane sometimes wrote love poems to Ralph that incorporated simplistic notions about the glories of emotional liberation. She would proudly set herself up as the "feeling" one, next to his frightened avoidance of intimacy. In one such poem, she warns:

Know that at this moment in your life, you are choosing
                    death over life
                    ugliness over beauty
You have created your life to be an elaborate prison
and it's been so long since you've known freedom
                    that you've lost the desire to be free
Why?
Know that your commitment to "us" still exists until you
face me,
Look into my eyes, and tell me that you don't want our
love
I am here, laughing, crying, feeling completely alive,
sending
you the courage to love yourself

I recognize your fear and it is not valid

Diane closed the poem in Spanish:

Cuando Tu Conoces la Verdad de Estas Cosas
Esteras Libre
(Only when you know the truth of these things are
you free.)

Yet Diane was only truly that "laughing, crying, feeling completely alive" person when she drank. And her
drinking increased as the seventies advanced, years in
which emotional strength and autonomy in women became increasingly valued, only to illuminate and exacerbate
Diane's inability to give her life definition and dignity.
Diane must have felt as she had leaving the comforts
of South Bend for the rude exposure of Birmingham,
Michigan: as if the jig was up; as if now her protective
veils of popularity and romance had been pulled aside
to reveal that she couldn't make it. "Charming" self-
destructiveness was becoming discredited. It would not
do, not for a single woman in her early thirties, not for
the long haul. It was the unflashy girls, armed with advanced degrees, genuinely earned confidence and the
ability to take themselves seriously, who were perhaps
best able to handle life in an era that was both post-
traditional and postpsychedelic.

In the language of alcoholic recovery, there is a term
called "cover behavior," which refers to the superachiev-
ing outer self that does a very successful job of hiding the
latent illness for a limited time. It would be reasonable to
apply the term to Diane.

According to Ralph, Diane was, beneath that often
captivating persona, "so insecure, anyone could put her
down." She knew her job at the Parks Commission was
a waste of her talents, but she appeared unable to *want*
to advance past it. She wanted to write, to take the character she had made of herself and put it on paper, but
she was afraid of trying, afraid perhaps of succeeding.
When she drank, she would become bitterly derisive

about people she had known from her *Life* magazine days who were now successfully published. It was clear to those close to her that she secretly despised her own jealousy as well as her own cowardice.

Diane tried to set herself on a positive course. Full of malaise about her work and self-worth, she nonetheless remained the dutifully organized girl who had created the Nancy Drew Library in grade school. "She was structured and perfectionistic," remembers Ralph. "She would make lists and goals—I'm going to do A,B,C,D. One morning, she was so determined to make the perfect sunnyside-up egg that she stood at the stove, cracking, then throwing away it must have been two dozen eggs before she got one 'right.' "

She tried bio-energetics, est and other seventies self-realization therapies. But none of these reached her deep-rooted, difficult-to-define pain or helped her to heal it. Increasingly, in the apartment on Riverside Drive in the Nineties where Diane now lived, Ralph would waken to hear, dimly in the next room, the clink of ice cubes over the sound of mournful, twangy ballads. Diane was staying up long into the night, slowly and quietly downing Tanqueray on the rocks while listening to the country-western station. She loved the songs of Kris Kristofferson, a Rhodes scholar with a severe drinking problem. Perhaps she identified with his combination of intelligence, education, looks—and overriding self-destructiveness. She talked maudlinly of how she was "damaged goods": how her mother's overindulgence had ruined her, had created the condition whereby she could act *out* but could not act.

"As an alcoholic, there's a perversity you come to recognize in yourself," says Maggie Gari. "It's as if a piece of your intelligence is missing, no matter how bright you are otherwise. You can't seem to do what everyone else around you does effortlessly: Make your life run constructively. You have to sabotage it."

Diane's pent-up anger, vulnerability and melancholy came out in cathartic explosions when she drank and when she and Ralph argued. He manipulated her by clouding himself in mystery and witholding information as basic as where he was living when not at her apartment. Early in 1975, Diane, provoked by Ralph's elusiveness, screamed that she wanted them both dead. Her outburst resulted in Ralph's breaking off contact with her. Immediately after her moment of powerful assault, she suffered great guilt, remorse and abject terror at having lost everything. In a long letter she expresses fear of her aggressiveness *and* her helplessness. It is a letter riddled with desperation, self-blame, and melodrama.

March 13, 1975

My dearest Ralph,

This letter . . . is the last thing I know how to do in trying to contact you, without being utterly rash and possibly destructive to you, and afterwards I'll feel totally helpless in the situation, which is almost unendurable to me . . .

I have loved you for four years. I never stopped loving you, even when I'd given up on the possibility of our having a life together. I will always love you, even if I never hear from you again. The not knowing [if you'll contact me again] is unhuman, it's worth [sic] than a death. Please don't let one day's hysterical outburst destroy all our chance for happiness. The incredible sweetness of life I had with you these last few weeks, I can't bear the shock of feeling it's all gone . . . I didn't mean what I said, even at the time, that I would never forgive you, that I was going to someone else, that I wanted us both dead. I only wanted to hurt you. I just couldn't tolerate the mystery anymore. I wanted to see where you live, know the truth, be able to reach you . . .

In the next lines she reveals that she knows why she drinks, and knows what drinking does to her.

I could feel it building up in me, but kept denying my feelings for fear it would spoil things. . . . I should have known better than to drink when I was in such turmoil—these are my problems, to deny feelings because of fear of loss and deep need, until they only get expressed when they've reached hysteria level and are totally destructive and nothing anyone can respond to.

Then, significant in its abrupt departure from the self-abnegating tone of the rest of the letter, she says, almost as a challenge: "I thought you knew this about me. Are you trying to punish me or teach me a lesson?"

Diane Whitmore, in the middle of a decade devoted to self-improvement and to feminism—and hardly alone among her peers—could articulate her weaknesses and yet couldn't stop running into the arms of the wrong men.

On June 29, 1975, a hot, humid day, on a boat moored at the Seventy-ninth Street boat basin, Diane and Ralph were married. A Lutheran minister presided and Nancy Kirkland was her matron of honor. Diane's parents, who had by now moved to a retirement community in Florida, were not present; they'd completed their yearly trip to New York just before the hastily planned wedding, and Diane did not want her father, a man who trusted his fate to cars, not planes, to make the tiring drive up the Eastern seaboard and back again. But they did send their blessings. Diane had just permed her hair, finding the loose mop of curls she would wear for the rest of her life. She had purchased a wedding gown but greeted Eleanor Lamperti in a slinky antique dress, saying, "Between the hair and the gown, I looked like the sugar plum fairy, so I wore this instead." Jamie Kleinberg watched the ceremony in the "awful, steamy river heat" and had an immediate bad feeling about Diane's choice of husband. "Then my heel broke on the wooden pier and I took it as an omen that this marriage would not be good for Diane."

Indeed, about a week after the wedding, as Diane's father remembers her telling it, Diane had come home from the office one day, opened the mail and stacked Ralph's letters, which she had not read, on his desk. "When Ralph got home, he got so mad that she'd opened his envelopes, he said, 'If you do that again, I'll push you out the window.' She called me in Florida, scared and crying. I said, 'Look, get out of this quick. I'll send you the money to get an annulment.' "

According to Ralph, "if I did say those words—and I'm not denying that I may have—it was in the same way that a mother at the end of her rope tells her kid, 'If you don't behave, I'm gonna break your legs!' I never threatened Diane seriously, and I never beat her; most of the time I walked away from her provocations in frustrated rage." They remained together intermittently for a year thereafter, during which period Diane's drinking got so bad that she was, as Ralph recalls, "knocking down a water glass of vodka every morning before she left for work, just to get herself going. Yet she never drank at work." And she remained the scrupulous secretary/assistant, digesting data that Joe Davidson gave her on the productivity of schoolteachers hired as part-time recreation field workers, and writing up memos on the subject; keeping Davidson informed on the progress of studies made of the adequacy of park lighting in Queens and Brooklyn; arranging for Davidson to be photographed at City Hall alongside Mayor Abe Beame. Diane hated the work—she thought it either drab or idiotic. But she never let on to Davidson. And he never even remotely suspected that she was an alcoholic.

By the end of summer in 1976, Ralph had moved out of Diane's Riverside Drive apartment. In September, Diane got a phone call at the office from her father in Florida. Her parents had just finished lunch, Don Whitmore was telling his daughter, with unusual emotion in his voice. Jane was standing in the kitchen doing the dishes when she suddenly fell over backwards. Don says he rushed in, "pounded on her chest and everything, and she finally started to come to, and I got her to her feet and onto the sofa and called our neighbor to come over as fast as she could. And then she said, with her hand over her heart, 'Oh my God, here it comes again.' That time, I couldn't revive her."

Within hours, Diane was in Florida, where she and her father took Jane Jackson Whitmore's body onto another plane to South Bend for the funeral. The next evening, she stood at her mother's grave in the family plot, not far from the Studebakers'. She was back home again, the sophisticated New Yorker. She had a job she didn't like, a salary she could not live well on, a bad marriage that was about to end, a penchant for men who treated her badly, and an addiction to alcohol. She was thirty-three years old: exactly the age her mother had been when she'd given birth to her.

*   *   *

Back in New York, Diane felt orphaned and desperate. Though her father was certainly alive and well, her sense of having a place to "go home to" was destroyed; it was always her doting, melancholic mother who took Diane back into the fold of those aqua rooms and listened and accepted unconditionally. Her drinking was now leading to blackouts and falls down stairs. A man who had known her, mostly as a friend, from her West Twelfth Street days would sometimes get calls from her, drunk, at 6 A.M. asking him to come over and keep her from being alone. But he was an AA member and he knew from the way she talked that she wanted him to drink with her. He pleaded with her to seek help.

At Christmastime, Diane's letter to Pat Jaudon was unusually brief. Gone was the chatty insouciance, the barely veiled delight in telling her conventional friend of the glories and ironies of her adventurous life. This letter had a terse and exhausted, almost a defeated, tone. "I do think of you and my negligence in not writing weighs heavy on my mind," Diane began. "I got married to Ralph in June 1975 but it wasn't very successful and we are now living apart. My mother died three months ago and that has preoccupied my thoughts since then."

On August 22, 1977, Diane had a lawyer serve Ralph with annulment papers. He did not contest. The annulment was awarded the following spring. According to these papers, "prior to the said marriage and for the purpose of inducing plaintiff [Diane] to marry him, the defendant falsely represented to her that if she would marry him the parties would cohabit as man and wife, have intercourse in the normal manner and have children." But Ralph in fact "refused to have normal sexual relations with plaintiff and insisted on the use of contraceptives . . . and prior to the commencement of this action, the defendant informed the plaintiff that he did not want to have children."

These were months of, as Diane would describe them in a short story, "desolation in the morning hours" and "despair . . . I could no longer face." It had been a particularly brutal summer in New York, with the blackout and the unremitting terror of the Son of Sam murders. In the midst of it all, Diane's old college beau Doug

Johnston recontacted her. He was the same clean-living "catch" he had been when she had spurned him; but now, after the battles she had been through, those qualities must have looked different to her. He had a plastic surgery practice in Florida, was a marathon runner, had just been divorced, owned and flew his own plane. When he called her at work in October 1977, while he was in town running the New York Marathon, and offered to pick her up at her father's house Thanksgiving weekend and fly her, along with another couple, to a skiing weekend in Vail, she leapt at the opportunity.

But when Doug saw Diane, he was disconcerted. "She seemed to have deteriorated physically. She had a funny kind of affect. Was it drinking? Drugs? I couldn't put my finger on it. And she almost immediately made a remark: 'With your money and my determination, we can go far.' I wasn't sure I was ready for that kind of come-on. It scared me a little."

As they boarded the plane and Doug took the controls, he had the sinking feeling that the girl he thought he'd never not be in love with had changed. When they landed at one airport to refuel, "Diane lagged behind. She seemed to be disassembled. The other woman we were with even whispered to me, concerned, 'Is she . . . talking to herself?'"

After the weekend, Diane, back in New York, sent Doug a flirtatious letter with a clipping of the marathon he had run. He kept the letter on his desk for several weeks before he realized he was not going to reply to it.

While Diane was waiting for the reply from Doug—or perhaps at the point when she understood it was not coming—she agreed to have lunch with a woman named Gloria Archer, who was a friend of her friend Nancy Kirkland. Nancy had helped Gloria get sober eleven years before, despite Gloria's initial stubborn protestations that she would somehow "lick the problem by myself." "This darling young friend of mine," Nancy now told Gloria, "is as stubborn as you were."

Sitting across from Diane at Wolfe's Delicatessen on Fifty-seventh Street and Sixth Avenue, Gloria saw in Diane Whitmore "someone who was me, but younger. Someone who could be a daughter to me. We reached each other."

Not long after that, one evening just after New Year's Day in 1978, Diane took the subway down to her old, favorite neighborhood, the Village, and walked into a little storefront with draped windows on Perry Street just off West Fourth Street. Informally dressed people sat on folding chairs. One member was "doing the coffee." Diane looked a little glossier, more "uptown" than most of the others. She was dressed in the madcap yet classy style then being popularized by Diane Keaton and Jill Clayburgh. For the first time in years she felt hopeful. "My name is Diane, and I am an alcoholic," she announced, standing, as the eyes of the others turned respectfully to her.

Standing in the back of the room was a tall man in a Burberry's trench coat. His name was Joseph Pikul.

PART III

A MARRIAGE FOR THE EIGHTIES

Chapter 5

I began to long for the security I thought a marriage could provide. Perhaps my mother had been right after all. My visions of glorious freedom dimmed. . . . Deep into a dead end career as a civil servant, I abandoned my drugs, got spiritual and pregnant.

My choice stayed constant, and my marriage was unkind. It was quite some time before I could admit this.

Diane Pikul, "A Fine Romance—The Fantasist and the Star"

The hundreds of rooms in greater New York City in which almost twenty-five hundred Alcoholics Anonymous meetings are held every week are as diverse as their demographics suggest. Meetings held in working-class communities in Queens and the Bronx are typically male and blue-collar. Those held in the Wall Street area at lunchtime brim with a distinctly white-collar group that includes brokers and traders. The evening meetings on the Upper East Side draw well-heeled and often very successful men and women. Indeed, the number of society matrons in designer suits attending meetings at Fifth Avenue's Church of the Heavenly Rest led it to be nicknamed, among AA members, "The Church of the Overly Dressed."

But of all the city's AA chapters, the chapter whose meetings Diane Whitmore chose to attend is one of the most colorful and distinct. It is referred to as the Perry Street Workshop—and sometimes, because of its dark, smokey, barlike atmosphere, and because so many of its members put in prior years at the desultory nearby bar called The 55, it's jokingly called "the 56."

The Perry Street Workshop is filled with actors, writers, Village bartenders and habitués. It is characterized by emotional energy, honesty, intellectualism, and, as one habitué says, "as much love and arguing as a family." Yet, despite its familial atmosphere, the members generally hold to the crucial AA maxim, designed for self-protection, that members not form any new romances or make any major life decisions during their first year of sobriety. This rule, Smithers director Ann Geller says, is especially important for women members, since "the vulnerability a woman experiences during recovery from alcohol is much stronger than that of a man. Her dependency needs are so great and her self-esteem so low that she's often desperate for someone to compliment her and 'make it all right.' "

Diane Whitmore's vulnerability was apparently too great for her to be able to hold to this important restriction. Shortly after she first stood up and gave her "qualification" (personal story) at the Perry Street Workshop—discussing her sense of aberrance, in childhood, from the blandness of her parents' lives; and the short distance she traveled from loving the accoutrements and rituals of drinking to becoming addicted to drinking itself—Diane met the eye of the man in the trench coat at the back of the room. They may have immediately sensed what they had in common: a desire for the good life, lived glamorously; a need to be loved, despite a lifetime's behavior to the contrary; and an almost uncontrollable penchant for violence in relationships.

The high-strung forty-three-year-old man with the Brooks Brothers wardrobe and the air of arrogance was a composite of all the disparate men Diane had ever been attracted to. Like her boyfriend Teddy, Joe Pikul's background was markedly different from hers, and he had suffered—not from a serious illness, as Teddy had, but from abuse: as a child, he had been beaten by his father. Like Doug Johnston and Doug Thompson, he held out to Diane the promise of entrée into a "better" social world—though, unlike either Doug, Joe Pikul's access to that world was not by birth but, rather, by the money he had earned himself. Like her first husband,

Ralph, he was mysterious and a less handsome man than her women friends felt she could attract. Also like Ralph, and like all the "sick" and off-center men she celebrated in her short stories and in her letters to Pat Jaudon, he was a potential provocateur of her fits of "hysterics"—and he was physically threatening.

And so, as Gloria Archer puts it: "In coming to AA, Diane was saved from a lifetime of drinking, only to meet a worse fate, and to have her fatal flaws emerge, in her sobriety."

Joseph Pikul had been sober for about two years when he met Diane at the Perry Street Workshop. Along with anonymity, confidentiality is the most sacred tenet of AA; the content of members' "qualifications" is not to go beyond the meetings' four walls. So it is impossible to know exactly what demons Joseph Pikul had to fight in order to achieve and maintain sobriety; but it is clear from the little that his fellow Perry Street members *are* willing to reveal that those demons were considerable.

"Joe was nervous, always on the edge when he spoke. He was, by his own admission, a very violent man—and he was clearly a very terrified human being," is the most that one Perry Street attendee, a man, will say to sum up Joe Pikul's character during those years. A woman remembers that Joe spoke of how, through drink, he had lost everything he had: his marriage and the success he had worked his whole life to amass. "He said he was starting all over again, from zero. He sounded both contrite and determined."

Perhaps the most revealing thing Joe Pikul ever said at Perry Street during those years was something he said not to the group as a whole, or even out loud. It was a remark a woman member overheard him whispering, as an aside, to the man seated next to him. "Sometimes," he whispered, "I think I'm looking at life through a killer's eyes."

Joseph Pikul was born on December 3, 1934, in the working-class town of Ware, Massachusetts. He was the second child and only son of poor Polish Catholic immigrants. The family was "very religious and old-world," remembers Sandra Jarvinen, whose own family was

upper middle-class, modern and prosperous. "Every holiday was celebrated. On Easter, Joe's mother, Bernice,
whom everyone called 'Bobchi' and who was a warm,
commanding, bustling old-fashioned matriarch, would
preside over a table with keilbasa blessed by the priest.
She'd always press me to take home her homemade
horseradish for good luck," Sandra recalls. "It was so
strong, I cried when I tasted it."

Elements of Joe Pikul's childhood are almost Dicken-
sian. His father worked in a textile mill as a weaver,
while Bobchi worked in a shoe factory to help make ends
meet; and Joe and his sister Janice would sometimes be
forced to play with buttons from Bobchi's sewing box
because the family could afford so few toys. Joseph
Pikul, Sr., was frequently drunk, at which time he would
take his anger and frustration out on his young son. During the custody hearings that ensued after his murder of
Diane Joe admitted, "My father punched me in the jaw
and knocked me around the room. . . . He used to chase
us out of the house at night. In an alcoholic household,
usually one kid gets the brunt of it. I was [my father's]
lightning rod."

Joe also told people that his father had been a Nazi.
(Once he made this admission to a Polish-born Jewish
hairdresser in a Greenwich Village hair salon. The startled young woman replied, "Well . . . that doesn't make
you guilty of anything." She did not know that he had
just been indicted for Diane's murder.)

From these miserable beginnings, Joe Pikul was somehow able to find in himself enough resilience, determination and self-esteem to vault past the abuse, the poverty,
the ceiling of his social class—past everything he knew—
in order to reinvent himself. Insistent on going to college
despite his parents' inability to pay, he worked for a year
after high school to earn money for school. Joe took
a day job as a construction worker for the local water
department. He would come home briefly for dinner and
to change his clothes, then go to his second job, working
the graveyard shift at a textile mill.

With the money saved from these jobs, supplemented
by an ROTC scholarship, Joe attended Boston's Northeastern University, sharing an apartment on Beacon
Street with a friend, Henry Sawoska. On a blind date in

1955, when he was twenty years old and a sophomore, he met Sandra Jarvinen, then eighteen and a freshman. Both sides of Sandra's family had come to America from Finland at the turn of the century. Her father owned a trucking and construction company, and the family spent two to three months of each year in Palm Beach. Sandra had had her own car since she was sixteen, and she was an accomplished horsewoman. Her higher social class, Sandra thinks, enhanced the struggling scholarship student's infatuation with her.

Sandra was impressed with Joe as well. "He was not your typical coddled middle-class college student," she recalls. "He worked around the clock: in factories, for the highway department and as a gravedigger. He ran the radio station for the ROTC and was a brilliant student, and he was driven by the desire to make money. He was extraordinarily charming, funny, intelligent, so clearly on his way to success. He called me Sandy; I called him Joey. He had a zest for life back then—we both did. And he was not yet drinking any more than the rest of us college students. At the ROTC ball, we entered the hall arm in arm and walked regally under the crossed military swords—he in his pink officers' uniform, me in my frilly gown. We had so much fun walking under those swords, we went back and did it again!"

But there were dark flashes beneath all that gaiety. When, shortly after they started dating, Sandra mentioned that she and some girlfriends were taking an annual spring trip to Bermuda, Joe became deeply upset. Sandra took the trip anyway, "and when I got back, we had a big scene about it. It was the first time I got a glimpse of his enormous possessiveness." Sandra's parents did not like Joe. "His hyper quality and overbearing nature made them nervous," she recalls. "They didn't like the fact that he was a man who always got his way, and they didn't believe his big dreams of financial success would materialize."

According to Sandra, Joe graduated number two in his class at Northeastern. He was accepted, with financial aid, to the MBA programs of Columbia and Wharton, both of which he turned down to go to Harvard Business School, even though no financial aid was offered. After graduation, he took six months off to do his active duty—

first at the Army School of Finance in Indianapolis, then at Fort Devens, in Ayer, Massachusetts.

In late summer, 1959, he and Sandra married in a simple ceremony at a Catholic church in Boston—Sandra in a white gown, Joe in his ROTC officers' uniform. ("God, he was handsome," Sandra remembers.) Hank Sawoska was the groom's best man. Joe's cousin Charlotte attended Sandra. A small reception was held at Joe and Sandra's new apartment on Beacon Street, right around the corner from the Ritz Carlton. Sandra's parents' unyielding disapproval of Joe led her to not invite them to the ceremony or the reception. "My childish anger at my parents, and my overwhelming loyalty to Joe at their expense, should have been a sign to me that, from the very beginning, he wielded too much power over me," she says today.

The newlyweds spent a short honeymoon at a romantic château in Quebec. "We rushed back in order for Joe to register at Harvard, only to find out he had an extra week to do it."

The Pikuls settled into the Beacon Street apartment, and Joe started his graduate classes at the most prestigious business school in the country, while Sandra worked as a secretary at the New England Mutual Life Insurance Company to pay the tuition. Joe Pikul, abused son of a poor alcoholic millworker, was off to what looked like a glorious life of wealth, status and accomplishment.

It is rare for a person from so grim a childhood to salvage his ego without the help of a nurturing and healing presence. For Joe Pikul, this lifeline may have been his mother, who, at least by Sandra's account, was the light of the Pikul household. According to Sandra, "Bobchi was the most wonderful person—an absolutely devoted mother with the most giving nature and a radiant warmth. She was full of love. She could never do enough for you.

"When Joe and I would come home from college on weekends with a bag of dirty clothes, she'd not only do our laundry, but she'd hide little goodies between the folded clothes." This kind of maternal doting is strikingly similar to that of Jane Jackson Whitmore. "She was fiercely devoted to Joe—a real 'my children are everything; they can do no wrong; they're my *life*' kind of mother."

But Sandra didn't meet Bobchi Pikul until Joe was twenty years old; by then, family secrets were swept under the rug in order to yield the image of the bustling, loving old-world family. ("I had no idea there had been family violence against Joe," she says. "No one acted that way, and Joe did not mention it.") But Joe did reveal those secrets much later. Says a Perry Street Workshop attendee, "It was generally known that *both* parents had beaten him when he was a child—his mother as well as his father."

This complicates the image of Joe's mother significantly. Bobchi Pikul was at the same time her young son's emotional life raft *and* a source of danger, fear and trauma to him, a contradiction that goes some way toward explaining Joe's becoming a secret cross-dresser. Dr. Michael Berzofsky, a New York psychotherapist with a special interest in the issue of gender, explains, "By cross-dressing, the man gets to have it both ways. By wearing 'his mother's' clothes, by *becoming* her on the outside, he gets to keep his mother with him. But—and this is where the triumph and the revenge: hence, the thrill, comes in—by remaining a man *underneath* those clothes, he gets to grandly mock his mother and secretly thwart her power over him, as he never could do in his childhood. In cross-dressing, these two things operate at once: the deep comfort in remaining attached to the invaluable mother, and the scornful parody of the woman, that same woman, who pretended to be such a good, caring mother but who really, *he* knows, wasn't."

The hidden "badness" of the mothers of eventual cross-dressers usually takes the form of narcissism. "Typically, the mothers of such men were narcissistic and self-absorbed," Dr. Berzofsky goes on. "These same women do not think much of their husbands, even though such men might be apparently dominant, even brutal. And they maintain exclusive control over the child, almost as a stage mother does, projecting to him the message: 'You're my creation; you're part of me. We're not separate.' "

We cannot know the exact trauma of Joe's childhood, but his relationship with his mother would seem to conform to the clinical prototype above in most ways—certainly in the fusion of mother and son, her dominance in his early development, and her cross-signaling of both enormous love and brutality. According to the late Dr. Robert J. Stoller, author of the book *Perversion: The Erotic Form of Hatred* (Pantheon, 1975), "Every perversion has at its heart a childhood trauma. The perversion is an attempt to correct it."

Joseph Pikul may well have been secretly cross-dressing by the time he met Diane Whitmore. Sandra Jarvinen, however, does not think he was doing so during their marriage. But their marriage did have a measure of violence, which escalated as Joseph Pikul became more successful.

Joe left Harvard Business School after only one year, when a bad knee injury from a touch football game led to a surgeon's suggestion that Joe take a year off. He got a job at Standard & Poor's in New York, where he demonstrated a talent for managing high-risk funds. He was beginning to drink heavily and to more consistently exhibit the "hyper" quality to which Sandra's laughing equanimity and stability was always a "safety net." Eventually, he and Sandra opened their own securities analysis firm, Argent. "We were running high-risk funds—hedge funds—which is like shooting craps," Sandra says. "Joe was absolutely brilliant at analyzing the risks. We covered as many as one hundred and fifty stocks at a time, flying all over the country to talk to limited partners and investigate new companies. Joe practically never went on a trip without me. I don't think there's a city in this country that I haven't been in."

In the late sixties, at the peak of their success, they handled $80 million in assets from their handsomely furnished, wood-paneled Wall Street office. Their commission was 10 percent of all profits. Joe swam victoriously against the tide of the 1969 Wall Street "disaster year," in which other managers of what were called "go-go funds" suffered drubbings in the bear market, which sent both the Dow Jones industrials and Standard & Poor's Index down. A feature story on him in *The New York Times* put it this way: "The average mutual fund showed a loss of 14.47% in darkest 1969 and the go-go funds had losses that often exceeded 25% . . . [whereas] Mr. Pikul

. . . managing a private hedge fund, turn[ed] in a 22.6% gain on about $2 million."

The Pikuls were living high. They rented a duplex penthouse at 2 Charlton Street, in southwest Greenwich Village, and they purchased a country house in Monterey, Massachusetts. Joe had his suits made to order at Dunhill and Sandra bought antiques and art.

But Joe's drinking was soaring out of control, as was his temper. The two elements, together, produced orgies of destructiveness in which every piece of furniture in the house was overturned or broken. "You never knew what he was angry at or why those rages would come on," Sandra recalls. "I'd be sitting across the table from him and all of a sudden his face would change. I could tell by his eyes and by the color of his skin that I should step back and run out of his way. Usually he couldn't hurt me, because I moved too fast.

"He would smash anything in sight. Once, in 1967, right after we had finished spending a lot of money having a decorator do our apartment to make it look just like a country home, Joe went on a rampage. He ransacked everything. The whole place was ruined, including one of only six coffee tables the sculptor Noguchi had made. The next morning our housekeeper Molly, an Irish lady, walked in, looked around and sighed, 'Begora, he's lost his temper again. Do you want me to try to clean it up?'

"I said no, because how *could* anyone clean what was left of the furniture up? Then the doorbell rang. Molly went to answer it. There stood two delivery boys, loaded with flowers of every description—masses of lillies, chrysanthemums, tulips, yellow roses. But there was not a vase left in the house that wasn't broken! I awkwardly instructed the boys to step through the wreckage and lay all the flowers on the grand piano. As I was tipping the boys, the phone rang. It was Joe, sounding all back to normal. 'Hi, honey,' he said. 'I made kind of a mess last night, didn't I?'

" 'Well, yes,' I said. 'And where am I supposed to put the flowers you just sent?'

" 'Oh, just go to Tiffany's,' he said, 'and replace everything.'

"He was always like that after one of his flare-ups—

impervious to the destruction, not emotionally repentant but repentant through material gifts and lavish gestures."

"The entire cycle of outburst and renormalization," says Dr. Berzofsky, "shows the inability Joseph Pikul had to simultaneously experience positive and negative feelings toward someone. Certainly there also existed a strong identification with his violent father. Through the violence, Joe the victim became Joe the powerful aggressor." Not just the furniture but Sandra herself suffered his attacks. He struck her, threw heavy objects at her and eventually threatened to kill her.

Why did she, a canny woman with skills in the business world that would allow her comfortable independence, stay with him?

In those days—the late sixties and early seventies—the very notion of "domestic violence" did not exist beyond clinical and academic circles; the term "battered woman" would not be coined by therapist Lenore E. Walker until 1973. A man's use of force against his wife was more or less accepted. "When a man got a marriage license," Sandra puts it ruefully, "he got a beating license, too. That's the way the authorities, the policemen and the male lawyers and doctors, all looked at it. There were no female authorities, no battered-women specialists, shelters, hotlines, treatment centers: nothing that we have today. Those of us who were physically endangered by our husbands were the invisible people. At worst, we were told that we 'asked for' it; at best, it was just our tough luck."

Indeed, our society's current avowed concern with domestic violence, so deceptively high-profile in the media, obscures an understanding of how shockingly brand-new a woman's legal right to protection from a violent husband really is. It was not until 1984 that a U.S. District Court, in the landmark Connecticut case *Thurman* v. *Torrington Police Department,* ruled that "a man is not allowed to physically abuse or endanger a woman merely because he is her husband," displacing the centuries-old attitude upheld by Anglo-Saxon law: that a husband is entitled to "chastise" his wife and his children, since he implicitly owns them.

As the events around Diane Pikul's murder would reveal, the assumption of male ownership of wife and children is still subtly in place within the law enforcement and court system; back in the less enlightened days, when Sandra was married to Joe, the assumption was undisguised and flagrant. As she remembers it, "Police, lawyers, doctors: they all scoffed at me the few times I dared make a complaint against Joe, even when the evidence of Joe's behavior was glaring at them. Once, in 1967, after Joe trashed the house, I called the police. They took in the whole scene—the broken dishes, the upside-down couches—very matter-of-factly. Then one of them went upstairs to look for Joe and came back down and said, 'I don't know what you're pulling, lady, but that guy up there's sound asleep, so clean up this mess and get back to your marriage.' "

Despite their successful professional relationship, by late 1968, after ten years of marriage, Sandra was trying to keep herself as much out of Joe's way as possible. She knew he was having "loads of affairs" with women. She never accompanied him on his night runs, via limousine, to the Upper East Side spot Le Club. She had given up on her dream of having children "because both of us assumed that drinking had lowered Joe's sperm count." Often she would spend weekends alone in their country house, riding her horse and finding some kind of peace. At the end of one such weekend, she drove back to New York earlier than planned, still wearing her riding habit. Entering their bedroom, she caught Joe in bed with a woman.

The woman quickly left and Sandra, standing at the top of the stairs, told Joe: "I'm not going to put up with you rubbing your affairs in my face like this. Don't do it in my own bedroom." Joe lost his temper. The two argued, and Joe turned and picked up off its stand a sculpture that Sandra had recently given him as a present. It was a cast-iron bull and bear she'd comissioned to celebrate their Wall Street victories. "The sculpture was so heavy, he had to use both hands to lift it. He brought it down on the back of my head. I fell down the stairs and lost consciousness.

"When I came to, hours later, I was soaked in blood. He had left me there and gone to bed. I ran upstairs, got my purse, and drove off, trying to get to my parents' house in Massachusetts. But I couldn't make it. It took me eight hours just to get from New York to Mystic, Connecticut, because I kept having to pull over to the side of the road and vomit. Finally, I passed out and hit a divider on the Connecticut Turnpike; *that* woke me up. I drove to a Howard Johnson's motel and asked the desk clerk to call a doctor, which he refused to do, saying he had 'no authority.' So I checked into a room and called my parents, who called the Connecticut state police, who came and took me to South Shore Hospital.

"I told the doctor there, 'My husband smashed my skull with a large sculpture.' The doctor laughed. He looked at me in my riding habit and said, 'Come on, you just fell off a horse, honey.' "

By the early seventies, Sandra was living apart from Joe, in a rented house in Massachusetts. Officially, they still worked at Argent together. "As long as he owned me—as long as we were partners and I wasn't threatening to divorce him—I didn't feel endangered." But when Sandra did start to mention divorce, Joe threatened to send people to kill her, or to do the job himself. After one such threat, in 1973, she and her mother went to a lawyer to obtain a restraining order against him. "The lawyer, who is now very important in Massachusetts politics, gave me all these legal reasons why he couldn't do anything. Then he put his arm around me to usher me out and said, with a smile: 'Look at it this way: if he kills you, we'll be sure that he gets a fast trial.' "

By now Joseph Pikul was imbibing cocaine and amphetamines as well as liquor. He was losing his business and becoming probably clinically paranoid. He had grown his hair long, appeared hyper and unkempt on a daily basis. He began keeping guns in the office. His threats toward Sandra became grandiose and explicit. They were now witnessed by the limousine drivers he frequently hired. These men congregated at the B&H Garage on Houston Street where, between jobs, they traded stories about their customers. Few of these customers were more colorful—or more dangerous—than the fellow they called, in a reverse wordplay acknowledgment of his tipping generosity, "Joe Pike."

What a character this Joe Pike was, went the word at the B&H. He'd tip a driver one hundred dollars to do the damndest things. Once, for example, he had one of the fellows take him to a rustic area outside New York, then stop the car. While the driver waited behind the wheel, Joe got out, thumbtacked a photograph of his wife Sandra to a tree, pulled out a pistol—and started firing at the photograph until it was indecipherably scarred with bullets. Another driver got tipped the same amount to drive Joe *and* his wife upstate. During this drive, Joe told the driver to stop the car. He got out, holding a shovel. Then, employing the skills he'd picked up during his old undergraduate night job, he started digging a grave by the side of the road. According to the driver, he then informed his wife that after he killed her, he would bury her there.

Among the B&H Garage regulars who heard these stories was Malcolm Rattner. On August 14, 1973, Rattner got a call from his car service dispatcher to pick up this "Joe Pike," whom he'd never before driven, at his Wall Street office. Rattner figured he'd get a big tip and a funny story out of it. What happened—as Rattner revealed in his very reluctant testimony fifteen years later to the city's child protection attorney, during the Pikul custody hearings—was considerably different.

Rattner entered Joseph Pikul's office building after the end of normal office hours. When he walked in the Argent office, the man he had been called to chauffeur began to tempestuously accuse him of having an affair with his wife. Rattner vehemently denied this—he had never met the woman. Joe Pikul then pulled out a loaded .38 pistol, put it to Rattner's temple and ordered him to sit down and write on a piece of paper: "I have been having an affair with Mr. Pikul's wife and I am committing suicide."

When Rattner refused, Pikul began hitting him about the head with the loaded pistol while fondling himself. Rattner then grabbed for the gun and, in the process, managed to knock it out of Pikul's grip and onto the floor. Bloody and scratched from the fracas, Rattner says he then ran out of the office and down the stairwell.

When he got to the lobby he realized, in dismay, that the building's front door was now locked. He was trapped. He turned—and saw Joe Pikul behind him, crouched in a firing stance, the gun aimed right at him.

At the appearance of the building custodian, Pikul withdrew his gun and the custodian let the terrified driver out of the building.

Rattner went directly to nearby Beekman Downtown Hospital to have his wounds treated. He called the police from the hospital. Officers took the report and shortly thereafter showed up at 2 Charlton Street to question Joseph Pikul about the incident. The loaded gun was in full view in Pikul's living room during the interrogation. The police arrested Joe, whereupon he bailed himself out; the gun was taken into evidence.

Yet by the time the court date to try Joe arrived, the evidence had inexplicably disappeared and all charges against Joseph Pikul were dropped.

After Sandra finally went ahead with her plans to divorce Joe, she lived in terror. On January 2, 1974, the day the divorce became final, she was telephoned at her new home in Norwell, Massachusetts by both her lawyer and Joe's, both warning her to leave her home because Joe had sent two men out to hurt her. She refused to leave the house but called the Norwell police department, who sent a police car out, sirens blaring, just as two men in a car with New York license plates arrived on Sandra's premises. "One of them was in my garage, the other was in his car when they heard the police siren," Sandra recalls. "They sped away and never came back again."

On May 19 of that same year, Joe was arrested in upstate Messina, New York, by the New York State Police for intoxicated driving; controlled substances were found in his car and a shotgun in its trunk. Two months later, on July 15, 1974, after more threats by Joe, Sandra again called the Norwell police, asking for protection. She was obliged, by way of an additional patrol of her street.

Argent was disbanded. Sandra received her divorce, though not the $28,000 alimony settlement Joe was ordered to pay her. Suing for the money was a slow and expensive process, which Sandra only intermittently pursued. Joe's withholding of the money enabled him to continue to feel attached to her, Sandra believes. Thirteen years later, that debt—swollen by over ten thousand dollars in interest and lawyers' fees—would figure prominently in Sandra's decision to reenter Joe's life just before Diane's murder.

Joseph Pikul spent the next three quarters of the year drunk. In late 1975, at about the time he first went to Alcoholics Anonymous, he applied, hat in hand, for an almost entry-level job with Argus Research Investment, a Wall Street research firm.

Joe Macalendon, who interviewed and hired him at Argus, remembers that "Joe appeared in my office extremely nervous, high-strung, but also extremely well dressed. He was someone who had clearly been through a lot, and he admitted to me that he'd lost everything and had been living 'like a bum.' He said he was willing to start, from the bottom, all over again."

Macalendon knew how successful Joe had been as an analyst; the job he had to offer was the unchallenging one of following food companies like Campbell's Soup and General Foods, and the salary was a virtual pittance: $22,000 a year. (Ironically, this was the same as Diane's *Harper's* salary, which Joe was always denigrating.) Joe Pikul leapt at it. After Joe left his office, Macalendon called a stock salesman who had had a lot of dealings with Joe in '72 and '73 and described the nervous man in the conservative clothes who had presented himself so repentently before him. "You would have seen a very different Joe Pikul if you went along with him to try to sell him stock ideas," the salesman said. "He was a compulsive drinker of diet sodas, hyper as hell, and he looked like a hippie."

"Joe didn't mix much, he worked long hours; he seemed very, very humble and grateful for the chance to climb back up again," Macalendon says. "Our firm hired him opportunistically and we got our money's worth. Eventually, after a couple of years, he got more confident. He uncovered a couple of interesting situations for us—Toys R Us was one of them. He could communicate an investment's potential and make it entertaining. He relaxed a little. His sense of humor started coming out. We doubled his salary."

That was when he met Diane Whitmore.

At some point in the early months of 1978, Joe and Diane had their first date. On their second, as she would later tell friends, he spat on her in the course of an argument at a restaurant. This, she said, "fascinated" her. Early the next morning, as former au pair Carina Jacobsson recounts Diane's telling of it, "Joe called her on the phone, waking her up, and insisted she go to the ballet with him that night. She thought he was crazy—and she *liked* that." When Maggie Gari, years after meeting Diane and Joe, saw the movie *Blue Velvet*, she found "Diane's attraction to Joe was just like the Isabella Rosellini character's attraction to Dennis Hopper's. I told Diane, 'You must see this movie; you'll know why.' After she saw it, she called me to thank me for telling her about it."

By now, it seems, Diane had convinced herself that her taste in these "strange" men was a sophisticated quirk, part and parcel of her New York self. "She had never met a man without a character flawed to some degree, and so she was able to continue the affair on a pragmatic basis," she later wrote in a short story. The persona, and the words, reflect Diane's pride in finally becoming the decadent, cosmopolitan woman who could take such flawed men in stride.

Despite the image of the archsophisticate she nurtured, Diane was quaking inside at the time she met Joseph Pikul. "She was very vulnerable and anxiety-ridden about the prospect of dating just after her mother died, just when Ralph was finally out of her life, just as she was getting sober," says Barbara Martin, who knew both Joe and Diane and went on to become one of Diane's best friends. "It was Joe who pursued Diane. Diane didn't pursue him or anyone at the time. Giving in to his advances was one way of putting herself out of the misery of single life.

"Joe could be charming and warm, and we always got along," Barbara goes on. "He seemed to understand his violent temper was his fatal flaw. The main reason he wanted to get sober, I think, was to learn to control it. He had such self-loathing, such self-destructiveness; you could tell he'd experienced great hurt in his life. I felt for him, trying to overcome his childhood. I gave him credit for that. I didn't know how sick he was."

Neither did Diane, who was every bit as moved as Barbara by Joe's efforts to vanquish his demons—but with the dangerous added element of romance. As they began to reveal themselves to each other, she seems to have cast him as the brilliant, tempestuous underdog driven by childhood wounds and fierce ambition, yet with touching reserves of vulnerability and goodness. This is how she described Joe in a short story:

> Randy could be vicious, a bully, a tyrant. . . . He reserved his most generous spirit for those lesser than he, in age or position in life, but possessing the same hunger for greatness as he. [He experienced] flashes of painful envy . . . at the advantages life had bestowed upon [others who didn't have to] suffer the ravages of a desperately poor, desperately violent childhood, [who] didn't have to spend an enormous part of their energies still battling these ghosts.

She romanticized what she saw of his severe emotional problems and glamorized him for having them. She was a woman who still could not fully grasp that she had emotional problems of her own. She insisted on maintaining an image of her life as a darkly picaresque short story. She was giving up the very thing—liquor—that had always enabled her to make her life interesting and exciting. This was an enormous sacrifice of self-image and ego. "That's why it's so hard for a lot of people to live sober," Dr. Geller says. "They miss the dash, the peril. They're afraid they'll turn back into boring Joe or Jill again." Diane found, in Joe Pikul, a way to keep that excitement and peril despite the sobriety. And he found in her a person with whom to rebuild the personal side of his life at the same time he was rebuilding the professional side, a partner in the fashioning of a whole package of willed normalcy that would allow him to deny the depth of his destructiveness.

As they solved their drinking problems together, they began to create, in their coming together, a deeper problem, from which neither would ever recover.

Just a few months into their courtship, Diane became pregnant. Because Joe had been told by a doctor that his sperm count was too low for him to impregnate a woman, this was an astonishment to both of them. Maggie Gari believes that if the relationship had been able to run its course, Diane would have seen the depth of Joe's pathology and broken off with him. But the pregnancy forced them into a premature commitment. Diane was almost thirty-five and, Gloria Archer remembers, "so determined to have the baby, she was beginning to sound obsessed. I'd say, 'Diane, you hardly know this man. And he sounds difficult. And becoming pregnant isn't the sensible way to get a husband. Do you really think you should have this baby?' She'd answer, 'I am going to have this baby, no matter *what* happens. Even if the marriage doesn't last.' The pregnancy was a miracle to her, and she was very, very adamant. We were on the brink of a serious argument over it, and I knew that if I held to my oppositional stand, I'd lose her altogether."

So Gloria reluctantly gave Diane her blessings. On April 18, Diane's annulment from Ralph became official. Diane and Joe planned marriage. "Joe was so excited about the baby coming—both of them were," Barbara Martin recalls. "I could tell that he wanted his child to have the home life he never had. They were still living in Diane's apartment, on Ninety-eighth and Riverside, and I was the one who suggested they move down to the Village, so they could be near Diane's friends, who could help with the baby." Diane began apartment hunting; eventually she found a suitable $600-a-month apartment on West Eleventh Street near Seventh Avenue—a block away from each of Diane's two earlier apartments, on Charles Street and on Twelfth Street, and a block away from the Perry Street Workshop. Still, all was not well. According to Barbara, "Joe was so jealous, he accused Diane of having affairs all through her pregnancy."

Joe was still at Argus, now making about $50,000 a year; Diane was still with the Parks Department. Joe wanted her to quit the job; she agreed to, without much regret. Although the job would be held for her long after she gave birth to Claudia, she would never go back to it. In June, Joe met his future father-in-law, Don Whitmore, when Whitmore and his new bride, Gretchen, made a trip to New York. In a man-to-man talk, Joe staunchly announced: "Your daughter won't have to work anymore. I'll be able to take care of her."

Don Whitmore was impressed by those words; he liked

this new fellow, Joe—"He seemed solid, like he'd make a big success of himself"—far better than his daughter's former husband. According to Barbara Martin, Diane, too, was dazzled by Joe's past and imminent future success. "She sensed he'd be successful—that they'd soon have plenty of money." In the blinkered comfort they both drew from Joe's breadwinning prospects, father and daughter seemed to be alone in the front seat of the Studebaker again, on their way to the train or the allergist: the one relaying, the other absorbing lessons about the primacy of money learned from the Depression.

Gloria Archer, however, despite her obliged and perfunctory "approval," silently worried. As a young woman, Gloria had been married to a wealthy man and had lived a life with the right clothes and the right country clubs, yet she'd felt lost, unhappy and increasingly vulnerable. Finally, that first marriage had come apart. Gloria recognized that every gift had its price. She feared for her young friend, who was so infatuated with the status symbols and material things her future husband would provide.

On July 14, Don and Gretchen Whitmore flew to New York to greet Diane and Joe and meet Joe's parents for the first time. Within two hours of the meeting at the Riverside Drive apartment, they would all be related. The elder Pikuls seemed to Don "like people who had worked hard in mills all their lives and didn't have much education. His mother was very fat. They were both nice enough, but we spoke a different language." Judging from photographs, Diane looked lovely; soft ringlets framed her face, which had the glow of early pregnancy. Her mother's gold locket hung from a dark velvet ribbon around her neck, grazing the off-white embroidery-trimmed milkmaid's dress she wore. She would later write to Pat Jaudon, with evident pride, that everyone told her she looked just like Julie Christie. Joe looked distinguished in a navy-blue suit with a lily sprig in his lapel, a white shirt and a wide, silver-blue satin tie.

The six traveled by limousine to an estate called the Dreamworld Inn, in nearby Putnam County, where the marriage was performed by the town justice. The couple honeymooned in the Caribbean, then moved into the

Eleventh Street apartment, "which was really quite lovely," Gloria recalls, "with windows all around and a water bed." Not long after they'd moved in, however, Diane called Gloria, who was on Long Island, to give an anguished account of how Joe had taken all her mother's china, which she loved, and thrown it against walls and on the floor in a fit of temper. "Get to Penn Station and come right out!" Gloria ordered. Diane did not come that time, though later, after another argument, she did, spending the night and returning to Joe the next morning.

To counter Gloria's worry, Diane would reassure her, "But there's another side to him—a good side." One night, the Archers and Pikuls went out to dinner as a foursome. "It was a very pleasant evening," Gloria recalls. "Joe was knowledgeable, and he liked to talk about the things my husband liked to talk about. During dinner, it *was* hard to believe there was that 'other,' bad side to Joe. I came away realizing that Diane, who was so determined to have the whole package that Joe was presenting—a baby, wealth, that good life—probably found it impossible to believe the 'bad' Joe would be back again, during those times when it was absent."

But Robert Salisbury, Nancy Kirkland's husband, also met Joe in a similar context and immediately disliked him. "He struck me as odd; I didn't like him—and this is before I had any idea he was mistreating Diane. He professed to be a hedge fund manager with many similar interests to mine"—Salisbury is a venture capitalist—"but I got such a bad feeling from him, it was a strain just being around him."

Diane had her baby, a girl, on February 1, 1979, at St. Vincent's Hospital, right down the street from their apartment. She and Joe had taken Lamaze classes, and photographs show a devoted-looking Joe, first in hospital whites, then in surgical greens and sanitary haircap, leaning over the metal railing of Diane's hospital bed while she lies against the pillow, her face contorted from labor pains, her left wrist bandaged and connected to the IV drip. Right after the birth, Joe called Don Whitmore, sounding ecstatic. The baby was named Claudia Jackson, after Diane's beloved grandfather Claude Jackson, "the one person," as she had once written, "who loves me without reservation."

Not long after the birth, Joe left Argus for Arnhold and S. Bleichroeder, where he was poised to remake his fortune. Though they had hired a daily nanny, as the months of new motherhood passed it was becoming clear that Diane would not go back to the Parks Department job. Gloria Archer took this as a potentially dangerous turn of events: now Diane was entirely dependent on Joe's financial support. Diane talked to Gloria about trying to write, but Gloria was doubtful that Diane would ever make the effort. "Diane did have a delightful and original way of expressing herself," she said, "but, after all, how many people do we all know who 'want to write'?"

Diane expressed her career and identity fears most directly to Pat Jaudon, with whom she kept up her intimate correspondence though they rarely visited each other. Now divorced and reentering the workplace, Pat got this letter from Diane, dated October 8, 1979:

> I can identify with your career search/change—feel completely lost myself on that score . . . Joe has such dreadful temper tantrums that leaving him is a possibility—my fantasy if that happens is not another man but tranquility and an ordered existence. Am trying to find a cheap shrink at a training institute. In between fits [presumably Joe's], I'm happy with my life. Claudia ("Sweet Pea") is a divine baby with a super disposition, sense of humor, courage. Taking her out is like leading a parade—everyone flips over her blue eyes. Am contemplating return to work, hopefully not my former spot, but overwhelmed at finding a good housekeeper or day care. I feel like a real anachronism not working, yet something in me (exhaustion, probably) clings to these days of strolling around the Village, looking for the perfect food.

Thus, at the dawn of the eighties, Diane, at thirty-five, was an enthralled new mother, confused by the gap between her "correct" desire for a career and her inability to take that desire seriously. Her letter shows she was still unaware that her fascination with violence and her sensible, better self were on a collision course with one another. For the latter to finally outrun the dangers imposed by the former, she would have to do more than have a "fantasy" about "tranquility"; she would have to stop being "happy with my life" "in between fits"—she would have to, instead, put herself outside the realm, and the presumable charm, of those "fits" forever. But that would take more psychological honesty than she was yet able to muster. And it would take money and flexible time, the very two things her lack of career and new motherhood made impossible.

And so Diane had run around the world, only to discover she could not cross the street. None of those years of glamorous, irreverent adventure had purchased her any control over her life, or, it would later become clear, over her physical safety.

Her next letter to Pat, dated just a month and a half later—November 22, 1979—indicates just how narrow was the margin of freedom and safety in which she was living. Referring to a panicked telephone call she had made to Pat while Joe was having a temper tantrum, she writes: "Forget I ever told you Joe had a nervous breakdown, and burn this letter. He was appalled. His disposition is slowly improving, as is my organizational ability."

Joe and Diane had now temporarily drifted away from the Perry Street Workshop, but stories got back to members that he was beating her. Still, she kept what abuse there was under enough wraps to appear the enthusiastic upscale wife: In 1980, she and Joe moved to larger quarters in the neighborhood, the duplex at Sixth Avenue and Tenth Street, and Diane hired an interior designer to decorate it.

The designer, a well-bred East Side woman, saw Diane as "an efficient and upbeat woman who carried around a notebook and was excellent with details, had good taste but wasn't always secure about it." She and Diane used a palette of warm colors—mostly shades of oranges and pinks, as well as aubergine—for the living room/dining room on the lower floor of the duplex. A large sectional couch, with a profusion of pillows, was covered in a serpentine-flowered chintz and formed the focal point of the room. Joe's recliner, which he refused to get rid of, was recovered in eggplant-hued leather to match the dark carpet. A pink-hued lacquered-wood book and stereo cabinet was constructed to face the couch, and a French dining set was placed by the windows that looked out over Sixth Avenue. The effect was elegant but practical and unpretentious. The water bed was installed in the largest of the three small upstairs bedrooms. According to the decorator, Diane loved the whole process of nest-making—meetings at the D&D Building, lunches afterward while looking at the swatches, interviews with workmen "to whom she was always, unfailingly, nice." It was a part of life she had waited a long time for.

But that part of her life carried an enormous price. For by now, Joe—having, Diane reported to friends, stopped his physical abuse of her—had begun systematically abusing her verbally. "He would wake her up in the middle of the night and tell her that she was a piece of shit, that she must have been at the bottom of her class at Mt. Holyoke, that she would never amount to anything—and sometimes he'd threaten to lock her into the bathroom for the rest of the night," remembers Maggie Gari.

In the winter of 1981, Don and Gretchen Whitmore paid a visit. Ronald Reagan had just been sworn in as president, and even Greenwich Village was beginning to reflect signs of the frankly materialistic ethos that was sweeping America. Women like Diane, now almost thirty-eight years old, realized their own days of bohemian adventure on those same streets had passed on to a new generation of questing young women who lived in the East Village, wore retro clothes and went to meet their dangerous young men not at acid-rock clubs like the Electric Circus, but at punk clubs like CBGB.

Walking with her father through the Village streets, pushing Claudia in her stroller, Diane opened up about what was really going on in her marriage. "Joe's always blowing up at me," she said. "He insults me. He mistreats me. I don't think it's ever going to get any better. I'm thinking of leaving him."

Ever pragmatic, Don Whitmore remembers replying: "Diane, stick with it if you can. You've got a young child. You don't just run off and get a divorce at the spur of the moment. Besides, he's beginning to make money; that'll probably make him treat you better."

Chapter 6

She was never sure it could rightly be called love. Her rage and fear and need to possess were so entwined with the rushes of warmth she might have been able to call love, that she could only have said with certainty that she was in the grip of a passion. And more and more she wondered about the value of passion in everyday life. It was such a threat . . .

Diane Pikul, "The End of the Affair"

By the summer of 1981, Joe and Diane had purchased a summer and weekend house in Amagansett, Long Island, one of the string of fashionable communities on the island's East End. It was a mark of some privilege to "summer" in the Hamptons: wife, child and baby-sitter spending the whole summer at the house, husband commuting out on weekends. The status inherent in this arrangement meant a lot to both Diane and Joe.

"Doesn't your husband miss you while he's in the city all week?" Diane's high school friend Eleanor Lamperti asked, when Diane called and invited her out to the house.

"No, he likes it," Eleanor remembers Diane having replied. "He thinks it's a very sophisticated arrangement."

When Eleanor came out to the house—a converted fisherman's shack of turquoise wood, deceptively resembling a tract-house from the front but hiding a vast lawn with a pool—she got an uncomfortable sense of what Diane's second husband was like, and how her old best friend had changed. "Joe called the house all day long, and most of those phone calls were spent with him screaming at Diane," Eleanor recalls. "I didn't understand it. Here was this man with a powerful job—how could he spend all his time making these phone calls? And the screaming! I said, 'Diane, what do people in his office think about him screaming?' She just said, 'I don't know. I guess he closes the door.' "

But what most bothered Eleanor was that Diane fought with Joe on the phone as angrily as he did with her. "She was arguing, giving as good as she got. I thought to myself, This isn't Diane. She never used to scream. And she had too strong a self-image to be accepting behavior like this."

During one of Joe's phone calls to the house, Diane told Joe that she and Eleanor were about to go out to dinner at a restaurant that had just opened, the Laundromat. "He had a fit," Eleanor recalls. "He didn't want her to go—whether because it cost money or because he was too jealous to let her go out to a restaurant without him, I don't know. When Diane hung up the phone, she said, 'We can still go, but when he sees the charge on the American Express bill, he'll be furious.' I said, 'Diane, it's not worth it. Let's stay in tonight.' "

Diane went on to tell Eleanor "how Joe once had a girlfriend"—presumably during his heavy-drinking years after the divorce from Sandra—"who had stabbed him, and he had gone to a hospital and said he'd been stabbed by a stranger on the street. And then Diane laughed as she said, 'I can certainly understand why that woman stabbed him.' She *laughed.*"

Right before Eleanor left to go back home to New Jersey, Diane and Joe had another screaming match on the phone. "After she hung up, Diane said, 'You know, I don't know what it is, but I always pick the wrong men.' This time, she didn't laugh."

With the help of her decorator, Diane set to work designing the interior of her Amagansett house. Here, she used "sherbet colors"—light oranges, lime green, lavender—trying to create an airy but not overly informal summerhouse look. There were skirted tables, bleached pine pieces juxtaposed with antiques, a dhurrie rug and straw-type sisal matting for the bedroom floors. Diane did

Claudia's bedroom by herself, in Ralph Lauren prints. Actually, if all went well, it would be a room shared by Claudia and a sibling, for Diane was hoping to spare her daughter the loneliness she had known as an only child. Now that Joe had reversed the vasectomy he'd had after Claudia's birth, Diane hoped to become pregnant again soon. Gloria Archer worried about this eventuality. With *two* children, Diane would virtually seal her fate of dependency on Joe. But Diane resisted Gloria's exhortations not to try for a second child as adamantly as she had resisted Gloria's advice against marrying when she'd been pregnant with Claudia. (Over the next years, when both women beheld Diane's beautiful towheaded son, Diane often teased Gloria: "*See* what you didn't want me to have.")

During the days Eleanor Lamperti spent at Diane's house, they talked about the North Plainfield High twentieth reunion, coming up in the fall. "I'll go if you go," they agreed. They had gone together to the tenth reunion—Eleanor with her husband Dick, Diane with Ralph; but, from the tempestuousness that seemed to exist between Diane and this new husband, Eleanor doubted her old friend would want to come this time.

But in September, Diane surprised Eleanor by calling to say that Joe did want to accompany her to the reunion. Eleanor gave Diane directions to her house and hoped for the best.

The evening proved calamitous. It was already after six P.M., the time at which the reunion was to start, when Diane called Eleanor to report that Joe had become so mad at her over the directions that "they had a tremendous argument and Joe had pushed Diane and Claudia out of the car, right at the entrance to the Holland Tunnel, where they were almost run over, and had driven off alone." First by hitching a ride, then by cab, Diane had gotten herself and Claudia safely back to the duplex.

Eleanor was then stunned to hear Diane say that, despite the past hour's harrowing events, she was *still* planning to come to the reunion. By now, it seemed that violent fights with men served not to dampen but to fuel Diane's determination and aggressiveness; they impelled her to try to "win" by confronting the challenge, and danger, head-on. By now, too, violent scenes had attained a normalcy to Diane. She was so desensitized to their aberrance that she could emotionally "step around" such episodes en route to the regularly scheduled commitments and pleasures of her life.

Diane told Eleanor she was going to rent a car and drive to New Jersey with Claudia. A half hour later, however, Eleanor received another call from Diane. Joe had come home, she said, full of apologies. They were going to arrive as a threesome, after all. The next call to the Lampertis was at eight P.M. The Pikuls, lost, were calling from a diner a few miles away. Eleanor and Dick and their daughter drove out to pick them up, "and Joe was fuming, mumbling under his breath about the 'rotten directions,' " Eleanor recalls.

"Then we called the hotel where the reunion was taking place and had them hold dinner." The late arrival of the Best Looking and Most Sophisticated girls in the class, with their husbands, caused heads to turn. Eleanor recounts, "During the evening, all our old friends from the Clique kept coming up to me, baffled, saying, 'All Diane's been saying to her husband all night is, 'Get away from me.' " Back at the Lampertis' that evening, Joe and Diane sequestered themselves in the bedroom and proceeded to have another screaming match, audible throughout the house. "Uh-oh, they're at it again," Dick Lamperti hummed, under his breath. Later, just before they drove back to the city, Diane told Eleanor how she and Joe had recently started marriage counseling, "but all we do is scream at each other for an hour and then go out to dinner."

For a few moments at the reunion, however, all seemed like déjà vu. Diane was called to the microphone and handed the reunion book, from which she read a poem she had written about the innocent excitement of the senior prom: putting on her tulle dress and wrist corsage, waiting for her date. It was written twenty years, and a whole other lifetime, before.

As 1982 began, Joe was making a name for himself at Bleichroeder—and increasingly on Wall Street—by beginning to uncover the investment potential of small Scandinavian stocks. Between his company's deep roots in and familiarity with the European markets, and his own penchant for investigative travel, which had been the secret to Argent's success, he would eventually have that specialized market virtually to himself. His reputation was growing, as was his income—both circumstances, to judge from his past, auguring emotional torment ahead.

Though there had been no lapse in sobriety for either of them, Joe and Diane returned to the Perry Street Workshop, going to meetings several times a week together. He became the Workshop's treasurer. Two young women who attended meetings there at the time recalled that the Pikuls were objects of emulation. And they seemed to cultivate as friends other members who were "somebodies"—an actress who had had a supporting role in a recent movie, for example.

"Joe was like a big teddy bear," one of the women remembers. "There was pain on his face when he talked, but he didn't seem arrogant and he spoke well, and the other men there seemed to respect him for climbing back up from the depths. Diane seemed very feminine and small next to him, but full of bravado, someone who loved being in front of people. She seemed wiley and almost theatrically scatterbrained, as if she were playing a Sandy Dennis or Goldie Hawn character. But I could always see a fragile, shattered quality underneath. They say that when you become sober, you're back to the age you were when you first started drinking; you've 'lost' those drinking years. Diane seemed to illustrate this. She acted and dressed so young. She had an almost intentional superficiality."

The other young woman recalls that Diane was so arresting because of "how she managed to retain her savoir faire, her New York on-the-edge quality, despite her sobriety. A lot of people lose their style when they stop drinking. Diane had found a way to keep hers. She wasn't about to stop being interesting; she looked like she kept up with life outside AA. She was this almost gaunt-looking, chiseled-faced figure who talked eloquently and artfully. She wasn't aloof, but she wasn't warm. There was some barrier there. She never broke down the way other women did. When she stood and qualified, I remember always being very impressed. But I don't remember ever being moved."

As these women remember it, nobody ever asked Diane to be her sponsor. (A "sponsor" is the veteran member who helps, one on one, the newcomer through the difficult early steps to sobriety.) Since it is very unusual for a longtime member not to be asked to be someone's sponsor, this fact may be a significant indication of some lack of approachability that Diane projected. Joe, on the other hand, did have members that he sponsored. One, recalls one of the women, "was a beautiful and very vulnerable young man who was gay and who was in great turmoil about his sexuality. He eventually committed suicide. Given what we know now about Joe, I think it was so irresponsible of him to agree to sponsor someone who was so obviously vulnerable on those very issues that Joe himself was hiding. It's so ironic: here Perry Street is known for its lack of secrets, and yet Joe and Diane always came to meetings together [most couples go to separate meetings so they can talk about the relationship more freely] and they were harboring so many secrets about what they were all about."

Ann Geller of Smithers doesn't think this secret-keeping is unusual. "One of the problems with people becoming leaders and objects of emulation within a chapter, as the Pikuls seem to have become, is their investment in that image. It becomes hard for them to ask for help themselves. I've seen that happen—people who are Mr. or Ms. Sobriety, chairing groups, being looked up to: They're not able to talk in an honest fashion about their present problems, only about their problems in the past." Thus, while benefiting from the program and scrupulously maintaining their sobriety, Joe and Diane were nonetheless able to defer questions about their own problems and to disguise the darkness in their relationship.

In the spring and early summer of 1982, Diane, again pregnant, attended a shower for Maggie Gari. It was on this occasion that their friendship really began. Maggie had known Diane as a fleeting acquaintance for several years and thought her beautiful. After Diane left the shower, another woman asked, "*Who* was that woman? She said she was pregnant, but she looked too old to be." That's when Maggie realized, with a start, how suddenly and precipitously Diane had aged.

Joe's irrational jealousy was now something Diane was used to. Whenever she ran into male friends or former lovers and the talk was felicitous, she would abruptly say, as she once said to Doug Thompson, "I have this insanely jealous husband so *don't* call the house." Possibly because of his fraught, dependent relationship with his own mother, Joe's jealousy deepened when Diane was pregnant. One day, in the middle of her pregnancy, Geoff Bartholomew, the husband of her friend Pat Bartholomew, stopped by the duplex to return a book Diane had loaned to Pat.

In the middle of Bartholomew's visit, Joe called Diane from his office. According to Pat, after Diane got off the phone, "she told Geoff he had better leave—which he did, going on about his day. Then Joe called *me* at work and started raving at me, threatening to kill my husband. I was really quite worried." She tried to reach Geoff at their loft, but the phone just kept ringing. She called the bar that he managed, only to be told he wasn't there. Deeply concerned, Pat rushed home. Shortly after she got inside, "the buzzer sounded, and when I answered the intercom, it was Joe, saying he had a gun and was going to kill Geoff. I told him I was calling the police, that he should get the hell away from my house." Pat stood tensely and waited. The buzzing stopped.

Eventually, such abuse by Joe caused Diane's friends to retreat from the couple. At a time when most of these women grew disgusted at her reluctance to leave him, Pat was one of the very few who refused to pass judgment.

In the fall of 1982, Burke Jackson, Diane's cousin and Pat Jaudon's old flame, received a surprise call at his home in Provo, Utah, from a man identifying himself as Diane's husband. Joseph Pikul happened to be in Provo on a business trip, he said. Burke hadn't even known that Diane was married again or that she had a child, but he'd come to expect anything from his sarcastic, nonconformist cousin. He'd last seen Diane in 1968 on her stopover in Utah from Vail. At the time, Burke and his Mormon wife, who had the first two of what would be their seven children, had listened to Diane talk of her East Village life; they'd inwardly shuddered.

Burke invited Joe Pikul to his home. "When he

showed up at our door I was surprised at how physically unappealing he was: an older guy, balding and overweight," Burke recalls. "Yet he was very nice and pleasant, and he showed us pictures of their little girl. I thought to myself, Diane has always been adrift and searching for something strange and exciting; maybe she's finally come down to earth. After all the weird fellows she's had, looks like this normal, unglamorous guy is going to give her the security she needs."

After the business in Provo, Joe went on to San Francisco for more business. Diane, who was in her seventh month of pregnancy, flew out to meet him there, leaving Claudia in the care of the live-in Swedish baby-sitter, Analee. On the second evening of the trip, Diane and Joe went to dinner in Marin County. On the way back to the hotel, driving down a side road in the rain and darkness, they had an argument in the rental car, and Joe pushed her out and sped away. Diane sputtered these details out to her father on the phone when she managed to get herself to another hotel later that evening. "She was very upset; she'd been crying," Don Whitmore remembers. "Gretchen and I were amazed that Joe would do that, especially in a strange city and with her so pregnant."

Yet, instead of immediately flying back home to New York—with her father paying for the ticket if need be—Diane remained in that other hotel, "hiding out from Joe," as Whitmore remembers her words, for three more days. Was she unconsciously enjoying the brinksmanship—the chance to drive the already-angry Joe crazy by "disappearing"? Or was she refusing to let the incident spoil her trip to San Francisco in the same way that she had refused to let the *last* time Joe pushed her out of the car ruin her chance to go to the class reunion? Or was she just terribly confused about whether to stay and risk danger or to leave and risk poverty?

It was probably a combination of all three. Diane had a penchant for raising the stakes of conflicts that Joe initiated. In addition, the "normalization" of danger in her life made her unable to hear the obvious warnings and perform normal reality tests. Finally, a wrenching ambivalence about giving up an affluent lifestyle accompanied her deep fear that she wouldn't, alone, be able to take care of her children and herself. To the bewilderment and frustration of the many friends who wanted to help her, this tripartite motivation would guide Diane's actions toward Joe to the very last days of her life.

After calling the New York apartment repeatedly for three days, Joe finally called Whitmore, convinced that Diane had fled to Florida. "Well, if she does show up," he said gruffly to his father-in-law, "you tell her I said not to come home. She can just stay in *Florida* and have the baby."

Whitmore then called Diane and told her about Joe's tacit threat to abandon her, "and she hung right up and called him at his hotel and told him where she was." Then, expensive souvenirs for child and nanny and friends in hand, they boarded, together, the plane for New York—looking like any prosperous businessman and his stylish, pregnant wife. Still, the incident apparently stayed on Diane's mind from that day forward. In a memo she wrote to her lawyer a week before her death, she said: "Please note, the five years are almost up [with which legally] to use the cruelty [charge] when he pushed me, seven months pregnant, out of the car in the rain in California."

Blake Joseph Pikul was born on December 28, 1982. Right before the birth, the Pikuls' Swedish au pair, Analee, left because of conflicts with Joe and passed her job on to a friend from her homeland, an aspiring young clothing designer named Carina Jacobsson. "Watch out for that man," Analee warned Carina of Joe. But Carina would prove to be that very rare thing: a baby-sitter who *did* get along with Joe Pikul.

Still, Carina's main relationship was with the children, to whom she bonded immediately—and to Diane, who "was generous and lovely to me from the start and treated me like the little sister she always wished she had."

Carina says: "I noticed right away that Joe and Diane had a strange relationship. I think they really loved each other, but I never saw them kiss or hold hands or hug each other. And I never saw them sit down and talk. Maybe they did it in bed, before they went to sleep.

Maybe they didn't like to talk in front of other people. When I think about it, they were hardly ever in the house at the same time. Most weekday nights, they would go to their 'appointment' [their euphemism for the Perry Street meetings], then go out to dinner with separate friends. They almost never came home together."

Carina says, "I never saw Joe physically hit Diane, ever. But they had loud and terrible arguments. Usually he started them, with his temper. But she could provoke him by laughing in his face—or by acting as if she *felt* like laughing. She would hold out with that attitude for a long time, just to annoy him."

One of the worst of the fights Carina witnessed occurred early in her stay with the Pikuls, in the spring of 1983, during a trip she took with them and the children to Boston. Joe was proud of the city he'd gone to school in. As would continue to be the case on other trips, he spared no expense, booking a suite at the Ritz Carlton and giving Carina carte blanche with room service. The second morning of the trip—a misty day that required umbrellas be brought along—Joe, Diane, Carina and the children were window-shopping on elegant Marlborough Street. The family must have made an impressive picture: fair-haired, blue-eyed, well-dressed mother, au pair, preschooler and baby; distinguished-looking patriarch.

"Then all of a sudden," Carina recalls, "Joe and Diane started to fight. I wasn't paying too much attention to what they had been talking about, but it seemed like the anger just erupted out of nowhere. Joe started it, but then Diane got furious. They started hitting each other with their fists. I was shocked! Then Diane got so angry, she hit Joe with her umbrella and then he hit her back with his, and they just kept *doing that.* All the people in the stores were looking at them through the windows and even walking outside and staring in amazement. I was totally embarrassed. And I felt terrible that the children were seeing it."

When the umbrella battle finally ended, Diane took off with Carina and the children in the rental car. Carina fully expected that they were driving to the train station to go back to New York. "But then Diane turned around and drove us back to the hotel, where Joe was napping. We were all going to stay and go on with the trip. I was stunned. It was like nothing had happened between them." Carina never did learn what had triggered the argument, but tape recordings Joe made of an argument with Diane a few weeks before he murdered her reveal she had reiterated an old anger at his having had a homosexual affair while she was breast-feeding Blake. Diane was breast-feeding Blake during the Boston trip.

Somehow, despite these incidents, the Pikuls were able to present the enviable picture of a handsome, in-control couple with beautiful children, living a life that was glamorous and scrupulously correct. The duplex was cozy. (Like all nineteenth century houses in Manhattan, it had small rooms and low ceilings, but its charm and its three separate second-floor bedrooms counted for much.) The summer house, after the renovations and decorating were completed, was lovely, its pool literally ringed with toys proffered by a father who, it was clear even to those who saw his madness, loved his children above all else. Joe Pikul's love for his children was probably the only love untainted by hate that he had ever known. Understandably but ironically, Diane regarded this as positive and hopeful. She had no idea what his fiercely possessive stake in that "pure" love for their children was to mean for her.

Joe called Blake "Spike" and delighted in carrying him around on his shoulders. As the little boy grew older, Joe tried to get to Amagansett on Fridays during the summer early enough to pick him up from day camp. He was proud, too, of his articulate and outgoing daughter, insisting she take riding lessons, year round, so she would have the satisfaction of watching herself become consistently better at a sport. His valiant efforts to transcend his own father's miserable example of parenting seemed finally to have enabled him to face his own fury at the man. When Joseph Pikul, Sr., died in 1984, Sandra Jarvinen—who had never heard a word about the abuse in her ex-husband's childhood and who had often had her in-laws as weekend guests during her marriage to Joe—called Joe to express her sympathy. "I'm so sorry . . ." she began. "Don't be," he shot back. "He should've died sooner. The sunuvabitch didn't suffer enough for what he did to me."

Actually, Sandra's resumption of contact with Joe predated this sympathy call. A few years earlier she had called him, told him she was strapped and asked him to send her $500. He did so—and she used that payment to nullify the seven years statute of limitations on her unpaid $28,000-plus-interest alimony settlement. With the reinstigated claim, which Joe continued to ignore, Sandra was back in his life: wanting money and available to listen to his woes.

During his marriage to Sandra, Joe, then drinking, had vented his raging fear of abandonment in those orgies of destructiveness wreaked upon the Charlton Street apartment. Now that he was sober and married to Diane, he seemed to express that same fear by doing the opposite: hysterically *tightening,* rather than losing, control. His perfectionism took bizarre turns. He was so fussy, for example, about how Jerri's Cleaners downstairs did his shirts that Diane often entered the shop in tears, proclaiming to the owner: "He says you have to do them again; there's too much starch"; he had even taken to phoning the cleaners himself to check on the starch—from his hotel rooms, *overseas.* And when the sight of the stacks of green garbage bags from Tony Roma's restaurant next door displeased him, he hired a boy to come by at four A.M. every weekday and walk those garbage bags several feet away so they were beyond his line of sight when he left the house in the morning.

This extreme perfectionism was not entirely absent in his dealings with his children. As would be later brought out in the custody hearings, he once beat Claudia with a belt, and another time locked Blake in his room when he didn't get into the nursery of the desirable Grace Church School, which Claudia attended. Both events upset Diane greatly.

"Diane adored her children, and they adored her," Maggie Gari remembers. "There was a lot of hugging and kissing. They wrote little love notes to each other. She loved reading to them—*The Cat in the Hat* was her favorite—and she loved going to children's book stores to buy them, and her friends' children, books. She was a very resourceful, hands-on mother who was always taking them on outings—to the South Street Seaport, on hansom cab rides through Central Park, on nature walks in the Hamptons. She made sure they had the right after-school lessons. She was an important presence at Claudia's school—working as volunteer school librarian once a week and at all the fairs and bazaars.

"Our sons were in the same day-care nursery school, Buckle My Shoe, for a year. In good weather, after we picked them up we'd take them to Steve's for ice cream and then to the playground at Washington Square Park. Every Monday, we'd go to Diane's house for either order-out pizza or a dinner she'd cook. Those 'girls' nights'—feeding the kids and then sitting around with our shoes off, laughing on her big flower-print couch—were so happy. We felt like Kate and Allie, except, as Diane once put it: '*Our* jokes are funnier.' "

Yet Diane did not repeat her mother's mistake of losing herself in her children's lives. She had adopted a feminist consciousness, in one short story having a character remember "the inequity in her parents' marriage," whereby "her father, truly the less interesting and capable of the two, seemed to command luxuries and freedom simply by virtue of his maleness. The rage on her mother's behalf and resolve to be different now burned in her with as much strength as ever." Intent on claiming such "luxuries and freedom" for herself, Diane always had full-time day-time baby-sitting—a young black woman named Bernetta Seegars was hired when Carina moved out. She often had sitters at night so she could go to AA meetings, then perhaps dinner afterward. And she usually took Carina out to the house on weekends. If Carina wasn't available to go out to the house, she and Joe usually hired a local sitter there. Joe, with his traditional working-class sensibility and his abused-child's heart, never forgave Diane for her modern refusal to be martyred to motherhood as his own mother had been.

By the mid-eighties, according to his friend, businessman Marshall Weingarden, Joe was making as much as $800,000 a year. This affluence, to Diane, was a dream come true. "She was in love with the whole picture of her life," Gloria Archer says. "And, because of that, she was determined to make the marriage work. I remember her taking me to the beach club she and Joe belonged to in East Hampton. I had taken her several times to my club, and now she was so quietly proud to be able to reciprocate. She loved the whole process: having the young attendant unfold our beach chairs, signing for lunch. Joe offered her a life comparable to the jet set, and she was too impressed to see the thorns in it. She bought clothes in a way that people do when they want to prove something. I remember when she got her lynx coat. She came into my office with it on; we were going out to lunch. The coat, the hair—she looked *wonderful*. She looked *born* to that life, and she seemed to know it. She was not going to give it up."

As Diane herself phrased it in a short story, she now had "a fashion identity which . . . as Randy began to make more and more money in Wall Street . . . resolved itself into an expression of herself that had never been within her means. She found herself refining a unique, elegant and odd style dependent on the counterpointed genius of American and Japanese designers, and she had taken a surprising amount of pleasure in this development."

But if Diane was surprised at the way she loved and now depended on the fruits of Joe's income, Joe was not. He knew exactly how to manipulate the girl who had spent her entire childhood listening to cautionary tales about the Depression; the girl who wanted, then didn't want, then regretted losing an Oyster Bay, Long Island, fiancé; the girl who spent her twenties envying the family wealth of her college girlfriend Jamie Kleinberg. "Joe was like a controlling parent," Gloria says. "They'd have terrible fights; she'd vow to leave; and then he'd say, 'OK, I'll give you money.' " Or, Carina says, "He'd say, 'If you leave, where will you be? Back in your fifth floor walkup with the roaches?' Which I always thought was an odd thing to say, because *their* duplex had mice." Sometimes he threatened to go even further. Barbara Martin remembers him once vowing to drop out of Wall Street, hide his money where she couldn't find it and become a beach bum. That way, even if she scraped up the money to hire a lawyer to find him, there'd be nothing for her to *get*.

Joe's threats always worked. It was, according to her friends, Diane's fear of being destitute that kept her with him—that and his threat to take the children. Gloria recalls: "He'd say, 'You'll have nothing—and I'll take the kids,' and she believed him. She was petrified. *Petrified.*"

She eventually fought her fear enough to begin claiming her independence. She began to broach the idea of getting a job—an idea Joe had deemed verboten. "She'd say, 'How do I even start looking? It's been eight years since I've worked.' She seemed so vulnerable and unsure of herself," remembers Barbara Martin. "I realized, here was a woman who knew exactly what hairstyle and clothes looked most flattering on her, and who could tell you all about the restaurant of the moment and the right exercise regime. She had the whole outside of her life figured out. But she didn't know if she was worth anything underneath. I would give her little exercises to do: 'Write down the names of five people you know who have jobs they like and ask them how they got theirs.' "

She began thinking, as well, of simply taking the children and fleeing. On vacation in Washington, D.C., with Joe and the children, now seven and three, she met Pat Jaudon in Virginia. She confessed how unbearable life with Joe was becoming. But her fear that he would track her down if she left with the children was too great. "Come live down here with me," Pat said. "He'll never find you here." Diane told Pat she would seriously consider the offer.

She did begin to combat her fear of writing. She asked Maggie Gari, who wrote song lyrics for *Sesame Street,* detailed questions about the process of writing. When did she write? How did she warm up? What did she do when she was blocked? Did she keep notebooks of ideas? Warily, she began a few stories about her life. Eventually, she read parts of these to her friend Carolyn Gaiser, a poet and contributor to *The New York Times Book Review.* "She would say to me, 'Do you really think I can write?' " Carolyn recalls. "I'd say, 'Yes.' And she'd say, 'Some of the writing teachers at Mt. Holyoke said I had talent. . . .' letting the sentence trail off as if to convince herself. She was very fragile and touchy on the subject of her writing. It was clear that this was one area of enormous investment and insecurity for her." As long as she never tried to make good on her fantasy vocation, she had remained safe from failure. But at age forty-three, that "safety" had begun to feel cheap and transparent.

The writing was threatening to Joe. "She was very afraid of writing at home," Carolyn Gaiser recalls, "where Joe could snoop around and see what she was writing. And whenever I'd say to her, 'Why don't you write about your life with Joe?,' she'd say, 'No! He'll find out!' "

Yet Diane was snooping around a little herself—and uncovering outrageous things about her husband. One day in the spring of 1986, she found a pair of women's stockings in Joe's briefcase. They were extremely large stockings and, as Barbara Martin recalls, Diane laughed, dumbfounded when she unrolled them. She couldn't imagine any *woman* wearing them. Not long after, on a hunch prompted by the stockings, Diane went up to Joe's attic room, which had always been off-limits to her and the children. There she found pictures and videotapes of him wearing women's underwear, writhing in sexual ecstasy. Diane was disgusted and profoundly disturbed.

During Easter vacation in 1986, just before Diane's secret discovery, Joe, Diane, Carina and the children went on vacation to Key West, Florida. There were lavish accommodations and dinners at the best restaurants, as usual. Afterward, Diane stopped off with the children to spend a few days visiting her father and Gretchen near Tampa. Joe and Carina flew back to New York together, and high above the Eastern seaboard "Joe kept talking about how well he was doing, how he was on a roll, how he wasn't going to stop until he had fifteen million dollars," Carina remembers. "I thought, What a funny, in-between number; why not ten or twenty?

"He said he'd lost it all that time before. His money. His company. His reputation. His wife. He said he was never going to let that happen to him again. Ever."

Chapter 7

Deanna had never been able to understand crimes of
passion committed with a gun. So impersonal. One
would need to feel the flesh yield . . . the direct agony
of the loved one whose life you were taking, spirit
snuffing.

Diane Pikul, "The End of the Affair"

If all of Diane's New York City girlfriends knew of the
aberrances and dangers of her marriage and counseled
her to leave it, there was another group of friends who
were slower to discover that the Pikuls' marriage was
askew. Marshall and Barbara Weingarden, Frank and
Snow Piccolo, and Peter and Leslie Griffith all had young
children close to Blake and Claudia's ages, and Diane
and Joe often socialized with them in the Hamptons.
Weekends would find them having barbecues in one another's backyards, playing Trivial Pursuit, hiring babysitters and going out to dinner together. The men talked
about business, local real estate, and things in general,
"like if our car phones got reception in Montauk and
where we got our firewood," says Marshall Weingarden.
The women, closer because they spent summer weekdays
together as well, discussed adult exercise classes, children's horseback riding classes and the merits of the local
day camps and summer nursery school. Joe was big on
stock tips, and Diane, whose weekends often started with
a stop at Bookhampton, could give authoritative capsule
reviews of the latest novels, especially those written by
women. The Pikuls would take the kids miniature golf-
ing, and Diane would attend lectures at Town Hall given
by weekend neighbors in the art and publishing commu-

nities. Snow Piccolo says, "I thought we had a normal couple on our hands."

The Weingardens for the most part did, too. "Joe was a little odd and nervous," Marshall says, "but I chalked that up to work pressure. And he was such an indulgent father—overindulgent, really. There wasn't a toy those children didn't have. The backyard of their house looked like Pennywhistle in Bridgehampton. I was Diane's biggest fan. She was really fun. I would introduce her as the best Trivial Pursuit player ever." Barbara thought the two were mismatched, "because she was so vivacious and he was so tense," and she was taken aback once when, after Joe laughed at a joke during a Trivial Pursuit game, "Diane told him, 'Your laugh is so phony, just like everything about you.' " But Barbara assumed that was the residue from some earlier argument—all couples occasionally argued, didn't they? Similarly, Snow Piccolo dismissed a remark Diane once made—"Joe likes lingerie even more than I do"—as "some kind of joke that went over my head, that I didn't think twice about." How could such people—an urban high-bourgeoisie couple who grappled with the pleasures and inconvenience of weekend-house family life—be anything but normal?

On the Fourth of July, 1986, the Piccolos, Pikuls and Weingardens celebrated by going to a dinner party at the Piccolos' and then to Main Beach for the fireworks show. Snow remembers how Joe leapt up at the sight of a souvenir vendor in the distance, jogged down the beach and came back with sparkling pinwheels for all of the children. He was dressed, as usual, in loafers, chinos, a Brooks Brothers crewneck sweater over a Lacoste shirt: Wall Street Prep. Diane looked glamorous in a designer sundress. The children, tans accentuating their white-blond hair, were beautiful. As the fireworks broke brilliantly over the ocean, no one there knew that this was to be the last day that the Pikuls could hide behind the splendid surface picture of their marriage.

Days later, Leslie Griffith said to Diane, "Joe is so great." Diane shocked her by replying, "You don't know him." She then revealed that in the middle of a recent argument—an argument that started when she said she wanted to get a job—Joe had taken Diane's contact lenses out of their case, thrown them down and stepped on them until they were virtually ground into the bedroom floor. A few weeks after that, standing in the playground of a local day camp, watching their children on the climbing bars, Diane told Snow Piccolo she wanted to divorce Joe. She had just had an "eye tuck" to make her look younger, and she was still wearing dark glasses to protect the scar tissue; Snow felt that the aura of anonymity provided by those dark glasses enabled Diane to open up to her. Snow, surprised at first, listened to Diane talk "about how she was trying so hard to come up with some plan, some way to put it all together—money, job, child care—so she could leave him. Then she said, 'But I *can't* leave him.'

"Why can't you leave him?" Snow asked, confused, since Diane seemed to want to so badly.

"Because," Diane said, "if I did, he would kill me."

Snow recalls, "I instantly knew, from the tone of her voice, that she wasn't exaggerating. That she meant it and that she was frightened to death. I'm a person who always has an answer for everything, but I just stood there, shocked silent."

Diane had by now written about her turbulent marriage to an old friend from her Vail days named Judy. Judy still lived in Vail, where she owned a clothing store. Diane asked her if she and the children could stay with her for a while, if the need suddenly arose; in exchange, Diane would work in her boutique gratis while she got herself and the children more permanently situated in Colorado. Judy wrote back saying yes. (It was important, Diane had written, that their entire exchange pass by letter, so Joe would have no long-distance phone record of the place to which Diane might flee.)

"As soon as that was done," Leslie Griffith says, "Diane came to my house in Montauk with three soft suitcases packed with some of her, Blake's and Claudia's clothes. I kept them in my hall closet for her. These would be her 'getaway' bags, in case things with Joe suddenly got so bad, she had to leave at a moment's notice. I gave her a key to my house and we discussed how it was a shame that getting to my house for the suitcases would take her an hour and a half out of her way before she could get on her way to the airport."

A far bigger impediment than the location of Leslie's

house was the fact that Diane had no money of her own. "She explained how Joe kept her almost like a concubine, with virtually no money in their joint checking account," Leslie continues. "She did say that there were certain odd days when, in the process of transferring funds from one of his holdings to another, Joe *did* keep money in the joint account—briefly. Diane started calling the bank-by-phone number every day that summer to wait for such a day, which would be the only day she could hope to get her hands on enough money to hire a lawyer and buy the plane tickets to Vail."

Diane didn't think Joe knew about her daily calls to bank-by-phone or her intention to flee to Vail, but one incident on a late July day when Joe was in the city gave her a powerful scare. Having gotten into her car to take the children to a local fair, Diane found that it wouldn't start. The engine had been jimmied so it wouldn't turn over, and air had been let out of the tires. Joe arrived at the house the next day, and when Diane's accusations about the incident led to a fight, Diane drove with the children to Gloria Archer's nearby weekend house where they spent the night.

Two days after Diane and the children returned from Gloria's, Diane drove back to the house from her exercise class at the exclusive Radu studio to find their housekeeper, Bernetta Seegars, running down Windmill Lane. When Diane stopped the car to ask what had happened, Bernetta said, "He was screaming at me—he must have thought I was you!" Eventually, out of loyalty to Diane and the children, Bernetta remained, though she finally did leave a year later. Carina spent the next week at the house, during which "Diane and Joe had such a bad fight, she ran out of the house. I ran after her. She was sitting in the car. I had never seen her cry before. She was just crying and crying—she couldn't stop. I hugged her so she'd calm down. Then she said, 'I just can't take this any longer.'" After composing herself, Diane walked inside and called Manhattan's top divorce lawyer, Raoul Lionel Felder.

A tall, lean man in his fifties, with Slavic eyes and a folksy and flamboyant manner, Felder has a master publicist's instinctive ability to ingratiate himself with the media. He dresses like a dandy and speaks in fast, emotional sentences that combine hyperbole, pith, sprinklings of Yiddish and quotes from stand-up comics and Supreme Court justices. Principals in the divorce sagas he orchestrates often wind up in the tabloid headlines, and sometimes in criminal courtrooms. Diane sought him out, having read about him in *New York* magazine. Felder had recently represented theater impressario David Merrick and movie director Brian DePalma in their divorces. Later, he would represent Nancy Capasso in the divorce in which Bess Myerson's status as the "other woman" led to the disclosure of improprieties that prompted Myerson's criminal trial. Later yet, he would represent actress Robin Givens in the divorce that capped her short, stormy marriage to heavyweight champion Mike Tyson.

Felder hadn't quite reached this level of celebrity, nor his eventual fee of five hundred dollars an hour, when Diane Pikul walked through his office door that morning in early August 1986. After a brief wait in a reception room lined with framed magazine articles calling Felder (variously photographed—always smiling—in homburg, safari suit and varsity letters sweater) "The Duke Of Divorce," "The Dean of Divorce," "Captain Divorce" and "Dr. Estranged Love," Diane was ushered into his massive office.

"She was a willowy, fragile, very simply dressed, very *very* frightened woman—dependent on her husband, worried for her children, habituated to terror," was Felder's first impression of Diane.

Diane was not after money, Felder insists. "Fear and protection was the leitmotiv of her case—not getting big bucks out of this guy. I've listened to hundreds and hundreds of women and I *know* when it's about money; you can't miss it—it's a skein that runs through every conversation; you don't have to be Clarence Darrow to figure it out. Anyway, the money thing was a miasma created by Joe. He created this aura of immense wealth—the limousines, the flying around.

"The woman was *scared*. I said, 'Let me help you.' I told her I could get her an order of protection, barring him from coming near her, from Family Court that afternoon. He did not commit physical violence on her—or if he did, it was not remarkable or else I would have taken pictures of it (the law loves a broken finger), but if we went to court, ex parte, and she told her story to the judge, what with her husband's history of alcoholism, violence and crazy behavior, she had a good shot at getting the protective order. Then, I proposed, I would try to bootstrap that protective order into an order of exclusive occupancy to get him out of the Amagansett house; she could leave the children with relatives or friends and we could get a private detective to bodyguard her.

"She asked me, 'Will the order really protect me from him?' I told her the truth: 'It's just a piece of paper, so the actual protection is an illusion, but it works if the man is rational and law-abiding.'

"She turned it down. She said, 'My husband is a very strange, bizarre person. He could kill me; he could run away with the children.' It was clear she was privy to some private madness that no one else could see, that living with him was like living with a volcano. Then she said, 'All you have to do is look at him to know something's not right,' and she—hesitantly—gave me the Polaroid pictures she had. At a later meeting, she gave me the videotapes. It was a very big move for her to yield these things up; she seemed to feel, as many frightened wives feel, that her husband was possessed of this great omniscience, that he would find out she'd done so. As I got to know her over the next year, I realized she was totally controlled by this man; he had to know where she was every single minute."

Looking at the pictures of Joe cross-dressing, Felder was baffled. "He was a most unattractive person, and a degenerate. What was she—this nice, sweet, physically attractive woman—doing with *him*? She was someone who could have had almost any man she wanted." In the videotape, Joe was wearing a garter belt and panties and masturbating to a recording of "Here Comes the Bride." Felder made no plans to do anything with, or reveal his access to, the pictures and videotapes.

Felder's initial retainer, to take on Diane's case, was $10,000. Diane made that payment with money she was apparently able to rescue from the joint account. (She told Felder that it came from her "mad money.") Leslie Griffith remembers the day Diane drove into the city to get the $10,000, along with an additional $5,000 for an emergency fund that would cover, among other things, the three Vail plane tickets. It is not known how Joe reacted when he noticed, as presumably he must have, that the money was missing.*

Diane's friends were greatly relieved that she was finally taking the momentous, long overdue, step of divorcing Joe. "And she was so genuinely ready to leave him," Maggie Gari says. "Emotionally and spiritually, she had arrived at that point that we were all hoping she'd get to. She was beyond being angry at him—so leaving wouldn't just be a dramatic retort. She had thought it through; she was able to reconcile the good and the bad parts of Joe; she was experiencing real sadness that her marriage finally couldn't be salvaged, that she'd have to do without some of the things she'd gotten used to. We felt confident that this was the *right* time, that she would do it correctly. We also felt that, in case she had a last-minute change of heart, Joe's reaction to being served the papers would be so inflammatory that she would know beyond a doubt that she was doing the right thing by leaving him. In a way, we were relying on Joe's own personality to be the final confirmation of her decision."

But Joe foiled that plan. Felder served the initial divorce summons to Joe at his office at Bleichroeder on an August weekday. Although Felder himself says, "Diane was afraid Joe would kill everyone in the Western Hemisphere once he got that summons"—and she was presumably prepared to get the suitcases from Leslie's closet, and the children, and head for the airport—things happened differently. Far from being enraged, Joe was contrite and conciliatory. Apparently leaving his office right after the papers arrived, he drove from the city to the house on Windmill Lane with flowers, profuse apologies and proclamations that he would reform for her. "It was a masterstroke," Maggie says bitterly. "And Diane fell for it."

---

*Diane eventually paid Felder $18,000 in all. After her murder, he returned $10,000 of that to the children and retained $8,000 as token recompense of the $300,000 worth of time he spent battling Joe's custody claims on the children.

She softened toward Joe and her will dissolved. "She had trouble making the follow-up phone call to Felder"—to sustain the divorce action—"just as she'd had trouble deciding to hire him in the first place," Gloria Archer recalls. " 'Things look better between us,' " she told me. 'Joe is going into therapy. . . .* She was particularly heartened that Joe accepted the fact that she knew about his transvestite activities. Her knowing, she said, was almost a relief to him. Now all the terrible secrecy was over with."

Diane's friends were dismayed and frustrated when, intent on saving the marriage, she and Joe entered couples' counseling with Dr. Shoshona Comet, her own therapist. Diane began laughingly telling her friends that Joe had become a "sex fiend," waking her up in the middle of the night to seduce her. "Looking back on it later," Maggie says, "this is probably when he began using cocaine."

Diane and Joe arrived together at the christening of Snow and Frank Piccolo's new baby in early September. "Joe looked terrible," Snow recalls. He looked just as bad when, a few nights later, he and Diane arrived at the Weingardens' Labor Day party. "They came so late, the party was breaking up as they walked in the door," Barbara Weingarden says. "Joe looked all scruggy and scruffy. They had apparently had a big fight; Diane had read him the riot act about what she wanted from him in return for a reconciliation." Having never been to Europe, Diane was, as Barbara recalls, "bound and determined she was going to travel." Joe was scheduled to take an extensive international business trip through Scandinavia, the Netherlands and the Far East in less than two weeks. It was decided that night that he would take Diane along, that it would be first class all the way. Barbara was "worried that her attitude seemed to be, 'I might as well get the perks I want from staying with this lousy character.' "

On hearing about the impending trip from his wife Nancy Kirkland, Bob Salisbury remembers, "I threw my

---

*Joe had been in therapy intermittently since 1980 with Dr. Ethel Harnett of Manhattan; later he would become a patient of Dr. Daniel Schwartz of Queens.

hands up and said, 'There's no accounting for what goes
on between a husband and a wife, but I think she's nuts
to stay with him.' " Diane informed Felder of her change
of plans, and he thought "she was one of those wives
who says, 'Help me, help me, help me . . .' and then
when you do help they say, 'I changed my mind; I don't
want it.' "

In the second week of September, Diane stopped by
the Griffiths' house in Montauk to finally pick up her
three packed suitcases; back at the duplex, she put her
and the children's "getaway" clothes back in drawers and
closets and repacked the suitcases for her and Joe's "second honeymoon." She went to the doctor to get innocul-
ations for the trip and also, she mentioned to Pat
Bartholomew, to get a physical exam required by an insurance company. When Pat Bartholomew asked her
what the latter was all about, Diane explained that Joe
had just taken out a million dollar life insurance policy
on her. "Diane," Pat said haltingly, "I'd be very nervous
if *Geoff* insisted on getting a million dollar policy on
me.' "

On September 15, Carina and her friend Inga Davidsson moved into the Pikul duplex to look after Claudia
and Blake for the month. "Joe had really changed," Carina noticed. With the help of his therapist, he had em-
barked on a new regime in which he tried to include
relaxing activities in his day, one of which was the reading of suspense novels. "He was much calmer. I felt
hopeful."

The trip was a dream for Diane, according to the post-
cards she sent to her father and Gretchen. In Amsterdam, their first stop, they had a "lovely room
overlooking a canal" in the majestic Amstel Hotel.
Diane toured the museums, ate Indonesian food, and
sent her father tulip bulbs. After a few days, they flew
into Oslo "on a beautiful, clear morning," settled into
the equally majestic Grand Hotel, and while Joe was
having daily business meetings Diane took "two afternoon tours and shop[ped] for toys and sweaters."

The Far East, where she and Joe arrived on September
29, was more exotic, bringing out the provincial Indiana
girl in Diane. Her first morning in Tokyo, "this intrepid
traveler," she confessed in a postcard, "is afraid to leave

the hotel room." Eventually she did so, among other things to dine with Joe and Joe's "big boss and three others, all of whom I found extremely attractive and charming. . . . Our dinner with them, high-class Japanese, was disgusting beyond my wildest dreams. I ate some raw octopus filled with mucus!" A day later, she got into the swing of things—she "rubbed good luck smoke in my hair and tied my bad fortune to a rack and said two prayers in a temple." None of these Japanese rituals was to intercept her destiny.

In the very short run however, the good luck balms worked wonders. In Kyoto, Diane stayed at the Hiiragiya Inn. She wrote her father: "Charlie Chaplin stayed here, and the Japanese royal family. It may be the most expensive place I will ever stay in. The service was sublime." And in her last missive before her October 15 departure—a letter written on stationery imprinted MRS. J. PIKUL—Diane waxed elegiac from her room in the Mandarin Hotel in Hong Kong:

Dear Daddy and Gretchen:
   You will notice the personalized stationery. It was waiting for me, along with the flowers, the basket of fruit, the Chinese tea served and the little man who immediately arrived to see if I had any pressing to be done. If you need something you don't call on the phone, you just push a button by your bed—you don't sign downstairs, they escort you to your room and let you do it sitting down.
   I can't believe that I, Diane Whitmore of South Bend, Indiana, have been fortunate enough to get to these places in my life—especially here. I love it.
   Before I unpack and while I'm waiting for Joe to arrive from his business appointment, as I watch twilight descend over Hong Kong Harbor from the balcony of our suite, I thought I'd just write to tell you that it doesn't get any better than this.

Indeed, it would not. One year and one week later, it would become sadly clear that she had bartered her life for this one month of glorious luxury.

Back in New York, Diane began to get serious about the

personal missions she had been postponing. With Blake now in nursery school all day, she bore down on job-hunting. Her old Parks Department boss, Joe Davidson, got a call from her asking if he'd be willing to give her a recommendation; he said he'd be happy to do so. Hiding her efforts from Joe—just as she hid her short-story writing—she combed the *New York Times* and *Village Voice* want ads every week. Of the Parks Department job, she wrote on her resume. "My specialty was seeming to say something while saying nothing," and of a smattering of freelance work she'd been doing for *Sports Illustrated*'s Picture Sales department, "a total inability to recognize sports figures hindered me." She covered the last eight years of her life with the job description "Mother & Domestic Administrator." Whoever was going to hire her was going to get the real Diane Whitmore. She went on eleven job interviews without Joe's knowledge.

In February, when spring semester started, Diane enrolled in a writing workshop at New York University's School of Continuing Education. "She was gay, bouncy and friendly—yet slightly distant, and she was a very promising writer with a strong voice," novelist Nahid Rachlin, who taught the class, remembers. Yet Ms. Rachlin recalls one of Diane's otherwise fine stories being almost unanimously criticized by the class for what seemed to be one glaring flaw: "The man in the story was so unlovable and unattractive that the protagonist's attraction to him didn't make sense. It wasn't literarily justified."

As their children played in the Washington Square Park playground one afternoon, Diane told Maggie Gari: "What difference does it make if I find a great job, and become a writer, and leave Joe? I'll just end up with another man like him. I don't know how to break this cycle."

In mid-March, *Harper's* magazine editor Lewis Lapham's assistant Ann Stern put an ad in *The Village Voice* for an assistant to publisher Rick MacArthur. The starting salary—$22,500—was so low and the cachet of working at *Harper's* so high that Ann expected to screen dozens of twenty-three-year-olds who lived either with their parents or in small apartments with three roommates. "Young kids and crazies who clearly couldn't hold down a job" started calling the minute the *Voice* hit the stands, Ann remembers. But one caller sounded distinctly different—"she sounded intelligent, sophisticated, articulate, good-humored, very literate, very literary—and *grown up*" Ann recalls, with relief on the last adjective. They made an appointment. Ann knew she'd like her. Diane knew she wanted *this* job, badly, Maggie Gari remembers.

It was raining the day of Diane's interview. The elevators of 666 Broadway open onto the *Harper's* reception room. Catherine Hopkins, an editorial assistant sitting at the reception desk during the receptionists' lunch break, remembers "this fast-talking, friendly, eccentric-in-a-nice-way woman walking out of the elevator and immediately changing her shoes. 'Here, hide my rain boots,' she said, 'so I can make a better impression.' We both laughed. I liked her immediately."

So did Ann Stern. "She came into my office with the ease you see in people who are very talented and well-practiced at making entrances. She was wearing a fur coat, but it was casual, like something you'd wear to a football game, and she wore it as if she wasn't afraid to have a baby spit up on its shoulder. She was breezy and friendly. There was no insecurity that came across. When I found out later how desperately she wanted the job, and how she had to job-hunt on the sly, I was amazed at how well she hid all this."

Ann did pick up a clue that day as to the appeal terror held for Diane. During the course of the interview, Diane mentioned that as she was leaving her apartment an ambulance and police car converged out front, sirens blaring. There'd been some crisis in the street, Ann says. "I remember thinking—because I'm a working mother—My God, you've just left your children, you're off to a job interview; then, *plunk,* right in front of your door is this introduction to the intimacy of horror. I said to her, 'That must have been upsetting.' "

But, far from sharing Ann's alarm, "Diane just threw back her head, smiled, and said, 'No, not at all. That's what I love about New York.' And I thought, How interesting . . . and strange: She still has that young infatuation with 'New York.' She doesn't have that sober, maternal feeling that danger is danger. Romance still covers *everything*."

Ann saw that Diane's aspirations were literary. Since the job open was strictly secretarial with no opportunity to eventually move into editorial, Ann recommended an applicant "who only wanted to be a secretary." Diane left the interview with the sense that she was not Ann's first choice; she went home and called Maggie Gari to say: "I'm going to call them up and convince them *I'm* the one they want." Maggie felt "proud and surprised that Diane had such a wonderfully aggressive attitude about being hired."

Before Diane could make that call, however, Ann called to offer her the job. Ann's first choice thought the salary too low and Diane was next on the list. Diane accepted the job on one condition: that she be able to leave the office twice a week from two to three thirty to accompany her son to appointments with his new speech therapist. The condition was met, and Diane started work at *Harper's* in April.

Predictably, Joe hated the thought of Diane working; it took her out of his sphere of control. Diane laughed to her new coworkers that the plant he'd sent her on her first day of work was a gift she had to *make* him send her. She quipped about Joe being so mad that she was working, he might burn the *Harper's* building down— and received nervous, uncomprehending laughter from her new colleagues. Diane made Joe's increasingly aggressive paranoia fodder for black humor.

In the meantime, believing all Diane's friends were lesbians bent on seducing his wife away from him, Joe hired a man to tail Maggie and Diane on their weekly jaunts to the SoHo restaurant Food. "There was always this same guy, sitting behind an opened newspaper one table away," Maggie says. She and Diane surmised Joe's actions. "Diane and I were tempted to start pretending we were lesbians in the middle of the restaurant just to watch him drop his paper." Joe's false accusations downplayed his own furtive return to homosexual liaisons and the escalation of his habit of cross-dressing.

Raoul Felder, with whom Diane continued to consult, now saw Diane as "a woman consciously trying to resurrect and restructure her life: to get back on track and do positive things. She wanted to leave her husband but she was reluctant because she was terrified. I said at one point, 'Is this the kind of thing where we're going to meet for the rest of our lives and never really get a divorce going? Because if so, I have better things to do with my time and you have better things to do with your money.' I say this to clients not to be cruel but to force them to make some kind of decision. Diane made it very clear that she was going to do something at some point, that she felt she was making progress."

And she *was* making progress. On the weekends, at night and in the hours after work, she was writing her stories. In June, she sought out Jamie Kleinberg Kamph, recently remarried, whom she'd never quite stopped thinking of as the Mt. Holyoke intellectual wunderkind. "She said she was reorganizing her life and she really wanted to talk to me about how to balance some of the different tensions," Jamie recalls. "When I suggested we get together with our husbands, who were both investors, she seemed to shy away from it." They put the date off until after the summer. They never got together.

Also in June, Diane enrolled in a second fiction workshop at NYU, this one taught by the writer Elizabeth Henley. When Diane read her assigned autobiography to the class, "She did so with a sense of humor and the class cracked up" at its black wit, Henley recalls. Like Nahid Rachlin, Elizabeth Henley thought Diane very talented. "But while she wanted to write very much, there was some conflict about her being able to do so. She expressed but never explained it."

At *Harper's*, Diane ingratiated herself to the women in their twenties. "She was their buddy, their nurturing older sister who was breezy and witty and worldly and could also say outrageous things about her husband," Ann Stern says. When editorial assistant Catherine Hopkins began dating *Harper's* assistant editor Rick Marin, Diane was her eager confidante. Catherine was well educated, stylish, an aspiring writer herself, and her beau, now the television critic at *The Washington Times*, was just the kind of handsome and promising "comer" Diane met, and rejected, in numbers at those long-ago Columbia parties she went to with Mary Beth Whiton.

When Catherine and Rick Marin became engaged,

Diane, who had known Catherine only two months, almost entirely organized the wedding and arranged for them to honeymoon at the Windmill Inn, right down the street from her house in Amagansett. Arriving at their room at the inn, the newlyweds found a basket of gourmet items, fruit, funny maps and descriptions Diane had drawn of Amagansett. A note said, "The elves have been here." It was as if—now past the point of no-return with her own, very different choices—Diane had wistfully carried out a road-not-taken romance and wedding by proxy.

But it was with advertising assistant Linda McNamera that Diane developed her closest friendship at work. Linda found Diane "generous, funny, protective; we became close immediately." Diane regaled Catherine with tales of her days at *Life* and her nights at the psychedelic-era discos, and she told Linda, who'd been dating a rock singer, about her romance with pop star cousin Tommy.

Linda loved Diane's style, her stories, her clothes. "There was one brown dress of hers I loved so much, I would kiddingly say, 'I hope you'll will it to me.' Diane laughed and said, 'When I'm dead, you and Claudia can fight over it.' " "Diane," Ann Stern says, "used irony like a dazzling sword. She could deflect all her deepest fears with it."

By the beginning of the summer, Diane had stopped regarding Joe's actions with cool black humor. She had become quietly but solidly terrified. The man who was following her unnerved her, and she suspected, from the strange clicks she heard when she picked up the phone, that her conversations were being monitored. Diane warned all her friends not to say anything negative about Joe when she spoke to them from the apartment.

Raoul Felder arranged for a private detective named Bo Deitl to come to the duplex and check for taps, but Diane was so worried that Joe would come home in the middle of the procedure, she cancelled the appointment with Deitl five times until, on July 30, she finally let Deitl and his electronics engineer, Guy Capalupo, come over.

Deitl found his new client "a lovely woman but as scared as a rabbit. I was a New York police detective for years before starting my agency; I've seen a lot of women who've been beaten or threatened by their husbands. They all have a certain look on their face, and she had it." Deitl listened while Diane "talked and talked about this maniac she was married to, like she just had to get it out, like I was a psychiatrist," while Capalupo began his electronic sweep of the duplex, "going through the house,"—as he would later recall on the witness stand at the custody hearing—"measuring for line voltages and currents."

Finding a suspicious "off" voltage in the living room, Capalupo set to work "dismantling all telephone equipment, inspecting all telephone lines and finding where they terminated," he recalls. "I finally wound up in the attic, where I found a tape recorder hidden under a pile of clothing. The tape recorder was hooked to the telephone line which was under a pile of cushions." Pushing a wicker basket away from the wall, Capalupo uncovered the last component of the impromptu device: a phone jack.

When Capalupo went downstairs to inform the client that he'd found an apparatus that automatically tape-recorded every incoming phone call, he—and Deitl—fully expected, from their years of experience, that Diane would become enraged at her husband's duplicitous invasion. But "Diane wasn't angry," Bo Deitl remembers. "She was just frightened and panicky. She wouldn't let us remove the tap. She said, 'Put everything back where it was! My husband can't know that I found this!' "

Still, despite her fear, Diane immediately told Joe about her plans to divorce him. But he talked her into renewed marital counseling, and they operated with the self-contradictoriness that was now so familiar and that fueled the tension between them: They stepped up the counseling even while he was starting to move his belongings out of the duplex and into the apartment on Rector Street. During their weekends in Amagansett, the Pikuls awkwardly tried to sustain their performance as the happy couple, but the Weingardens were increasingly aware of the precariousness of their friends' reconciliation. They saw Joe's emotional instability, and suspected chemical dependency. "Joe's the mystery man," Diane complained to Barbara Weingarden. "In the city, I get up in the morning to go to work and there's a big limou-

sine with darkened windows waiting outside for him.
Sometimes he disappears for days at a time."

One evening in Amagansett, Joe called Marshall
Weingarden and asked him to come over to help him
figure out how to use a foreign videocamera he'd recently
bought on Forty-second Street. "It was the craziest thing
to buy!" Weingarden says. "All the labels, the buttons,
the instructions were written in Japanese. I couldn't believe that someone as brilliant as Joe—who'd recommended all these stock purchases to me—would have let
himself be ripped off like the most naïve tourist." Diane
simply murmured to Barbara: "I'm sure Joe was on drugs
when he bought this."

Another evening, Joe kept jumping up from the Trivial
Pursuit game they were all playing in the Weingardens'
living room. "He went to the bathroom ten or fifteen
times," Marshall recalls, "but most of the time I didn't
hear the toilet flush." This was the classic behavior of a
cocaine addict.

It was in August that Joe's eccentricities began to turn
into real madness. He was abroad frequently now, in-
vestigating Scandinavian condom manufacturers because
the AIDS epidemic had made such companies promising
investments. His phone calls to Diane from hotel rooms
were fevered and threatening. By now, he knew that he
himself was HIV-positive. The eventuality of his death
plagued him, and he sought release by confiding this to
the one woman who was somehow always there for him,
Sandra Jarvinen. Placing overseas calls at all hours of
day and night, he would ramble to Sandra, bitterly berat-
ing Diane for, as Sandra recalls it, "leaving the children
with a different baby-sitter every night." Sandra, not
knowing Diane or the situation, waxed sympathetic. She
didn't discourage these middle-of-the-night phone calls;
in fact, she had developed ways to cope with them. Once,
years before, when he had called at 3 A.M., Sandra left
the phone off the hook and went back to sleep. She was
awakened hours later when a telephone company
worker, concerned about the length of the call, sent
someone over to knock on her door. On the other end
of the line, Joe Pikul was still talking.

It was Joe's calls to Diane, however, that most clearly
revealed his mental state. Pat Bartholomew was visiting

the house during one afternoon barrage of his calls. Twenty minutes after Diane hung up from one call with Joe, Pat lifted up the receiver to make a local call of her own. Instead of a dial tone, Pat heard dim heavy breathing. Joe, it turned out, had never surrendered the line. He was stalking his wife, at exorbitant cost, from his hotel room across the ocean.

Joe returned from these trips with suitcases full of sample brands of condoms, many of which he stored in drawers in the Amagansett beach house.

By early September, Raoul Felder and David Slavin, the younger associate who directly handled Diane's case, approached Joe's attorneys to obtain a statement of Joe's net worth. Joe's lawyers stonewalled. Joe was now telling Diane he fully intended to sue for custody of the children—and that she would lose against him because, except for what he called her "laughable" salary, she was virtually penniless. Felder, however, had the videotapes. "The value of those pictures and videotapes was in the custody situation," Felder explains. "What I would have done—if Diane had permitted me to do it; and I've done this in the past—was go to her husband's lawyer and say, 'Look, here are the pictures we have. You don't want to see them in a courtroom. These pictures demonstrate that this man is not a good influence on these children. I don't want to have to produce these pictures in court, but my client and I intend to protect these children.' "

"Diane was trying to do everything she could to *not* have to resort to using those pictures," Gloria Archer says. But Joe knew that Felder had them.

By early September, Diane suspected Joe might have the AIDS virus. "She kept telling me she wanted to get an AIDS test and that she was so worried about the children getting AIDS, but I never knew why," Maggie Gari says. It didn't seem unusual, though, since, at that time, AIDS panic and misinformation were rampant in New York. Some people were even bringing their own silverware to restaurants. In a tape recording that Joe secretly made in the Amagansett house, we hear Diane confront him:

"You're hiding your AIDS from me," she says. Then, after lamenting her age and her salary, she says: "I probably have the AIDS virus, too. I'm too scared to go for a test."

"Well, how do you know [I have AIDS]?"

"Because somebody told me."

Joe then stammers: "That, that, that is of course ridiculous." He continues to repeat "absolutely ridiculous" as she asks him to get an AIDS test.

Finally, Joe warns her: "You haven't seen anything yet, Diane . . ." By now, he was trying to talk Sandra Jarvinen into signing a document agreeing to become legal guardian in the event of the death of both of his children's parents. In addition to complaining to Sandra about Diane's shortcomings as a traditional mother, Joe had three other confidants: his chauffeur Jim Burns; his old Charlton Street neighbor Ramona Craniotis; and a young French junior analyst at Bleichroeder named Jean-Jacques, to whom he functioned as a professional mentor and big brother.

Later on the same tape, Joe, apparently making the recording for his own legal benefit, provoked her into telling him just what she thought of him. "You are a faggot—you're worse than a faggot, you're a bully," is how she begins her string of contemptuous accusations. "You're a nasty, cowardly bully. You're a liar. You're a cheat. You're dishonest. You're dishonorable. You're mean, you're nasty and psychotic, and I don't want to live with you and I want to see you as little as possible." She rebukes him for borrowing her clothes, including her sanitary napkins.

"Retaliate, Diane," he then dares her on tape. "Kill me. You don't scare me."

"I'm living a bad life," Diane finally says, bitterly and sadly. "I've had a bad decade, Joe. I've had a real bad decade."

"Go share your bad day with one of your friends," he then advises her, sarcastically. Finally, he reminds her, "You're making twenty-two five; I make a million two. . . ."

Joe had mostly moved to Rector Street now, and came for the children at unannounced and unpredictable times, spiriting them off in limousines, plying them with toys and stuffed animals at F.A.O. Schwartz. Often he didn't bring them home until the next morning. "Diane would say, 'He's disappeared with them again'—'disappeared' was her word," Barbara Weingarden recalls. "Once, he was gone with them for three days. She thought he had them in Minneapolis, where he was going for business. She was on the verge of hysterics."

Another time, after instigating a fight with Diane, Joe blindfolded the children to take them to what Diane would later deduce was the Rector Street apartment. (They told her they could "see the Statue of Liberty out the window.) "When Diane told me that story," Raoul Felder says, "I insisted on getting her a protective order. I had done so in the past, but now I knew she had to have one. I was also now sure we could also get her the order of exclusive occupancy. I remember standing in the hall of my offices, with her leaning against the door— and saying to her, 'Diane, this goes beyond the pale. This husband of yours is a raving lunatic. Let me get this protection for you.' I *almost* had her convinced, but in the end she still turned it down. She was afraid it would only provoke him more."

"The woman who knows her husband is serious when he says, 'If you leave me, I'll kill you' is like a woman locked alone in a cubicle, screaming," says domestic violence specialist Dr. Penelope Grace, a psychologist at Harvard University Medical School's Children's Hospital, "The people outside the cubicle's walls can hear her screams in a dim, muffled, general way—and they respond to what they hear with advice based on good intentions. But they can't hear the clarity and the bottomlessness of her terror. And they don't know what she knows in her bones: That he's going to make good on his promise." Diane was that woman in the cubicle.

In early September, Joe took a series of measures to "step up his attempt," as Gloria Archer would later see it, "to isolate Diane from anyone who could help her." First, just before Labor Day weekend, he screamed so heatedly at Bernetta that the baby-sitter—in a gesture that distressed Blake and Claudia, who had grown so attached to her—felt she had no choice but to leave the employ of the person she now considered a "madman." Then he stole Diane's appointment book and phone book; she later found them in his car's glove compartment. Finally, he started keeping the guns that he had in Amagansett in the duplex; when Diane told Maggie Gari, Pat Bartholomew and Barbara Martin about the guns, they had no choice but to stop sending their own children over to the Pikul house for playdates with Blake and Claudia.

Barbara Martin got a call one day from Diane, "whispering into the phone that Joe was following her around the house, shouting horrible things about her." Carina got phone calls, too. In one, "Diane said, 'Oh, Joe's so crazy, he's ripping the suitcases up with a knife!' Another time, she said, 'You know what he's doing *now*? He's on the floor with his sweat pants rolled down, eating a watermelon and . . .' and then she indicated, in an embarrassed way, that he was masturbating." Carina was able to see for herself Joe's escalating pathology. When she and Inga Davidsson took Diane and Joe out to dinner at the trendy restaurant Barocco as a thank-you gesture for the Pikuls' financial support of their new design business, Carina recalls, "I was shocked when I saw Joe. I had been out of the country for several months, but a person doesn't change *that* much in a couple of months. He was skinny and so hyper I thought he'd jump out of his skin. And he kept rubbing white powder under his nose. Diane acted as if she didn't notice."

Carina, Barbara Martin, Maggie Gari, Gloria Archer, Pat Bartholomew and Linda McNamera continually let Diane know she *must* leave Joe: divorce-in-the-works or not, she simply could not wait any longer. Gloria took her on the futile house-hunting search in Port Washington. All offered their homes and apartments as temporary way-stations for Diane and the children. But way stations to where? To each of them, Diane reiterated her fear that Joe would find her *wherever* she fled, and the more makeshift her attempt, the easier it would be for a man of Joe's resources to trace her. Doug Thompson, with whom Diane stayed in touch, says that Diane had turned to her father for financial help and had judged from his response that, while he could help her out a little, as a retiree with a wife to support he was in no position to assume major support of Blake and Claudia. Neither was he able to put them up for an extended period.

Thus, Diane had to cling to her assets. If she left the duplex, then the duplex became Joe's—as well as the Amagansett house, which was legally his purchase. He could also sue her for abandonment. With the claim of abandonment, with both domiciles in his possession and with his overpowering income, he'd be in an excellent position to get custody of the children. No, she told her friends. She couldn't just pick up the children and go. The stakes were too high. She had to craft as airtight and viable a leavetaking as possible.

On September 15, Diane wrote a letter of application to Allan Gurganus, director of the distinguished Writers Community workshop. "I am forty-four, the mother of two small children and am nearing the end of my second marriage," she began. "Six months ago I resumed working outside the home after a child-rearing hiatus of eight years. . . . My job is interesting but not editorial. I am not sure where it will lead or where I would want it to." After telling Gurganus about her two writing courses, she said, "At this turning point in my life I would like to seriously explore the possibility of writing for a living or at least writing seriously and regularly." She enclosed three short stories.

Gurganus, as impressed as her previous teachers Rachlin and Henley had been, called to accept her into the workshop. This was an achievement Diane had dreamed of all her life—but it was an achievement now lodged in the midst of a gathering nightmare.

That same week, Barbara Martin paid a visit to the Pikuls to pick up the stroller and toys Diane had offered to pass on to Barbara's young children. Almost alone among Diane's friends, Barbara had remained on good terms with Joe. "How are the children?" Barbara asked Joe, who was home alone. "They're great," he replied. And then, "That's what life's all about."

Toward the end of September, Maggie called Diane at home. Almost immediately after answering, Diane whispered, "Joe says he's going to have me killed, and then he'll have my body disposed of where no one can find it." Diane's need to whisper—so that neither Joe, in the next room, nor the tape recorder rigged to the phone, would pick up her words—forced her to also speak slowly, so that Maggie could understand her. This manner of speaking, along with the fact that Maggie, not Diane, had initiated the phone call, would constitute Joseph Pikul's greatest pretrial triumph.

On October 3, Carina and Inga hosted a birthday party for Inga's boyfriend at the Hudson Street loft the couple shared. Joe came up to Carina during the evening and told her, "Diane's leaving me—and I don't want her to." Joe's awkward confession made Carina cry. She felt she *had* to get out of the miserably uncomfortable position she occupied between the two of them.

On Saturday, October 17, when Joe again disappeared with the children, Diane went to her office at *Harper's*. But instead of working on a short story, as she often did there now on weekends, she first called her father, telling him she was very upset. Then, in her windowless cubicle made cheerful by Blake and Claudia's drawings and Claudia's big I LOVE YOU, MOMMY sign, she sat for several hours and, on her IBM Selectric, typed a cogent five-page single-space description of the horror her life had become.

TO: Raoul Felder/David Slavin
FROM: Diane Whitmore Pikul
DATE: October 17, 1987

On the days of September 26 and 27, . . . the evenings of Sept. 30, Oct. 14 and 15, and the day of Saturday, Oct. 17th, I did not know the whereabouts of my children. They were taken suddenly and with no planning to unknown locations by my husband. He made no attempt to notify me of their whereabouts and refuses to tell me where they went. In addition . . . on the afternoon of Oct. 6 he took Blake, then called to tell the babysitter he had him at the airport [Joe was leaving for Zurich] and would send him home by limousine, to be expected about 6:00 P.M. He did not arrive until about 7:00 and I had no way of knowing the number of the limousine service. In most cases the children are sent for by hired car and taken away from previously arranged babysitters or playdates.

On the Sept. 30 occasion an older woman from a babysitting agency attempted to call me when he . . . shouted at her that her job was to take orders and she should get out. Her supervisor at the fox Agency reported to me later that she had been terrified. . . .

On the Sept. 26 and 27 instance, [Joe's absconding with the children] occurred after I got out of the car at midnight and refused to drive to Amagansett [with them] in a state of fatigue while being called "bitch" and "moron." My first knowledge that they were not in Amagansett was the next day, when . . . our houseguests* . . . said there was no sign of the family having arrived . . . I . . . called all police departments and highway patrols covering the route they would have taken to see if there had been any fatal accidents. I did not receive a call until Sunday at about 11:30 A.M., at which time Joe said he would bring them home in an hour. At about 2:00 P.M. he called to say he wanted to get them bathing suits so they could go swimming. When I asked where they were he hung up. They did not arrive home until 8:30 P.M. . . .

We attended marriage counseling on Tuesday, Oct. 13, which we have done weekly for a year. In the session the therapist expressed alarm over the environment in which the children are living and insisted that we agree upon a schedule for the weekend in which everyone will know who will be with whom and when. At the end of the session Joe said he refused to pay for anymore sessions or babysitters for them . . . and subsequently said he would refuse to adhere to any schedules because of my bad attitude toward marriage counseling.

But no sooner had Joe become belligerent than he turned suddenly flexible, and continued on a manic back-and-forth mood-swing for the next few days. Diane continues:

On Thursday evening he brought me a flower and asked to arrange a schedule for the weekend. we agreed that I would have [the children] Friday night,

*Those "houseguests" were Edleen Powlowski bergelt (Joe's sister Janice's daughter) and her husband, Keith Bergelt. they lived in a small apartment on the Upper East Side."

Saturday after 12:30 and until midday Sunday. He came home in the middle of Friday night for two hours, expressing hostility toward me. On Saturday morning he arrived home as promised at 9:30 A.M. but [the children] were not returned at 12:00. He called and suggested we go to the country, and get a baby sitter for Saturday night. When I said he'd have to make all financial arrangements . . . he said he'd bring the children right home. At 1:20 I left for a 1:30 appointment, to which I'd planned to bring the children, leaving a note as to my whereabouts. I heard nothing and arrived back home at about 3:30, then left again an hour later, leaving a note that I would be at my office. It is now 9:00 P.M. and they have not called the office and there is no answer at either of our homes. I consider this excessively cruel behavior toward me and a bad environment for the children's well-being to say the least.

Joe frequently spends the night out, and usually seems to arrive and depart by limousine. . . . I played back one tape he made of the home telephone conversations in which he repeatedly gave directions to the children, drivers and babysitters to do things and not to tell me. . . .

She picks up this concern several paragraphs later as well:

He is attempting to turn my children against me, tells them he took me off the street, that I lived in slovenliness with cockroaches when he met me, that they will never see me when I get a boyfriend, that he will fight for the house in Amagansett and for custody of them, that they will get to live with him, that I care nothing for them but only for myself. . . .

Joe says he is planning to sue for custody on the basis of my having too many babysitters. What babysitter help I do have, I must point out, is never for the purpose of carousing, rarely even for socializing, and never to a place where I cannot be reached. . . .

His erratic behavior indicates drug abuse. Called me from Zurich the night of either Oct. 7 or 8 and asked me to go to . . . Antigua with him, just to be nice to him. . . . He said [the hotel management] had put him in a little room so he had called and said if they didn't move him immediately he would jump out the window so now he was enjoying a beautiful view of Zurich from the presidential suite. The next day he called to express anger at some domestic detail. After arriving home from Europe he called Amagansett, wanted to go to a disco with me, said he would meet me in the bookstore at 10:30 and never arrived until 2:30 the next afternoon. He was in a rage because we were not there (although we left a note as to our whereabouts), overturned furniture, broke a toy rifle and when we returned grabbed the children, refused to wait for their coats or homework and left. When he called later he refused to let me talk to them.

At approximately the same time Diane had begun writing this memo, Carina had come to the duplex on orders from Joe. Diane did not know this. Joe had called Carina from Zurich some days before, asking her to baby-sit for the children. Diane, he said, would be in Amagansett. Although Carina had vowed to remove herself from Joe and Diane's battleground, she couldn't say no to a request to help the children. She waited in front of the unaccountably empty duplex for two hours, then went home, angry, her day ruined. An hour later Joe called—and the same irrational anger he had expressed to Diane when *he* had stood *her* up in the Hamptons was now repeated to Carina. When Carina hung up after Joe's tirade, she decided she could never be in his presence again, even at Diane's behest. Within an hour of Carina's inadvertently fateful decision, Diane typed these next words, expressing fear of her children's exposure to Joe's violence and perversity:

After hearing the nature of our current home life, my therapist urged me to ask you to make some intervention on the basis of psychological abuse of the children. This is a situation in which their babysitters are subjected to extreme anger or dismissal, their mother is belittled and denigrated, they have no ability to predict their schedule or whereabouts, no constancy in human relationships, just a constant round of limousine pickups, late hours, junk food and presents.

Their father exhibits extreme and unpredictable behavior. He is frequently sadistic, abusive, violent, paranoid, antisocial, controlling and sexually perverse. He is probably abusing amphetamines [especially dangerous in a recovered alcoholic with a history of violence], possibly practicing homosexuality and constantly engaged in covert behavior in one form or another. Claudia has mentioned to me that her father looks at women's cosmetics in drugstores. I don't know if he is spending time with men, women or alone in nightgowns. I want this unwholesome, disruptive presence removed from our lives so my children can grow up without emotional scarring.

I find my plans continually sabotaged, along with my peace of mind. After not being in the workplace for nearly ten years, with a history of alcoholism myself, and asthma, I am struggling to build a career, go to school and raise normal happy children in a confusing environment in which the threat of abuse and violence of one kind or another is constant.

Despite her clearly demonstrated understanding of the emergency her life had become, Diane also raised the prosaic issues of finance with her lawyers. With the single-minded pragmatism her father had long ago taught her, she asked: Did she still have a share in Joe's pension? Could she become "irrevocable beneficiary" of his life insurance policy? Could Joe be made to pay for her therapy? And should she challenge his attempt to sell the Amagansett house, half of which was rightly hers? Those questions were the calmly self-interested questions of a woman pursuing a *normal* divorce from a nonviolent man. While her realistic, appropriately frightened self was willing to run for her life, another self was trying to do battle and not lose any ground. Both Dianes ended the memo, in alternate sentences:

Please help me to resolve this horrible situation as quickly as possible for all of our sakes. It is now time, I fear, for the World War III you promised me we would have if necessary.

Thus she entered the week that began with Wall Street's Black Monday. She called the Chappaqua realtor, Helen Richards, then failed to pursue Richards' lead on a cottage to rent. And as Joe, his emotional state further aggravated by Black Monday, brought Sandra Jarvinen to town to press her once more for that "favor," Diane wrestled with the question of going out to Amagansett for a showdown over the sale of the house.

On the heels of the fight that ensued after Joe prevented her from going to her writing workshop, Diane made her decision. She made plans to meet Barbara Weingarden the next day, with their children, at the East Hampton library for story hour. She cancelled her dinner plans with Maggie Gari. She held to her course, even when Carina called to say she would not be along. At the very end of the day, just as all her friends at *Harper's* were covering their typewriters and putting on their jackets to leave, she told receptionist Karen Hoffman, "I'm going to Amagansett to have it out with Joe." But that certainty and bravado slipped when she said good-bye for the weekend to Linda McNamera. "I don't really know *why* I'm going. . . ." she said softly.

Then she went home, where she fed and bathed the children and kissed them good-bye as they drove off to the house with their father. She remained in the duplex: straightening up, changing her clothes, quite possibly mentally replaying the same ambivalence she had expressed to Linda. Then she took herself out to dinner, got money from her bank's cash machine, walked to the parking garage.

And finally—just as she'd oared, as a child, on Lake Huron, neither wearing a life vest nor able to swim; and just as she'd courted an unwanted pregnancy right before college graduation; and just as she'd walked, drunk and barefoot, after fighting with Ralph, into the Amazon jungle—just as she'd done all of this and more, Diane stepped on the accelerator and drove into the night.

PART IV
MURDER AND CAPTURE

Chapter 8

"I am mad and I am brokenhearted and I tried as hard as I could. . . . Do I *look* like I feel powerful?! I don't feel powerful at all. If I were powerful, I wouldn't have to act this way. I feel totally unpowerful." —*Diane*

"You haven't seen anything yet, Diane. . . . Go ahead. You'll be left with your memories. Nothing. Zero. Zilch. Go. Go ahead, Diane. Diane, you're powerful. You in your corner, Diane. You've got a chance. Come get me." —*Joe*

From a tape-recorded confrontation in Amagansett, late August 1987

Saturday, October 24

No one knows for certain where Joseph Pikul strangled Diane to death, and he has given conflicting accounts of the act. But it most likely occurred in or right outside of the Amagansett house. This is where both Donald Delaney, a senior investigator from Long Island's Troop L of the New York State Police—one of the first investigators on the case—and Alan Joseph, the Orange County assistant district attorney who prosecuted the case, believe Joe killed Diane. This is also where Joe himself stated he killed her when he took the stand at his trial.*

*Seventeen months before taking the stand, however, Joe gave a conflicting account to Newburgh-based New York State Police Senior Investigator Joseph Tripodo, the last of the string of detectives who finally wrested his confession. Joe told Tripodo he killed Diane on the beach.

173

Yet if Joe and Diane argued loudly in the house between 1:15 and 1:30 A.M. before he began beating and strangling her, whereupon she fought back so hard she managed to knock out one of his teeth before he killed her—then *why* didn't any of their neighbors hear the loud recriminations? And why didn't the children wake up? And why did the police find such minimal evidence of strife in the house?

Perhaps there was *no* accidental, escalating argument at all—just a brief, provoked prelude to a planned ambush. This theory is supported by Joe's musing to Sandra Jarvinen that Diane "might have to have an accident" and by his flying Sandra in the day before to meet his children, ostensibly to become their guardian should both parents die. It is also supported by his calling the Travelers Garage to find out exactly when Diane left, the better to prepare for her arrival, by the alacrity with which he came up with an alibi and the way he proffered that alibi to everyone he spoke to over the next four days, even strangers. Carina Jacobsson believes "Joe was planning to kill Diane that weekend, and the reason he wanted me there so badly was that I could have the children somewhere else while he did it." But Carina did not come, and Joseph Pikul had to make do with killing Diane while the children slept.

Bypassing the divorce court, which he knew would have proved troublesome, Joseph Pikul tendered a custody bid for his children through a simple and grandiose tactic: He murdered their mother. Whether he actually knew it beforehand, or just sensed it, or was too determined and desperate to care, the law was squarely on his side. Though a confessed killer, he would soon be awarded sole custody of them. Four things abetted his daunting legal position: (a) those aspects of the criminal justice system (initially and notably the bail system) that are prodefendant by design; (b) a body of custody law that overwhelmingly favors the natural parent—even if that parent is accused of murder; (c) the terror that can silence potential witnesses (especially mothers of young children) when the person they would be speaking out against is back in the neighborhood, free, and has just proved himself willing to kill for the very thing—custodial parenthood—that their testimony would be intended to deprive him of; and (d) the manner in which hearsay can operate in the courts: to nullify the rights, integrity, and past pleas and warnings of the victim, who is dead, and to benefit the defendant, who is alive.

Joseph Pikul initiated his "suit" not by filing papers with an attorney but by waiting for Diane to enter the living room, delivering at least ten blows to her head, then strangling her with his hands until she died, and, finally, afterward, strangling her a second time with a pink plastic utility cord.

Diane's murder was messy. She was bleeding from the head wounds, and the strangulation had induced vomiting and a bowel movement. So Joe—by his own admission when on the witness stand—cleaned his dead wife with towels to "prevent any fluids that might come out." On the witness stand Joe claimed he then wrapped her, right after the murder, in many towels, as well as in the Mazda's tarp and a plastic lawn cover for eventual burial.* Then "I cleaned up the bedroom as best I could since I was rushing. I cleaned the rug, the pillow, straightened the bed out. There was vomit on the pillow."

According to a portion of his witness-stand account, which the prosecutor believes to be true, Joe then put Diane's body in the Mazda, along with a small barbell and an inflated raft, and drove down Windmill Lane, past the cemetery, left onto the eastbound Montauk Highway, then left again into the woods separating Amagansett from East Hampton. He continued driving through a series of narrow serpentine paths in absolute darkness, to a tiny clearing that opens onto the bay beach, called Little Albert's Landing.

"People who commit murders can think they've planned everything, but they almost *never* plan what to

---

*D.A. Alan Joseph believes Joe's serious wrapping of Diane's body did not occur until later, that his witness-stand scenario was implausible and self-serving: an attempt (a) to explain away Diane's head wounds, positing them not as the result of his striking her but as the mere by-product of her head banging against the walls and stairs as he struggled to get her thickly wrapped body out of the house, and (b) to convince the jury that he had wrapped Diane for a permanent, not temporary, beach-burial, to counter Sandra Jarvinen's incriminating account of their visit after the murder.

do with the body afterward," says Investigator Don Delaney, expressing a well-known police truism. Joseph Pikul, for all his prior boasts that he could dump Diane's dead body "where no one will ever find it," was no exception. He would later say on the stand that he took the barbell and raft to cast her body out into the Atlantic Ocean. But the tiny peaceful inlet that is Little Albert's Landing hardly boasts a turbulent sea that can carry a body away without a trace. Wearing jeans and a sweatshirt, Joe dragged Diane's body through the sand close to the shore, but he never put her body in the water. Sometime during the approximate hour he spent "in the moonlight" on the beach, Joe apparently had a change of heart about the efficacy of the barbell-and-raft maneuver on so tame a body of water; he simply buried Diane's wrapped body in the sand and drove back to the house at about 3:30 A.M. where, according to his trial testimony, he "cleaned the raft off, hosed it, cleaned the bathroom [and] checked on the children, of course."

Next, he changed his clothes and, as he said on the stand at his trial, "I kind of hung around and sat in the comfortable chair in shock." What little sleep he got that night—indeed, all the sleep he would get for the next thirty-four hours—was in that chair. "Claudia woke me up," he would recall on the stand. "I told her that her mother had run out of the house. I fixed her breakfast and put her in the baby-sitter's room to watch TV. I got the garbage ready to go to the dump . . . to throw away the jeans and shirt" in which he'd committed the killings. He then "watched some TV with Claudia."

By 8:30 or 9, Blake was up. He, too, was put in the baby-sitter's room with the television. By 9:30, the children dressed, Joe drove them in the station wagon to the town dump. There, he tossed the trash which included his incriminating clothing. After this, Joe drove with the children to the Amagansett Hardware Store. At 10:30, he charged $325 worth of items, including a shovel, a wheelbarrow, plastic lawn bags, fishing gloves, a flashlight and rope to his American Express card. His next stop was Felicia's, a delicatessen also on Main Street, where he purchased twelve bags of ice—to keep Diane's body (by his own later admission) from rotting and smelling while he thought of how to dispose of it more permanently. Then he drove the children back to the house.

Now Joe called his home security service to have the house's alarm codes changed. It is unclear whether this act was a naïve effort to keep the police out or was calculated to make it seem as if Diane had stormed off in a rage and he was now retaliating by blocking her from reentering the house. Anxious to replace the tooth suspiciously absent from his mouth, Joe called the office of local dentist Dr. Allen Katz for an emergency appointment—and left a rambling message on the dentist's answering-machine tape. (When the dentist's office manager Patricia Sarlo returned his call at 12:30, he launched into a story about how he had found another man's condoms under his bed and how his wife had walked out on him. Sarlo thought the conversation strange, to say the least.)

He also called his old Northeastern roommate Henry Sawoska—best man, all those years ago, at his wedding to Sandra—who now lived with his wife and their two children in the Orange County town of New Windsor. Joe told Hank Sawoska that he had just had word from his doctor that he was dying, that he had found another man's condoms under his bed, that Diane had just walked out on him. Joe and Hank hadn't seen each other in nine years; neither Hank nor Louise had ever met Joe's children; and their house was, under the best of driving circumstances, four hours away from Amagansett—yet Joe now asked Hank if he could drive his children up to stay overnight with the Sawoskas while he dealt with his traumatizing circumstances. Concerned and upset for his old friend—and hardly given much choice—Sawoska said yes and invited Joe and the children for dinner.

At 11:45 A.M., Marshall Weingarden called the house on Windmill Lane. Barbara Weingarden had stepped out on some errands and had asked her husband to call and confirm her plans with Diane to take the children to story hour at the East Hampton library. "Joe answered the phone and I said the story hour at the library seemed good for the kids, and he agreed," Marshall recalls. "But Joe seemed very nervous. Of course, this was not unusual. Then he told me Diane had 'disappeared'—I remember thinking that was a strange word to use. He said she hadn't arrived at the house until after one A.M. last night, and when he asked her why she was so late, she became angry that he was checking on her and stormed out of the house. I asked him, 'Did she take the car?' He said, 'No.' Which was also strange; you can't get anywhere out there walking. Then he told me he found condoms in the living room—he would tell everyone else he found these same condoms in the *bed*room, but he told *me* the living room—and that he suspected she had a boyfriend whose house she went to."

When Marshall expressed the possibility that the condoms belonged to one of the baby-sitters' boyfriends, Joe "just kept on trying to give the impression that she had a boyfriend and that's why she left without the car." Joe occasionally interrupted his conversation with Marshall to talk to a man from the alarm company who was now at the house, changing the security codes. Before hanging up, Joe told Marshall he had just had a bad doctor's report that week and that he was bringing the children to a friend's house upstate and he had to hang up because he had a lot of packing to do. "I suggested he bring the children to our house, to the swimming pool." Joe thanked Marshall and said he would call him back later.

When Barbara Weingarden returned from her errands, Marshall told her about the distressing conversation. It troubled Marshall that Joe had used the word "disappeared" to describe Diane's leaving. "That's the word Diane always uses—'Joe's *disappeared* with the children,'" Barbara answered. "I'm sure he just picked it up from her." Diane had probably gotten mad and was now back in the city, Barbara suggested to her husband.

Shortly after lunch, Joe left the children in front of the TV set to go back to Little Albert's Landing. "I told them," he later said, "that I was just going out for a ride, that I'd be right back." Prosecutor Alan Joseph and most of the investigators who worked on the case believe that Joe now drove back to Little Albert's Landing, where Diane's body had been buried since 3 A.M., to remove the body from the sand. D.A. Joseph believes he then laid some of the many towels he had taken from the house on one of the plastic tarps; put Diane's body on the towels on the tarp and laid the newly purchased ice on top of it; rolled the body over; put more ice on; and rolled the ice- and towel-packed corpse tightly in the plastic tarp, tying the entire "package" up with the rope he'd just bought from the hardware store. Joe then loaded the body into the back of the station wagon.

"Then I started to pack things for the trip—clothes, toys and a shotgun," Joe testified later. The gun, purchased in 1984, was to be used for the suicide he claimed to have been contemplating. Joe also packed a household knife. That knife, when later found in a car wash dumpster, would form the basis of his defense at his trial. Joe left with the children for the Sawoskas' house somewhere between 4:30 and 5:00 in the afternoon.

Not long after he started his journey, he pulled off the Long Island Expressway to make the first of many phone-booth toll calls he would place over the next three days—all, like this one, paid for in coins, since he did not want a record of his desperate inquiries on his telephone credit card. The number he dialed was Sandra Jarvinen's. "He said he had something to hide, and could he hide it with me," she would testify. Sandra indicated that she would welcome his visit.

Joe got lost several times on the way to New Windsor; his lack of sleep and his desperation to find a place to dispose of Diane's body couldn't have made the long drive, with the children in the car, easy. What, one wonders, did Joe Pikul say to deter Blake and Claudia from climbing into the backseat where the five and a half foot long oblong tarpaulin-wrapped package lay? Did the children ever ask what was in that package? If so, how did their father reply? Given the news of their mother's disappearance, the mysterious purpose of the long drive, and the addled behavior of their unkempt and sleep-deprived father, the Pikul children must have felt they were in the midst of a bad dream.

From a phone booth, Joe called Hank Sawoska and asked him not to have his wife, Louise, hold dinner, that they would simply have a snack when they arrived there. At about 9:30 P.M. he dropped his two tired children with the Sawoskas, whom they had never met, and said he would pick them up the next day.

At about 10:20 P.M. he began a six-hour drive to the south shore of Massachusetts.

Sunday, October 25

At about 3:30 A.M. Sandra Jarvinen, at home in Norwell, Massachusetts, alone in bed, was awakened by the ringing telephone. It was Joe, calling from a phone booth off the turnpike in Hartford, Connecticut. He wanted directions to her home, which she gave him. About a half hour later he called again, this time from a pay phone in Norwell. He couldn't find the house. "I said I would come down and get him," Sandra later recalled on the stand. "So I put on my raincoat and went down. He was driving a new station wagon with a telephone antenna on top. I hit the horn very lightly. He followed me but stayed at a great distance. We arrived at my home at about 4:30 A.M.

"He came in the house with a canvas bag, a shoulder bag, and kept walking back and forth in the house. He said, 'Where can I bury it?'

" 'Bury *what*?' I asked.

Joe repeated: 'Well, where can I bury it?"

At which point Sandra says she remembers telling him, "Joe, you're going to have to tell me what it is you have to bury.' "

When he did not reply, Sandra suggested storing the item in a safe-deposit box. "He said, 'It's too big for a safe-deposit box.' I went into the library area [of the living room], sat on the floor. I said, 'You really have to tell me what it is you have to bury.'

"He slumped on the wing chair. He said, 'I had to eliminate her.' "

"I said it wasn't a good place to bury anybody on my property, because of the high water table." This absurdly matter-of-fact rejoinder was relished by the tabloid reporters during the trial; Sandra rationalized it by saying, "I just had to get him out of the house." Sandra seems to have had some other burial suggestions handy: a nearby park and the section of the Berkshires in which their own weekend house had been located. She also offered to put him in touch with her friend and sometimes-beau Vinnie Federico, a Quincy, Massachusetts, former policeman who was now a lawyer. Despite the fact that Joe knew, and regularly used, a number of powerful Manhattan lawyers, he appeared to want to hire the smalltown litigator Federico. It is impossible to know whether this was because he was too desperate and scared to calmly comb through his own list of sophisticated legal contacts—or whether he hoped Sandra's personal relationship with Federico implied that the man might be enlisted to protect their interests in covering up their actions.

After spending about forty-five minutes in Sandra's house, Joe finally left at 5:30 A.M. "It was getting light out," is how she later recalled it on the witness stand. "I sat in the library, stared out the window and froze. Within an hour a car came back, stayed in my driveway, then left. I came out of my shock, got dressed to go to the state police." This assertion may be self-serving. "Then I realized I didn't have anything to tell them. I drove home."

Sandra was scared. She had managed to reverse her own years of victimization by Joe by becoming his confidante, only to have let herself become dragged into a murder case. What had gone on in her mind during those months she let herself empathize with Joe's complaints about Diane's "too many baby-sitters"? What was she thinking when he asked her to take custody of his children in case he and Diane should die?

Sandra will only say today that the entire episode was "very painful" and that she has entered psychotherapy to "find out how it happened and why Joe had such a hold on me." One can speculate that the game Joe engaged her in tapped her vulnerability. Quite likely Sandra, single and middle-aged, was susceptible to the flattery conferred by her ex-husband's renewed attention.

Joe called Sandra several times again on Sunday. During the first of these calls, he asked if she'd been able to reach Vinnie Federico yet; she said no (eventually that day she did reach him) and gave him Federico's number. She would later testify that she suggested he turn himself in and that he hung up on her. Sandra then left to take care, as she routinely did, of her aging mother. When she returned home that evening there were two messages from Joe on her answering machine. In the first message, Joe stated that he was in his hometown of Ware—on a drive that, he later told investigators, included a sentimental foray to the cemetery in which his grandmother was buried. He mentioned on the tape that he'd found one promising burial site but, as Sandra would testify, "he said he couldn't leave the package there [because] it was too close to the road." The second message Joe left was from Tyringham, the rustic Berkshires community in which he and Sandra had once spent weekends. "He said he couldn't do anything there because it was hunting season and people were walking around there."

Desperate, exhausted and running out of time, Joe spent the rest of the late evening driving around—all the way from Massachusetts to upstate New York and back, looking for a safe burial site for the body. When he failed to find one, and with the children still at the Sawoskas', he returned to Manhattan, going to the Sixth Avenue duplex after midnight for the first real sleep he'd had since Thursday night. It is believed that Diane's tarp-wrapped body was still in the back of the car, which was parked on the street.

Before she went to sleep Sunday night, Sandra Jarvinen erased Joe's messages from her answering machine. No investigator ever heard them.

Monday, October 26

At 9:30 A.M., the men and women who work in the business and editorial sections of *Harper's* magazine began filing into the office. Several were dimly aware that Diane—who was usually one of the first to arrive, after delivering her children to school—was not yet at her desk. As she began her work day, Kathryn Crowley remembers thinking, Maybe my mom's friend Helen Richards found her a house in Chappaqua . . . Maybe she just slipped away to it with the children. . . .

Karen Hoffman, at the reception desk, remembers that one of the first calls that came through the desk that morning was from Joe. Speaking from his car phone, he stammered, "Uh, uh, Diane disappeared over the weekend. . . ." "The minute he said that," Karen remembers, "I suspected the worst."

Joseph Pikul had good reason to be stammering: Moments before he called *Harper's,* he had taken Diane's wrapped body out of the car and rolled it into a culvert on the side of the New York State Thruway, about three and a half miles south of the Newburgh exit. He needed to get the body out of the car before he had to pick up the children from the Sawoskas. After his two-day search for an ideal site, he arbitrarily chose a ditch. He put a spare tire over the body to try to camouflage it. Before driving on to pick up his children from the now concerned Louise Sawoska, he made the first of several more pay phone calls to Vinnie Federico. He was desperate to talk to Sandra's lawyer friend and to fly him into New York.

After retrieving Blake and Claudia, Joe placed a second, abrupt call to *Harper's,* again getting Karen Hoffman. When, moments later, Linda McNamera stepped off the elevator into the reception area, she encountered the worry on the receptionist's face. "The minute Karen said, 'Linda, Diane hasn't come in yet and Joe's been calling, acting like he's worried about her and looking for her,' I was scared to death. I went to Randy Warner and said, 'Randy, you know, Diane's not here.' Randy said, tensely, 'Yes. I know.' " By the time Ann Stern arrived at ten A.M., "the worry had ripened," Ann remembers, "into a kind of agitated suspicion. This was *serious,* we all realized."

Ann immediately called both the East Hampton and New York City police departments. She told officers from both departments of Diane's fears of Joe and of her protracted divorce plans, and she vouched for Diane's organization and her reliability as a worker: *No one* with Diane's talent at juggling details would fail to call to say she'd be late for work. *No one* who was prepared to turn down a job unless she could have regular time off to take her child to speech therapy appointments would walk out on her children. Ann was told there was nothing the police could do. An employee's late arrival—even her unexplained truancy—from a relatively new job didn't warrant police action.

Meanwhile, phone calls from Joe continued. "He called about twenty times throughout the day," Linda McNamera remembers. "And he kept changing his story. First he kept saying, 'Where *is* she?' Then it was, 'She has a boyfriend and she ran off with him this weekend.'

Then it progressed to, 'We had a fight and it got out of hand.' Then he made a reference that scared us to death, something about her 'rolling over.' " The *Harper's* women fruitlessly tried to ascertain whether or not Joe had the children with him. By noon, they had given up on doing any real work and had divided up the leaves of Diane's large Rolodex, ferreting out those names that sounded more like Diane's friends than Rick MacArthur's business contacts and calling all of these people to see if any of them had any idea where Diane was.

Maggie, Gloria, Carina, Pat Bartholomew and Barbara Martin were all called. Almost to a one, they concluded that their friend had been murdered. Carina suspected that Joe had locked Diane in the basement of the Amagansett house. She reported this fear to Ann Stern, who was by now the hub of the telephone operation. Ann, worried that this scenario sounded logical, pressed Carina to try to find someone to go over to the Amagansett house. Carina called the number of the Windmill Inn and several local baby-sitters, but no one answered.

Everyone's great concern now was: Where were the children? Were they safe? Did Joe have them? The task of getting this information—and protective access *to* Blake and Claudia—fell to the likeliest candidate for the job: Carina. Starting at around noon, she called Joe's secretary at Arnhold and S. Bleichroeder repeatedly, each time to be told, "He's not in—I don't know where he is." She left a message: "Can you tell him, the minute he comes in, to *please* call Carina?"

While Carina made her calls, Joe drove back to New York, stopping at Stewart Auto Wash in Newburgh, not far from where Diane's body now lay in the ditch. Joe wanted to have the station wagon thoroughly cleaned before he drove back to the city. He was also anxious to get rid of Diane's belongings, along with some questionable belongings of his own. To the cleaners and manager of the car wash, Joe's nervous behavior, his gratuitous talk about his wife having just run off with a man whose condoms were found under his bed, and the extensiveness with which he wanted the sandy trunk of the car cleaned triggered the idea that this was *not* your ordinary customer. The staff of the car wash then watched as Joe walked first to a nearby metal garbage can, then to a large dumpster and started throwing out what seemed to be an unusual variety of debris—not the few paper cups and empty Kleenex boxes customers usually swept from the seats of their cars. Two of the car washers made a mental note to check out the bin as soon as the weird guy's car pulled away.

Finally, the customer reached into the car and took out a mint-condition shotgun. He told the car wash manager, Jimmy Mitchell, that he could have it for just twenty-five dollars. It's not every day that a customer offers to sell you a perfectly good shotgun for one-sixteenth of its price, and Mitchell was a hunter. He gladly paid and took the gun. (This sale, Joe would later say, signaled his resolve not to commit suicide.)

While Mitchell went off into the surrounding woods to test his new weapon, two of his young workers, curious, commenced a casual search of the dumpster. Amidst the debris they found in a maroon plastic card holder, a batch of credit cards in the names of Diane Pikul and Diane Whitmore. When they mentioned the cards to Mitchell's wife, Laurie, who served as the wash's cashier, she became concerned. She told her husband about the cards when he returned from testing the gun. Mitchell got the cards from the boys. They also gave him a knife and a large rubber glove, and they told him that a number of pieces of women's clothing were also in the dumpster. That customer sure was strange, was the discomfited consensus.

Before leaving the car wash, Joe called Sandra and left a terse message on her answering machine: "The package is down."

Joe returned home with the children at about three P.M. By then, from a phone booth along the way, he had contacted Vinnie Federico, who agreed to represent him. Invoking attorney-client privilege, Federico will not reveal how much Sandra's first husband told him he had done; he'll only say, "I didn't question him." Plans were made for Federico to be flown into Manhattan that day and put up at a hotel at Joe's expense. Vinnie Federico did not know that his new client, who now held out to him the prospect of a career-making case, had a habit of changing lawyers. Joseph Pikul did not pause to remember his own beginnings and consider how wounded and angry an ambitious, up-by-his-bootstraps Massachusetts working-class man could be if humiliated and summarily fired. That lapse of memory and judgment would eventually cost him dearly.

As soon as Joe and the children got home, Barbara Martin got through to him by phone. "Oh, hi, Barbara, I really can't talk right now," she remembers him saying. "The car is double-parked and the kids are downstairs. Can you call back in half an hour?" He hung up, got the children upstairs, and then, while he was out moving the car to a permanent parking space, Claudia Pikul did what she apparently had not been able to do in her father's presence: She picked up the phone and called her mother's workplace.

"Do you know where my mommy is?" she asked Randy Warner. The plaintive words cut the woman's heart to the quick. "We're your friends and we're trying to find your mommy," Randy assured Claudia. Meanwhile, Ann Stern began a series of insistent calls to the Sixth Police Precinct, where she had earlier encountered no luck beyond having a patrolman drive over to the Pikul house and fruitlessly ring the doorbell. She vowed not to take no for an answer.

While Ann, from three P.M. on, was having her calls fielded by a number of officers who were awaiting the arrival of a Detective Bill Glynn, Don and Gretchen Whitmore, having been called in Florida by Randy Warner, began phoning Joe and asking him where Diane went. Gretchen, less threatening to Joe, tried first, but after several of her inquiries were deflected by Joe saying, "I can't talk now; I'll call you back," Don himself took the phone and pressed Joe for his daughter's whereabouts. "What damn business of *yours* is it where my wife went?" was Joe's response.

Whitmore called the East Hampton Police Department. He now had the same suspicions as Carina. "Look, I got a hunch he killed her out by the side of the house, in the shed where they keep the bikes—you've got to go to that shed," he told the desk officer. One officer ventured a trip to the house; when Whitmore called back, the desk officer said that the basement was padlocked and that he had no authority to remove it. "Well, good God, take a hammer and knock the damn padlock off and *find* my daughter!" Don shouted. "You have *my* permission!"

At about 3:30, Carina got through to Joe at home. "Why were you calling my office all day long?" he asked challengingly. "I was worried about the kids," Carina answered, adding, "And do you happen to know where Diane is?" Joe launched into the condoms story and Diane's flight to the mysterious boyfriend. Carina started shaking; "I knew he was lying. All I was thinking about was getting to the children. 'Don't you want me to come over and give the kids dinner and put them to bed?' I kept asking. He kept saying, 'No, I'll be okay.' Then he finally hung up on me."

Not long after, Snow and Frank Piccolo called Joe, as did Marshall Weingarden. These friends did not yet suspect Joe of murder, and it showed in their voices. (Snow, for one, was hoping that Diane had fled to Vail, as she'd planned to do sixteen months earlier.) "You're the only people who are being nice to me, who aren't accusing me of anything," he said to both Marshall and Snow. Perhaps softened by their apparent sincerity and convinced that not everyone was on to him, he relented when Carina called back at 5:30. Yes, he said. She could come over and take care of the children.

Just as Carina was canceling previous evening plans in order to be with Blake and Claudia, ninety miles upstate in Newburgh, a police patrolman named Greg Crisci decided to get his patrol car washed. Crisci and carwash manager Jimmy Mitchell had once worked together as ambulance technicians and Crisci had gone to high school with Mitchell's wife, Laurie. The patrolman's chance arrival gave Mitchell the opportunity to sort out the strange goings-on that day with a policeman who was also something of a friend.

Mitchell gave Crisci the credit cards, knife and glove his young employees had reported finding in the dumpster and suggested it might be worth the patrolman's while to wander over and take a look.

Crisci quickly saw that what was in the dumpster was not your normal pre-car-wash clutter. Officially off-duty, he called in an on-duty team, Patrolman Gary Cooper and his partner, Patrolwoman Margaret Hansen. Cooper and Hansen sifted through the contents thoroughly. They found a lot of women's clothes, jewelry, underwear and shoes. "As Gary and I were picking through the dumpster, we looked at each other," Hansen recalls, "and I said, 'There has *got* to be a body that goes with this.' " They agreed that the contents of the dumpster should be impounded and taken back to precinct headquarters.

Back at the white clapboard Newburgh precinct headquarters, Cooper and Hansen spread out on desktops and studied the disparate collection of fifty-five items. To Cooper, the odd thing was that the credit cards were found *with* the jewelry and clothing; in purse snatches and robberies, the kind of crime such discarded items would usually indicate, credit cards are almost always discarded separately. Hansen found something else odd: The holder of the credit cards was, according to the driver's license they also found, a slightly built woman—five foot three, 110 pounds. But the clothes that were found were those of a much larger woman—an *enormous* one, in fact. Even stranger—and perhaps, Hansen thought, you had to be a woman to be struck by this—the credit cards were all for good stores like Bloomingdale's and Saks Fifth Avenue, while the large clothes and especially the jewelry were cheap stuff that would never belong to someone with the taste or the means to patronize those shops.

By six P.M., Hansen and Cooper had decided that these discrepancies warranted their calling in Sergeant Mike Clancy, who had recently left for the day. They reached him by phone as he was settling down in front of the TV set in his house down the road, looking forward to the sports news and thinking of cracking open the books he was reading for the State University courses he was taking toward a business degree. In minutes, Clancy, a boyish-looking man with red hair and freckles, was on his way back to work.

The discrepancies that Hansen and Cooper had found puzzling registered with Clancy. So did an even odder thing: The various brassieres found were of widely divergent cup sizes. "Whoever she is, she can't figure out what *size* she is," Clancy muttered, embarrassed.

Clancy phoned his on-call detective, John Smith, who also lived nearby. "Cooper and Hansen found some fishy stuff at a car wash—we need you to take a look," he said. Smith, a burly, good-looking, open-faced man, drove over and scanned the items on the desks. He picked up an extremely large woman's pump and put it next to his own foot. "This shoe," he observed, "could fit *me.*"

But what bothered Smith the most was the discarded wallet-sized picture of a blond little boy in pajamas. Smith's own two sons were blond; he remembered when they were younger and wore pajamas like those of the child in the picture. He'd never spent a day without their pictures in his wallet. If his wallet had ever been picked off him, he'd feel violated. He'd want to punch out any guy who stole his kids' pictures. Sure, it was a sentimental response, but Smith had learned from his nineteen years on the force that sometimes your sentimental responses pointed you in the right direction.

"Who would throw away a picture of a child?" he asked himself out loud.

Only someone, he realized, who was very, very angry at the parent whose wallet that picture had come out of.

Mike Clancy and John Smith are clean-living guys from a semirural town in which intentional homicides occur about once every two years, where the precinct house is a former school house on a maple-tree-lined road, and where a major homicide could be stumbled upon through a local cop's chance encounter with his old buddy, a car wash manager. Their counterparts at the Sixth Precinct in Greenwich Village are very different animals. Detective Bill Glynn and Detective Sergeant Ken Bowen speak in gravelly tones and swaggering New York accents. Both smoke hard, pepper their conversation with expletives, and go about their jobs with an air of relished cynicism. After a respective seventeen and thirty-nine years as New York cops, they'd seen it all—and it showed on their faces: Bowen's pink with broken blood vessels; Glynn's amply pockmarked, his eyes deeply lidded.

The night before, at midnight, Glynn, Bowen and two

other detectives from the Sixth—"a skinny, outspoken guy," says Glenn, named Richie Composto and Ronnie Finelli, a wry veteran with thirty-four years as detective first-grade—had gone after work for a few rounds of rye and ginger at Marylou's, a restaurant on Ninth Street. While there, a call for Glynn came in on the restaurant telephone: "Possible body in water off Sanitation Pier." So he, Bowen, Composto and Finelli rushed over to the pier, better known as the Saltlines, off Gansevoort Street in the far northwest Village. This out-of-the-way wedge of Manhattan is a round-the-clock meat market, both figuratively and literally. From six A.M. to three P.M., animal shanks and carcasses swing on hooks from wooden-awninged rafters outside the meat wholesalers. From two A.M. to five A.M., hardcore gay hustlers paraded their own flesh outside of the night-blooming S&M bars, not yet closed down by the city's concern about the AIDS epidemic.

At one A.M., Glynn and the others parked their squad car by the pier, then walked around, training flashlights on the rotting wood planks until they finally found— "Hey, I got it!" Composto had shouted—the wrapped body that had floated up to the river's surface and had been hospitably deposited on the dock by a sanitation worker. Since detectives aren't authorized to cut ropes— only medical examiners can do that—they had groped around the wrapped corpse, guessing first at body parts, then at the whole pedigree. The guessing game turned, as it often did, into a betting pool by the time they got to the Bellevue morgue. Between rounds of drinks at the next-door bar, Glynn, Bowen, Composto, Finelli and the morgue attendants kicked in ten dollar bets. There was two hundred dollars in the pot by the time the pedigree was ascertained (male, white, fifty-one) and it wasn't till five A.M. that the killer, a Brooklyn woman, was found. Glynn said he "knew all along it was a woman, because the body was naked and so neatly wrapped, like a fucking Christmas present."

Tanked up on the coffee, potato chips and Winstons that always got him through homicides, Glynn didn't return to his Brooklyn home until dawn. He fell asleep at seven, only to be awakened at eleven A.M. by his youngest son, Matthew, whom he baby-sat for while his wife, Rosemary, was off at her part-time bookkeeping job.

Tired and still hung over, Glynn arrived in the second floor squad room at the Sixth Precinct's West Tenth Street headquarters at six P.M. and was handed the telephone by the detective going off-shift. The last thing he wanted to have to do was diplomatically get rid of some well-meaning pest of a caller, but this appeared to be the task at hand. The person on the phone—one Ann Stern, from *Harper's* magazine—had been calling all day, insisting that her co-worker, a woman who was thought to have a dangerous husband, had disappeared from her Long Island house over the weekend, and that those who knew the husband believed her to possibly be locked in a shed on the premises: harmed, or dead. "Everyone we've talked to today, including her father, is *very* concerned—and they're not overreacting; they're looking at this in a very measured way," she reported earnestly.

Glynn immediately pegged Ann Stern as "a lily-white liberal broad who thinks husbands and wives don't fight and take off from each other every day of the week." He couldn't even count the cases he'd had that *did* qualify as Missing Persons but which had, after all the paperwork was done, dissolved when the spouse walked back in the door. And this one, as he patiently explained to Ann Stern, didn't come close to meeting the guidelines: There was no evidence of foul play; the reported woman, Diane Whitmore Pikul, was over twenty-one years of age, of sound mind and not physically handicapped; Ann Stern was not a family member—nor even a close friend, but a distant co-worker of a mere six months standing; and twenty-four hours had not elapsed since the woman's alleged disappearance.

Glynn, who prized himself as being a "great appeaser—I can bullshit the best of them," carefully concealed his great initial skepticism from Ann Stern. "He wasn't the least bit dismissive of me or short with me," she recalls. "I felt he was taking me seriously." What he was really doing, at first, was letting her talk and trying his best to assuage her fears. "Look, maybe she's just out partying," he said, thinking of the sales executive whose husband, in a panic of worry, had filed an MP three weeks ago when she didn't return from a client meeting. Two days later his wife turned her key in the apartment lock, after her forty-eight-hour fling with the client.

When Ann Stern wouldn't hear of that, Glynn went right to the next likely scenario: "You say she and her husband fought a lot? She probably just went somewhere to cool off." Just a year before that's what had happened between Glynn and his own wife, Rosemary. After a week of bickering, they'd had a big fight. "Screw this," Rosemary said, "I'm leaving with the kids." Bill said, "Here's the door." Four days later, Rosemary was back, and all was forgiven. Didn't this woman on the phone know?: This was the way *regular* married people were with each other.

But Ann Stern would not be appeased. She spoke now of the calls Joe had been making to *Harper's* all day, but they didn't seem to Glynn to necessarily be suspicious. After all, he knew from his own life that a guy whose wife walks out does some strange things. When he'd first tracked Rosemary down to a friend's cottage in the Poconos, he'd dialed the number—and when his son answered the phone, Glynn hung up. If hanging up on your own kid like some goddamn heavy breather wasn't weird and suspicious, then Bill Glynn didn't know *what* was.

"I must tell you, Detective Glynn," Ann pressed on, "not one of the people we spoke to today who know Diane well believe she would ever leave without taking the children, or that she would *ever,* especially now, leave them with Joe." At this point, Glynn recalls, "I'm thinking, What is she, busting my balls . . . ? Enough of this already!" He made himself calm down, loosen up and let go of "my ego, my tight fix on the thing." After all, weren't he and Bowen always reminding themselves that the worst thing a catching detective* can do is get tunnel vision? "So I started thinking, Maybe she's not letting up 'cause she's got a sixth sense. Maybe she *knows* something." Finally, Glynn succumbed to the logic and passion of Ann Stern's words and began to take notes for an investigation. "It was Ann Stern's persistence—

---

*Police jargon for a detective who's next in line to take on any case referred to his or her squad for investigation.

she just *would not let go*—that turned it all around for me."

While Glynn was listening to Ann Stern, Detective John Smith in Newburgh had just gotten Joseph Pikul's number from directory assistance. Posing as a private citizen—he'd borrowed his sergeant's last name and called himself "John Clancy"—and calling from his private line, Smith dialed the Manhattan number. A man with a low, stern voice answered before the end of the first ring. Coldly correcting the caller's mispronunciation of his last name, he warily conceded that he was Mr. Pikul. Now, humbly, Smith said that he was a Newburgh resident calling because he had just found a Mrs. Diane Pikul's credit cards in a garbage can.

"You *what*? You found *cards*? You *what*?" this Pikul fellow stammered, dropping all previous hauteur. Then he audibly dropped the receiver, during which interval Smith high-signed to Clancy that something was up and quickly attached his tape recording device to the telephone.

Joseph Pikul got back on the phone, more composed, thanked "John Clancy" and said he would be sending his chauffeur immediately to claim the lost cards and to bring a cash reward. Within five minutes after Smith hung up, Pikul's chauffeur, one Jim Burns, did indeed call to get directions. Smith and Burns exchanged descriptions and planned to meet at Stewart Auto Wash in three hours: 9:30. Before he hung up, Burns—apparently reacting to his boss' urgent fervor to get the cards back and worried that he and "Clancy" might somehow miss each other— gave "Clancy" the license plate number of the Lincoln Continental he would be driving and the phone number of the small car fleet, the Great American Dream Machine, that he owned.

After "Clancy's" call, Joe Pikul must have panicked. Someone had Diane's credit cards—he'd have to make up for lost time in playing the concerned husband. So he obtained and dialed the number of the Sixth Precinct.

It was only a few minutes after Glynn had concluded his conversation with Ann Stern that he picked up his ringing phone and heard a male voice say, "My name is Joseph

Pikul and I want to report my wife missing." Glynn was startled by the coincidence. *Now* things were cooking.

Pikul started somewhat undefensively, "I got your name from someone at *Harper's* magazine," he said truthfully. "I don't really know why I'm calling; I've never done this before. I'll explain the situation and you can guide me from here." He then went on to tell Glynn of Diane's "disappearance," the lover, the condoms. Relaying the story, he began sounding more nervous—but then Glynn himself had been a nervous wreck after Rosemary left: "smoking, drinking, pacing around, going crazy." Similarly, it made sense to Glynn that Pikul hadn't made the call to the police until his wife's colleagues prodded him to do so. None of the guys Glynn grew up with in Brooklyn and Queens would go running to the cops after they'd had blowups with their wives; guys just didn't *do* that. When Rosemary split, Glynn hadn't called anyone.

As Pikul talked on—identifying himself as a prosperous professional man, saying he had the children with him—Glynn kept thinking his story checked out for the most part. Still, Ann Stern's stubborn belief continued to nag at him. Finally, Glynn took a procedural leap. Instead of making the standard "scratch" Missing Persons, which involves simply calling Missing Persons Unit (MPU) to see if any unidentified females of appropriate description were lying in morgues or hospitals, Glynn told Mr. Pikul he would come over to his apartment and take the report in person.

Since residence calls require a two-man detail, Glynn tried to persuade Richie Composto to join him. Composto would not be moved. "It's just an MP," he said. "What's the big deal?" Glynn remembers thinking: Aw shit, Richie's gonna razz me. I'm letting this ivory-tower dame lead me around by the nose. Then Pikul called back and asked if the appointment could be postponed until eleven P.M. because he was taking his daughter to her neighborhood religion class and then had to get both children settled in bed afterward. Glynn agreed, relieved to be spared Composto's ridicule.

Just as Glynn was hanging up from this second call from Pikul, John Smith called the Sixth Precinct in Manhattan, in whose jurisdiction Mr. and Mrs. Pikul of 446 Sixth Avenue would fall. He was eager to know from his Manhattan counterparts if, at the very least, the Pikul apartment had been recently burglarized. A woman detective named Chris Margillo, one desk over from Bill Glynn, took the call. Had anyone in her precinct named "Pikul" been a crime victim recently? John Smith queried. With the name "Pikul" on a scratch pad, Margillo walked over to the "60 sheet," where all crimes in Sixth were posted.

Deciding to stretch his legs and get a cup of coffee, Glynn lit up a Winston and walked across his room. Encountering Margillo at the 60 sheet, he glimpsed the name "Pikul" on her scratch pad and did a long double-take. "What's with this 'Pikul'?" he asked. "I just been on the phone almost an hour *about* this guy and *with* this guy." When Margillo told him, Glynn immediately called the Newburgh officers.

"Margillo says you just called about this 'Pikul.' Whaddya got?" Clancy and Smith remember Glynn asking. The two men told Glynn about the strange contents of the dumpster, the call to the stammering Pikul, and the planned meeting with Pikul's chauffeur at the car wash in three hours. Glynn told Clancy and Smith about the adamant phone calls from Ann Stern, the MP report filed by Pikul, and the scheduled eleven P.M. interview with him. Except for the large women's clothes and the cheesy jewelry, which no one quite knew what to make of, the Newburgh and Manhattan leads—all of which were acquired in the hour between six and seven P.M.—fit together like the start of a foul-play jigsaw puzzle. With three jurisdictions involved—Newburgh, Manhattan, Long Island—it was time to call in the state police, fast, to coordinate things.

I *knew* there was a reason I let that Ann Stern bust my balls, Glynn remembers thinking.

Smith, Clancy, Glynn and Detective Sergeant Ken Bowen (who was briefed via telephone at home by Glynn) all agreed that, since the missing woman was last seen on Long Island, the job should go to someone in that jurisdiction. But who? Bowen thought of an NYPD lieutenant he knew whose wife was a state police investigator; he called her and she led him to William Cahill, who'd just nine months before taken over the job as BCI (Bureau of Criminal Investigation) captain at the state police's Troop L, and who was known for his tight investigations. By 7:30 P.M., Bill Cahill was filled in and at the helm.

Cahill's work would consist of overseeing events in and communicating moves between Newburgh, Manhattan, and Long Island, and he wanted someone he trusted from his troop to handle the investigation in a hands-on manner. He immediately called Donald Delaney, the senior investigator of Troop L's Major Case Unit, at Delaney's home in neighboring Nassau County. Delaney, a specially trained polygraphist with a master's degree in human relations, was considered an authority on interviewing suspects and determining guilt or innocence. With his wholesome face and his earnest, polite demeanor, he was to lend the balance of a light, trustable presence to Glynn's dark, cynical one. But Delaney was plenty streetsmart; he had the easy jocularity of a classic urban Irish cop, and his normal caseload was heavy on racketeering and homicides, with body dumps a specialty. (Long Island's wooded parkways were often used as impromptu cemeteries.) Still, as part of the more conservative state police, Cahill and Delaney shared a methodical approach to their work. They were exquisite proceduralists. They understood that the sum of an investigation was only as good as the ability of each of its parts to reach—and then to stand up in—court.

This meticulous, by-the-book style made them as different from the flamboyantly macho guys from the Sixth, who sometimes bent procedure and sacrificed means for ends, as the guys from the Sixth were from the local officers from Newburgh. From the beginning—and continuing over the next seventy-two hours, the friction of different approaches would prod the investigation forward, and the way each style took turns augmenting and covering for the other would provide the investigation's depth.

Cahill briefed Delaney by phone, gave him Bowen's home number and told him to go into Manhattan to join Bowen and Glynn in interviewing Pikul. By 8:15, Delaney had spoken to Bowen, showered, and was on his way out the door for the hour and a half drive west on the Long Island Expressway. "There may be a body," he told his wife, Kathleen. "I may not be back tonight. I'll call you when I know I'm coming home." He had a feeling he was in for a long, sleepless run.

Approximately forty-five minutes earlier, Joe Pikul buzzed Carina Jacobsson into the duplex. She anxiously walked up the narrow stairs to the living room, where Joe stood on the landing. "His front tooth was missing, he was really really nervous, just stampering around, slurping Coke from a can and panting," Carina recalls. "I rushed past him upstairs—my heart was pounding so fast!—and I saw Blake but no Claudia."

Carina felt better when she discovered Claudia was at a neighbor's house for Bible class, where, after bathing Blake, she later went to bring Claudia home. "Claudia's hair was very dirty. And she was very tired. Walking home, I tried to ask her about the weekend. She was usually so talkative, but now I could sense that she knew I was fishing. She just said she had had a good time— not spontaneously, but as if she'd been programmed to say that. I asked her about Mommy and she just shrugged her shoulders.

"When we got home, Blakey was asleep on the floor and Joe was making phone call after phone call." Many were calls to Newburgh Detective John Smith's private line, which Pikul believed was citizen "John Clancy's" residence. For a good part of the time between seven and ten P.M., John Smith sat in the precinct house listening to his phone ring ten times, stop for 40 seconds, then ring ten times again. As Joe continued the compulsive phone-dialing, Carina set out the Chinese food that Joe had ordered in for the family's dinner. "I had to wake Blakey to eat and Claudia wasn't very hungry. It was so terrible, so strained—trying to pretend things were normal. Joe saw me looking at his mouth; he told me his tooth had somehow loosened and he'd accidentally swallowed it.

"Then suddenly, in the middle of dinner, someone buzzed the front door. It was Jim Burns, Joe's chauffeur. Joe leapt up and said, 'I'm unhooking the phone. Leave it off the hook. Don't answer it! I'm going out.' And he ran out." Burns drove Joe to meet Vinnie Federico, who had just flown in from Massachusetts, and who would pocket five thousand dollars for an initial lawyer-client meeting. Then the chauffeur drove off to Newburgh, expecting to exchange his boss's reward money for the credit cards "John Clancy" had found in the nearby dumpster.

While Joe was out, Carina tucked the children into their beds. "Daddy told us that he would take us away if Mommy ever left, and now Mommy left us," Blake said drowsily. "She'll come back," Carina reassured him, feeling in her bones it wasn't true.

At 9:40, Sergeant Mike Clancy, wearing a white Stewart Auto Wash uniform, was behind the cash register at the Newburgh car wash when the grey Continental with the plates he had memorized drove in. The plan now was to get a good look at Pikul's chauffeur but not to hand over any of the confiscated possessions. Smith, at headquarters, stood ready when called to drive over in an unmarked car and tail the chauffeur.

So when Jim Burns, a stocky man of 5'11", walked over to the cashier—the only employee visible on the premises—and said, "I'm looking for a guy who found some property belonging to my boss and I'm supposed to meet him here," the "cashier" put down the receipts he was counting and said that some fellow had been "hanging around the front of the parking lot for a couple of hours, then he looked all disgusted and left."

Burns threw up his hands in frustration, then went back to the Continental to wait. Clancy picked up the cashier-stand phone and called Smith. Smith left the post by his ringing private line and drove over. He parked in the dark just outside the car wash and watched Burns sitting in the Continental for over half an hour. Finally, forty minutes after he first arrived at the car wash, Burns turned on his headlights and engine. Smith proceeded to follow the Continental into the parking lot of the Howard Johnson's across the road. Parked twenty yards away from Burns, Smith sat behind the wheel and watched as the chauffeur made short trips from his car to the phone booth. The scenario was always the same: Burns would dial a number, then hang up and go back and lean on the car door, then back to the phone booth to try again. With each successive trip to the phone booth, Burns grew more frustrated, slamming the phone down and stomping back to the car. He was trying to call Pikul who, home again after his meeting with Federico, was keeping the phone line busy with his continual ten-ring phone calls to "Clancy." Watching from his darkened car at a discreet distance, Smith smiled at the game of cat and mouse he'd set up.

When Burns got in the car and slammed the door resolutely, Smith followed him back across the street to the car wash where Burns sat in his parked car until, at ten minutes of eleven, the "cashier" came and knocked on the car window and told him, "Hey, we're closing up now. If you want to stay here, it's okay with me, but it's going to be real dark."

Burns emitted a growl of disgust, gunned his engine and, an hour and ten minutes after he'd first arrived, drove off, the cash reward still in his pocket. Smith tailed him to the New York State Thruway southbound entrance. Certain that Burns was returning to his boss Pikul, Smith and Clancy called in a flatbed truck to take the dumpster back to the station house where it would spend the night chained to a maple tree, its contents to be sifted through in the morning.

At eleven P.M., just as Burns's Continental disappeared from Smith's sight on the Thruway, Carina Jacobsson was on her way back home to her Long Island City apartment, and State Police Detective Donald Delaney was getting in the Sixth Precinct squad car to accompany Detective Bill Glynn and Sergeant Bowen over to 446 Sixth Avenue to interview Joseph Pikul. The three officers had agreed that their only objective that evening was to try to determine if Pikul was involved in a homicide—and, if so, where the body was. They did *not* want to get a confession, even if Pikul seemed on the brink of giving them one. It was not that the confession would not have stood up. It would have, for two reasons: since the interview was conducted at Pikul's home, it could not be construed that he was questioned in a police-dominated atmosphere, and since the three officers were making the visit in response to a call for help from Pikul himself, they could not be perceived to have been in his house over his objections.

Still, a needlessly early confession meant the detectives would be stuck with a weak case. "We didn't yet have a body; we hadn't yet conducted a search of the house; we hadn't collected any corroborative evidence," Delaney explains. "And, as a man of some means, Pikul would call an attorney the minute he was arrested—and that would cut off our chance to interview him again or to get his consent for the house search. So we were just going over there to play, 'Hey Joe, relax, it's just a Missing Persons—we want to help you find your wife.' "

Delaney, Glynn and Bowen were admitted to the duplex by a young man with a French accent who identified himself as a co-worker of Joe's in the securities business. This was Jean-Jacques, Joe's protégé, whom he'd apparently invited over to the house because he believed he might be called to the police station—indeed, even arrested—and he wanted the children to be left in the care of someone who was loyal to him and who would believe the story of Diane's "disappearance" with her "lover." The three officers took a seat on the flowered sectional couch to help achieve the casual, unintimidating atmosphere they desired. Pikul seemed calm—that was good. The officers chatted a bit about the stock market. Joe said his losses weren't bad and he was going to come back from them.

With the warm-up talk on the couch having ensured that Pikul was not immediately about to slip into the nervous suspect mode, Glynn casually suggested they all move to the dining room table where the closer seating configuration would allow for their more attentive hearing of his account of his wife's disappearance, the better to help find her. Having Pikul face his questioners foursquare would increase the pressure on him enough to, hopefully, produce gaffes and inconsistencies in his statement; but that pressure had to be undetectable. Thus, the three officers remained relaxed, never exchanging looks. By prior arrangement, only Delaney took notes—unobtrusively, in his small spiralbound notepad.

Joe began by saying that he and Diane had had a brief argument when she arrived about an hour and a half after midnight; that he had then gone to bed, had awakened the next morning and gone to take a shower—and only then, when he'd called to her from under the

Diane Whitmore at eight, against the family Studebaker. (Courtesy of Donald Whitmore)

Senior at North Plainfield High School, 1961: valedictorian, honor student, "Most Sophisticated." (Courtesy of Donald Whitmore)

Mount Holyoke College, 1965: a strong B average, high recommendations from faculty, a decision to break her engagement to a handsome young doctor, a job waiting for her at *Life* magazine. (Courtesy of Mount Holyoke College)

1967: caught up in the sixties' spirit of adventure, romanticism and excess, which would bring out vulnerabilities in her character. (Courtesy of Donald Whitmore)

After a stormy romance, Diane marries Ralph Schnackenberg in summer 1975. Annulment follows. (Matron of honor Nancy Kirkland is at left.) (Courtesy of Ralph Eric Schnackenberg)

Three years later, a second marriage—in a similar old-fashioned dress—to fellow recovering alcoholic Joseph Pikul. On July 14, 1978, Diane is newly pregnant and desperately hopeful for a happy future. (Courtesy of Donald Whitmore)

With Claudia's birth in 1979, Diane and Joe are delighted new parents, hiding problems under his business success, the happy distractions of family life, and their mutual concerted sobriety. (Courtesy of Donald Whitmore)

With Blake's birth at Christmas time 1982, the perfect family picture is complete. (Courtesy of Donald Whitmore)

Diane spends the eighties with her adored children, fearful that if she leaves Joe, she'll lose his money and her life. (Courtesy of Donald Whitmore)

On the 1986 Hong Kong trip designed to woo Diane back from the brink of divorce, Joe exhibits his sense of power. (Courtesy of Donald Whitmore)

Diane's murder and Joe's arrest are announced to New York City on October 30, 1987. (From the *New York Post,* reprinted with permission)

Justice Kristin Booth Glen, the active feminist divorced mother who initially allowed Joe Pikul to keep custody of his children despite his murder indictment. (© 1991 Faye Ellman)

Joe and his new wife, Mary Bain Pikul, enter Justice Glen's courtroom on September, 1988, ready to assume permanent custody of Blake and Claudia. At day's end, startling complications develop. (© 1988 Al Raia/*Newsday*)

Sandra Jarvinen, Joe Pikul's first wife, takes the stand at his winter 1989 murder trial and testifies that he drove to her house with something to bury in the back of his car, and that he admitted, "I had to eliminate her." (© 1989 Dick Kraus/*Newsday*)

In surprise testimony at his murder trial in Judge Thomas A. Byrne's courtroom, Joe is asked, "Did you cause the death of Diane Pikul?" He answers, "Yes," but denies he is guilty of murder. (© 1989 Jeff Golding/*Times Herald Record*)

Boyish prosecutor Alan Joseph (left) and husky defense attorney Ron Bekoff separately wield the knife Joe claimed Diane tried to kill him with. (© 1989 Dick Kraus/*Newsday*)

Mike, Kathy, Claudia, and Blake O'Guin, 1990. The children are healing and happy with their adoptive parents, the hairbreadth victors in the custody case that had so many outraged for so long. (Courtesy of Mike and Kathy O'Guin)

streaming water and heard no answer, had he realized she had gone off. But as the interview wore on, Joe—possibly worried that the admission of an argument would lead to incriminating inferences—started to shift his story a little: First he said there wasn't much of an argument; then he changed his account to one in which he and his wife had no heated words with each other at all.

The shift in the story was a good sign, and the officers took in each successive version respectfully, straight-faced. To keep Pikul unaware that he was increasingly contradicting himself, they gently and subtly prodded him into digressive conversation so that by the time he got back to the subject of Diane's disappearance he would forget how he'd described it just ten minutes earlier. Eventually, the half-hour's skilled questioning did its intended job of getting Joe to change his story 180 degrees. When he started one sentence about what happened after she'd gotten to the house with, "And then she stormed out . . ." none of the three officers turned so much as a quarter of an inch to each other. There it was: Their nonsuspect had now entirely contradicted his earlier assertion that he had *not* witnessed his wife leaving. Furthermore, he was now saying she had left (or he noticed she'd left) not in the morning but *right after* she had arrived at 1:30 A.M. And the heated argument that he'd spent a half hour erasing from his first account was now ("stormed out") stuck back *in* the scenario. This was—bingo—a major double contradiction plus a backpedaling.

Once Joe lost control of his story, it slid around, every which way. When asked if a car came to pick Diane up, he said no—she had walked off. He wasn't sure if she'd walked off because she couldn't drive the stick-shifted Mazda or (suddenly he remembered she'd taken stick-shift lessons) because her lover lived close enough to walk to his house. Other than his curiously convenient knowledge of that lover's highly coincidental residential proximity, he knew nothing else about the man—not his name, profession, physique, nor how Diane had met him; a peculiar absence of detail for a man who claimed to have long been suspicious of his wife, and for a wife who, the man claimed, loved to taunt him.

Ken Bowen, who, with almost forty years on the force, had a professional wisdom that could cut through the facts of an interview to enable him to judge the situation by instinct, says that he kept thinking the same thought over again: *He just doesn't seem that concerned about her.* That woman on the phone from *Harper's*, Ann Stern: now *she* legitimately cared about this woman, Diane. But not this guy, the husband. He's just going through the motions.

Joe cooperated with the three detectives' request to search the Amagansett house. He signed the consent-to-search letter as soon as Delaney wrote it out. But their request for a photograph of Diane was something else. This made him exceedingly nervous. Searching through manila envelopes for a picture of his wife, he became so highly agitated, he could barely select one. Then Joe responded to Delaney's request for an article of Diane's clothing by bringing a pair of panties from the bedroom. "She wore them jogging and they haven't been washed—the dogs will get a good scent of her," he volunteered. The detectives were startled by Joe's clumsy overeagerness to please, his deep violation of his wife's privacy.

The three officers took the panties, stood up, thanked Pikul and assured him they'd work hard to find his wife. Out on the sidewalk, Glynn slyly asked the two others: "Did you guys hear two different stories like I did?"

Bowen allowed as to how Pikul didn't seem to give a shit about finding his wife.

But it was Delaney who leapfrogged over both men's implications to what was now his clear deduction. He said: "She's dead, and he did it."

Chapter 9

"Unless the guy confesses immediately, you're going to solve the case by sweat—sweat and really good police work, where no single strand of action by one cop stands out from the collaborative fabric of the whole."

Attorney Michael Schwartz, veteran prosecutor and law clerk to People v. Joseph Pikul *judge Thomas J. Byrne, commenting on the police work on the case, 6/4/90*

Tuesday, October 27

Close to one A.M., Delaney headed back out to Troop L headquarters to put together a team for the house search and grab two hours sleep. He planned to start the search at daybreak. Pikul would be left to sleep in his duplex all night, soothed by his assumption that no one was on to him. Any future lawyer Pikul hired would be ultimately forced to concede that his rights had not been violated in the slightest: the questioning had been done in a noncustodial atmosphere and no confession was elicited. Meanwhile, while he slept, plans would be put into motion on Long Island for forensics men, dog handlers and troopers with spades to start combing the probable crime scene.

That, at least, is what Delaney—after having stopped at the Sixth to plan strategy with Bowen and Glynn—assumed was going to happen.

But Bowen and Glynn did not quite share their colleague's faith that Pikul had swallowed the "It's just a Missing Persons" bait and was willing to rest with the hook in his mouth all night. In fact, they thought he could be getting ready to split, right this minute, for the airport—passport in hand. At the very least they had some additional questions to ask him—things that weren't made clear during the interview at the duplex. So, remembers Detective Ronnie Finelli, "When Kenny and Billy got back to the precinct, me and Richie Composto and them started talking and deciding we gotta go back there and try to take this guy away from his home ground. Bring him back to the station to make him squirm a little. See what else we can get from him. Maybe if we had him for three or four hours, it would give the other guys a chance to find the body. We wanted to have our hands on him while things were developing.

"So Richie and I went back to his house—this is now about three in the morning—to try to convince him to come with us. If he said no, that was the end of it. We woke him. He didn't say no, but he was hesitant—kept saying he'd rather come in at twelve the next day. Now we figured he was definitely going to flee. So we tried to be nice, tried to use a little cream on him. 'We want to show you a few things and it will be more comfortable for you at the precinct . . .' Finally, we got him to come with us." Pikul's protégé Jean-Jacques remained at the house to baby-sit the sleeping children.

Back in the Sixth squadroom at four A.M., Composto and Finelli now took over the questioning, purportedly trying to figure out where Diane went and trying to affect an atmosphere of a couple of guys shooting the breeze with a concerned husband. The successful conveyance of that noncustodial atmosphere was crucial; it was the thin thread by which the legitimacy of their questioning hung. For now they had Pikul out of his residence, in a police-dominated setting, and they themselves suspected he was guilty of a crime. But he was not an official suspect and he hadn't been, as the police describe the obligatory reading of rights, "Mirandized." Under those weighty circumstances, Pikul's rights could only be considered *not* violated if he himself experienced the "situation" as *not* a "custodial" one—if, throughout the questioning, he perceived himself free to leave at any time.

The fellows at the Sixth took a lucky gamble on their own finessing skills and on Joe Pikul's deep need to be affirmed as a "guy." (Later his defense attorneys would say that, to distance himself from his self-loathed streak

of homosexuality, Joe always "macho'd it up.") Joe
bought the line. He boasted to Finelli and Composto: "I
knew that that guy who called with the credit cards in
Newburgh was really a cop. He couldn't bullshit me. I
was just playing a game with him." Yet, he had tipped
his hand in the playing—for his chauffeur's license plate
and phone numbers had been obtained by the Newburgh
detective. This would prove to be important information
for the police.

Casually, the officers walked Pikul back through his
story, which Finelli remembers as "terrible." This time,
they took a six-page statement. Now he wove in his long
winding trip from New Windsor to Massachusetts, back
to New Windsor and back to New York. (In the earlier
interview, at the duplex, Joe had said he'd spent the
whole weekend at the Sawoskas'.) Now they had a geo-
graphical lead that would within twelve hours help them
understand the significance of Vinnie Federico and,
within forty-eight hours, of Sandra Jarvinen.

While Composto and Finelli kept the banter up,
Bowen, in the next room, got on the phone with the
Newburgh PD. Clancy answered the phone. "We have
the motherfucker here," Bowen announced to his upstate
counterpart.

Clancy was concerned. "Well, did he ask for a lawyer?" he asked.

"He didn't ask for no fucking lawyer, we don't want
a fucking lawyer," was Bowen's reply. The recording device Detective Smith had attached to the phone earlier
was still intact. Later, this tape-recorded verbal report
would be used in court as part of Joe Pikul's defense.

As the hours ticked away toward dawn, Joe dropped
what looked like a bombshell. "I have another apartment," he began.

"Can we see it?" Finelli asked politely. "Maybe Diane
went there."

"No, she wouldn't go there," came his quick, nervous
reply.

"Can we go anyway?" Composto pressed on.

Now Pikul became reluctant. Finally he said, "Well
. . . just don't be surprised by what you find there. . . ."

Finelli and Composto tried hard to contain their excitement. Were they going to see the body? So *soon*? But

their hopes were dashed by Pikul's next words: "I like to dress up in women's clothes." He claimed Diane encouraged this habit, photographing him in women's clothes and blackmailing him with those pictures.

When Finelli and Composto went down to the Rector Street apartment, they saw, in Finelli's words, "a bedroom with no bed but all cluttered with large-sized women's clothes and lipstick and shoes—on every surface, all over the floor: everywhere."

So there it was—the mystery of the large woman's clothes and the cheesy jewelry: solved. But that was all that was there. After sifting through the storehouse of secret obsession, Finelli and Composto could find nothing to connect Joseph Pikul to any murder. The two detectives took Pikul out to breakfast at a diner, and then they dropped him back off at the duplex.*

When Cahill and Delaney found out the next morning what Bowen and Glynn had let ensue, they were not delighted. They arrived at the house on Windmill Lane at about 8:30 A.M. and began a cursory search as precise and by-the-book as their Manhattan counterparts' late-night questioning had been fast and loose and risky. When red stains appearing to be blood were found on the kitchen floor, they immediately stopped what they were doing, secured the house by leaving a trooper at the door and drove back to state police headquarters in Riverhead, where they drew up an affidavit for a search warrant enabling them to test blood, hair and fibers (the

---

*What the officers at the Sixth had done was risky. For, had Pikul confessed during that early-morning questioning, Finelli and Composto would have then had to inform him that he was not free to leave. That he *was* free to leave he'd inferred *but had not been explicitly informed.* Thus, that thin thread on which the legitimacy of their questioning hung would have been snipped; and, on the basis of what has happened in similar cases, there is probably a 50% chance that a judge would have found that Pikul's rights had been violated during the questioning. Then, under what is known as the Fruits of the Poison Tree doctrine, everything obtained from that flawed questioning—not merely the confession but the physical evidence, including the body itself—would have been thrown out of court and Pikul would not have been able to be successfully prosecuted at all.

consent-to-search letter Pikul had signed the night before hadn't covered this) and cleared the warrant through the Suffolk County D.A.'s office. Their caution delayed the search seven hours, but the prudence was well grounded. "We wanted to make sure we were on very good legal ground, that any evidence we found would be admissible in court," Cahill recalls.

Returning to the house at around six P.M., Cahill and Delaney brought another detective, Investigator Joseph O'Neill, and two forensics specialists with them. These "ID men," as they're called, would photograph and collect any item the detectives felt significant.

Just as Pikul had promised, there were condoms under the bed and in the nightstand drawer. But Delaney, having heard Pikul talk the previous night of his condoms-market research in Scandinavia, did not take these seriously as evidence. As for the red stains on the kitchen floor, ID man Roger Chilemi cut out a piece of the floor and administered an on-site field test on it. The test registered positive for blood. (A later test done in the serology lab would contradict this finding.) This led Delaney to think that Diane had been killed with a knife or a gun.

Then, playing back the unerased answering machine and hearing the callback from dental assistant Patricia Sarlo, Delaney called Sarlo and was told of Joe's call to have his tooth fixed. Next, Delaney found the tooth itself—on top of the bedroom dresser—and in the kitchen drawer he found a set of knives to which the knife found in the car wash dumpster belonged. Now Delaney had a connection from the house to the dumpster. More important, he had a scenario: "Pikul was standing over Diane, trying to kill her; in an effort to free herself, she stuck an elbow, or a blunt object, into his face and broke his tooth." The scenario made sense. And, aside from his assumption that the death was by knife or gun, that scenario held all the way through the trial.

Meanwhile, 150 miles east in the Sixth Precinct squad-room, Bill Glynn, with Ken Bowen at his side, picked up the phone and, at seven P.M., dialed the dispatch garage of the Great American Dream Machine in Queens. When the fleet's owner Jim Burns answered the phone, Glynn said, "We have information that you were upstate in Newburgh last night trying to retrieve some property that belonged to Diane Pikul." Burns confirmed the trip, said he had made it at his boss's behest and that "when I got up to the car wash no one was there so I just turned around and went home." When Glynn asked Burns to come to the Sixth Precinct to aid their investigation, Burns became reluctant. *Extremely* reluctant. He was loyal to his boss. He did not want to get involved.

"Look," is how Glynn then put it, "I don't want to have to break your balls. You can drive in and we can sit down and discuss this. Or my partner and I are gonna come out to your house. And when we come to your house, we're *not* gonna leave."

Burns said he'd come right in.

When he arrived, Glynn did his best to loosen the guy up. They'd both grown up in Rosedale, Queens, so Glynn did a few easy lobs of "Did you know so-and-so . . . ?" But the banter didn't work—Burns was nervous, stoic and unswervingly loyal to Joseph Pikul. In his opinion, Diane had just up and walked off on her own. Glynn thanked Burns for coming and reminisced further about Rosedale as he walked the nervous driver to the precinct parking lot and watched, smiling, as Burns drove his Dream Machine east on West Tenth Street. If Burns had looked long and carefully in his rearview, which apparently he didn't, he would have seen he had acquired a tail.

Meanwhile, back in Amagansett, with a preliminary crime scenario set, the officers' next major concern was the whereabouts of the body. Delaney went to check the Mazda, still parked in front of the house. The inside backseat was loaded with sand—this was telling, Delaney thought, since Pikul had mentioned nothing the night before about either he or Diane being at a beach before her "disappearance." Under the car, a mass of mud, beach grass and red clay-like sand that matched the sand in an adjoining field was found stuck to the wheels. All of this indicated to Delaney that the car had been driven off the road in an initial effort to dispose of the body, which Pikul later rejected as being too obvious.

Still, it was tempting to consider the most obvious

place first: the cemetery that directly abutted the house. There was a freshly dug grave there. But digging in a graveyard required time-draining court permission, so Cahill decided to save that search for a last resort.

Another investigator from Troop L, Steve Oates, a hefty, balding man, arrived and combed the surrounding woods. In the meantime, Delaney continued his detailed search of the house, and Cahill drove out to a nearby potato field where car tracks had been noticed by the East Hampton PD. Cahill was sufficiently interested in those tracks to have plaster casts taken of them, to see if they matched the Mazda's. (They did not.) He also sent dog handlers with bloodhounds to comb the fields— to no avail. Cahill and Delaney decided they would keep the house continually secured, even after the body was found. That way, they'd never have to worry that some initially insignificant item would be deemed inadmissable as evidence simply because it happened to have been removed from the house while the trooper was not standing guard. Given the case's eventual long-circumstantial nature, this foresight would prove valuable.

Back in Manhattan, Glynn and Bowen paid a mid-morning call on the women at *Harper's* magazine. Ann Stern, first disappointed that Glynn was so "rumpled and unprepossessing looking," soon "saw how extraordinarily intuitive and charismatic he was." He started to rein in and bring focus to the emotional remembrances of Ann, Linda McNamera and Karen Hoffman. "The high seriousness of Billy Glynn's attention," Ann says, "his ability to focus the search, to quiet our panic and to patiently and methodically guide us away from the hearsay and back to the facts, as well as his understanding of the dark side of human nature and the difference between appearance and reality: all of these things were the match of the most enlightened therapist I had ever met." From Ann, who was married for many years to an eminent psychiatrist, this was no small praise. As for Glynn, he was moved and impressed by how deeply Diane Pikul's colleagues at *Harper's,* especially Ann, cared for this woman they had known so briefly.

Glynn left *Harper's* with a pile of confidential papers of Diane's that Ann had retrieved from her desk: her

short stories; her list, made at the behest of Raoul
Felder, of Joe's transgressions and threats; and the financial statement that Felder and Slavin had finally been
able to extract from Joe's attorneys. When he got back
to the squadroom, Glynn leafed through the latter and
discovered how wealthy Joe really was. No wonder he
said the stock market crash hadn't hurt him, the detective
said to himself, mentally erasing financial ruin as a partial
reason for the homicide. "The cocksucker has hundreds
of thousands salted away in Mexico and Switzerland," he
said to himself.

Joseph Pikul's financial and business statements made
the man a likely candidate to flee the country. He had
money harbored abroad; he had business connections
there also. Added to this, investigators from the state
police's Troop F in Newburgh had just come up with
some newly disturbing facts. Interviewing the Sawoskas,
they learned that Joe had spoken of a "terminal illness";
and interviewing the workers and manager at Stewart
Auto Wash, they learned that he kept guns. In their interviews with Maggie Gari, Gloria Archer, and Inga and
Carina later that day, Glynn and Bowen would learn that
Pikul had guns in the duplex itself. When the policeman
who'd been tailing Jim Burns's car all afternoon called
in with a report that the chauffeur had just picked up a
man wearing a business suit at the Boston–New York
shuttle exit at LaGuardia Airport and driven him to the
Barbizon Hotel at 63rd Street and Lexington Avenue, all
the investigators were concerned and pressed for an ID.
  The man, the Barbizon desk clerk said, had registered
as "Vincent Federico" of Quincy, Massachusetts. He was
an attorney. Had Pikul brought him to New York to get
his affairs in order so that he might flee? Investigators
from the state police and the NYPD began "sitting on"
the Barbizon. One, disguised as a hotel employee and
using a "suitable context," went to Federico's room to
get a look at the lawyer and to determine if he was there
alone. He was.

Marshall Weingarden called Joe again at home on Tuesday. Marshall and Barbara had just spoken with Joe's
old friend and confidante Ramona Craniotis, who told

them how she had recently had lunch with Joe and he'd
seemed hopeful that the marriage could be saved. They
were still giving their friend the benefit of the doubt.
Marshall talked with Joe about Halloween. Because Joe
was too distracted by Diane's "disappearance" to have
made plans for the children, Marshall said Barbara would
get costumes for Blake and Claudia. He also offered to
take the children to the Village Halloween parade and
keep them overnight. When Barbara got on the phone,
Claudia picked up the line and asked her if she knew
that her mother was missing and when did she think she'd
come back?

Carina and Inga had offered to take care of the children that night and Joe agreed to this. When they asked
if they could take the children to Inga's boyfriend's Tribeca apartment because someone had to be home to
await the delivery of cabinets, Joe did not see this request
as what it was: a ploy worked out by the young women
in concert with Detective Bill Glynn, who had elicited
their eager cooperation in his efforts to gently debrief
the children. Perhaps Joe was distracted by the plans he
was now making for himself: He was in the process of
dropping the services of Vinnie Federico, virtually before
they'd begun, for those of the powerful Sam Dawson,
who had defended (though fruitlessly) the heads of several major crime families in the recent Mafia Commission
trial; and he was arranging for the children to stay, for
a few days, with his sister Janice's daughter, Edleen Bergelt, who was eight and a half months pregnant, and her
husband, Keith, in their Upper East Side apartment. A
month before, Edleen and Keith had helped Diane call
highway patrol and police departments in her distraught
attempt to track the children down when Joe left for
Amagansett with them and did not arrive as expected.

Inga came to fetch the children at the duplex, where
she was met by a peculiarly expansive Joe who now suggested he come along to the Tribeca apartment and have
a pizza dinner with them. Inga panicked; she and Carina
were awaiting Bill Glynn at the apartment. "I'll go get
the pizza!" Inga insisted, and on her way to the pizza
parlor, she called Glynn and warned him that Joe might
be there.

But at the last minute, after a brief foray to F.A.O.

Schwarz to buy toys for the children, Joe begged off, and
at 7:30 he dropped Blake, Claudia, Inga and the pizza
at the Tribeca apartment, where Carina was waiting.
Glynn was promptly alerted that the coast was clear for
his visit. Weaponless, in his off-duty clothes, posing as a
friend, he soon "dropped in" with his "girlfriend," Chris
Margillo. When offered a piece of the pizza, Glynn said,
"No thanks—I lost a tooth eating pizza once." To which
Claudia forthrightly chimed in: "My daddy broke *his*
tooth, too. But he broke his on a piece of candy." The
man suddenly seemed very interested—not just in her
daddy's tooth but in what the whole family had done that
weekend. The children, especially Claudia, seemed to
sense a hidden agenda in this "friend's" curiosity. They
clammed up, and the pizza party proceeded in mostly
awkward silence.

Glynn hated pumping children who may have been at
crime scenes; whatever those poor kids had to witness,
he figured, they were entitled to forget. Returning to the
squadroom, he thought of how those kids reminded him
of his own kids: two sons, three and six, and a daughter,
eight. Before lying down on the squadroom cot for the
few hours of sleep he could afford, he called his wife,
Rosemary, and told her about the children.

"Can I stay with you tonight?" four-and-a-half-year-old
Blake asked Carina after the visitors were gone.

"Of course you can—if it's okay with your daddy,"
Carina answered.

"Can Claudia stay, too?"

Carina nodded. But Joe, she knew, was on his way
over to pick them up. She rocked Blake in her arms.

"I'm thinking about Mommy," he admitted. "Mommy's never coming back."

"Don't think that," Carina said hopefully. But she was
crying as she spoke.

At eleven P.M., a lieutenant from the East Hampton police reported to Delaney that what looked like a freshly
made sand grave had been found under a kiosk at a
public beach directly south of the house. Expectations
were high as officers from Troop L and the East Hampton PD drove through a light rain to Main Beach and,

in continuing light precipitation, dug in the sand where the Pikuls—and the Piccolos and Weingardens—had sat during the 1986 Fourth of July fireworks.

Bill Glynn phoned Ann Stern late that night, as he would many other evenings during the investigation and afterward. He had just come from interviewing Gloria Archer and Barbara Martin, and wanted to doublecheck what Diane had worn to work last Friday. They talked easily, the reader of Yeats and Auden and the maker of bets on the IDs of washed-up corpses. "You must really know Diane by now," Ann remarked, after Glynn said he'd just read her short stories and her memo to Felder. "Yeah, well," he said offhandedly, "you get a sense of a person when you put all the pieces together." Then he added, "I like her." Ann was struck by the poignantly ironic present tense.

As the rains on Long Island became heavy, the diggers from Troop L and the East Hampton PD called it a night and went back to their respective headquarters. There was no grave there, they realized. It had just been a false lead.

At about this time, a few hours after midnight, Blake and Claudia Pikul were asleep in the Bergelts' Upper East Side apartment, where their father had dropped them off after picking them up in Tribeca.

And then, for almost two full days, Joseph Pikul disappeared.

Wednesday, October 28

At approximately 2:45 P.M., William Heller, a New York State Thruway Authority light equipment operator, was riding in a slow-moving Thruway Authority dump truck on the shoulder of the northbound lane of the Thruway, three and a half miles south of the Newburgh exit. Heller was inspecting the drainage ditches for obstructions such as fallen tree branches that might have resulted from the previous night's storm when something out of the ordinary caught his eye. It seemed to be a canvas or plastic covering, wrapped around what he guessed from the long oblong shape might be a human body. He told his partner, Douglas Pfleger, to stop the truck. Heller got out, walked down the slope of the culvert, crouched, and groped around the thin extremity of the wet package. His hands touched what he was fairly sure were human feet. With a sense of nervous foreboding, he took out a pocket knife and cut the covering. A pair of women's legs in black hoisery were revealed. Moments later Heller was back in the truck, radioing the Thruway Authority dispatcher.

When state police trooper Jerome John arrived and surveyed the scene, he instantly sent out a general call to any and all troopers who might be listening, describing what he had discovered.

At about 3:15, word that a body had been found reached a Newburgh banquet hall where a farewell luncheon honoring a member of Troop F was winding down. Senior Investigator Joseph Tripodo, commander of Troop F's Bureau of Criminal Investigation—an avuncular, cigar-smoking twenty-six-year veteran—heard Trooper John's call on his hand-held radio. John's call erroneously described the body as having been exposed for a very long time, perhaps weeks. So even though Tripodo had already been tangentially pulled in to aid in the Pikul Missing Persons investigation (he'd interviewed Henry and Louise Sawoska the day before), he didn't make the connection. He was almost apologetic when he asked Investigator Robert Venezia to leave the party, go to the scene and take a look. "It's probably gonna be a bag of bones," Venezia remembers Tripodo saying.

Venezia—tall, mustached, and, like his commanding officer, softspoken—had had twenty-three years in the Trenches, as Troop F's BCI is called, where his caseload ranged from chicken coop burglaries and airfield accidents to homicides and rapes. What you drew was what you drew and if it was a bag of bones, Venezia reasoned, so be it. But when he got to the crime scene at 3:30, it looked to be bigger than that. The little patch of highway was swarming with troopers. Venezia looked down into the culvert and saw the body of a woman, which had since been revealed by three ID men who had cut the tarp, taken all the evidence, conducted the crime scene search. Her body had been packed in towels; her wrists and ankles cord-bound. What surprised Venezia was how fresh the body seemed—he'd expected a highly decomposed corpse.

Venezia wasn't the only one surprised. A pair of investigators from Long Island's Troop L—Larry Shewark and Pete Person—had been sent up to Newburgh to work on the disappearance of Diane Pikul. They'd just left the Stewart Auto Wash, where they'd garnered a positive photo ID of Joe Pikul and the children from the manager and workers, when they heard Trooper John's radio call. Shewark drove over to the culvert. He was just as startled as Venezia was by the freshness of the corpse. He also happened to have with him a photograph of Diane and a list of her vital statistics. He and Venezia looked closely at the corpse, the photo and the listing of height, weight and age. "The connection," Venezia remembers, "was right on the mark."

Orange County Coroner Mary Ellen Wright had just ordered the body removed to the St. Luke's Hospital morgue in Newburgh, and Venezia and Shewark made sure they were at the morgue when the body arrived. By 5:30 P.M., they were all but completely certain—from the physical description of Diane and the clothing (plaid shirt, dirndl skirt) Joe had told Delaney she was wearing—that this was indeed Diane.

Suffolk County, within which the town of Amagansett lies, could have pressed to get the case, but in order to be able to successfully prosecute it, Suffolk's D.A. Pat Henry would have had the risky task of proving that the murder had been committed there. In a series of phone conferences, Henry and his Orange County counterpart Francis Phillips agreed that it would be a much surer prosecutorial bet to give Orange County the case. The jurisdiction in which a body is found always has the right to prosecute the crime, no matter where that crime may have occurred. Orange County Chief Assistant D.A. Alan Joseph, thirty-three, was hungry for the case. A slim, boyish, blunt-spoken man, Joseph had recently been robbed of a murder trial when an accused juvenile tendered a guilty plea before jury selection. As he puts it, "You always want a big case; you always want a murder

trial." It would be left to him to orchestrate the unwieldy
Pikul case.

When Captain William Cahill got word that Diane's
body had been found, he immediately left the Amagansett house for Orange County, where a case command
post was set up at Newburgh's Troop F on Stewart Airfield. Cahill brought sample towels and bed clothes from
the Pikuls' Amagansett house to Troop F's forensics lab.
The lab established that one of those towels—with a pattern of blue stripes on white—matched those in which
Diane's body was wrapped. These towels were soon
found to be Brazilian imports, sold at only a few East
Coast department stores. Alan Joseph was excited; their
distinctive origin would make it almost impossible to con-
tend that anyone but the victim's husband wrapped the
corpse in the same towels that the Pikul family used.
Even more compelling as circumstantial evidence were
the specks of glitter found in one of Diane's makeshift
shrouds. When the forensics lab later found stray specks
of that same glitter embedded in the trunk of Pikul's
station wagon and among the debris in the Amagansett
house vacuum cleaner bags as well, Alan Joseph had a
follow-the-dots diagram with which to link Joe Pikul to
the enshrouding of Diane's body and its subsequent disposal on the New York State Thruway. Joseph would
doggedly cling to those towels and to that "glitter trail"
throughout the next fifteen and a half months.

Don Delaney and Investigator Tom O'Neill* were already en route to Manhattan when they received word
via radio, at 4:15 P.M., that a body found in a culvert by
the New York State Thruway was thought to be Diane
Pikul. By the time positive identification was radioed to
them at 5:30, they were impatiently negotiating the traffic-
jammed streets of the city's east twenties, rushing to the
Sixth Precinct. There they were to meet Bowen and
Glynn, who had already driven to the duplex, the Rector
Street apartment, and the Bleichroeder offices—and
found Pikul at none of these places. He was either on the
run (possibly already out of the country, it was feared) or

_____
*Not to be confused with Investigator Joseph O'Neill, who aided
him in the house search the day before.

he was being "made unavailable"* by his lawyers. Blake and Claudia Pikul *were* at the duplex, however, with a baby-sitter hired from an agency who was waiting, on Joe's instructions, for some third party to relieve her.

When Delaney and O'Neill met Bowen and Glynn at the Sixth at six P.M., the safety of the children was on all their minds. The four men with two very different approaches to police work unanimously assented to a simple truism: "Anyone involved in a homicide who is not a career criminal," as Glynn puts it, "can, under pressure, go off the deep end. Children are in imminent danger when they're left in the care of a man like this." The officers immediately called the city's child protection agency, the Special Services for Children (SSC), to meet them at the apartment and, adding a few patrolmen to ensure the children's safety, Glynn and O'Neill went to the duplex to effect an "emergency removal" of the children. What seemed instinctively right to these policemen, what made such common sense to them, would turn out to be far more ambiguous, indeed dispensable, to the judges and psychiatrists who were later drawn in. Such firm, preemptively protective action would never be repeated on behalf of the Pikul children again.

When Glynn, O'Neill, their backup team and a social worker got to the duplex, Edleen Bergelt and her husband, Keith, had also just arrived, ready to take pajama-clad Blake and Claudia home with them on her uncle's orders. When Glynn displayed his badge and told the couple that the children would be going first to the Sixth Precinct, then to protective custody for the night, the Bergelts clasped the children to them and demanded to know why. O'Neill made a gesture toward the children and indicated that the reason could not be explained in their presence. Glynn looked into the bewildered eyes of the boy and girl, pressed to the bodies of relatives they did not seem to know very well, suddenly surrounded by uniformed adults who were communicating in ominous

---

*Accepted euphemism for a criminal lawyer's tacit hiding of a client who has just become a suspect. The burden then shifts to the police, who must now amass enough probable cause to get an arrest warrant before they can talk to the client/suspect again.

gestures. His heart ached for their confusion and their vulnerability.

The officers escorted Blake and Claudia and their aunt and uncle to the precinct where an Emergency Children's Services (ECS) worker soon arrived. Tom O'Neill tried to question the children about what they might have seen, but the children were silent. After interviewing the children in a private room, the social worker told O'Neill and Delaney: "They have nothing to say. Please leave them alone." Meanwhile, knowing that Blake and Claudia wouldn't be allowed to stay with Joe's niece and her husband while Joe was still in hiding, and knowing how disorganized and inefficient the city's emergency child welfare agency could be, Bill Glynn called his high superior, Captain Michael Gardiner, Commander of the Second Detective Division. "Instead of putting the children in foster care for the night," he asked, "would there be a problem with me and my wife taking them into our home?"

There would be a problem; it wasn't procedure, Glynn was hardly surprised to be told. So, at ten P.M., the two tired children whose mother had "disappeared" five days before and whose father had disappeared that day were led out of the police station in their pajamas by the ECS worker and taken to the agency's center on Church Street. As the hours passed and a suitable foster home was still not secured, Blake and Claudia spent the entire night in the agency's wooden office chairs while the Bergelts remained at their side, concerned and dismayed.

While the children slept fitfully in their uncomfortable surroundings, Dr. Mark Taff, a forensic pathologist, was performing an autopsy on their mother's body at Newburgh's St. Luke's Hospital morgue. She had died not from knife or gun wounds, as the blood on the Amagansett floor had suggested to Delaney, but from strangulation. This was clear from the marks on the skin of her neck, the buildup of fluid in her lungs and the fractures and breaks in the bones of her neck. The murderer had used hands and a cord and, to effect the strangulation, the grip on the victim's throat had to have been maintained for thirty seconds or more. From internal examination, Taff found ten bruises about the victim's head, indicating blows struck there.

Nearby, at Troop F, Investigator Venezia and Senior Investigator Tripodo had begun pulling up the toll calls Joseph Pikul had made. Two brief phone calls to Norwell, Massachusetts intrigued them. One was made at 12:16 P.M. on Sunday, October 25; the other, thirty-four minutes later that same afternoon. Given that Pikul had attested to his wife's "disappearance" early Saturday morning and that the coroner had estimated, from the wrinkled but intact skin on Diane's hands and feet, that she had lain exposed to the elements for approximately two days, these phone calls appeared to have been made at a crucial time between the murder and the body drop. Both calls were so short in length—forty-three and fifty-two seconds, respectively—that Venezia and Tripodo believed them to be messages left on an answering machine.

Venezia realized he would need some help in the Norwell area and, after calling Massachusetts State Police, came up with an experienced homicide and narcotics investigator, Trooper Bill Gorman of the Plymouth "C-Pack" (Crime Prevention and Control Unit). Venezia called Gorman and asked for help in identifying, then interviewing the recipient of those phone messages. Gorman called Venezia back within the hour and told him the phone number was residential, unlisted and belonged to a Miss Sandra Jarvinen.

Thursday, October 29

With the autopsy report in, by midnight the task was clear: Find Joseph Pikul. Cahill sent orders to the Sixth Precinct squadroom to find and escort Pikul to Newburgh to identify the body, but not to arrest him yet. Plainclothed officers from NYPD Nightwatch, from Narcotics and from Troop L were sent to "sit on" the Bergelts' apartment (the children had finally been released into their custody), Kennedy Airport, the Hotel Barbizon, where Vinnie Federico was registered, and the Warwick Hotel on Fifty-fourth Street, to which Pikul's chauffeur Jim Burns had also been tailed. Delaney and Tom O'Neill, each paired up with a partner from Nightwatch, headed out to slowly cruise the streets and check the parking lots and garages of the upper seventies and eighties, near where the Bergelts lived, looking for Pikul's station wagon.

At 2:30 A.M., O'Neill and his Nightwatch partner joined the team at the Barbizon. The talk among the team of NYPD and Troop L men in the lobby had it that Pikul was there, checked in under the name "Joe Pike," his old nickname among the car service guys at the B&H Garage. O'Neill's partner borrowed one of the hotel's bellhop uniforms, went to Joe Pike's room carrying a room service tray with a sandwich and beverage on it and knocked on the door. The man who answered the door said, "I didn't order room service"; the "bellhop" then handed the man the room service bill and said, "You'll have to sign here, to confirm that you didn't call." The man signed "Joseph Pike."

The detective returned to the lobby and showed the signature to O'Neill, who found its nearly identical match in a photostated sample of Pikul's signature that he'd brought with him. O'Neill radioed this news to Delaney, who was still cruising the East Side streets for the station wagon, and Delaney sped to the hotel, ready to position himself in the lobby and wait however long it took for Pikul to come downstairs. But after waiting two hours, Delaney realized that he had been awake now for almost forty-eight hours and was simply too exhausted to make the arrest; he called Cahill, who told him to go home and get some sleep—fresher troops were on the way.

But "fresher" did not mean "fresh" in this already long investigation. Steve Oates, the Troop L detective who had combed the Amagansett woods for the body the day before, had already logged two twelve-hour days on the case when he got in his car to drive from Long Island to the Barbizon. His partner, Jim Probst, a tall man with a delicate face and a drooping mustache, had logged long hours, too. Driving the hour and a half in darkness, Oates fingered the radio dial and found a pop music station. After years enduring squad cars that had no AM/FM radios, Oates was grateful for the addition of music on these marathon details to keep him awake.

When Oates and Probst reached the Barbizon at 4:30 A.M., they discovered from the other detectives that

something had gone very wrong. This Joseph Pikul was
a cannier, more devious suspect than any of these experienced men had anticipated. It seems that a guest had
come down to the lobby and had signed his name "Joe
Pike" at the desk, whereupon the clerk made a prear-
ranged signal to the officers. These particular officers,
however, did not include the Nightwatch detective who'd
dressed up as the bellhop, and they hadn't seen Pikul in
person. The officers moved in on this "Joe Pike," only
to find out he was, in fact, not their suspect at all. Meanwhile a *second* man was sighted slipping out of the hotel's
side door. A detective chased after him but lost him
when he jumped into a cab. "It was Pikul, all right, and
we blew it," Delaney was told. It was later attested by
other detectives checking telephone calls that Pikul was
at *another* hotel, the Warwick, under another borrowed
name, for at least the second half of those predawn
hours. To this day, Delaney remains convinced the suspect set up a complicated ruse: Either he had two decoys
("Joe Pike" and the fleeing second man) at the Barbizon
while he was at the Warwick, or *he* was that second,
fleeing man and ended up at the Warwick. Just who the
decoy could have been—Vinnie Federico? Jim Burns?
Jean-Jacques?—remains a mystery.

But, even more than such cat-and-mouse chases, good
police work often involves sense-numbing patience: the
ability to wait and sit and loiter for hours on end, all for
what could be minimal payoff. Oates and Probst spent
the rest of the night milling around the Barbizon lobby,
examining the exits and refraining from standing near or
talking to one another. Troop L BCI and NYPD Narcotics people were positioned outside. The entire assembled
team were waiting to find and put a tail on Vinnie Federico, figuring he'd eventually lead them to the elusive
Pikul. As two, four, then six and seven uneventful hours
ticked by, Oates drank coffee and kept reminding himself: "This is a murder case, and murder cases aren't
boring, even when they are."

While the two investigators kept watch in the Barbizon
lobby, across town and twenty blocks down, two NYPD
detectives picked up Inga Davidsson from the O. P. Andersson showroom at eleven A.M. and brought her to

Newburgh Hospital to identify Diane. From an undisclosed hiding place, Joe had sent word to Bill Glynn through a friend who identified himself as William Schwartz, an attorney, that he was "too upset by Diane's death to identify her body himself"; and since neither any of the detectives nor Diane's friends thought it wise to ask Diane's elderly father to fly up from Florida for the emotionally taxing task, the identification fell to one of Diane's friends.

Inga walked into the small morgue room, with its ten refrigerators. The sheeted body was inclined by a morgue attendant so Inga could see only Diane's neck and face, all her curls brushed back. The angle made it appear that Diane was sitting, as if for a conversation—yet all color and animation was gone from her face, now a gaunt, pasty mask barely resembling the vivid, expressive woman Inga had known. Inga had volunteered to go because she was by nature more stoic than Carina and Maggie. She cried all the way back to the city.

At 11:45 A.M., Steve Oates rode up to Federico's floor to locate his room in case he and Oates should later have to enter it. As he walked down the long hall taking note of room numbers, a solidly built man of six feet two inches with dark curly hair and a mustache, attired in a business suit, walked out of the very room he was looking for. Now Oates knew what Federico looked like. He took the next elevator down and waited in a corner of the lobby while Federico left his key at the reception desk. As Federico waited outside for the hotel's doorman to hail him a cab, Oates "detailed" one of the five other plainclothesmen to follow him. The officer hurried out a side exit to one of the two unmarked cars parked on opposite sides of the Barbizon. He followed Federico's cab, until he had to radio to Oates that he'd lost it in midtown traffic.

During these same prenoon minutes, a Manhattan-based detective monitoring Pikul's bank and stock accounts told Captain Cahill that significant withdrawals had just been made from at least one of those accounts. The question of whether Pikul was getting ready to flee the country was now deemed pressing.

*   *   *

Oates and Probst saw Federico reenter the Barbizon shortly after two P.M. The lawyer went right to the hotel bar, which occupies a corner of the ground floor. From a discreet distance Oates kept his eyes both on Federico and on the bar's one separate outside door—"I just watched him . . . you know, maybe Pikul was going to walk in and join him for a drink." Probst monitored the front entrance and the lobby itself.

Federico had two drinks, which he downed quickly. Then he rode the elevator up to his floor. Frustrated and impatient, Probst and Oates began the tenth straight hour of their stakeout. In the eleventh hour, at 3:30 P.M., Oates called Cahill. "Bottom line is, Captain, we've come to a standstill. Things are dead in the water. We'd like to be able to talk to Federico." Cahill said he'd call them right back.

Now Cahill had to weigh his desire for an impeccable case against the need to move quickly, both for the sake of the investigators' morale and out of concern for the suspect's likelihood of fleeing. Cahill called Delaney, who agreed that a case isn't closed with handcuffing but with the prosecutor's ability to convince a grand jury that *this* man may well have committed *this* crime. The two meticulous investigators were aware, as Delaney put it, "that we didn't have all our ducks in a row yet. We wanted to tie up some loose ends, to do a complete review of all evidence before we made an arrest." On the other hand, the officers' perfectionism was risky at this late hour. Cahill quickly arranged a conference call with D.A. Alan Joseph and Troop F's Lieutenant James O'Donnell. Recalls Cahill, "We were now seriously running out of people and time. Most of our men had been working twenty-hour days on this case, and we believed Pikul was getting ready to leave town." Joseph and O'Donnell recommended quick action. Cahill called back Delaney, who agreed. "We *do* have enough probable cause," Cahill decided. "Let's make our move." Cahill now called Oates back and instructed him: "Go question Federico. We've got nothing to lose."

At approximately 3:50, Oates and Probst knocked on Federico's door. They introduced themselves, showed their shields and ID cards, and said they were attempting to find Joseph Pikul. "Federico expressed great surprise," Oates recalls. "He had no idea he'd been under any type of surveillance. We entered the room with the game plan of talking to him as long as we could, to see if we could glean any information about Pikul's whereabouts."

Initially, Federico was reluctant to talk, but his reluctance soon gave way. It turned out that he had just had lunch at the Plaza Hotel with Joe Pikul and, to his surprise, he had been eased off the case. This case could have made his career.

After almost forty-five minutes of conversation, Federico finally revealed that Pikul was with his new lawyers Sam Dawson and Charles Clayman at their offices at Madison Avenue and Forty-second Street. Before Oates and Probst could make a move, they needed confirmation of their suspect's location. How would they get that confirmation? Federico told the men that Clayman had said he would call him at five P.M.; Oates figured the dumped lawyer shouldn't be holding his breath. Now Oates and Probst had two choices, each involving a risk. They could have Federico call Clayman before five P.M.; but such an eager, preemptive call might signal Dawson and Clayman that Federico was not calling by and for himself. Or they could have Federico wait until 5:10 to call Clayman; except most office switchboards close at five, and Federico did not have Clayman's direct extension; therefore, says Oates, "the chance to capture Pikul would be completely blown for the night."

At 4:45, Oates had Federico make the call. Clayman's private secretary told Federico that Mr. Clayman would have to call him back. Oates, Probst and Federico waited tensely for five minutes. The phone rang. As Federico lifted the receiver, Oates wrote directions on a legal pad: Ask, Is Pikul okay? was the first. "Federico complied and nodded his head to indicate: Yeah, Pikul's fine," Oates remembers. "Then I write: Ask him if Pikul is there. Federico does, then nods. My next note to Federico is: Tell him you want to speak to him just to say hello and ask him how he's doing—because I want to hear Pikul's voice myself.

"Now, as a result of Federico's request, Pikul gets on the line and there's a three-way conversation taking place between Federico, Clayman and Pikul. I'm overhearing Pikul's voice saying, 'Yeah, I'm fine.' *So now it's written in stone that Pikul is there* . . . although, in the back of my head, I'm thinking: Maybe Federico's got one of those conference phones, and he just put Clayman on hold and called Pikul—who isn't really at the law firm; he's two rooms down in the hotel . . ." At 4:55 P.M., Oates did not have time to indulge this paranoia. "I had to go with the belief that Pikul *was* at the law firm, and that if we didn't get over there right away, the office would close, they'd all be leaving, and that would be it. If we had let Pikul slip through our fingers that evening, we would have lost our ability to track his whereabouts— maybe even for good."*

Oates now called the Newburgh command post. "We know where Pikul is," Oates told Cahill. "Get over there," Cahill ordered. "Let's do it!"

It wasn't easy getting twenty-one blocks downtown in New York City rush hour traffic in an unmarked car at 5:05 P.M. Oates kept thinking, "Pikul probably's leaving that building right now. . . ." After a twenty-five-minute drive, they arrived at 305 Madison. "We park the car anywhere, rush into the lobby. There's a Chase Manhattan Bank there and a big bank of elevators," Oates recalls. "We were planning to go up to the office—Suite 1301; I'll never forget that number, somehow. But I look up at the lights indicating where each elevator is and I see all eight elevators are coming *down*. So the decision is made for us: We just stand there and wait for the elevators to open one by one, hoping Pikul will be in one of them."

The first elevator opened. No Joe Pikul. The second elevator opened. There he was. Oates and Probst walked up to the middle-aged man they recognized from the photograph. Both showed their shields and their ID cards.

---

*If worse came to worst and Pikul, tipped off by Federico's phone call now suspicious of Federico's phone call, had fled the country that evening, "we would have gotten an indictment but possibly never prosecuted the man," says Alan Joseph. "As far as holding the lawyers accountable, all we could do is file a complaint with the Grievance Committee of the New York State Bar."

Oates said, "Mr. Pikul, I'm Investigator Steven Oates from the New York State Police and this is my partner, James Probst. We're taking you into custody on the charge of murder." Pikul looked briefly surprised, then concertedly unemotional. A man at his side, an associate of Dawson and Clayman named Michael Katzenstein, asked Oates if the arrest was on a warrant; Oates said it was.* Pikul said nothing. He looked rumpled, Oates thought, and almost as exhausted as his pursuers. And possibly just as relieved. He did not resist.

Amid the mushrooming attention of the flood of office workers streaming off the elevators, the two investigators, the suspect and the lawyer all rode the elevator up to Suite 1301, where Pikul officially surrendered to custody. Oates called Cahill at the command post. After Cahill talked briefly with Clayman, he got back on the phone with the tired but triumphant investigators. Cahill knew the pair had worked thirty-four straight hours; he wanted to get a relay team to come in and relieve them for the drive to Newburgh, where Pikul would be processed, arraigned and jailed; but, with dozens of men spanning three jurisdictions and accounting for several thousand man-hours already depleted, "we didn't even have any fresh horses left to send."

At about 6:30, Oates and Probst flanked their suspect and ushered him down the elevator and into their car. Probst sat in back with Pikul; Oates took the wheel for the hour-and-a-half-long drive. Now this is where these new AM/FM radios come in handy, Oates thought, as he turned on the sound.

Almost exactly as Pikul was being arrested, Sandra Jarvinen answered her ringing front doorbell. Two men in different uniforms flashed badges and identified themselves as Trooper Gorman from the Plymouth County District Attorney's Office and Sergeant Bongarzone from

---

*According to Captain Cahill, the warrant Oates mentioned was not on his person but was still in the paperwork stage. But the legality of Oates's arrest, had it ever been questioned, would be covered because the warrant was being processed and because the arrest was made in a public place.

the Norwell Police Department. Gorman said: "Miss Jarvinen, we want to gather some information if we could on one Joseph Pikul."

"Is Joe in trouble?" she asked.

"Yes," Gorman replied, getting right to the point. "He's a suspect in the murder of his present wife."

Sandra then said: "I'm lucky it wasn't me. I knew that someday his temper was going to get the best of him."

Seated in the living room of what Gorman perceived as a "very nice," clearly "upper-income" two-story house, Gorman and Bongarzone walked Sandra briefly through the story of her marriage to Joseph Pikul. She seemed nervous. She spoke of his brilliance, his drinking, his violence and the terrorized complaints she had lodged with the Norwell Police Department. She spoke of the 1974 divorce and mentioned that she was now in the process of suing him for back alimony. She said that she had flown into New York on Thursday, October 22—exactly a week ago—to discuss the lawsuit; that he had met her at the airport in his limousine; that they had then gone out to dinner with his children; and that he'd mentioned that he and his wife, whose name she said she did not know, were having marital problems. She then returned home and had not, she said, spoken to him since.

Gorman sensed that something about Sandra's story did not add up. It was strange that a childless marriage, terminated thirteen years ago by a woman who was now quite wealthy, would produce such a freshly-pursued alimony claim. It was also strange that a man of Pikul's resources hadn't settled the suit long ago. Then there was the mixture of the adversarial lawsuit and the friendly evening with the children. Jarvinen's story simply did not make sense. "I felt that she was not telling us everything," Gorman says. "That they were really at that restaurant talking about something else."

Sandra said she had not spoken to Pikul after she flew back to Boston a week ago, but that he'd left one message on her answering machine—"How are you? I'll call you back"—later in the week. Gorman left Bongarzone to finish the questioning and went back to the C-Pack's headquarters. He called Venezia in Newburgh to report that Miss Jarvinen had voluntarily vouched for one of the phone-machine messages, but failed to mention the other one. Gorman returned and questioned her about that second call. Oh, yes, she said—she had simply forgotten it. It was the same type of call, just a felicitation. She had erased both messages after she heard them. But then, she said, she routinely cleared her machine's tape every day. At this point, "I felt there was something she was withholding. She knew more than she was saying," Gorman says.

Gorman now questioned her about Vincent Federico, since there were toll calls traced from her to him and from Pikul's credit card to him as well. "She said he was a personal friend of hers, that she was dating him; in fact, she was expecting him that evening to take her to dinner and to a show." (Federico, of course, was two hundred miles away in Manhattan.) Did Federico maintain contact with Pikul after that initial credit-card phone call? Gorman now asked. Sandra said that, as far as she knew, he did not. In fact, Federico had gone so far as to get angry at *her* for going to New York to see her ex-husband last week.

As Gorman and Bongarzone were leaving, they handed Sandra their calling cards and asked her to call them if she heard from Joe. (Word of his arrest had not yet reached the pair.) She might also call them, Gorman said, if she happened to remember anything else that they might want to know.

Oates was wending his way out of New York City, according to Joe Pikul's directions. Once over the George Washington Bridge, Oates and Probst started talking about their young children. They were killing time. They mentioned Sesame Place, a children's amusement park on the Pennsylvania–New Jersey line. "That's when Pikul began to chime in about his two kids and how he loved them," Oates recalls. "How he wanted to take them to Sesame Place, too. 'My children are the best part of me,' he said." He began to sob, and launched into his standard rant against Diane's allegedly hiring "a different baby-sitter every night." Now the words started pouring out, "That's why I did it. She's such a bitch. She deserved it. I never did anything wrong before in my life. Well, I can't change it now. How much will the bail be?"

Probst, seated next to Pikul in the back of the car, heard every word of this remarkable outburst. The words would almost certainly be admissable in court because they were spontaneous and unsolicited, he realized. Oates, in the front seat, felt the same excitement. He could hear the general incriminating nature of Pikul's account; it's just that he couldn't make out every word because of the music on the radio. Pikul's most important confession, "I did it" was lost to Oates.

Oates and Probst delivered Pikul to Venezia and Tripodo at the Troop F barracks at about 8:30 P.M. Tripodo remembers he thought the new prisoner "seemed so hyper and excitable, we thought he was on amphetamines. First thing he wanted to do was use the bathroom. When he came out he was already talking—just splurting things, really. Mostly, he was knocking Diane—rambling on about her all night: How she was only working for her ego and because she wanted to get out of the house. How he hated that she went back to work, how he was so jealous she had a boyfriend, he would question her if she came home ten minutes late. He shot back and forth in time. You'd be talking to him about one thing and he'd be talking back when he was in Switzerland: 'Oh my God, I was over in Europe and she's getting baby-sitters all the time. . . .' That was it: the baby-sitters. To him, that was the very worst thing."

Joe's talking presented a problem; Tripodo and Venezia were not supposed to interrogate him because they knew he had a lawyer and that lawyer was not present (a fact that seemed odd to both investigators). Yet it looked like the prisoner was dying to talk—should they be saint-like pillars of procedural virtue and actually shut the guy up? Venezia himself had been recently divorced—his wife had gone all the way to England when she left him; mentioning this, Venezia knew, would get Pikul talking about his own wife. But Venezia had to get him processed first, and called in a uniformed trooper to take Pikul to be fingerprinted and photographed. While he sat waiting, Joe Tripodo, Jr., also an investigator, was Pikul's guard. Later, on the witness stand, the young Tripodo would testify that the prisoner, sometimes sobbing, said during this time that his wife was an "evil and malicious person"; that "she tried to kill me, not physically but mentally. . . . She tried to break me down. I just couldn't take it anymore. I don't care if you guys give me ten or twenty years. I don't care what penalty I have to pay. I think everybody's just better off without her."

A few miles away, Alan Joseph came home to a message that Charles Clayman had called. The Chief Assistant District Attorney got on the phone to the Manhattan lawyer and told him his client was being arraigned, but that it might take some time. "This isn't like Manhattan, with twenty-four-hour arraignments," Joseph explained. "They've got to bring him to a local justice court when they get a judge lined up."

While Pikul was pouring his heart out to Tripodo, Jr., he seemed to have developed an appetite. No problem, the F squad men said. In fact, were it not for Oates and Probst bringing him in, the F troop investigators would right now be at a colleague's retirement party at a restaurant down the road. "Since we'd already paid for our tickets," Tripodo, Sr., says, "we just had trays of cold cuts sent in." The prisoner scarfed down "three or four" sandwiches from the fixings on the festively garnished tray during what may have been the only catered murder prearraignment in Orange County history.

Joe was returned from processing to Robert Venezia's office in the barracks at ten P.M. Venezia read him his Miranda rights—the first time they had been read to him—and filled out an arrest report, a short list of questions known to investigators as the General Five. Once Venezia completed the report, his prisoner took the opportunity to begin complaining about his newly hired attorneys. "I had to sign over $250,000 to them," Pikul said (the figure presumably accounting for the large withdrawal of stock funds discovered earlier in the day). "The least they could have done was come here with me." Then he smiled. "But they won't get the money—I stopped payment on the check."

Pikul's rueful smiling wasn't reserved for the matter of his lawyers alone. "There's a hook to this case. . . ." he said, leadingly. Venezia did not rise to the bait; clearly the "hook" he seemed so proud of would emerge.

"Where did you bring her?" Pikul demanded.

Venezia answered: "The St. Luke's Hospital morgue."
"Was an autopsy done?"
Venezia said, "Yes."
"Was she checked for AIDS?"
"I don't know," Venezia said. (She was not.) Venezia thought he understood what the "hook" was now.*

Pikul asked if the autopsy showed whether or not his wife had had sex recently. Venezia, again, said he did not know.

"What's the charge against me?" Pikul asked. Venezia said: "Second degree murder."

"My only hope is to beat this thing on a technicality," Pikul mused. "I killed her for no particular reason." Yet he did give Venezia "reasons": "This whole thing," he said, indicating the marriage, "began to go bad in July." He mentioned the incipient divorce, the "blackmailing," the private detective Diane had hired. He told Venezia that he was a cross-dresser, that his wife had betrayed this secret to all her friends. "My life is over," he said, and he requested that someone take him out and shoot him.

At 11:15, Joe asked if he could be taken to see his wife. "Let's go see the stiff," were his words to Tripodo, Jr. The Tripodos and Venezia drove Joe to St. Luke's Hospital, and the two investigators led their prisoner to the window through which Diane's body was visible, propped upright on a reclining table. "Yes, that's her," Venezia recalls him saying, emotionlessly. "She has no makeup on," Pikul said to Joe, Jr. "She'd be very upset if she knew we were looking at her like this."

At about the same time Joe was making these remarks in the hospital morgue, Sandra Jarvinen—unaware of Joe's arrest—stood at her front door, bathrobe over her nightgown, letting in two policemen. The Norwell PD was responding to an anxious telephone call they had received from Jarvinen some minutes before. She showed a photograph of Joe to the officers, requesting protection

*By ruling of Judge Thomas J. Byrne, after motions by Pikul's eventual attorney Ron Bekoff, Venezia was not allowed to testify about this portion of the conversation either at the pretrial hearings or at Pikul's criminal trial.

from him. It was like 1974 all over again, except now
Joe had proved he could live up to his threats.

Friday, October 30

The Tripodos and Venezia drove Joe back to the Troop
F barracks at 12:30 A.M. The sight of Diane's body, the
deepening understanding of his predicament and the lateness of the hour had made him vulnerable. He stopped
obsessing angrily about Diane and turned his worried
thoughts to his children and himself. Where were Blake
and Claudia? he asked Venezia. After their one night in
foster care, he was told, they were back with the Bergelts. What would happen to them now? That was up to
the child welfare authorities and the court. Where was
he going to be arraigned and what jail was he going to?
New Windsor Town Hall and Orange County Jail.

Joe Tripodo, Sr., considers himself an easygoing man
who always gets along with people, even men arrested
for murder. With his disarming manner and polite approach—"after almost thirty years on this job, I still
don't have the lingo down," he says with canny self-ef-
facement—he is a highly skilled interrogator who inspires
people to drop their guards. He and Pikul had been developing a rapport, and Pikul had liked his son Joey,
who had offered sympathy when Pikul broke down and
cried. The three Joes were connected, they joked. Pikul
was surely too worn out and frightened to become taciturn now, Tripodo reasoned.

Tripodo pulled up a chair, positioned it facing Pikul,
sat down and moved his head as close to Pikul's as he
could get it. "When you're far away," Tripodo explains,
"a person can lie; but when you're close up, he can't."
Touching Pikul's arm Tripodo gently urged Joe to talk
about the moments before the murder. They'd been at a
beach called Little Albert's Landing—they'd gone there
to finish an argument so the children wouldn't wake up.
(He was "so emphatic about being at that beach, and
'partially burying' Diane in the sand," Tripodo recalls,
that Tripodo, alone among all the investigators, remains
convinced that Diane was murdered there and not in or
around the house.)

Tripodo listened sympathetically. If Glynn's gift to the tag-team investigation had been streetsmarts, and Delaney's, meticulousness, and Oates's, doggedness, then Tripodo's was intimacy.

"How'd you do it, Joe?" he asked, in almost a whisper.

Joe tried not to fall for it. "*You* know how . . ." he said.

"No. No, I don't know. You tell me," Tripodo softly pressed.

"You *know*," Joe insisted.

"No, I *don't* know. How'd you do it?"

"You *do* know."

"No, I don't. I want *you* to tell me." This volley of insinuation and coaxing went on for several more minutes. Finally, Joe Pikul gave in. He simply put his two hands to his own neck and simulated a choking motion.

We've got him, Tripodo said to himself. *We've got him—and it's all admissible.*

He was wrong.

At 2:15 A.M., Judge Donald Suttlehan phoned to say he was in the courtroom, ready to arraign. "Okay, Joe," Tripodo said, "before we leave here, you've got to take all your clothes off."

"I *can't* take my clothes off," Joe said. After all the wild, confessional talk that had gone on over the last six hours, this sudden modesty surprised Tripodo. "Can't I do it in the bathroom?" Joe asked.

"No, Joe," the investigator said. "You've got to do it right here."

"Look, I'll come *out* naked," he pleaded.

"No dice," said Tripodo.

So, warily, in the back of the squadroom, the suspect submitted to the stripdown search. He slipped his shirt over his head, dropped his pants, and there Joe Pikul stood before the officers—in a woman's bra, panties and panty hose. The officers noted what Venezia now calls a "scratch from his stomach to the back on his right side. I really wasn't sure what it was from." Tripodo asked Joe how he got the scratch; Joe said that he'd gotten it playing with his kids. Later, in Joe's defense lawyers' hands, that innocent scratch would be significantly transformed.

Diane's murder covered the full front page of the final edition of the *New York Post*. WIFE SLAIN—NAB STOX WHIZ went the headline. In one edition, an unflattering photograph of Diane—apparently taken just before her "eye tuck" of 1986—appeared to the left; in another edition, that same picture was superimposed next to a photograph of Claudia Pikul as a toddler. The story took up all of page three, half of which held two pictures. One showed a trench-coated Joe in glasses, hiding his face in his hands, being led to the arraignment; the other was of Diane's recently hired housekeeper/baby-sitter, Carolyn Murray, dabbing a tear in front of pictures drawn by Claudia.

Among the many people whose eyes went right to that headline that Friday, October 30, was Paul Kurland, a portly forty-year-old corporate securities lawyer and teacher of trial advocacy. Who was this STOX WHIZ?— someone he knew? Kurland wondered. It turned out Kurland *did* know the accused man. Joe Pikul had come to Kurland's office at the firm Snow, Becker and Krauss last June, "looking a little unkempt, unfocused, in a rumpled tan raincoat," Kurland recalled. Pikul was seeking a lawyer through whom to sue the organizers of a tax shelter he had bought into. Since a lawsuit had already been brought by a group of the tax shelter's other investors, Kurland had talked himself out of a job. "I discouraged him from retaining us to represent him. I said, 'Why underwrite the cost of the whole suit yourself and take the risk of getting nothing?' I never heard from him again."

By midafternoon on Friday, Kurland received a call from the same mutual friend who had sent Joe to him in June. Kurland was asked to help raise the $35,000 bond money for Joe Pikul's $350,000 bail. By the end of the day, Kurland was on the phone with Joe himself. "He asked me if I would make sure his children were okay— that was his one hundred percent overriding concern," the lawyer says. " 'I want to make sure they're all right. I want to protect them,' he said."

*　　*　　*

While Kurland, in his Manhattan office, talked to Joseph Pikul about his children, Trooper Gorman, at Plymouth County C-Pack headquarters in Massachusetts, received a call from Hugh Scott, who explained that he was representing Sandra Jarvinen, and Ms. Jarvinen *did* have more information to give Trooper Gorman. Scott, Gorman recalls, "said his client 'was almost an eyewitness to the murder of Mrs. Pikul,' and she wanted to give us a statement." The minute he got off the phone with the Boston lawyer, Gorman called Tripodo, Sr., and Venezia, who put in a strategy call to Alan Joseph. The two investigators then made the four-hour drive to Boston to meet Gorman and Norwell police sergeant Bongarzone in Hugh Scott's office.

"Sandra was there in the office but we were talking to her lawyer first," Tripodo recalls. "He wanted me to call Alan Joseph and make sure that she wouldn't be criminally responsible for holding back information. He ran down her story. I called Alan Joseph and ran it by him. Joseph gave a tentative okay* and I relayed that to Scott.

"Then we took an actual written statement from Sandra. I asked the questions; Bobby [Venezia] typed her answers on Hugh Scott's typewriter. Although she implicated Pikul—no question about it—she didn't really come out and say that much. When he spoke of 'getting rid of' and so forth, you knew what he was talking about, even though he never actually said 'Diane.' We all knew in our minds what Pikul was talking about but on paper that statement was a little vague. She didn't really implicate herself that much. Reading it, you couldn't say, 'What—you mean you *knew* he was looking to bury a body?' "

After she left Scott's office, Sandra began to worry

*Alan Joseph says today that an immunity assurance for Jarvinen was unnecessary. "Sandra Jarvinen had committed no crime," Joseph explains. "New York State doesn't have accessory-after-the-fact. If you witness a crime or if someone admits to you that he committed a crime, you're under no obligation to come forward to the authorities. Only if someone tells you, 'I committed a crime—here, hide this gun,' can you charge the recipient of the gun with hindering an investigation." Sandra's erasure of Joe's answering machine messages wasn't considered akin to gun-harboring.

about her safety. And Alan Joseph, who would fiercely protect the identity of his star witness during the months ahead, tried to avoid thinking about the possibility of another female body being found in Orange County once Joseph Pikul was released on bail.

On Sunday, November 1, knowing nothing of the statement Sandra had made and her planned appearance before the Orange County grand jury, Joseph Pikul waited, in jeans, a sweater and running shoes, in his cell at the Orange County jail to meet two lawyers to talk about rounding up bail money. Paul Kurland was one of these men; the other was Paul's friend Ronald Bekoff, a former Nassau County district attorney. Kurland had spoken highly to Joe of Bekoff's skill as a criminal lawyer, and Joe had asked to meet him.

Once the two arrived, Kurland recalls that Joe talked mostly about his children. "I made some phone calls to make sure they were situated with the Bergelts and left Joe to talk about the criminal stuff with Ronny."

Neither man was officially retained by Joe Pikul. Dawson and Clayman, still in Joe's employ, were currently preparing his bail motion. In addition, Joe had asked Kurland his opinion of other criminal lawyers. (Juggling a lot of attorneys at once, Kurland soon came to see, was part of Joe Pikul's modus operandi.) But Kurland and Bekoff agreed to act as advisors regarding Joe's respective civil and criminal options. If Joe Pikul's dilemma identified him as a desperate man, his professional stature, wealth and arrogance marked him as a man accustomed to winning. Moreover, the bizarreness of his circumstances foretold, to both men, an attractively challenging, high profile case.

Before they left, Joe asked Kurland to help make sure his children were all right. Impressed by the prisoner's fatherly earnestness, Kurland said he would do so.

This would mark the start of a unique legal battle during which Diane Pikul's final grim premonition would come true.

PART V
KILLER TAKES ALL

Chapter 10

When one person kills another . . . in a time so short as to seem indecent . . . the dead person ceases to exist as an identifiable figure. . . . She is only a figure in a historic event. We inevitably turn away from the past, toward the ongoing reality. And the ongoing reality is the criminal. He usurps the compassion that is justly his victim's due. It is not so in the world of the poets. They understood the necessity of maintaining the balance of sympathy. With them, the voice from the grave is . . . a reality as profound, as startling, and as real . . . as the figure of the murderer. But the courtroom is a drama without the voice of the poet or the voice from the dead.

Willard Gaylin, M.D., psychiatrist and ethicist, and director of the Hastings Center, from the preface to his 1982 book, The Killing of Bonnie Garland: A Question of Justice

Diane was buried in the Whitmore family plot at River View Cemetery in South Bend, Indiana, on Thursday, November 5, a cold, misty day. Services were held at Westminster Presbyterian Church, which she had attended as a child. None of Diane's childhood friends—the girls with whom she'd lip-synced in the mirror to the Crewcuts' songs and traded Nancy Drew books—learned of her death in enough time to attend; the gravestone carver, not otherwise instructed, hewed literally to the name on her death certificate, Diane W. Pikul, obliterating the only name by which she was known in her hometown. She was buried in an arbitrary dress, hastily purchased by Gretchen Whitmore at a Tampa mall dress store. Heavy winds prevented the mourners from going to the grave site. Diane was buried, unattended, by the undertaker.

Blake and Claudia flew to South Bend with their grandfather and, after the funeral, the assembled relatives held a small meeting in the Whitmores' room at the Marriott Hotel. There the fate of the children was discussed. None of Diane's relatives objected to either of Joe's sister's children and their spouses—the Bergelts in Manhattan, with whom the children had been staying, or Joe's nephew Ed Pawlowski and his wife, Lauren Pawlowski, in Washington, D.C.—becoming Claudia and Blake's guardians. In fact, these two couples were cited as such in Diane's own will. Since Diane left her entire estate to Joe, however, it is likely that he had controlled the will-making, and that she had acquiesced to his choice of guardians as a matter of course. But what if neither the Bergelts *nor* the Pawlowskis proved willing, or suitable, to be permanent guardians?

"In that case, Michael and I will be happy to take the children," said Kathleen Norman O'Guin, Don Whitmore's niece. A delicate-featured brunette, Kathy O'Guin physically resembled the cousin with whom she had been in pleasant if intermittent contact; but their sensibilities were very different indeed. If Diane was style, then Kathy was substance. Where Diane had an amateur writer's eager irony, Kathy had a scientist's serene pragmatism. She was a forty-three-year-old former nurse and schoolteacher who had recently received her master's degree in developmental genetics and was now a molecular research technician. William, her husband of three years, had a Ph.D. in cell biology. A Southerner and a gentleman, everyone called him by his nickname, Mike. Both he and Kathy worked at the Albert Einstein College of Medicine in the Bronx, she researching Alzheimer's disease, he doing advanced studies on cell structure and cancer. They had no children of their own.

The O'Guins owned a three-bedroom house with a backyard in Yonkers, New York, drove a sensible American-made economy car and travelled often to see their families in the South. Both were active in their local Episcopalian church and participated in local charities. "We are very normal," Kathy would later say.

After Kathy and Mike said they would be willing to act as parents to Blake and Claudia, Don Whitmore called Raoul Felder in New York. Whitmore had not known the name of his daughter's divorce lawyer until that very morning. By sheer coincidence, he was watching *Good Morning America* just before the funeral and saw the divorce lawyer being interviewed. "Do you always win your cases?" Felder was asked. "I wish I could say that were true," he answered, solemnly. "Just a week ago, in fact, one of my clients was strangled and bludgeoned to death by her husband." Realizing that the attorney was talking about his daughter, Whitmore listened hard for Felder's name, then immediately called the attorney's New York office.

When Whitmore was put through to Felder, he bluntly asked how much of Diane's retainer was available to be refunded; Felder told him that nothing was left. On her funeral day, it was perhaps the perfect conversation between the first and the last male protector of a woman whose life was bookended by an overriding concern about money. But, twenty minutes later, Felder called Whitmore back and said: "I have good news for you—I checked, and there's ten thousand dollars left." He would give it to the children, he vowed, adding: "I will do whatever fighting I have to do to make sure that those children are taken care of properly."

Back in Florida after the funeral, Whitmore called Felder again—this time with the names of the O'Guins as contingency custody petitioners. Neither man imagined the protracted court battle to come, or that this phone call would pave the way for Raoul Felder's unlikely transformation from an extractor of copious alimonies into a champion of children's rights.

Two days after the funeral, on Saturday, November 7, Diane's New York friends held a memorial service at St. Luke in the Fields Church on Hudson Street in the Village. It was a sad and tender ceremony, with organ music at beginning and end. Diane's last writing teacher, Allan Gurganus, came. So did her once bohemian lover, Doug Thompson, now a successful stockbroker. And so, on his own time and in his off-duty clothes, did Bill Glynn. Gloria Archer read the "To every thing there is a season . . ." passage from Ecclesiastes; Linda McNamera read the "New Jerusalem" verse from Revelations; Barbara Martin read from the Book of John; Inga Davidsson sang a solo hymn; Carolyn Gaiser read a selection by Gerald Manley Hopkins; and everyone stood and together read the Twenty-third Psalm and the Lord's Prayer. But it was Maggie Gari's reading from Diane's own short story, "A Fine Romance—The Fantasist and the Star," about her friendship with her hairdresser, that provided the emotional high point of the service. For this was the story in which Diane equated her attraction to "glamorous" violence in men with flight from her drearily normal Midwestern destiny. She had foretold her fate in that story. Listening to it, Ann and Linda and Carina had the same anguished thought: Why couldn't Diane's knowledge have been power? Why couldn't she have just gotten out?

In the section Maggie read, Diane envisioned the city as a field of lights, in which "the lights that represent my children seem brighter than the others." Meanwhile, in Washington, D.C., those very children, just back from their mother's funeral, were getting to know the Pawlowskis. It was thought by Joe and Paul Kurland that they would be better off there, away from New York, out of the limelight.

Two days later, on Monday, November 9, Joseph Pikul made bail. He had put up $180,000 of his own money, and a group of investor friends had arranged for the balance. The $350,000 bond required by Orange County was now guaranteed. Immediately after he walked out of jail, Joe told Paul Kurland, "I *want* to see my kids."

Kurland knew this would not be easy—and that it would have to be delicately arranged. For one thing, a condition of Joe's bail was that he not leave the state. Even if the Pawlowskis sent the children to New York to be with Joe at the duplex, Kurland knew that their reunion in Greenwich Village would make Pikul a sitting duck for the press—and not merely because of the notoriety of his case alone. A week ago, another murder had occurred in the Pikul neighborhood. Six-year-old Lisa Steinberg had been beaten to death, allegedly by her illegally adoptive father, attorney Joel Steinberg. Steinberg had also consistently battered the woman he had lived with for twelve years, former children's book editor Hedda Nussbaum. Steinberg and Nussbaum lived around the corner from the Pikuls, a half block east on Tenth Street. The horror of this second crime had moved Diane's murder clear off the public-attention map. The anomoly of fatal abuse inflicted on a child of educated professionals, and by at least one of those parents; the revelation of a den of iniquity in a choice landmark building on one of the loveliest Village streets; the fact of such senseless squalor and brutality in the midst of seemingly enviable lives: All of this, at once tragic, lurid and entirely incomprehensible, had riveted New York. Lisa Steinberg's death was in the air the city had breathed all that week and indeed for many months thereafter. People were up in arms about the bureaucratic and attitudinal failings that allowed abused children to go undetected and unrescued.

Wreaths and hand-written letters collected on a makeshift shrine to Lisa on the stoop of the Steinberg apartment, regularly visited by local TV camera crews. Much attention was turned to the "cracks in the system" through which Lisa's case had "slipped." The city's Special Services for Children was called on the carpet, its unwieldy bureaucracy full of tired workers who were bound by a greater, hidden culprit—the law itself.

In the midst of their grieving, Diane's friends felt Lisa Steinberg's death as a second awful tragedy. How do you explain these deaths to children? Maggie Gari wondered as she walked her five-year-old son up Sixth Avenue, past the press-besieged Steinberg apartment and the shuttered Pikul duplex, to P.S. 41. There, a "grief counselor" was now trying to help the children deal with their schoolmate Lisa's death.

Not only had Diane and Lisa Steinberg been murdered and Hedda Nussbaum severely battered, but the trial of noted minimalist sculptor Carl Andre—accused of pushing his Cuban-born wife, artist Ana Mendieta, out the window of their thirty-fourth floor apartment two years before—was about to begin. So was the trial of "preppy" Robert Chambers, who strangled young Jennifer Levin to death in Central Park in early September 1986. Like Diane, both Ana Mendieta and Jennifer Levin had been feisty, expansive women. Among their multitude of female friends was a deeply unsettling hunch that these deaths were spontaneous male paybacks for feminist advances during the last twenty years. Was the "buck" of women's liberation really stopping "here"—in the deadly power of latently psychotic middle-class men's fists? "Thank God for our normal passive-aggressive husbands" became the grim but grateful joke among Diane's friends.

Amid the swirl of tragedy, these women tried to steady themselves with what seemed like a logical assumption: The outrage at the "system" that was engendered by the Steinberg tragedy would *have* to work in favor of Diane's children. After all, the SSC, charged with monitoring Blake and Claudia, was obviously being held to the highest standards right now; they would not be permitted to make so profound a mistake again.

Diane's friends' logic would prove to be naive. However many "cracks" were patched in the system, a formidable chasm remained: the body of case law, in New York State, and in most others, that recognizes a fundamental, constitutionally protected right of natural parents to keep and raise their own children, and demands an almost impossibly strong case be made by petitioners who seek to take that right away. Legal affirmation of the primacy of parental rights goes back one hundred years, to cases like the U.S. Court of Appeals' *Finlay* v. *Finlay*. Furthermore, U.S. Supreme Court cases such as *Stanley* v. *Illinois, Wisconsin,* v. *Yoder,* and *Pierce* v. *Society of Sisters* have affirmed at the highest level that the parent-child relationship is a fundamental right protected by the Constitution, with which states cannot interfere without compelling necessity.

But if we are a country that fiercely believes in family privacy and civil liberties, we are also, as De Tocqueville noted, a country of optimists. American laws are written from the assumption that parents, *by their very nature,* will act in the best interests of their children. Indeed, the very first child-abuse case prosecuted in this country occurred in 1874, when a New York girl named Mary Ellen was scissors-stabbed by her parents. An animal-protection advocate named Henry Bergh, who had recently founded the ASPCA, convinced the courts of the novel idea that children ought to be deemed just as needy of protection from abuse as cats and dogs.

One century and fourteen years later, a different social reality—high rates of divorce, single parenthood, poverty, stress and drug addiction—had brought the frequency of child abuse to alarming levels; but the tacit optimism of early America, which gave a kind of blanket protection to parents, still held sway.

Most child-abuse cases severe enough to reach the courts today are committed by men: either the child's natural father or its mother's boyfriend*; and the overwhelming majority of spouse violence cases are also committed by men. Thus, abusive family men can be considered one of the few groups in America who have benefited from this mutually unintended marriage of right and left: Between the pro-patriarchal-family stance of the conservatives and the liberals' reverence for defendants' rights and due process, a violent husband/father entering the court system stands a good chance of going unprosecuted. As Dr. Vincent J. Fontana, head of New York's Mayor's Task Force on Child Abuse during the Koch administration, explains, "The defendant is always protected, while the burden of proof is on the child who has been abused or is at risk of it."

Word of Joe's release from jail was late to reach Diane's friends. Claudia and Blake were with the Bergelts from the time their father had gone into hiding on October 28 until they were flown to South Bend for their mother's funeral on November 5. Claudia's school lessons and homework were couriered back and forth to her by the mother of one of her classmates, a woman we will call Sarah Brockton. Sarah had learned from the Bergelts that Joe was about to make bail. Alarmed, she went to the school's headmaster, Kingsley Ervin, but the head-

*According to the preliminary results of a major survey being done by Barbara E. Smith, Ph.D. and Sharon R. Goretsky, M.S. under the auspices of the American Bar Association through a grant from the National Center on Child Abuse: Of those prosecutors (in American counties of a population of 50,000 or more) who replied that they're prosecuting more child-abuse cases now than they have in the past, most said the perpetrators in these cases are usually males in a primary caretaking relationship to the child (i.e., father, stepfather, mother's romantic partner). The preliminary findings reflect three hundred jurisdictions.

master was in favor of giving Joe the benefit of the doubt. He told Sarah Brockton that she had no proof that Joe had done anything to cause his wife's death and later called her with what he thought would be reassuring news. "I've just spoken to Joe," Sarah remembers his words, "and he's cheerful, he's rational, he says everything was a dreadful mistake and will be cleared up." Sarah was aghast. *"Cheerful?"* she said. "Cheerful is hardly the proper state of mind for someone whose wife has been dead for only two weeks."

Sarah turned to Laurie Jones, managing editor of *New York* magazine, who had two sons at the school. Laurie was appalled. Later that week, when Sarah and Laurie learned that Joe would also get the children back that weekend, the two women, Laurie recalls, "became insanely emotional about the injustice of it." A similar feeling had been developing among other mothers at Grace Church, especially after a midweek parents' meeting. There, emotions ran high, yet, Sarah recalls, "Kingsley Ervin said Joe was a kind and loving person." "He did seem to be taking Joe's side," says another parent of the headmaster's attitude that evening and on subsequent occasions. Ervin says, "The feeling on the part of many parents is that they wanted nothing to do with him. Most people assumed he was guilty. But the law is quite clear on the subject [of innocence-until-proved-guilty]."

The two women mobilized. Laurie called Manhattan D.A. Robert Morgenthau and made sure he knew Joe would be with his kids that weekend. Sarah called detectives in Orange County to find out where Pikul was planning to take the children. Sarah had no qualms about pushing until she got answers. "A number of us mothers discussed it, and we agreed that if we were in the situation Diane was now in, we'd want the same thing done for our kids."

Morgenthau's Assistant D.A., Mary O'Donoghue, of the office's Child Abuse Unit, made a mission of getting the kids away from Pikul. The oldest daughter in a family of fifteen children, and the mother of three young sons, Mary was energetic and unflappable. She blended a feminist's perspective on patriarchal law with deeply traditional values—and brought both to her work against domestic abuse. She reacted passionately to the fact that

Pikul's arraignment for murdering his wife could not be used to legally impugn his fitness as a father. "What's more abusive to children than taking their mother!" she would frequently exclaim over the next months. She searched for a minor act of neglect Pikul may have committed. "Did he ever leave the kids in the car for ten minutes while he went into a store for a pack of cigarettes?" she would ask Diane's friends. "I can't get him for murder but I can get him for *that.*"

Given the atmosphere of outrage among Diane's friends and supporters, Paul Kurland did not want the freshly bailed Joe Pikul to resurface, hand in hand with his children, in the neighborhood. "You'd be better off seeing them in a structured environment far away from the Village or the Hamptons—somewhere the press won't be camping out," Kurland advised Joe. Joe knew the attorney was right about this, and he accepted the suggestion that he rendezvous with the children at the Concord Hotel in the Catskills.

By Thursday, November 12, it was ascertained by Sarah Brockton, Laurie Jones and Mary O'Donoghue's spadework that Blake and Claudia had been flown into New York and that Joe was on his way with them to the Concord Hotel, in the Sullivan County town of Monticello, where he had made reservations under an assumed name. The next day Mary O'Donoghue called the Special Services for Children's child abuse hotline and filed a report through the central register in Albany that two children who may have witnessed their father's murder of their mother were now with the man at the Concord Hotel. That night, a Sullivan County caseworker reported back to Mary that Pikul and the children had been located at the Concord, but that since there was no evidence of neglect or abuse, or of the children's being in "imminent danger" from him, there was nothing that office could do.

By now Morgenthau and O'Donoghue were very concerned. They applied further pressure and, at 1:30 A.M. on Saturday, November 13, three state troopers and the caseworker entered Joe's room at the Concord with orders to take the children into protective custody for the night. The children were asleep and Joe indignantly refused. He called Ron Bekoff at Bekoff's home on Long Island. Bekoff knew that Pikul's lawyer Paul Kurland—"by coincidence," Kurland says—was staying at a neighboring Catskills hotel, Kutsher's, with his wife and a group from their Long Island temple. He told Joe he'd get Paul over there fast.

Kurland, wakened by Bekoff's call, quickly dressed and drove over to the Concord to confront the troopers. "I said, 'Look, just don't wake the kids—that would be traumatic. They're tired from a long day and a Washington-to-New York flight. They're only visiting their father for the weekend. There's nothing to be concerned about, but *if* you're concerned, why don't you search Mr. Pikul for weapons and then stay in the room here until the children wake up and then we'll all go to court.' "

.he troopers and caseworkers turned down Kurland's invitation to wait in the room for seven more hours. Kurland then phoned the Sullivan County Family Court judge, Anthony Kane, at his home, waking him up. Kane declined to interfere, so the children were wakened and taken into foster care.

Clearly, the timing of the troopers' arrival was unfortunate; waking the children and spiriting them off in the middle of the night can't have been good for them. Kurland saw the event as positioning his client as the wronged and reasonable father struggling against a child protection system shifted into overdrive by the Steinberg case.

A hearing took place Monday morning, November 15, at Sullivan County Family Court. Judge Anthony Kane was to decide if the children, in foster care for two days, would be returned to Pikul or not. By now, Bob Wayburn—the Associate General Counsel in charge of Family Court operations for New York City's Human Resources Administration (HRA), the parent agency of the SSC—was watching the case with concern. Pleasant-faced and even-featured, Wayburn grew up on a farm in Pennsylvania and had barely set foot in Manhattan before attending NYU Law School. His calm and deliberate manner belied his twenty-year-long career as a tough and fervent litigator on behalf of children in situations of abuse and danger. It was Wayburn's job to oversee the city's hundred and ten attorneys who prosecuted about twenty thousand child abuse and neglect cases yearly in Family Court.

On the morning of Judge Kane's upstate hearing, Wayburn was in Manhattan, knee-deep in litigation on behalf of Joel Steinberg and Hedda Nussbaum's "adopted" baby son Mitchell. His natural mother, Nicole Smigiel, wanted to resume custody. (She won that right and renamed her son Travis Christian Smigiel.) Soon, he would begin actively litigating another highly publicized case—this time taking a position against the forcible return to Zimbabwe of the nine-year-old son of an attache to that country's mission to the United Nations. The boy, Terence Karamba, was placed in foster care by the SSC after teachers at his Queens school found his body profoundly scarred and welted ("his back looked like a venetian blind," said one Legal Aid lawyer), the result, according to city officials, of beatings by his father administered with an electrical extension cord while he was suspended from a ceiling. Terence was terrified of the man and wanted to stay with his foster family. Wayburn began an abuse proceeding.

But Terence's father, Floyd Karamba, who returned to Zimbabwe, had diplomatic immunity—a privilege the U.S. State Department, with thousands of its own employees abroad, did not want to rescind. Wayburn's child abuse suit was dismissed and the State Department, acting on behalf of Zimbabwe under diplomatic law, ordered Terence returned to officials of the Zimbabwean mission to the UN. During his foster care agency's attempt to comply with the State Department—on New Years Day, 1988—Terence opened the door of a moving car in which he was being transported. Upon returning to his foster home, he wrestled away from the grasp of his foster father and attempted to jump out the second floor window. Several days later, U.S. marshals served Terence's foster father with a writ of habeas corpus; in reaction, Terence crawled under his bed.

Bob Wayburn would spend most of his time from December 1987, through February 1988, on the Karamba case, fighting the State Department in five separate appellate, circuit and district courts, as well as serving a futile stay application to the United States Supreme Court.*

The Sullivan County Family Court hearing turned into a bench conference during which that county's child protection agency, the Department of Social Services (DSS), conceded that it had no grounds at all for charging that Joseph Pikul had either been neglectful toward or posed an "imminent danger" to the children. Paul Kurland had now won important affirmation of his client's custody rights. Hearing the news in Manhattan, Morgenthau and O'Donoghue were dismayed, as were Bob Wayburn and his boss, HRA commissioner William Grinker. " 'What do we *do*?' Mary O'Donoghue asked me," Wayburn recalls.

Knowing that Pikul's arraignment on murder charges was not in itself grounds for a claim of child abuse, Wayburn devised a plan: If it could be *proved* that Pikul had driven the children around while the wrapped corpse of Diane was in the back of the car where the children were at risk of seeing it, then that single fact itself could be claimed as abuse. He got on the phone with Orange County D.A. Alan Joseph. But Joseph told Wayburn he did not have clear proof that the children and the body were ever in the car at the same time. Wayburn now knew he had no case. Rather than fight and lose, as the Sullivan County DSS had done, he vetoed the idea of seeking a remand of the children from Pikul's custody, choosing instead to get what he could—the right of the agency to monitor Pikul's weekend New York visits with his children—until he could think of something else.

Meanwhile, hearing from Kurland of Pikul's victory in Judge Kane's court, Ron Bekoff offered to drive the three and a half hours from Long Island upstate to Sullivan County in order to bring Pikul and the children back

---

*Enough delay was granted for Terence to receive counseling so that his return would not be traumatic, and for agreement to be worked out to ensure monitoring of the family in Zimbabwe. As SSC workers crossed their fingers, Terence boarded the plane for his homeland and father on February 28. He is alive and reportedly well in Zimbabwe, attending a boarding school and spending holidays, weekends and some vacations with his parents.

to Manhattan that afternoon. The reason he did so, he says, was his nervousness about Pikul getting his children back. He wanted to observe this particular father-child relationship with his own eyes.

Six foot three, husky and laconically self-assured, Ron Bekoff had the style of a lumbering Queens street kid. After eighteen years on both the prosecutorial and defense sides of Nassau and Suffolk counties' criminal courts, he was known to be strong on direct examination, scathingly sarcastic on cross. He relished winning unpopular cases: One of his proudest victories as prosecutor was the guilty verdict for perjury he got for Nassau County judge Martin Ginsberg, a wheelchair-bound, locally beloved former Assemblyman. He liked murder cases, too—he had been the original lawyer for Adam Berwood, the Long Island man who, after vowing to do so, killed his estranged wife when he got out of a prison mental facility on a one-day pass. Bekoff quit the case because he had a hunch Berwood would try to kill any lawyer of his who could not get him off—an instinct that proved correct when, immediately after his conviction, Berwood went after his next attorney with a baseball bat.

Not that Bekoff always chose to play it safe. He worked hard to get the sexually abused young daughter of the leader of a pornography ring to trust him enough to testify to her father's abuse. ("Once a week, for a year, I would buy her an ice cream cone and we would talk.") When the guilty verdict that resulted from the child's stinging testimony was read, the defendant jumped Bekoff from behind and applied a chokehold to his neck.

These victories had had one thing in common: They were Long Island cases, Long Island clients, Long Island courts. And, to the media, even a showcase trial in Long Island was somehow second-rate. Winning Joseph Pikul as a client would give Ron Bekoff a valuable plum: a high-publicity case with a Manhattan-based client. Such a case might put him on the map, right up there with Jack Litman, who was now defending Robert Chambers, and Barry Slotnick, who had defended organized crime heads and "subway vigilante" Bernhard Goetz.

Bekoff drove Pikul and the children back to Manhattan, where he took them out for a late lunch. He observed easy affection between father and children—as Kurland had before him. "You could see this guy just lived for these kids—it was very touching," he recalls.

Joe Pikul now had two excellent lawyers ready to jump when he called, as well as two others—Dawson and Clayman—still working on retainer. He had two children who helplessly loved him and would from now on commute back and forth to him from Washington. He had a nephew's wife, Lauren Pawlowski, who was taking care of those children in Washington, and a niece in New York, Edleen Bergelt, who had just done the same thing. And his custody rights had just been roundly confirmed by a judge.

That Joe had the temerity to move back to the duplex, that he'd been given the children back, struck Diane's friends as simply outrageous. Maggie Gari was particularly incredulous. She lived closest to Joe and usually walked her son Andrew past the duplex to get him to school and back, though now she changed to a circuitous route to avoid running into him. Maggie also understood that Joe knew Diane had confided in her—and therefore knew she might have information damaging to him in a custody fight. Joe's threats to Diane had always suggested a contract killing—he always said he would "have her killed." Now Maggie stayed up nights imagining that Joe might call out a hitman on *her*. "When your best friend has been murdered by her husband and he's out there walking around again," she says, "all bets of 'unreasonable paranoia' are off."

Most of all, Maggie feared for her five-year-old son, Andrew. For two years, Diane had kept Maggie's last name and address secret from Joe, planning to hide in her apartment if necessary. It would be easy for Joe, with his retinue of lawyers, to find out where she lived. Maggie overcame her fear enough to try to help Mary O'Donoghue get Blake and Claudia away from Joe. But when Mary pressed Maggie to testify about Joe's past violence and threats, Maggie couldn't bring herself to take the stand. "I can just see it now," Maggie mused wearily one day to a circle of other mothers. "I refuse to testify so I'm held in contempt of court. I'm held in contempt of court so I lose custody of Andrew. I lose

custody of Andrew and *Joe* gets custody of Andrew."
Rolling her eyes heavenward she asked, "Diane, are you
ready for this?"

At the end of the first week in December, the Pawlowskis informed the SSC that they could no longer keep
Blake and Claudia: They were sending the children back
to live with Joe full-time on December 22. Now Bob
Wayburn snapped into high gear. After the failure of the
Sullivan County DSS to get Pikul's custody remanded,
and with Mary O'Donoghue still unable to come up with
a usable incident of neglect, Wayburn knew that a petition of parental unfitness in Family Court would never
fly. For help, he called Raoul Felder's office and had a
lengthy conversation with Felder's associate, Steven
Beiner, about the possibility of finding relatives of Diane
who might be willing to fight Joe for custody. Beiner
spoke to Felder, who called Don Whitmore, who called
Mike and Kathy O'Guin.

Wayburn's plan hinged on the 1976 appellate court decision, *Matter of Bennett* v. *Jeffreys.* "Intervention by the
State in the right and responsibility of a natural parent
to custody of her or his child is warranted," reads *Bennett,* "if there is first a judicial finding of surrender, abandonment, unfitness, persistent neglect, unfortunate or
involuntary extended disruption of custody or [emphasis
added] *other equivalent but rare extraordinary
circumstances. . . .*" With the finding of such circumstances, a best interests hearing could be called in State
Supreme Court.

In *Bennett,* the extraordinary circumstance had been
the mother's protracted separation from her child. A
man's killing of his wife had to be at least as worthy of
consideration, reasoned Wayburn. There was something
else in *Bennett* that heartened Wayburn—a cautionary
paragraph about a factor that "although not present here
often complicates custody dispositions." That was that
"[t]he resolution of cases must not provide incentives for
those likely to take the law into their own hands. Thus,
those who obtain custody of children unlawfully, particularly by kidnapping, violence or flight from the jurisdiction of the court, must be deterred. Society may not
reward, except at its peril, the lawless. . . ." To Way-

burn, this meant one thing: Joseph Pikul could not be allowed to benefit from killing the wife who stood in the way of his getting his children. A best interests hearing would have to place petitioner and respondent on equal footing: with Pikul allowed no natural parent's advantage, with the O'Guins positioned as stand-ins for the murdered Diane and thus bearing no burden of proof in the proceeding.

"Yet," that paragraph of *Bennett* continued, "even then, circumstances may require that, in the best interest of the child, [emphasis added] *the unlawful acts be blinked [at]*."

"Don't blink at murder of mother!" Bob Wayburn had scrawled in the margin of a Xerox he made of the *Bennett* citation.

Now he and Raoul Felder had to be lucky enough to draw a judge who believed the same thing.

On December 14, the O'Guins, through Felder, filed for custody of Blake and Claudia Pikul, citing that they were doing so "with a heavy heart and [we] wish to God that it wasn't necessary to do so. . . . We are not seeking to pass judgment on Joseph Pikul nor do we assert that all we have heard and read is entirely true," the two scientists said, " . . . [but] because of our love for Diane, our great concern for the immediate safety of the children, and our genuine belief that we can provide a safe, loving, normal family environment for the children," they were asking for custody. Concurrently, Wayburn petitioned that Pikul's murder of Diane be considered the "extraordinary circumstance" needed to trigger the hearing.

Both petitions were made to State Supreme Court justice Kristin Booth Glen, who was drawn, as is custom, through lottery. At a time when most lawyers for battered women were calling the country's plethora of old, conservative, male judges their single biggest stumbling block, Kristin Glen, an attractive woman in her forties, was a mother, a survivor of divorce, and an active feminist. She admonished lawyers for sexist language in her courtroom and, in writing her decisions, changed the usual pronoun progression from "his or hers" to "her or his."* A case she decided early in her State Supreme judgeship called *Rudow* v. *Commission on Human Rights* was one of several reflecting that feminism. It established that a worker can claim sexual harrassment even if she (or he) does not object verbally to the overtures and even if the harrasser does not issue threats. That decision was cited as precedent, and praised by Justice Elliott Wilk, in a major subsequent case, *Thoreson* v. *Penthouse International.*

Before her elections to the New York Civil Court in 1980 and to the State Supreme Court in 1986 (after being appointed acting justice thereon in 1983), Glen had been a highly regarded attorney with a strong reputation as a legal scholar. She was associated with the firm Rabinowitz, Boudin and Standard, known for its interest in liberal and progressive causes, and she was a professor at NYU Law School. She was also something of a champion of the unempowered and of consumer and environmental groups. She successfully represented a residents' group in a class-action suit to keep developers from destroying public parks and, vigorously but less successfully, she championed a jazz-listeners' group in their grass-roots attempt to save New York's sole all-jazz radio station from transformation to a more lucrative country-western format. In another case, she argued that if the New York utility provider Con Edison were to be allowed to continue to send pronuclear power enclosures in their bills, then groups with opposing views would have to be granted access to Con Ed customers as well.

The same social consciousness she had demonstrated as a lawyer continued, to some degree, to distinguish Glen's career as a judge. She had ruled for a group of rooming house tenants in their fight against lease termi-

---

*On behalf of a judicial antibias committee of which she was cochair, Glen would later write a letter to the editor of the *New York Law Journal* expressing "extreme distress" at an ad which carried the copy line, "We have the girl any lawyer would love to court." Wrote Glen, "The suggestion . . . that all lawyers are men is outmoded and clearly disproven by the large number of women . . . in our profession. In addition, the use of the word 'girl' is inappropriate—unless the ad is suggesting that lawyers should be corrupting the morals of minors."

nation by a realty company; another time, she had jailed
a landlord for thirty days on a contempt-of-court charge
for not repairing apartments damaged by fire. Making a
fairly pointed distinction between the rights of the truly
vulnerable and the calculated risks taken by those who
are not, Glen had ruled that a "well-educated" attorney
"presum[ably] responsible for his own difficulties" could
not be protected by the anti-usury laws intended "to keep
desperately poor people from the consequences of their
desperation."

On first view, then, Glen might have seemed to Diane's friends and supporters like a judge dropped from
heaven itself. But such view does not take into account
the paucity of laws protecting the children of abuse victims, a potential constraint on even the most otherwise
sympathetic judge. More important, the common assumption that progressive politics subsumes child advocacy forgets something else: The same concern with
protection of natural parents' rights that runs through
American custody law also runs through the liberal and
civil libertarian position—as does concern for protecting
defendants' rights. When someone wants to take away
the children of a parent about to be indicted for murder,
especially a parent whose sexually unconventional habits
make him a likely target for knee jerk castigation, then
a judge might well view such a party as in need as much
of *protecting* as being protected from. And when a judge
with a strong legal mind and a respect for the letter of
the law approaches a case in which common sense is not
written into the law, she can be expected to make a legally sound though not emotionally satisfying judgment.

In a review of Glen's cases long after the fact, two
particular decisions she made—one after, one before
1987—might be said to shed light on the way she would
approach the competing risks and rights *O'Guin* v. *Pikul*
would raise. In a 1989 decision, Glen declined to appoint
a financial conservator for an elderly woman despite a
Guardian Ad Litem's recommendation. The eighty-
three-year-old woman in question was diagnosed with
"organic mental syndrome." "I am concerned about her
situation," Glen wrote in her decision. "I also believe
that her life would be substantially improved by the pro-
vision of [the home health care worker the woman did

not want but whom the conservator would hire.]" But Glen found the woman "lucid" and "coherent," and the conservatee status implied loss of liberties. It was not the court's function, Glen concluded, to deprive the woman of her liberties "simply because it would be in her 'best interest' " to do so.

"The integrity of the elderly . . . should not be invaded," Glen wrote, "nor their freedom of choice taken from them by the state simply because we believe that decisions could be 'better' made by someone else." Thus, when the issue was individual rights or best outcome, Glen made the former choice.

Even more instructive was a decision Glen made in April of 1986. A fifteen-year-old boy was arraigned before her on charges of first degree robbery after stealing bicycles at knifepoint in Central Park. The boy had spent time in a residential treatment center for juveniles and had been discharged after repeated attempts to run away, but this was apparently not information to which the parties at the arraignment were privy. The assistant district attorney, Katherine Scheuer, told Justice Glen, who was temporarily serving in Criminal Court, that the boy, Shavod Jones, "appear[ed]" to have an "open felony" for second-degree robbery (also of a bicycle), had been positively identified in a photo array and line-up, and had made a statement "tending to indicate his guilt." Scheuer recommended bail be set at $3,000, an amount that, according to Ivar Goldart, the Legal Aid Society's deputy attorney-in-charge, would have been "absolutely" prohibitive to him—or to any other youth similarly adjudicated indigent, as evidenced by the fact that he was assigned an attorney at the public's expense. If he could not raise bail, Shavod Jones would be detained in a juvenile facility.

When the boy's Legal Aid attorney, Maryann Wong, said that Jones's "open felony" had in fact been dismissed and that he had appeared in court to answer that charge, Justice Glen chose to waive bail. Citing his prior appearance on the dismissed charge and the fact that he had court-verified ties with his grandmother, she released Shavod Jones on his own recognizance. "So far he has not betrayed our trust in coming to court," Glen reasoned, with characteristic specificity, "although he may have betrayed our trust in committing crimes."

In the opinion of a number of Manhattan criminal defense attorneys, Glen did the right thing. The purpose of bail is not to preventatively detain but to ensure the defendant's return to court. Someone who has previously returned to court when ordered has proved he is likely to return again—and someone who, because of youth, is facing a limited period of incarceration is considered to have a greater incentive to return. Both qualifications applied to Shavod Jones. Still, the Legal Aid Society's Goldart estimates that, because "it's never been a political asset to be considered a judge who is 'soft' on crime," only half of all Manhattan judges in 1986 would have ruled as Glen did. Attorney Norman Reimer goes further, calling Glen "one of a diminishing number of judges who have the guts to be *real* judges—who aren't just political puppets, blowing in the wind." Glen's aggressive hewing to strict constitutional standards, even when the resulting decision might be unpopular, would augur her stand on *O'Guin* v. *Pikul*.

But so would something else: the unhappy fact that the recipients of such judicial benefits-of-the-doubt do not always feel compelled to return the trust. Less than three months later, after pleading guilty and while awaiting sentencing, Shavod Jones was back in Central Park. This time he had a gun. When a young police officer flashed his badge, asked questions, and bent down to feel if the bulge in Jones's companion's pants cuff was a weapon, Shavod Jones shot the officer three times.

The officer, Steven McDonald—who went on to become a national hero—was paralyzed for life.

Justice Glen agreed that the murder of Diane was an "extraordinary circumstance" that properly merited a hearing. The battle lines were drawn. *The Matter of Kathleen and William O'Guin* v. *Joseph Pikul*—with Felder representing the petitioners, and Paul Kurland, the respondent—received a calendar date of December 17.

Raoul Felder rushed to assemble his witnesses, but many were Diane's friends, mothers of young children, too fearful of Joe to testify. Paul Kurland, however, felt confident: For one thing, he read *Bennett* in a different way than Wayburn did and felt that Pikul's natural parent's primacy still held; therefore, the burden of proof on his opponents was "tremendous"; for another, he'd just uncovered a 1979 New York Court of Appeals case, *A Matter of Leon R.R.* This termination of parental rights case was unremarkable but for one small thing that caught the astute lawyer's eye: the fact that it deemed hearsay testimony (statements that a witness testifies have been made by a second party to her or him) inadmissible in a custody hearing. Finding this precedent, for Kurland, was like finding a diamond on the beach.

Among the group of women who were close to the case, there was a rising sense that some grass-roots effort was necessary to focus attention on the plight of the children. A friend of Maggie's, a former caseworker named Laura Berzofsky, drew up a "Petition to Protect Diane Pikul's Children." The simple, three-paragraph document called for authorities to take seriously, and counter, the unfair vulnerability the children would face if left to live with Joe. Copies were circulated for signing at the gates of Greenwich Village schools. Almost everyone who saw it immediately signed—one hundred and seventy-one people in all, many saying they would be willing to take off from work to carry signs at a demonstration outside State Supreme Court. The petition addressed two separate issues: that children's rights to assured personal safety be given precedence over a criminal defendant father's "ownership" rights to those children; and that the dead mother's voice be "heard"—that justice not be allowed to mock her wishes and take advantage of her in the grave. It didn't have to be said to any of the people who signed the petition that Diane did *not* want her killer to raise those children. They knew this, and signed the petition on her behalf.

Copies of the twelve pages of signatures were sent to fourteen city and state agencies and officials and to the media, leading to an article in *The New York Times*. At the same time, a number of concerned women began to research domestic violence as it affected custody law. It was found that while nine states* and the District of Co-

---

*Alaska, Arizona, California, Colorado, Florida, Illinois, Kentucky, Iowa, Washington.

lumbia had laws on the books making spouse abuse a factor in custody designation, New York was not one of these ten jurisdictions. Though such legislation had passed the Democratic subcommittee of the New York State Assembly, it was yet to go to the Republican, which was less likely to second it. It was discovered that in a number of cases in those ten states and others, men who were wife-batterers and murderers had been denied or stripped of custody of their children, several in advance of being found guilty in criminal trials. But there was a hitch—in all of those cases (which Justice Glen could be asked to consider as precedent but would not be bound by, since none were New York appellate courts), at least one of three conditions held. Either the mother was still alive and thus a legal coequal, if not advantaged, custody petitioner; or the father had physically wounded the child as well; or the child had witnessed the mother's murder by the father. In the Pikul case, only the latter was a possibility. If it was determined that either Blake or Claudia had witnessed the murder, then two cases could prove extremely relevant: In the 1970 Kentucky case, *Bramblett* v. *Cox,* custody was temporarily denied a father while he was under a charge of murder of his wife because the daughter had witnessed the strangulation and was thus a material witness against him; and in the 1980 California case *In Re Sarah H.,* children were declared free of their father's custody, in a "best interests" hearing, because the father had been determined to have fatally beaten the mother in the children's presence.

Six weeks after Diane's murder, it was still not known whether Claudia and Blake had witnessed the crime, and to Kristin Booth Glen, this was a pressing question. She spent the first recorded day of the case—December 18— trying to get that question answered, starting with a phone call to Alan Joseph, which she made from her robing room. The case's principals waited in Justice Glen's chambers: Kurland and Felder (both of whom had briefly gotten on the phone to question Joseph), Bekoff (now officially Pikul's attorney), Bob Wayburn, social worker Jose Flete—and Joseph Pikul and his children.

"From my perspective," Glen said to Joseph, after he'd outlined delays he was encountering in getting a psychologist to interview the children, "whether or not [Pikul] did commit this crime is not the only issue. The issue is whether he is possibly dangerous to his children, and obviously one piece of that would be if the children have evidence which might be used against him. Presumably that gives him a motive to do them harm.

"I mean, this is obviously a worst-case scenario," Glen reassured Joseph, "and I don't mean to suggest that's what I think. But it certainly is a possibility and one that's suggested by the petitioners. So if the examination of the older child* is going to be conducted in the near future and if it is going to be memorialized in some way, whether by tape or by stenographer, so that any information which is given would be usable in the event that something happened to the children, [then] whatever motive there is to do harm to the children disappears once the testimony or information is given."

Thus, Glen was suggesting that quickly securing the children's account of the night of the murder might protect them from their father, either by relieving Pikul of the fear that the children had anything to say that might incriminate him or (to attribute the worst possible thoughts to Pikul) by rendering any harm he might be thinking of doing them futile, because they had *already* testified. This suggestion might give cold comfort to Diane's friends, who wanted to think that fathers do not need special motivation to prevent them from harming their children. Some might argue that if such means are determined by a judge to be so important to ensure children's safety, then that fact itself argues for the children's removal from their father.

"I can't memorialize it," Alan Joseph responded. "The only method I have in criminal practice of memorializing anything would be by a conditional examination in which both [prosecution and defense] are present and able to cross-examine the witness. I just can't take a deposition from [Claudia] or even put her in front of a grand jury and have her testify and have that testimony survive some unforeseen event that may occur to her."

"There is *no* way it can be taped or videotaped with

---

*Only Claudia was to be interviewed; Blake was not a candidate for an interview, on grounds that he was too young and nonverbal.

the consent of the parties so that it could be used at trial?" Glen asked again.

"The only way that could be done," Joseph said, "would be assuming that the parties are able to ask whatever questions they want to ask." Kurland and Bekoff, Joseph knew, would surely object to the prosecutor being there to question the defendant's daughter. Just three days earlier, Bekoff had filed, in Orange County Court, a "Motion to Quash a Grand Jury Subpoena to Compel the Testimony of the Defendant's Two Children." Whatever it was the children saw, or heard, or knew, Bekoff clearly did not want it admitted into evidence.

"They can waive the conditional, can't they?" Glen pressed on.

Only, Joseph replied, if he himself knew what information Claudia had and was therefore prepared to assert that she possessed information directly relevant to the prosecution. And this was not the case.

"This certainly puts a different wrinkle on the situation than I thought earlier," Glen mused. Apparently, she had come to view the memorialized interview as a linchpin of the children's safety with their father.

Joseph now detailed his "very strong circumstantial" case against Pikul: running through the investigation and the evidence, eventually mentioning that Pikul showed "absolutely no" remorse for the murder ("his indication was that she deserved it") and that the D.A.'s office had just gotten an unsolicited call from a former neighbor of Pikul's who volunteered information about Joe's beatings of Sandra Jarvinen.[*] He also mentioned that the child protection worker who had spoken to the children the night they were taken from the duplex had said that Pikul had told Claudia "that he had a fight with their mother and that [Claudia] was not going to see her mother anymore." Claudia had also indicated to that worker that "Mommy and Daddy were arguing" or "Mommy threw a fit and Daddy said, 'Don't talk about it any more.' " Whether or not Claudia heard the argument or was told this version of it by her father, Alan Joseph did not know. "Basically, we are told by Claudia that 'Daddy

---

[*]In the pretrial hearings in Orange County, Joe's violence against Sandra was deemed inadmissible.

said there was a lawyer' and she was not to speak to the police."

Joseph laid out a variety of available inferences. "It's possible the kids actually witnessed the homicide; or it's possible the kids heard portions of what actually led up to the homicide even though they didn't witness it; it's possible that Mr. Pikul told them things that he may later be regretting; it's possible that they know nothing."

Eventually the conversation, despite its tone of amiability and cooperation, edged toward areas of difference. When Glen asked, "Is there anything in any of his statements to the police or anyone else, whether relevant to your case or not, that would indicate that he is any danger to the children?" Joseph seems to have been surprised by the question. "Well, he never told anybody he was going to kill the children, if that's what you mean," he responded. "That's kind of a wide-open question."

"I certainly understand that all of our concern is that if he were capable of killing his wife, then he is at least a potentially dangerous person," Glen reassured Joseph, her language here, as it would be throughout the proceedings, carefully reflective of the accused's right to the presumption of innocence. "But so far what you have said [when recounting Pikul's remarks to the police investigators] is that he said the children were the best part of him, that his wife was in some way neglecting the children by leaving them with all these baby-sitters. . . . I don't mean that any of this is positive from my standpoint, but it's all sort of concern for the children as opposed to anger which might in any way be directed *at* the children."

Joseph was not having Glen's logic. He had a murder case to aggressively prosecute and a violent defendant free on bail who'd made threats to flee the country. That he was going to have to worry about Sandra Jarvinen was bad enough; the very last thing he wanted was to have to worry about two young children's safety as well. As far as he was concerned, those children should not be with Pikul. With logic of his own, he countered: "He was angry toward the person he was in the process of getting a divorce from. You can get angry at anyone."

"That's a leap," Glen reminded the D.A., "which *I* have to make or not make."

After more talk about the case, Joseph gingerly floated one more hint of his position: "I can tell you what *my* personal opinion is . . . but on the other hand, I really think it's *your* function to decide whether someone who is charged with murdering his wife—possibly being guilty if we are to believe his admissions—should have custody of his children. But, again, that is your decision, that is your province."

After stressing yet again to Joseph that "I really wish you could work out the situation with getting the psychiatrist [to interview Claudia] as soon as possible," Glen came up with an interim alternative: that she, in the course of the talk she was scheduled to have with the children anyway, would see if any information emerged about the night of the murder—and that the conversation be memorialized by a court reporter. Alan Joseph liked the idea very much—hopefully it would "kind of shortcut any further interview with them" unless "they know something major, like they're eyewitnesses." Felder, thinking such a conversation would drive home to the judge the children's vulnerability, agreed to it, as did Kurland.

And so, after her phone conversation with Alan Joseph, Kristin Glen had a conversation with the children. She emerged from the session concluding that, as she would soon say, "the kids . . . adore their father, miss their father" and were looking forward to going with him that weekend to the christening of Edleen Bergelt's newborn baby. Furthermore, she had observed the children "sleeping in [Pikul's] arms when the courtroom door was open." From what Glen could tell thus far, they had seen or heard nothing of their mother's murder.* Glen would later relay her conversation with the children to Alan Joseph, resulting in the decision that Claudia not be

---

*The children's adoptive mother, Kathy O'Guin, says today, "It's not clear to us, from what the children have told us, that they did not wake up that night or that they were unaware of a fight or unusual activity. And it's clear to us that Claudia would not have revealed to anyone, including Justice Glen, anything she might have seen or heard, not only to protect her father, but because she knew that such revelation would have put her security, in terms of her life with her father, in danger."

called to testify before the grand jury. Whatever the children had seen or heard that night would now never be legally uncovered, and neither *Bramblett* v. *Cox* nor *In Re Sarah H.* could be deemed relevant as precedents through which Glen could be asked to remove the children from their father's custody.

During parts of the two attorneys' brief time on the phone with Alan Joseph, Glen, with the wry exasperation and firm hand that would characterize her handling of all the attorneys throughout the hearings, had reined in both men: Kurland for his gratuitous reminders of his client's Sullivan County victory ("Mr. Kurland, this is *not* a criminal trial") and Felder for his seeming eagerness to use Diane's autopsy pictures for his own purposes ("*Forget* it, Mr. Felder; this is not a sideshow") and his apparent attempt to highlight Pikul's two kinds of strangulation as a sign of extra savagery. ("Let that go. I understand what [Alan Joseph] said, Mr. Felder. I have tried many, many felony cases in my life.") Now Glen opened her chambers to these two men and to Bekoff, all three bristling with their separate agendas: Kurland, eager to solidify his client's right to his children; Felder, wanting to strip Pikul of custody immediately; and Ron Bekoff, invested in making sure Joe's custody fight wouldn't in any way jeopardize his criminal defense. From the bench, Kristin Glen now coolly prepared to ride herd.

If she and Alan Joseph had politely differed on the breadth or narrowness of the concept of potential danger, then this next session was a virtual crossfire of conflicting interests. Glen's pressing concern was for access to any and all of Joseph Pikul's current or past psychiatrists and psychologists, especially his most recent therapist, Dr. Daniel Schwartz. She wanted to be able to speak *in camera* with Schwartz about Pikul's potential for violence, including the way he felt and behaved toward Diane. "Obviously there is a Fifth Amendment problem here, and there is certainly a doctor/patient problem," she acknowledged. Somewhere in the middle of which lay the children's welfare and safety.

Bekoff and Kurland had initially objected to such an interview, fearing it would be construed as a casewide waiver of physician/client privilege; but Alan Joseph had assured them that he would not construe it thusly. Felder objected to the *in camera* nature of such an interview; he certainly wanted access to Pikul's therapist's assessments.

Now Bekoff told Glen that, while he and Kurland were wholeheartedly supportive of her interviewing Schwartz on the subject of Pikul's relationship with his children, "we both feel anxious to convey to Your Honor that neither one of us wants you to talk about [Pikul's] relationship with his former [sic] wife or any of the surrounding circumstances of her death."

"You don't want that?" Glen asked, apparently somewhat dismayed, having been led to believe the issue had already been approved in prior conversation. When Bekoff said, "That's correct; we do not," Glen seems to have become somewhat frustrated. "What good is [such a circumscribed interview] going to be to me, then?" Glen asked. The doctor's view of Pikul's relationship with his children would merely be an opinion; he had never observed the three together. "My concern," she said, as she had to Alan Joseph, "is possible danger to the children—and there are very few ways I can ascertain that." She firmly informed Bekoff: "I have heard the evidence which the district attorney in Orange County has against your client and there is no question it is very powerful evidence. And, based on what I've heard, I have no question that he will be indicted. I [also] believe there is certainly a possibility that he will be convicted.

"I have said from the first here that we have a presumption of innocence, and that the law in this state is that parental misconduct unrelated to the children is not relevant and cannot be used in a custody proceeding . . . [and] although I would be personally appalled and horrified if this man did kill his wife, that is *not* what I have to look at.

"What I have to look at is *whether he poses any danger to the children*. If he did kill his wife, that is perhaps some evidence of his propensity to violence, although we also know that spousal killings may be a one-time-only event. I don't mean to make light of it. I just mean statistics show that repeat violence is of a different sort than that.* There is a possibility that [spouse killers] would never engage in violence toward the children. It may be that [Pikul] fears that his children might reveal something," she said, echoing her words to Alan Joseph. *"That* is what I need to know in terms of danger. . . . It's absolutely critical for me to know this."

Glen gave Bekoff a few minutes to think over his answer to her request for full access to Schwartz. Bekoff and Kurland then conferred with each other and with Pikul. Returning to the bench, Bekoff said: "Your Honor, I am going to have to stick by my guns. . . . Every instinct I have as a defense attorney does not allow me to give Your Honor that latitude. I am sorry."

Glen responded that the negative inference she would draw from that refusal would go right to the issue of Pikul's right to custody. She then laid out the legal foundation by which, according to her interpretation, she would be bound. *Bennett* v. *Jeffreys*, she made perfectly clear, was a "two-step proceeding. The court may not consider the application until it ascertains that there *are* extraordinary circumstances." Furthermore, "The courts are very clear that 'extraordinary circumstances' per se do not mean that the best interests of the child would *not* be for the child to be with the parent. For example, [in the case *Wohlfahrt* v. *Drees*] when the trial court found a father selling drugs and the woman he was living with selling drugs and gave custody of the child to some relatives, the appellate division reversed that, finding that . . . the court had erred in not going on to ascertain

---

*It is not known what statistics Justice Glen was referring to. Neither the FBI nor the Bureau of Justice Statistics keeps statistics on recidivism or prior recidivism in spouse murderers, but, according to Dr. James Alan Fox, Dean of Criminal Justice at Northeastern University and a widely regarded authority on murder, "Murderers in general tend to recidivate less than other criminals and this is particularly the case when the murderer kills someone he knows." But even if spouse murder is a low-recidivistic crime, this does not mean that its perpetrators are not dangerous to others. "Criminal recidivism and dangerousness to others are two separate things," Fox explains. "Professional thieves are not dangerous to others but they recidivate all the time. On the other hand, spouse murderers, though they may have no criminal record, can be dangerous people at the peak of their history of violence."

all the relevant criteria as to whether the best interests of the child required the custody to be given to another. . . . The mere fact of the wrongdoing or misconduct [of] the parent—or whatever the 'extraordinary circumstances' are—are not, by themselves, enough. They must be weighted in the totality of the circumstances."

Glen seemed to indicate what later bench conferences would make clear: She strongly believed that *Bennett* v. *Jeffreys* merely opened the door to a best interests hearing by which petitioners could challenge the natural parent's custody, but it did *not* take away the traditional advantage of that natural parent, and it required the petitioners to shoulder the burden of proof. This was not Bob Wayburn's interpretation.

Next, Glen went into her robing room with Wayburn and caseworker Jose Flete, and examined the files the HRA had amassed on Pikul since the district attorney's office's call to the SSC hotline. The great frustration Mary O'Donoghue had felt in her search for one technically usable charge of abuse or neglect was borne out by this session. When Glen returned to chambers, she reported that she'd found "no evidence whatsoever of any abuse or neglect of the children, nor have they found anything other than the [murder] charges made against the father and the obvious fact of the arrest that would indicate in any way that he is not a competent parent." The "extensive investigation" done by the HRA and Glen's own conversation with the children "allay[ed] my fear that there is any reason here to be concerned about the situation." The proceedings had run overtime; it was now seven in the evening. Given the lateness of the hour, further testimony could not be given until Monday. Therefore, "persuaded that there is no danger to the children this weekend," Glen ruled that Pikul could have, with caseworker Flete's supervision, custody of the children for the balance of the evening and for Saturday and Sunday.

Glen stated she believed that, despite Diane's pending divorce and the "clearly very substantial differences" between her and her husband, "there was," the judge said, "no question in [Diane's] mind that the children were [not] in danger." (Glen did not yet know about the five-page memo Diane had written to Felder just before her murder. The next week, when the memo was brought to Glen's attention, she would decline to consider it because it was hearsay.)

"In some ways," Glen continued, "[Diane's] voice from beyond and her willingness to leave the children in that household for well over a year after retaining Mr. Felder . . . indicates to me that these children are not in any greater danger from this man than any child is from any parent in the city at this time." This was "ironic," Glen said. But perhaps not as ironic as the fact that it was an active feminist who was drawing this conclusion.

Most ironic of all was that the desperate fear and ambivalence that had made Diane initiate, call off, then resume her divorce did not come through in her "voice from beyond"; the only thing heard through that silenced voice was her poor judgment.

Raoul Felder, of course, was outraged about Joe Pikul's weekend custody. "I'm against it," he said forcefully. "I do not have the investigative resources of the HRA or maybe the wisdom of the court, but I do have a gut that feels things. I do have, I think, a sense of logic and common sense. . . . We were all in the room when we heard [from Alan Joseph] that Mr. Pikul was not only accused of the murder, he also confessed to the murder, several times. A most brutal murder, and the murder of the mother of these children. . . .

"His remorseless attitude . . . the method of the murder: ten blows to the head, two different kinds of strangulation, burying the body, digging it up . . . that sort of suggests that maybe these kids are not as the court suggested in no more danger than any other child in the city."

Felder was being intuitive and emotional—everything Justice Glen felt she must keep *out* of the proceedings. "I don't want to respond to Mr. Felder, because I take this as seriously as you do," she said evenly, "but in the end the weight of whatever happens is on my shoulders and that's an awesome position and a frightening one, and I think it's very easy to take the easy way out. If I were not absolutely convinced, as I am, that the children are not in danger, then I would not do this. I would not risk it for a second."

Felder took Glen's claim of earnestness on behalf of the children's safety as an invitation to a contest. "I think nobody is more concerned about these kids than I. In the American tradition, I've put my money where my mouth is and I'm working for nothing, which doesn't happen too often in our business."

In the meantime, it was access to the *press* that Felder wanted for his cause. The Pikul case had been buried under the Steinberg case for six weeks now; beyond the immediate circle of Diane's friends, people in New York were not aware that the rich stock-expert wife-murderer still had custody of his children; and, with Justice Glen's blessing, would have them all to himself this weekend, as he had for the last three weeks. In the city's new domestic-abuse-conscious climate, this news had a terrific potential to incite a groundswell of legitimate outrage. Felder was critical of the agreement, worked out between the others, that made Pikul's confession to murder unmentionable to the press. The claim that this was being done to protect the children, he said, was bogus, because "they're going to be exposed one way or another. The concern seems to be to protect Mr. Pikul." Even more than Pikul's confessions being made unmentionable, "I don't see why the press can't know the children are with their father this weekend, if that is the court's ruling," Felder challenged Glen. "The only one who is troubled by this is Mr. Pikul. With all due respect, I don't think that's our concern here. Your concern *should* be for the kids. Whether or not he gets a fair trial, let him fight *that* out up in Orange County. I don't see how you can muzzle us here or muzzle the press on that basis."

"I think it's admirable that Mr. Felder is working for nothing," Bekoff responded, trying to keep the sarcasm from his voice. "I am a criminal lawyer. I am not on the clock. I am also here for free."* When Bekoff heard that the children were being released to Pikul in Monticello, "I got in my car in Long Island and drove all the way up there. I wanted to see with my own eyes that he

---

*Shortly, Bekoff would be paid a $75,000 retainer by Pikul, who liquidated a pension fund for that purpose, with a promise that he'd pay the balance of his defense fee with the bail money. Kurland received a retainer of about $25,000.

wasn't going to be a danger with these kids before I went on my merry way. I drove back with him for *two hours.* I took him and his kids out to a late lunch . . . and I looked and listened. So please don't say you're the only one concerned about the welfare of the kids. Everyone standing or sitting in this courtroom is concerned about the kids.

"We are in America, judge. I have the right to a fair trial for my defendant. . . . He is accused. That doesn't mean he is guilty. We can't have that right to a fair trial subverted by Mr. Felder going out there and saying, 'Hey, this homicidal maniac'—which I just heard him say two minutes ago—'confessed up there.' "

Now Glen stepped into the two lawyers' altercation with her own perspective. "*My* position here is actually somewhat different than everyone else's. . . . I cannot in my wildest imagination conceive of how telling the press that Mr. Pikul has confessed to this crime will aid the children. It can only make their lives utterly miserable. . . . It must be a nightmare for them and certainly if [their father's confession] comes to their attention it will be the *worst* nightmare." On the face of it, this argument was irrefutable—except for one thing: Protecting the children from the extremely ugly facts of their father's deed *also* protected their father. This concommitant feeding of the guilty living parent from his half-orphaned children's trough would persist throughout the custody hearings. The reasoning that the "children have already suffered the loss of *one* parent" would soon effectively hold the opposing petitioners hostage—and would therefore reward the very person who had been responsible *for* that "loss."

In murdering Diane and then fighting for his children, Joe Pikul gained the privilege of *containing* his children—making a wound struck at him felt by them. Bob Wayburn recalls thinking he would like to draft legislation to correct such situations as Joseph Pikul's free ride on his children's best interests—if not in time for this case, perhaps in time for the next.

In concluding her session with the three lawyers, Glen unhappily conceded that if Felder insisted upon telling the press the children were going to be with Pikul the coming weekend, "I can't stop you; you have First

Amendment rights"; but, she added, imagining a headline, "The fact that the 'lunatic judge' gave the kids to the 'homicidal maniac': I don't think *that* is a good thing for the kids."

But what *was* "a good thing" for the children? And who truly spoke for them? What if they really wanted to stay with their father? Were the wishes and desires of children so young and so victimized to be taken at face value as their "best interests"? On the other hand, were certain seekers of justice focusing too exclusively on the assumption that a man who murders someone he's loved is a danger to all his other intimates? Could it be possible that an accused and confessed wife-murderer might still somehow be a safe father? These were some of the issues that *William and Kathleen O'Guin* v. *Joseph Pikul* would raise.

But the overriding question was this: What comes first? Protecting the young children of a violent adult who is also a murder defendant? Or protecting that adult's parental custody rights and his rights to an impartial criminal trial?

One person left out of this debate was the victim herself. The loss of Diane's rights due to her murder was writ large over the proceedings of the first custody hearing, called to order in Justice Glen's courtroom the following Monday, December 21.

Diane was absent from the old-fashioned wood-paneled courtroom in more than the obvious way. She had no posthumous right to have her desires for her children presented in court; Joe alone was the client-parent whose unilateral wishes for the children were to be catered to. Diane had also, through death, lost her rights to have anyone refute accusations made about her by Joe; there is no rebuttal-by-proxy available to dead spouses maligned on the stand by their widows or widowers, even when those surviving spouses have been arraigned for their murder. (That same widower/accused murderer may be protected from accusation by invoking the Fifth Amendment.) Even written statements in which the deceased has pleaded her case—like the memo Diane wrote to Raoul Felder—are handicapped by being rendered "hearsay."

And here, with regard to the pivotal matter of hearsay, is where Paul Kurland's discovery of the New York Court of Appeals case *Matter of Leon R.R.* would come into play. Hearsay is customarily inadmissible in *criminal* trials because the speaker whose story is recounted secondhand is unavailable for cross-examination. The policy in noncriminal proceedings, however, has always been vague. *Leon* set a precedent in New York State by which hearsay was deemed inadmissible in *custody* cases. In *O'Guin* v. *Pikul*, the admissibility of hearsay would be critical to the petitioners. For when the person who was most threatened by another person's violence is permanently out of the picture, usually the only record left of those threats and that violence are either police reports (here Diane's failure to get the restraining order Felder had urged her to get would posthumously work against her) *or* hearsay, recounted by friends. Once that hearsay becomes inadmissible, there is no recourse. In the eyes of the court, it did not happen. Thus, as Bob Wayburn put it: "By killing Diane, Joe Pikul effectively destroyed almost all of the file on his own violence."

Kurland's first words in court that day were therefore not surprising. "I object to the hearsay statement, Your Honor!" He had leapt to his feet when the first witness, a matronly looking woman named Sharon Space who had been Diane's AA sponsor, took the stand. "Did Diane ever tell you anything Joe did to Claudia?" Felder had asked her. "Yes," was Space's answer. Kurland's objection was sustained by Glen.

Felder, speaking more wishfully than factually, countered: "There is no hearsay when the welfare of children is at stake. Furthermore, the only reason Mrs. Pikul is not here today [to say these things herself] is because she was murdered."

"Your honor!" Kurland protested again. Sustained again.

Glen did let the body of Sharon Space's testimony stand—only to strike it as "hearsay and double-hearsay" later. Space was one of the very few friends of Diane who did not have a child herself and was therefore not afraid of taking the stand against Joe. While Joe sat staring at her, just a few yards away, Sharon Space told of five incidents of Joe Pikul's violence—his kicking a chair into a wall at an AA meeting, making verbal threats to a building security guard, randomly firing guns indoors and throwing eggs at people on the sidewalk outside his window; but only one, the first, was an incident that she herself had witnessed, and some had occurred before he stopped drinking. When Sharon said Joe had told her that "prior to entering AA, he was on cocaine," Joe himself leapt from his seat. "It's a lie!" he said.

Felder now approached the bench with a copy of the long memo Diane had brought to him five days before she was killed. Filled with examples of Joe's instability and redolent of Diane's extreme dismay at the children's being alone with him, it would be eloquent testimony. He wished to submit it into evidence. It was "admittedly hearsay," Felder said, but he was requesting that, since Diane's murder was the only thing preventing her from testifying in person about its contents, Glen make an exception to the hearsay rule. Glen later refused.

Then Kathy O'Guin took the stand. The O'Guins' own lives and characters would be hard to attack—last Friday, Justice Glen herself had called them "perfectly lovely, perfectly competent, and perfectly wonderful people"— so Kurland concentrated instead on sowing doubts about their suitability to sudden parenthood. Hadn't they been virtual strangers to Blake and Claudia? Wasn't Kathy's husband's work as a scientist at the mercy of grant-renewals and constant outside offers? Would they be willing to turn down a lucrative job offer in order to stay in the state that their father's bail order prevented him from leaving? As active Protestants, would they consent to putting Blake and Claudia into the Catholic school that their Catholic father required? Would they make efforts—undergo counseling, if necessary—to ensure that their own ill feelings against Joe would not hurt his right to a relationship with the children?

Kathy O'Guin met each challenge. She and her husband would accommodate each of Joe Pikul's conditions; they would make every reasonable sacrifice.

Where was her weak spot? Kurland seemed to wonder. Now Kristin Glen stepped in and, as perhaps only one woman at a sensitive juncture in life could do to another, located it. Did the O'Guins hope to have children of their own? Kathy answered affirmatively. The judge now asked: "If a therapist or family counselor" determined that "having a baby of your own would be frightening to [the children], would you take that into consideration and be willing to postpone [becoming pregnant]?"

Kathy answered, "Certainly."

Glen continued. "I'm aware of the ticking of the biological clock and we are of not dissimilar ages, and I have many friends who are now having babies . . ."

Kathy bit the bullet and said, "If I were informed that an addition to the family like that would be unsettling, I would be willing to do some waiting."

Not long after Justice Glen had secured Kathy's promise that she would wait to have her own child in order to give Blake and Claudia a home, Kurland said that he had no further questions. From his seat, Bob Wayburn pondered the "sadly amusing" fact that Justice Glen, while able to hold a pure best interests hearing, was, instead, holding the O'Guins to a much higher standard. Glen's reading of *Bennett* v. *Jeffreys* was that it did *not* strip Joe Pikul of his natural parent's advantage—and that in order for her to give custody to the O'Guins, she'd have to find clear and convincing proof that the best interests of the children were served by taking them away from their father.

In a series of bench conferences begun that day and continuing throughout the hearings, Wayburn disagreed with the judge. "I kept saying, 'You don't have to decide it like that! He killed the mother,' " Wayburn said. " 'He wanted to take the kids from his wife and he didn't want to go through a divorce court. *He murdered her for that reason.* He's created a vacuum and he's taking advantage of it! Why should a parent have the advantage when he's the perpetrator? In property law, if you murder another person, you can't inherit from their will. If this is true in property law, it should be at least as true in custody cases.' She indicated that she might like to rule that way but that she was a judge, not a legislator, and her reading of the law prevented her from doing so. I said, 'But you *can* rule that way.' In the absence of statute and dealing with children, she could have fashioned an appropriate procedure and let the appellate courts decide if she was right or not."

Glen was not swayed by Wayburn's arguments. The burden of proof remained on the O'Guins.

When Joe himself next took the stand, his testimonial advantage over his dead wife enabled him several victories. Unimpeded by dissent, he could speak for the record that he, not Diane, was the reasonable spouse who sought marriage counseling "to see if there was anything to salvage in the marriage and, if not, to see what our dialogue would be in the divorce action. My wife was reluctant in this issue all the time." He lost no time in claiming that Diane "beat on" the children "verbally all summer." He even claimed, with no possible rebuttal, that Diane "told the baby-sitter to beat the kids." When Felder inquired as to why the rent on the Sixth Avenue duplex had remained unpaid for months, resulting in an eviction notice, he replied: "One of my wife's only responsibilities was to write the checks, and she had an unfortunate character defect of procrastination. If a check was not paid, it was because it was not presented to me to be signed."

On the subject of his own character, however, the witness proved rather less begrudging. In testimony drawn out by his own lawyer, Kurland, Pikul stated: "I am a wonderful father [and] I am a wonderful caretaker, and . . . I don't have any doubt of my ability to take care of my children."

Justice Glen's perceptive—occasionally even skeptical—inquiries went some way toward unearthing the flaws in Joe's glowing portrait of himself as single parent-/provider. For example, she bore down hard on his presumption that his disability insurance would somehow pay for child care when time-consuming preparation for his criminal trial made employment impossible. Still, if you took away the reason for his newly single fatherhood (which the law, under Glen's interpretation, instructed the court to do), then Joe Pikul, particularly under his own attorney's gentle questioning, sometimes appeared as any other concerned, if high-strung and nervous, father might when sorting out the logistics of schools, baby-sitters and schedules.

Raoul Felder, however, avidly went about unseating

this Joe Pikul and interrogating the other, more notorious one.

"Did you ever blindfold your children?"

"Of course not," the witness replied.

"Did you shoot off a gun into the ceiling of your apartment?"

"Ridiculous."

"Have a temper tantrum at an AA meeting and kick a chair into a wall?"

"Ridiculous."

The egg-throwing Sharon Space recounted?

"No truth [to it] at all."

The verbal altercation with the security guard?

"Innocuous."

Pikul explained that the source of these "very amusing" allegations, Sharon Space, had, when they first met, "wanted me to be her lover, and I went out with Diane instead. I guess she harbors some kind of resentment."

Had Pikul, Felder asked, bugged and taped Diane's phone conversations?

Kurland asserted his client's privilege to take the Fifth Amendment.

Had he ever threatened Sandra Jarvinen's life?

Kurland took the Fifth for his client again.

"Were you ever arrested prior to this present episode?"

Once again, Kurland asserted the Fifth.

"Overruled," said Justice Glen.

Joe seemed startled. "Was I *what*?"

"Ever arrested prior to the situation with Diane," Felder repeated.

"Prior to the situation with Diane?" Joe asked nervously. "I believe I was."

Felder picked up the pace. "When was that?"

"I don't remember specifically."

"Give us a date. Ten years ago?"

"More than that. I was drinking."

"Were you arrested for intoxication?"

"I'm not sure. I think it was fighting."

Excited, Bob Wayburn* made a mental note to try to

---

*He had at this point been officially asked in on the case, by Justice Glen, in the capacity of *amicus*.

track down that prior arrest, while Felder pushed on: "Did it have anything to do with drugs?"

Pikul stiffened with hauteur. "I have never taken drugs, Mr. Felder."

"Never taken cocaine?"

"I don't know what cocaine is."

Had he ever dragged Diane around by her hair?

Fifth Amendment.

Did he ever tell anyone he had AIDS?

Fifth Amendment.

Felder was now casting a wide net. Did he ever sleep outside a cemetery in an automobile? Objection. Sustained. Lie on the kitchen floor, eating watermelon with his pants down? Objection. Sustained. Did he drive the kids around with the body of his wife in the car? Objection. Sustained. Did he kill his wife? Objection. Sustained. Did he drive to the hardware store and buy rope and shovels? Objection. Sustained.

Felder—who, as an Orthodox Jew, is something of a Torah scholar—took another tack. "You say you say prayers with the children at night, that you read the Bible with them," he said, picking up on Pikul's previous remonstrances against the children being raised Protestant. "Do you ever read the Book of Deuteronomy? How about Deuteronomy 22:14: 'A man shall not put on a woman's garment, or a woman a man's.'[sic]?"

"Objection!" Bekoff shouted. That Justice Glen, in closed session, had seen the videotape of Pikul dancing around in women's underwear and manipulating a dildo was bad enough, but Pikul's cross-dressing could *not* be permitted to spill over to the criminal trial. No jury in America, no matter how objective and open-minded, would fail to hold sexual deviation against a murder defendant.

But Felder pushed on with the cross-dressing questions through a hailstorm of sustained objections from Bekoff and Kurland: How many times last month did he wear women's clothing? Did he ever take his children with him shopping for undergarments? What was a bassinet doing in the background of the videotape? Then Felder came to the real point. "Do you think it's important that people have examples in life? Role models?" he asked. "Do you think you're a good example for your children?"

"Yes," Joseph Pikul answered.

"Do you want little Blake to grow up like you?"

"*Just* like me?"

"Yes," Felder managed to affirm before Kurland raised—and Glen sustained—that last objection.

Still, Felder's heated questioning had yielded two leads for Wayburn. The first was Pikul's prior arrest. Given its lack of known date, details or jurisdiction, it would not be easy to find, but Wayburn would start hunting. The second lead was more immediately usable. Felder had gotten Pikul to admit he had physically punished his children. When Wayburn took over questioning, he developed this last charge, and got Pikul to describe the physical abuse he himself had suffered from his own father. "Do you think history has affected you with Claudia?" Wayburn now asked.

Pikul answered: "No, I think if anything, it's given me a desire to avoid [physical abuse of children]." The contrary reality, long known to authorities in the field—that abused children often grow up to abuse their own children—was not a point Wayburn could raise for the court record; nor was a finding, independently confirmed in two different academic studies, one British, one American, nine years apart and identical almost to the percentage point,* that slightly more wife-abusers go on to become child-abusers than do not. Rather, Wayburn focused on getting Pikul to admit that he'd spanked Blake once because the child had failed to answer a call to get ready to go to his speech therapist; and that he'd spanked Claudia twice—once, because "it really disturbed me" that she had found out there was no Santa Claus and had thus ruined Pikul's fatherly pleasure in keeping her innocent; another time because she was lying in support

---

*"In a survey of one hundred battered women, 54 percent said that their husbands had committed acts of violence against the children as well," Gaylord, *Wife Battering: A Preliminary Survey on 100 Cases,* British Medical Journal, 194 (1975); and in Dr. Lenore E. Walker's National Institute of Mental Health-funded study of 403 battered women, published in her 1984 book *The Battered Woman Syndrome* (Springer Publishing Co.), 53 percent of the women responded that their batterers had battered their children as well.

of a baby-sitter "and I wanted her to know lying was not an acceptable way of life. I wanted her to tell the truth."

When Bekoff had his chance with his client, he asked: "Did the children ever ask you, 'Is it you [who killed Mommy], Daddy?'"

Pikul answered: "Claudia said, 'I *know* it's not you, Daddy.' "

Wayburn sat wondering: Might Claudia have learned from those two beatings by her father that some fictional wish-dreams, like that of Santa Claus, were imperative to maintain? That it was not lying, per se, but rather disloyalty to her father that was "not an acceptable way of life"?

Chapter 11

The conduct [of the father] serves as a beacon to the trier of fact of his potential for violence and physical harm.

Illinois appellate court decision Williams *v.* Williams, *1982, affirming that a trial court acted properly in admitting evidence of a mother's severe beating by a father into proceedings through which the father lost custody of the child*

Blake and Claudia Pikul moved from the Pawlowskis' in Washington, D.C. to the duplex in New York with their father in time for Christmas. After the holidays they would be reenrolled in their respective schools and their welfare would be monitored by concerned teachers, fellow parents and staff.

Diane's friends were not unappreciative of these advantages but felt they paled next to the main, uncorrected outrage: Joe still had custody of the children. The women believed they had to organize a demonstration protesting this decision. A permit to picket in front of the State Supreme Court on the morning of the next hearing, Wednesday, January 6, was obtained by Laura Berzofsky. Ann Stern and Randy Warner gathered the troops at *Harper's;* dozens of calls were made to women professionals and to local school parents who had signed the petition. But the element of fear was enormous. Sarah Brockton declined to attend because she was afraid Joe would see her as he mounted the Supreme Court steps, and "if he gets too angry at me, I'll be afraid for my daughter." Maggie herself planned to demonstrate wearing a disguise.

Fear is what kept many of these women from testifying in court. Between this fear and Glen's ruling on the inadmissibility of hearsay evidence, Felder and Wayburn found themselves with only a small pool of potential witnesses. Wayburn tried to get Sandra Jarvinen to testify, but two things hampered him—Sandra's own terror at appearing before her ex-husband, and Alan Joseph's desire to save Sandra as his own secret star witness. To get Sandra on the stand, Wayburn would have had to go to a Massachusetts court to subpoena her, and he was understandably reluctant both to compromise Alan Joseph's criminal prosecution and to make Jarvinen any more nervous than she was already. One domestic violence authority, postdoctoral fellow Dr. Penelope Grace of Harvard University's Children's Hospital, regretfully turned down an invitation to fly in to be an expert witness. "If you'd asked me two months ago, I'd have definitely said yes," she explained. "But I have a daughter, and I just did a custody evaluation in which the man I spoke against said he would 'take things into his own hands' with me and my family. It's *women* professionals who are always bullied by these guys."

At least one male professional was also afraid—but not of Joe. Raoul Felder was afraid of Justice Glen. He was extremely anxious that the publicity-wary judge not learn that he knew anything about the forthcoming demonstration and the inevitable attention that would follow. He was already pushing things with Glen, who'd clearly expressed her feeling that sensational press coverage would be "the worst nightmare" for the children. He didn't want to provoke the judge's anger.

Still, why would an outspoken, media-friendly attorney like Raoul Felder—a man whose matrimonial clients swap sensational diatribes in the tabloids—be so afraid of revealing what he knew about a group of earnest women with picket signs? The answer lay in two recent trends in custody cases involving allegations of child- or wife-abuse. The first was that claimants—if they could not win in the courts or through the social agencies— were taking their plight to the media. The second was that judges in such cases were, with increasing frequency, issuing gag orders to the women who were doing just that—and sometimes to their attorneys as well.* This was a step that Kristin Glen had thus far refused to take.

But enjoining a party from publicly saying negative things about her ex-spouse (or about the judge's decision) was one thing; construing that talk as an index of parental unfitness was another. And this, to the dismay of such women and their attorneys, is what custody judges had the liberty to do. Some judges interpreted the garnering of media coverage as intentional violation of the child's privacy, a perception that could directly affect the custody decision itself.† In this intimidating new climate, Raoul Felder—whose clients were petitioning *against* the natural parent—straddled two fences. He knew the women would be picketing and did not dissuade

---

*Joan Pennington, staff attorney for the National Center on Women and Family Law, says, "I have noticed an increase in these gag orders. Most of the women who talk to me now relate that the judges have ordered them not to become involved with the media." Janet Dinsmore, communications director for the National Center for the Prosecution of Child Abuse, says, "Whether there are more gag orders now is something we have no statistics on, but on the basis of anecdotal information, this appears to be true."

†For example; In June of 1989, Virginia LaLonde—who'd spent six months in prison rather than surrender her seven-year-old daughter Nicole to the father the child said had abused her—lost legal custody to the child's father, Stephen. (However, she won shared physical custody.) Boston judge Mary C. Fitzpatrick found that the immense publicity surrounding the case had intruded on Nicole's privacy. She wrote: "Virginia . . . has done more than tolerate this publicity, she actively courted it and even orchestrated her own actions to suit its needs."

In protracted hearings, it was asserted that "positive signs" of abuse were found on Nicole and a psychologist who examined Stephen LaLonde said that the father had a "highly romanticized and erotic relationship" with his daughter. Stephen LaLonde, however, asserted his innocence—and a psychiatrist who talked to Nicole once for an hour backed up his claim.

Judge Fitzpatrick termed the physical abuse findings "inconclusive" and wrote, "This court has determined that Stephen did not sexually abuse Nicole." Fitzgerald concluded: "As much as Nicole has learned that she can say 'no' to sexual abuse if her father initiates such . . . [she] has yet to learn to say 'no' to the emotional pressure her mother has placed on her to see life and Stephen through her mother's eyes."

Virginia LaLonde appealed the decision. She lost.

them from doing so, while at the same time he told reporters he thought the demonstration was a "bad idea."

On Monday, January 4, 1988, Joseph Pikul was indicted in Orange County on second-degree murder. This is the most serious murder charge normally available in New York State.* After the brief proceedings, while Pikul was driving back to the Village to pick his children up from school, Maggie Gari was delivering press releases describing the demonstration planned two days hence to the city's five local TV stations and to *The New York Times,* the *New York Post,* the *Daily News* and *Newsday.* Later, Maggie and two others assembled at Maggie's apartment and stapled and felt-penned thirty picket signs. The television news was on as the women worked. They watched a young middle-class man named Matthew Solomon lead a large contingent of police and neighbors in a search for his young bride. He claimed she had walked out of their Long Island house and disappeared into the woods on Christmas Eve. "Watch," one woman looked up from her sign-lettering to say. "They'll find out that he strangled her." Several days later, they did.

A psychiatrist appointed by Justice Glen, Dr. Michael Kalogerakis, had recently examined Joe and each of the children and was set to make his custody recommendation to the court. He would be performing the task that Glen had been so concerned about during her December 18 conversations with the attorneys: determining whether or not Pikul was dangerous to his children. Bekoff had initially expressed his and Kurland's concern because the doctor and Raoul Felder were on a first name basis; Kalogerakis, in fact, had once worked on a case with Felder and had been paid by Felder's client. Justice Glen, however, said, "There are not many people I would trust. . . . [Kalogerakis] comes very highly recommended to me. He told me he doesn't have a problem" with conflict of interest. Furthermore, he had time to evaluate Pikul, the children and the O'Guins during the Christmas court recess.

---

*Only killers of policemen and on-duty corrections officers and killers who are already in prison serving life sentences may be charged with first-degree murder.

* * *

On the morning of January 6, thirty-five people, mostly women, stood in six-degree weather on an icy mound across from State Supreme Court, holding signs protesting Joseph Pikul's court-affirmed custody of his children. Inside, Paul Kurland was relishing a significant victory—one he was "totally shocked" by: Dr. Kalogerakis had just given the judge his confidential report, which was implicitly supportive of the Pikul children's remaining with their father. The report had an inauspicious prelude. Kalogerakis learned from Joseph Pikul about his abused childhood, alcoholism, and five years of transvestism. Furthermore, the evaluation

> gradually unfolded [as] a picture of a troubled man who, while successful in business, seems to have experienced continuing failure in his personal life. . . . He seems not to have experienced great success with women before or between his marriages. He was given to moments of rage, some of them explosive . . . tended to be reclusive and secretive, at least with regard to some aspects of his life . . . [and] displayed considerable nervousness, only some of which could be accounted for by his current legal problems. . . . [His] emotional life appeared turbulent, labile and confused. . . . There is also evidence suggestive of an impulse disorder and [in the past] at least one . . . paranoid disturbance requiring antipsychotic medication. . . . It is possible to entertain a diagnosis of mixed personality disorder but additional supportive data would be necessary. Mr. Pikul made it clear that he felt very vulnerable to humiliation and his entire character structure is consistent with someone who could become enraged at denigration or even being opposed.

Kalogerakis noted that

> on at least one occasion, he lied to this examiner, at first denying and then admitting that he had used a strap on Claudia. He changed his story only after I

informed him that Claudia had told me that a belt was used.*

Still, Dr. Kalogerakis was very impressed that

despite all the above, the overwhelming bulk of the evidence is that Mr. Pikul's relationship with his children has been fundamentally good. He claims to love them very much—his first words to me were that he was "willing to risk the criminal case" to hold on to his children. . . . I could find no evidence of warped attitudes to children, of sadistic impulses or of any tendencies beyond those already described which could prove inimical to the children's welfare.

Moreover, Kalogerakis was struck by the fact that "the children are emphatic in attesting their love for their father and their insistence on remaining with him."

The doctor labeled Pikul's "caretaking" "adequate" on the basis of "all the evidence available to me," yet he was forthright in admitting that "time constraints made it impossible to conduct an exhaustive exploration of the relevant issues with the principals." In this "admittedly short" observation time, "the overall tenor of the relationship to the children . . . was well within the normal appropriate range" and that "there was warmth, tenderness and an ability, albeit imperfect, to control the children's behavior."

Getting to the crucial issue of Pikul's possible dangerousness to his children, Kalogerakis wrote: "Though no one can predict dangerousness, numerous factors may be taken into consideration in arriving at a decision in this very difficult matter."

Kalogerakis then cited a number of factors. He said that one of these, the presence of a history of violence,

---

*At the next court session, Kurland promptly put Pikul on the witness stand, where the repondent nervously admitted that "upon reflection of my testimony," he'd made a mistake when he'd said that he "spanked" Claudia; in fact he had struck her with a belt. Justice Glen exacted Pikul's promise not to revisit the experience on either of his children.

is the factor which correlates best with future violent
behavior. Inasmuch as Mr. Pikul has not been convicted and innocence is presumed on the current criminal indictment and there is no other verifiable history
of significant violence (nor is any admitted to by Mr.
Pikul), there is no basis for assuming a peril to the
children on this account. It is also important to remember that violent behavior is often highly specific
and may well be directed at one person but never
anyone else. This is probably truest in violence between intimates where the dynamics that operate between two members of a family may differ markedly
from those with other members of the family.

Kalogerakis concluded his report with two key observations—that the children "displayed no fear, behavior-
ally or in their statements to me, but on the contrary
were quite comfortable with [their father] and vigorously
defended their wish to be with him"; and that a "healthy
love" seemed to exist between Pikul and his children.

Dr. Kalogerakis had ample experience in forensic and
adult psychiatry. He was a diplomate of the American
Board of Psychiatry and Neurology and a clinical professor of psychiatry at New York University School of Medicine. He also had experience in adolescent psychiatry,
having been in charge of the Adolescent Service at Bellevue for sixteen years and having served as the Assistant
Director of Child and Adolescent Psychiatry at the NYU
School of Medicine at Bellevue. After the latter director-
ship, he was the Associate Commissioner of Children and
Youth of the New York State Office of Mental Health.
He had been a member of the New York Citizens Committee for Children for twenty years.

However, as impressive as Kalogerakis's résumé was,
Raoul Felder was able to pinpoint an area of weakness
in the doctor's credentials: his recent clinical experience
with young children the ages of Blake and Claudia Pikul
was extremely limited. Early in his questioning during
the morning of January 6, Felder asked, "Doctor, when
did you pass your boards in child psychiatry?"

"I am not boarded in child psychiatry," Kalogerakis
admitted. However, he was, he said, board eligible "on
the basis of experience."

More pointedly, Felder prompted the doctor to disclose the fact that he was not presently seeing any five- or eight-year-old children. Felder accentuated this point by moving backward in time. "In 'eighty-seven, how many eight-year-olds did you see in consultation?" he inquired.

"I would say one at most," Kalogerakis replied.

"How many five-year-olds . . . in 'eighty-seven?"

"Perhaps one."

"Let's go back to 'eighty-six. How many eight-year-olds . . . ?"

After remarking that the attorney was testing his memory, Kalogerakis allowed: "It may have been one."

"How many five-year-olds in 'eighty-six?"

"No more than that."

"How many eight-year-olds in 'eighty-five?"

"I do not remember."

Felder was caustic; Kalogerakis seemed annoyed—whatever relationship they'd enjoyed seemed to have melted away with their sparring.*

Bob Wayburn then took the floor and asked Dr. Kalogerakis whether he had any recommendations, in the event that short-term custody be given to Pikul. The doctor described a plan consisting of therapy for the children, psychiatric monitoring of Pikul "separate and distinct from" his ongoing therapy with Dr. Schwartz, strong communication with the schools, and some preparatory work with the O'Guins "by the psychiatrist supervising the overall plan," since they might one day assume custody. Kalogerakis noted that the O'Guins, whom he'd also evaluated, were "eminently suitable to undertake [the] responsibility" of custody.

When Felder resumed questioning, the doctor's commendation of the O'Guins proved a fertile opening. Assuming the O'Guins won custody, "do you have any worry that the children will be physically harmed?"

"I don't think that's the question," Kalogerakis responded.

---

*Moments later, Bob Wayburn elicited from Kalogerakis that he had served as an expert witness in about fifteen cases involving children younger than adolescence.

"That's *my* question," Felder retorted. "Do you have a worry that they will be physically harmed?"

"Absolutely none."

Having set up a nice base of comparison, Felder now asked, "If Mr. Pikul retained custody, do you have maybe an itty bitty worry that something could happen to the kids?"

"Yes," the doctor replied. "I think this is an open possibility."

When Kurland took the floor and asked the doctor to explain "open possibility," Kalogerakis replied: "What I mean by that is this: To the extent that Mr. Pikul may already have manifested any hurtful behavior toward the children, and some of that was recorded in my report . . . it remains an open question as to whether he would be capable of acting in an injurious fashion toward the children." This less than reassuring answer dangled.

Now Glen had a question for the doctor, and with it she skillfully shifted from the issue of possible physical harm to the children to that of their possible emotional danger. "Is it your opinion," she asked Kalogerakis, "that there could be harm to the children from, number one, *removing* the children from his custody at this time, and, number two, does that outweigh in your view the 'open possibility' that something could happen to them in his custody?"

"Indeed, I do," Kalogerakis assented. "Because as far as the children are concerned, their father is innocent of any criminal charges. He is their daddy and they love him." Now Pikul's "containment" of his children came into play as the doctor continued: "They have sustained a terrible loss. It's a question of whether the state wants to act in such a way as to impose a second loss, [which] can have very serious consequences to personality growth and development."

Glen reiterated the question for emphasis: "Is it your opinion that the loss or harm to the children from removal of their father's custody outweighs the 'open risk' of some harm coming to them?"*

---

*In an affidavit filed with the court, Felder objected to Glen's questioning here, terming it an attempt to "virtually rescue" Dr. Kalogerakis.

"It does," Kalogerakis answered.

Now Glen turned her attention to the issue of Joe Pikul's AIDS status. She had "drawn a negative inference" from his taking of the Fifth on that question, and now she had to decide whether or not to compel him to take a blood test. Turning to her expert witness, she said, "Assume that Mr. Pikul is presently suffering from AIDS. Would that affect your opinion at all in terms of . . . whether . . . his shortened life span . . . might lead him to flee from the jurisdiction?"

Kalogerakis said no. But when further questioned he said that "suicide" was "a much more likely outcome." But even if Pikul's AIDS status did render him potentially suicidal, the psychiatrist said: "I don't think that would constitute a reason to remove the children from his care."

This reference to suicide led to worrisome implications. "Is there any possibility," the judge had to know, "that he might take his life and take the lives of the children with him?"

"I have no information about Mr. Pikul that would lead me to conclude any of that" was all Dr. Kalogerakis could promise.

Felder spent the rest of the session striding around in front of the witness stand, throwing Kalogerakis's own negative assessments about Pikul back to him. Hadn't he called Pikul "hostile"? Yes. A man of "general impulsivity"? Yes. A person "enraged at denigration or even being opposed"? Yes. "Secretive"? "Labile"? "Confused"? Yes. Yes. Yes. "So," the attorney exclaimed, "he has all the elements of a time bomb, ready to go off!"

"I did not say this was not a worrisome case," the psychiatrist conceded. "I think that Mr. Pikul needs help in understanding what proper child rearing consists of, and there's no question in my mind that I would not want to leave him with the children without assuring that there would be an ongoing education about child rearing."

The image of the seethingly unstable murder defendant dutifully curling up in bed with books by Benjamin Spock and Berry Brazelton prompted Felder to opine: "To quote Lincoln, 'The dogmas of the quiet past are inadequate for the stormy present.' " Then he asked: "What good is it if the system works for other people who are *not* killers?"

Ron Bekoff now, loudly: "Objection!"

Glen: "Sustained."

Felder rephrased that. "Dr. Kalogerakis, if there are ten thousand Mr. Pikuls out there and 9,999 don't kill their children and one does, the child he kills is just as dead, right?"

The doctor answered by asking: "Do we jail the 9,999?" Although remand of custody, not jailing, was at issue, the doctor's point was a good one.

So was Felder's. "Maybe," the attorney said. "If the one is that important."

As the conundrum of how to protect children from possible harm while assuring parents' constitutional rights hung in the air, Felder said: "I have no further questions."

Glen sustained Pikul's temporary custody of his children, with continued SSC monitoring. "The ultimate issue in this case," she said, "is whether a nonparent should be permitted to take custody of children from a parent and . . . an extensive body of law . . . affords the strongest constitutional provisions to the rights of natural parents, barring danger to the children. I am second to no one," Glen declared, "in my concern for the children."

The next day's *New York Post* featured an article about Glen's interim decision. Felder's words to her appeared as the article's headline: LAWYER SAYS JUDGE IN WIFE-KILL CASE IS PLAYING: RUSSIAN ROULETTE WITH KIDS' LIVES. The attorney was now too outraged to worry about Glen's imposing a gag order. And Glen was too committed to First Amendment rights to impose one.

At the hearings' continuing sessions on January 13, 15 and 23, Felder and Wayburn presented what witnesses they could gather. Because Diane's female friends were too afraid to appear; because hearsay evidence about Joe's violence was inadmissible; and because Joe and Diane's AA friends had less than pristine pasts, the details of which were known by Joe but not by his opponents' attorneys, the petitioners' witness list was full of vulnerability. They expected imperfection. They did not, however, anticipate disaster.

Bob Salisbury, Nancy Kirkland's husband, was the only person the attorneys could find who was not afraid to testify and who could offer an example of Joe's violence that did not involve hearsay. Though Salisbury's testimony would not speak directly to the issue at hand (Joe's danger *to his children*), Felder hoped it would at least drive across the point of the defendant's volatile temper.

Salisbury testified that he had been at the Pikuls' Amagansett house with his wife one day in the summer of 1985. Diane was there; Joe was in the city working. Diane asked Salisbury, who is an acknowledged computer expert, to teach her to work the PC Joe had recently installed.

Two days later, Salisbury got a call in his office. It was Joe Pikul, accusing him of having erased "data worth a million dollars" off the computer. "He started swearing at me, 'You fucking son of a bitch, if you ever come near me or my wife and children again, I'll kill you.' Finally, when I couldn't reason with him, I hung up on him. He called me back twice and reactivated the conversation in the same vein."

"What do you know about this guy?" Kurland whispered to Joe, as defendant and lawyer listened to the testimony. Joe replied that Diane had once told him a wacky story; he had no idea if it was true. "Tell it to me anyway," Kurland suggested.

To the surprise of all present, Kurland opened his cross-examination with a loaded attack: "Have you ever been confined in a mental hospital?"

Salisbury, warily, said, "Yes."

"Were you ever forcibly removed from Newark Airport for the way you were behaving there?"

Kurland could tell from the look on the witness's face that Diane's story to Joe—that Salisbury had once been pulled off the airport's runway for trying to direct traffic in the midst of an alcoholic hallucination—had been true.

Again: "Yes."

"And you were put in a straitjacket?" Felder and Wayburn were shifting uneasily. If they'd known about this incident, they'd never have put Salisbury on the stand.

"Probably," Salisbury allowed haltingly. The humiliating ease with which Kurland was pulling this large skeleton from the closet of a witness so minimally useful to begin with was making Felder rue having called the man.

Kurland queried on: "Isn't it a fact that you then tried to escape from the ambulance you were confined in in the Lincoln or Holland Tunnel?"

Salisbury said he did not remember. When he admitted to having been hospitalized thereafter for two to three weeks, Kurland said: "I have no further questions."

Next, Felder called to the stand Guy Capalupo, the electronics expert that Diane's detective, Bo Deitl, had called to the duplex last July to uncover Joe's phone tap. Capalupo described in detail his dismantling of the phone equipment, his detection of the "off" voltage, and his tracing of the tap to the attic where he found a tape recorder hidden under some clothing and a phone jack secreted behind a wicker basket. Capalupo's testimony was leading to one point Felder had sought desperately to get across from the very beginning. After all of this work, was Capalupo then allowed by Diane to remove Joe's bug?

"No," the witness answered.

"Why *not*?" Felder asked. "Was Mrs. Pikul *frightened* of anything?"

No sooner did Capalupo sneak in the word "yes" than Kurland was on his feet, objecting to the hearsay.

Glen sustained Kurland's objection.

Thus, from Felder and Wayburn's perspective, hearsay seemed to be a single-edged sword: All stories about Diane's fear of Joe were inadmissible, while any stories about Diane's friends' and Felder's witnesses' unstable past were grist for the mill of Kurland's cross-examination. Given this double bind, it seemed fruitless for Felder and Wayburn to call any more character witnesses; perhaps they'd do better with experts.

So Wayburn called to the stand Dr. Ava Sielger, a child psychologist who was contacted by Mary O'Donoghue after an attorney active in drafting feminist legislation had made the referral. Siegler stated on the stand that she held a Ph.D. in clinical psychology from New York University as well as postdoctoral certification as a psychoanalyst both for adults and for children and adolescents. Siegler also directed a clinic for troubled children and their families that handled fifteen thousand patient-hours per year, and maintained a private practice specializing in "the emotional consequences of trauma on child development." In aggregate, "I have direct experience in working with hundreds of" three- to eight-year-olds. Just prior to this court appearance, however, she had made the mistake of discussing the case on television. To make matters worse, she had spent portions of the last two days waiting outside the courtroom, asking Felder and Wayburn if she could testify. This naïve eagerness made Siegler putty in the capable hands of Paul Kurland, who went right for the bias he smelled.

Did Siegler have a "general interest in protecting the rights of children?" Kurland casually inquired.

Siegler said: "Yes. The rights of children are extremely paramount . . . and . . . the physical-emotional states of the children should not be in any way compromised even in a situation where the civil rights of a parent might be at stake."

"So you are really here as an *advocate* of the position," Kurland deduced. Flustered, Siegler demurred—she had never testified as an expert witness before; she didn't know the rules—but Kurland continued to wonder out loud whether she in fact had her mind made up.

When Felder objected, saying, "The witness is being cross-examined before she has testified on direct," Justice Glen overruled, saying Kurland's point was "important." Glen told Siegler that while she found Siegler's devotion to child advocacy work "utterly admirable," at the same time, "if I had wanted to appoint an advocate for the children, and if I thought that were necessary, I would have done so. I did not do so." Both Kurland—happily—and Wayburn—unhappily—noticed Glen's displeasure.

Then Glen asked Siegler: "Is it your belief that in any instance where there is any danger to a child, the child's safety—which may mean removal—is paramount to that of the natural parent's right to the child?"*

---

*The judge did not ask this question, which most people would be hard put to answer in the unqualified negative, to Dr. Kalogerakis or to the expert witness who testified next, Dr. Arthur Green.

"Let me think about that," Siegler said. "I've never had that question put so extremely to me." Then she allowed: "I would say yes; I think that's probably—"

"I thought that's what you were saying," Glen said abruptly.

Nevertheless, under questioning by Wayburn, Siegler managed to get across some points—points that Glen stated she might later, after determining the limits of the witness's expertise, choose to strike. "Children love us for all kinds of ways that we have," Siegler said. "We can be loved if we're cruel, we can be loved if we beat them." As if speaking to Dr. Kalogerakis's conclusions, she warned: "I have known children who have begged to be returned to psychotic mothers, children who have no trouble loving a father who whips them or whips their mother. So for a child to say, 'I love my daddy' is not something we should take at face value."

And, as if speaking to the judge's own surmise that the children hadn't witnessed or overheard anything to do with the murder, she cautioned: "Children love and protect people who are very dangerous to them. Children operate on the premise, What I don't know can't hurt me. A child of nine would most likely begin to rely heavily upon progressive denial in order to continually exist in a state of dependency. She might even cling much more poignantly to the remaining parent. [Thus] I do not think a child's conscious testimony [about what she witnessed] should be taken at face value."

Even highly trained evaluators cannot know how these children are really doing, Dr. Siegler stressed, because such children suppress so much; their measurable level of emotion often lags six months behind their feelings. Therefore, she concluded, it is wise to err on the safe side, to assume that "these children are at great risk [and we must not] permit them to be."

Next, psychiatrist Dr. Arthur Green was called to the stand by Bob Wayburn. Wayburn wanted a child psychiatrist to confirm or deny Kalogerakis's findings, and Green was the only one who returned Wayburn's call over the Christmas holidays. However, it might have appeared to some people—feminists and friends of Diane, for example—that Green was a peculiar choice of witness. The medical director of the Family Center and

Therapeutic Nursery of the Presbyterian Hospital of the City of New York and an associate clinical professor of psychiatry at Columbia College of Physicians and Surgeons, Green is highly controversial in the child-protection field. This is because of his methods of determining whether or not sex-abuse charges made against fathers are valid (for example, he advocates interviewing the child in the presence of the allegedly abusing parent) and because of his theories about the mothers of some of the children who make those charges: that they are sometimes "vindictive" or "delusional" mothers who "bombard [their] children with incessant interrogations and pressure them to accept their delusions" and who "foster abnormal dependency in the children to enhance their own narcissism and to compensate for their unsatisfactory love relationships."* Green testifies widely on behalf of fathers accused of abuse.

Arthur Green took the witness stand and concurred with Kalogerakis's psychiatric monitoring plan. The rapport that Kalogerakis observed between Pikul and his children was, Green said, "the best predictor of future harm" that might befall them. And while Green affirmed that "spouse abuse is strongly associated with the physical abuse of children," he noted that "there had been no indication of spouse abuse prior to this alleged incident," and even if there had been, "abuse is not synonymous with homicide." Green concluded that "if the father seemed adequate" and if a psychiatric evaluation showed him not to be dangerous, then "everything should be done to foster that relationship." He also stated, in re-

---

*Green put forth this theory in a 1986 issue of the *Journal of the American Academy of Child Psychiatry,* prompting nineteen other practitioners to sign a letter to the editor claiming that the "article contained many unsubstantiated claims that could mislead clinicians and legal decision makers." Rebutting Green, an article in the *Journal of Interpersonal Violence,* by the five founders of the American Professional Society on the Abuse of Children contended: "Green's formulation of characteristics that allegedly differentiate true from false cases of child sexual abuse contradicts our experience as researchers and clinicians. Our major concern is that Green's article is most likely to be misused in judicial settings to the detriment of a large number of children who are caught in custody battles and who have also been sexually abused."

sponse to questioning put to him by Glen, that the prospect of Pikul's being convicted rather than acquitted would probably be reason for *more* (even, in Glen's words, "constant"), not less, contact between the children and their father before the murder trial.

The last witness that afternoon was Bernetta Seegars, the children's longtime baby-sitter, whom Joe Pikul had recently rehired. Felder had heard from Diane's friends that Bernetta had fled the Amagansett house the past Labor Day weekend when Joe had lost his temper. Now the attorney wanted to know how much Pikul was paying Bernetta to have her back. Enough, perhaps, to dim her memory of his volatility? Bernetta was reluctant to reveal her salary, and Glen refused to permit Felder to press the issue. When questioned about the incident that had made her flee the previous September, Bernetta waffled: Yes, she had quit because Joe was yelling at her, but he was really only yelling because she was too far away from him in the house to otherwise hear him. Felder's attempt to trap her in an evasive self-contradiction yielded little. Then he asked: "Did you ever tell Mary O'Donoghue that he was a lunatic?"

"I might have said he was *acting* like a lunatic," the baby-sitter responded. "I didn't say he was a lunatic, specifically."

Glen closed the series of hearings by ruling that Joe Pikul did not have to get an AIDS test and that he would continue to have temporary custody of his children. Raoul Felder was furious: How could Glen have sustained Joe's custody after hearing from Dr. Kalogerakis that Joe's AIDS status might render him suicidal? And how could she honor Dr. Green's recommendation that an imminent conviction for murder would argue for *more* pretrial father-child contact? But then again, it was Kurland and Bekoff, not Felder, who had initially objected to Kalogerakis's appointment to examine Pikul and the children. And it was Felder's ally Bob Wayburn who had put Arthur Green on the witness stand.* Through all

---

*Wayburn says today that his bringing in Green could have opened the door for Felder to bring in another child psychiatrist, "thereby giving him a better leg to stand on." But this opportunity was not communicated to Felder nor perceived by him.

of this, Diane's friends had the awful sense that every oversight, misjudgment and stroke of luck in this case was working *for* Joe and against Diane's posthumous interests.

Little did they know that Joe was now cultivating what would turn out to be his biggest advantage.

Around the time of these hearings, there was a new development in the lives of Joseph Pikul and his children: the presence of a Grace Church parent named Mary Bain, the mother of one of Claudia's classmates. A plump, attractive thirty-three-year-old woman, Mary's fluttery movements and chirpy voice gave her an air of almost frivolous femininity that could obscure her keen resourcefulness. She was employed as a production designer for the fabric manufacturer Royal Silk—and her competence and organization enabled her to combine frequent business trips to Asia with full-time parenthood.

A hardworking Brooklyn girl from a modest background, Mary had gone to a local fashion-trade college and, at twenty, had married Steven Bain, a pharmacist several years older than she. Steven had a son from a previous marriage whom Mary often cared for and, at twenty-four, she had her own daughter, Jennifer, with Steven. When she began her career in fashion, the Bains moved to Manhattan. In 1979, when many young women in Manhattan were still experimenting and dreaming, twenty-five-year-old Mary was minding two children and working hard.

When Jennifer was five, Steven and Mary separated. After three years, however, in December of 1987, Mary and Steven were reconciled.

Mary knew that Steven's job as a pharmacist had "not much growth" potential. Mary had in fact been earning more money than her husband for some time. Too, problems had begun to develop between her and her seventeen-year-old stepson. These mundane pressures may have seemed tedious to Mary, who impressed others with quite another side of her nature. Sarah Brockton says, "There was always this real . . . starfucker quality about Mary. Anything that was controversial and that put her in the limelight she would revel in. She would join school committees and promise she could deliver certain incidental but glamorous things. And she was a stage mother—she sent Jennifer to school for the kindergarten class picture with makeup on and asked the photographer to take extra pictures."

Another mother remembers how perfectly Mary used to fix Jennifer's hair, even in nursery school; that "done-to-the-T's" look had always seemed slightly out of place—more suburban-striver than cool Manhattan. "Mary," Sarah Brockton says, "was considered flaky, a little laughable, but basically harmless." Still, there was an earnest streak of altruism in Mary. For years now, she had come back from her Far Eastern trips telling Jennifer about all the poor children in orphanages there. The idea of rescuing such a child from a grim destiny was very compelling to Mary. "When are we going to adopt our orphan?" Jennifer would ask. Mary would say she was working on it.

As Mary herself recalls it, it was Steven who had first shown her the *New York Post* item about the Pikul childrens' return to their father at Christmastime and who had suggested they be the first school family to volunteer to help them. "Steven knew Joe from picking up Jennifer from playdates with Claudia; I didn't know him—though I had the impression of this man running in and out of limousines, and I only knew who Diane was from my being class mother." In January, when Claudia had just reenrolled in Grace after holiday vacation, Mary and Steven—a little nervously—called Joe Pikul to invite Claudia over. An after-school playdate was made several days later.

When the playdate was drawing to a close, Mary called Joe. "I did *not* want to talk to that man. I just gulped and said, real fast: 'Hello-this-is-Mary-Bain. Steven-and-I-will-bring-Claudia-home-in-an-hour.' " To Mary's surprise, Joe Pikul started laughing. "Wait till you see this place," he said, "This is embarrassing. What will the Watchers [Joe's name for the concerned school parents] think? That I'm having voodoo practices?"

Mary says, "I thought, What a bizarre man . . . Then I asked: 'What do you mean? What's going on?' "

"They shut my electricity off," Joe Pikul explained. (His landlord's aggressive commencement of eviction proceedings, and the effect that might have on the children's stability, was an issue not considered by the court.) "I have three boxes of candles in my house." An hour later, Mary, Steven and Jennifer chaperoned Claudia back to the duplex. Under Mary's supervision, Claudia had done her homework and made cupcakes; Mary even loaned Claudia one of Jennifer's swimsuits for the two girls' upcoming swimming lessons. "Claudia seemed grateful," Mary says. So did her father, who was impressed with the neatly wrapped homemade cupcakes, the report of homework supervised and completed, the proffered swimsuit. Claudia's mother, he let on to this eager and helpful woman, was not quite so organized and nurturing. Joseph Pikul, Mary remembers thinking, was "not at all the horrible person the newspapers were saying those terrible things about."

"After that day, Claudia started calling the house all the time, asking to speak to Jennifer, then to me," Mary says, explaining her deepening role with the family. Being needed made her feel good. She was used to being needed by her own family, but this was something much more dramatic: Overnight, Mary became privy to the day-to-day life of this suddenly notorious family. Then there was Joe Pikul himself, who was emerging to Mary as radically different from the way the other parents were depicting him. It was exciting, becoming the only person who knew the *real* Joe—who could defend him. He was so "gentle," Mary thought. "So funny, and charming. And with charisma"—*Steven* "didn't have those qualities." But what most dazzled and moved Mary was the flattering contrast between Joe's worldliness and his blossoming reliance on her. "He was a brilliant, brilliant man, and yet he *trusted* my opinion, he *needed* me so much," she says now.

With Joe Pikul and his children, a whole package of Mary Bain's unconscious cravings could be answered. She could have the drama her premature responsibility had deprived her of. She could be the sole champion and rescuer of a man far more complex and sophisticated than her familiar pharmacist husband. She could be the saviour of two beautiful, blond motherless children. She would no longer have to hoist herself into an upscale world by volunteering as class mother, by coiffing her daughter to resemble a child actress. She could steal that world's limelight by walking right into the center of one of its most mysterious scandals.

One day in mid-January, Barbara Romans, the Grace Church School nurse, saw Claudia looking unusually unkempt, with scratches on her arm. Romans suspected abuse. She contacted the women at *Harper's,* who put in a call to Mary O'Donoghue; an SSC emergency call was made. As it turned out, the scratches were from the family cat, but additional inquiries by the SSC caseworker to the school led the worker to believe that Claudia was acting out and that her schoolwork was suffering. "The stress on her was increasingly evident," the school's headmaster Kingsley Ervin says. "Her sense of reality was gradually deteriorating. It was as if she were trying to deny what had happened, though she was old enough to know it."

Raoul Felder requested a special hearing, which Justice Glen convened on January 28. "We predicted this would happen, and it gives us no pleasure to see it," Felder gravely told the court. "The normal course of nature is that a child gets over the death of her mother—the pain is ameliorated by time. Here it is different. Every day that she's in the custody of the man who killed her mother, it's going to get worse."

Now Bob Wayburn had something to present that was relevant to Felder's last point—legislation he had just drafted that was now undergoing the long process of being approved by the city for presentation to the state senate and assembly in Albany. The bill Wayburn wrote accomplished two things. First, it solved the problem of how to protect the emotional bonding needs of the child whose parent has been murdered without letting the indicted remaining parent benefit from the child's new vulnerability. Second, it limited the indicted parent's natural-rights presumption without abridging that right either radically or unconstitutionally.

The heart of the bill was this: Once one parent was indicted for the murder of the other parent, he would not so much lose his custody "weapons"—his preponderant natural-parent rights—but would simply be compelled to share them, and never with people who were strangers to his children, but only with members of the dead spouse's family, with whom the children already had some relationship. A sister or a cousin of the murdered parent would be able to petition for custody *on an equal footing* with the indicted parent. The best interests hearing would not put the burden of proof on the latter petitioner; both parties' respective offerings to the children's physical and emotional well-being would be accorded the same weight by the judge. It would not be a foregone conclusion that the indicted murderer would lose custody.

This change, Wayburn said, was called for first of all for "moral" reasons—the law, in other words, had to stop being allowed to be common-sense-blind and ethically empty. Secondly—and getting right to the heart of Felder's interpretation of Claudia's stress, the law was needed because of the "difficulty the children will [have] coping with the fact of the knowledge that they are residing with the alleged murdering parent and dealing with the loss of the other parent." In other words, even if it *can* be ascertained that the child witnessed nothing, and even if the child believes that the parent she or he is residing with is innocent, *the sheer fact that the contrary belief has been bolstered by legal indictment* is enough to constitute a severe emotional strain that the child must not be forced to suffer. Claudia Pikul knew that her father was indicted for her mother's murder; according to Wayburn, that in itself would cause stress.

Justice Glen said that this change was a "position I might agree with" but that she was bound by the law as it stood.

By early February, Claudia started arriving at school at eight A.M. looking very well-kept, her hair done in the familiarly impeccable way Jennifer Bain had once worn hers. "Claudia," Sarah Brockton says, "had Mary Bain written all over her." Kingsley Ervin spoke widely about the admirable "support and sympathy Mrs. Bain was showing the Pikul children." When people called her at night, Steven Bain would take messages. He finally told Sarah Brockton: "She's hardly ever here anymore."

When Mary announced she was giving a birthday party for Claudia, the other parents were surprised and discomfited. One by one, they declined the invitation—no one wanted to be in the same room as Joe Pikul, whose lingering presence outside the school gates was unnerving enough. This was getting to be too much for Sarah Brockton, who finally called Mary and asked her, point-blank: "Are you out of your mind?! Why have you plunged yourself into this family?" Mary, Sarah recalls, replied by "going on at great length about people being innocent until proved guilty and how needy Claudia was. I finally said, 'Mary, you've already *got* a daughter! Don't you understand what you're doing to her?' She just answered, 'But they're so needy. . . .' "

The next time Sarah Brockton heard Kingsley Ervin talk of Mary Bain's helpfulness to the Pikul children, she retorted: "Just talk to Steven Bain—he'll set you straight."

Bob Wayburn now switched from long- to short-term tactics. Ever since Felder had gotten Joe to admit last December that he'd been arrested "sometime in the seventies," Wayburn had been trying to track down that arrest, a task which entailed the subpoenaing of records from Albany's Division of Criminal Justice Services. Then one day in the second week of March, Wayburn got lucky—a court worker called him with the case's docket number. Wayburn rushed to obtain the records.

The arrest had taken place in 1974. And, far from the evasive account Joe had given on the stand, it was for assault with a loaded .38 pistol. The complainant's name was listed as "Malcolm Rattner," and the hospital records indicated he'd been bruised on his arms and complained of blows to his face by Pikul. Right away, Wayburn called Justice Glen to ask that the hearings be reopened, not because a fourteen-year-old charge could be considered a reliable indication of a man's current propensity to violence but, rather, because Glen's sustaining of Pikul's custody had been so largely based on the court's and Dr. Kalogerakis's willingness to take Pikul's statements at face value. "And here—about this arrest, Pikul was clearly not presenting the truth about himself."

Glen granted a special hearing for March 2. But the process server returned to Wayburn's office with Rattner's subpoena still in hand. He couldn't find the man's office. With mere days to go before the hearing, Wayburn was desperate. "I've got to find this guy," he said to Doris McGarty, another lawyer in his office. Doris went out with the subpoena to the designated address, which turned out to be a gutted and desolate midtown office building in the earliest stages of reconstruction. McGarty stepped warily around the empty building until she found two construction workers who directed her to a trailer in a parking lot across the street: Malcolm Rattner's hidden interim car-service office. Outside the trailer were two Doberman pinschers. Doris McGarty girded herself and entered.

She handed the subpoena to the man—burly and bushy-haired—who identified himself as Rattner. Rattner read it, laughed, called Wayburn and said, "I'm not coming." Later that afternoon, his attorney called Wayburn and reiterated his client's position with considerably less amusement. Wayburn now went to see Rattner himself. The limousine driver who'd been forced to write a "suicide note" when Pikul had paranoically leapt on him with a gun was immensely upset at the subpoena and vociferous about his fear of Pikul. Finally, Wayburn got him to agree to appear in court on the condition that he could bring along his own bodyguard.

Wayburn hoped for the best. One thing he did not need was for another witness to backfire. Meanwhile, going over the records, he found a provocative detail: After the arrest, Pikul's loaded gun had been found in his office, vouchered to the police property clerk and judged to be ballistically operable. But then it was inexplicably "lost" by the police. When the time came for Pikul's court appearance, the D.A. didn't have a weapon to charge him with, and the case was adjourned in contemplation of dismissal after which Rattner settled out of court with Pikul, forfeiting any right to further action from the law.

The lost gun indicated to Wayburn that Pikul may have paid someone to get rid of the evidence. If Pikul had whitewashed his own record in that legal proceeding, could he not be capable of doing the same thing in this current one? As Rattner, with obvious reluctance, entered the courtroom, "bodyguard" by his side, Wayburn was cautiously optimistic.

So, it turned out, was Paul Kurland. Malcolm Rattner seemed to Kurland to be a jumpy, emotional man. During his direct examination by Wayburn, Rattner was asked if he'd served in the Vietnam War; he replied affirmatively. Wayburn elicited this information to show the court that Rattner was not a man easily cowed. Big mistake, Kurland thought happily. Excitable Vietnam Veteran: what a rich lode of vulnerability. Sitting with his client—now being described as a gun-brandishing madman assaulting a perfectly innocent messenger—Kurland formulated the aim of his cross-examination: to show *Rattner,* not Pikul, as the unstable one.

Kurland began by challenging Rattner's account of the injuries he'd incurred by Pikul. Rattner described bloody, dramatic injuries, while Beekman Downtown's records had merely listed bruises and scrapes. The witness defended his account and bristled at the implication.

Now Kurland zeroed in. "You've said you served in the Vietnam War, Mr. Rattner," he remembers asking. "Were you ever treated for post-traumatic stress syndrome?" It was just a guess. The witness answered warily in the affirmative. As Kurland pressed, Rattner appeared to be getting angry. He'd been *assaulted* by Joe Pikul. He'd been dragged to this hearing. Now Joe Pikul's lawyer was putting *him* on trial. "He seemed upset," Kathy O'Guin recalls. Finally, without being released by Justice Glen, Rattner rose from the witness stand. Kurland remembers Rattner moving toward him and a court security officer putting his hand on his gun. Having revealed a volatile man, Kurland calmly said: "No further questions."

Later that day, Paul Kurland put Mary Bain on the stand. Under oath, she described herself as a family friend and the parent of a playmate of Claudia Pikul. She was there to testify as to Joseph Pikul's good fathering and character. So confident was she of this man's equanimity and responsibility, Mary Bain said, that she had left her own daughter alone in his care on frequent playdates. This was positive testimony indeed.

Then, without any prompting from Wayburn, Mary Bain told the lawyer she had offered to adopt the children should Pikul be convicted. "I distinctly remember how it came out of the blue," Bob Wayburn says. "It was almost bizarre for this woman, a mere recent family acquaintance, to have made such an offer." Kathy O'Guin sat listening, "amazed," she recalls, "at this woman who had come out of the woodwork to testify and was now talking about adopting the children."

A week after she testified, Mary Bain was seen by another Grace Church parent walking out of the Pikul duplex at seven A.M. At about this same time, Sarah Brockton received a telephone call at home from Joe Pikul. He had somehow heard about her disapproval of his relationship with Mary. "I know what you're doing and you can't get away with it," he warned her. "I have a dossier on you and I've had you followed. I'll turn my information over to the headmaster of the school. I'll get you if you don't stop. I've done it before." Terrified, Sarah had her husband call Pikul back and tell him never again to call his wife. She then reported the call to Kingsley Ervin and to the Sixth Precinct.

That week, Carina Jacobsson called Joe to ask him if she could take the children for a day; her company, O. P. Andersson, was participating in a trade show at the new Javits Convention Center, and she knew the children—Claudia especially—would enjoy the event. Joe gave his consent. "The children were depressed," Carina remembers. "Blakey wanted to be carried everywhere—he had absolutely no energy. In the cab back to the duplex, he asked, 'Can I stay with you?' He didn't want to go home. I just said, 'Perhaps I can come and spend a weekend sometime. Daddy's waiting for you.' "

Carina recalls that when she got the children upstairs and into the living room, "Claudia was screaming; she didn't want to let me go. Then Mary Bain came in from another room and hugged her—ignoring her own daughter, who was sitting in the corner. I was flabbergasted. I wondered: Who *was* this woman and how did she get connected to Joe and the children so fast? When I told Mary I wanted to take Claudia out another day, Mary said, 'Well, plans will have to be made in advance.' She was telling me that she was now in charge and that my presence wasn't welcome." Carina did not call back.

*   *   *

By early April, Mary's relationship with Joe had accelerated. She and Steven Bain officially separated, and though she had not moved into the duplex, she was there a great deal of the time, creating a sense of home despite the fact that eviction proceedings were continuing. (Joe had still not paid his rent.) Mary's presence was particularly helpful on Sundays, during which Joe drove to the Mineola, Long Island, law offices of Ron Bekoff and Bekoff's associate, Steven Worth, where the three men would go over the explanation of the killing that Joe was to give in his defense. But if Mary was shoring up family life for the Pikuls, mothers at Grace Church School were dismayed at her apparent transfer of attention from her own daughter, Jennifer, to Claudia and Blake.

On April 14, Paul Kurland learned of a Chicago circuit court decision which set a godsend of a precedent for his client. This was the review of a case concerning a young Illinois man named James Lutgen who in December of 1984 killed his wife after she had obtained an order of protection against him. The couple's two young daughters witnessed the murder; James Lutgen pleaded guilty to voluntary manslaughter and was sentenced to four years in prison. The daughters were placed in the care of their dead mother's relatives while their father was in prison.

But last December 29—just as Joseph Pikul was celebrating the holidays with his own children—James Lutgen, released from prison early, sued for custody of his young daughters—and won. Despite the murder, despite the children's having witnessed the murder, despite Lutgen's guilty plea, his conviction and incarceration, Illinois circuit court judge Eric DeMar had just ruled that, "having paid his debt to society," James Lutgen "was a fit and proper person to have the care and control of his minor children."*

Not only had this landmark decision sprung fullblown from the Illinois court at zero hour (Glen was then writ-

---

*Carol Lutgen died of asphyxiation, the victim of what the prosecution called strangulation but James Lutgen called "a freak accident; she came at me and I pushed her away . . . and somehow her larynx got crushed." Hours before she died, she had filed for divorce.

ing her decision on *O'Guin* v. *Pikul)*, but, for Kurland's purposes, it provided extra legal berth within which his client's exceptional entitlement could be highlighted. For "Mr. Pikul is merely *accused* of the homicide. . . ." Kurland pointed out to Glen in a memo he wrote to her immediately after hearing of the decision. "In *Lutgen,* the defendant had already been convicted and incarcerated."

Fifteen days later, when she filed her decision, Glen indeed mentioned the Chicago circuit court's *Lutgen* ruling that "the conviction was not, of itself, sufficient to deprive the father of custody," and she sustained Joe's custody of the children through the summer. As she had decreed at the outset, Glen "assumed in making my decision that [Pikul] was guilty of the crime with which he was charged."

She began her discussion of the legal framework of her decision by stating, with citation references to *Bennett* v. *Jeffreys:*

> The law in this state is abundantly clear that a natural parent has a "right" to raise her or his child, and the child has a corresponding "right" to be raised by her/his parent. . . . The Court of Appeals has held that these "rights" are constitutionally protected, and that courts are "powerless to supplant parents except for grievous cause or necessity." . . . Thus, the courts may not even consider removing a child from a natural parent unless "extraordinary circumstances" are found.

She took a moment to acknowledge the press coverage and controversy of the case—to distinguish the just basis for her decision from extra-legal pressures, and to address the conflict between her duty to interpret the law as it stood and the desire of some for future, amending statute:

> [I]t is also important to state what is *not* at issue in this case which has received such wide public attention. First, the case must be decided on the record before me, not on press speculations, out-of-court

charges or the like. . . . [T]here is absolutely no evidence on this record either of abuse towards the children or of any abuse whatsoever toward Diane Whitmore Pikul prior to her murder. During the trial, advocates have picketed the courthouse and called for a change in the law which would require removal of children from a parent who has abused or who is charged with killing the other parent. It is, of course, the right of those advocating expanded legal protections for children, as of any other group, to demonstrate for changes in public policy and express their concerns. Indeed, no person of conscience can remain indifferent to the endemic problem of child abuse and familial violence, and the legislature may well be disposed to provide additional legislative protections. Nevertheless, the court is bound by *current* law . . .

And, according to that current law, the judge wrote, "I cannot find that Petitioners have met the heavy burden which would be necessary to deprive Joseph Pikul of custody of his children."

Glen relied considerably on the report of Dr. Michael Kalogerakis and both his and Dr. Arthur Green's testimony. She praised both men as "careful" and "thoughtful" and credited their mutual views that "if the relationship between the father and children was a strong and solid one, there was little or no predictable danger to the children" and "that to remove the children under these circumstances would be harmful, since the children are already grieving the loss of one parent; to leave them with no parent,* assuming the relationship with the remaining parent was a good one, would impermissibly† jeopardize their emotional health."

But what of the testimony of psychologist Ava Siegler? The specialist on children in trauma had come right out

---

*Since Felder, Wayburn, the O'Guins and Ava Siegler had all favored visitation by Pikul, the children would no more have "no" father (the wording "no parent" originated with Green) than do most children of divorced parents whose fathers are noncustodial.

†It is not clear from whose point of view this would be "impermissibl[e]." According to the transcripts, Green did not use this, or any, adjective in that particular sentence.

and stated her belief that "the rights of children are paramount" and that "[t]he physical-emotional states of the children"—emphasis here added—*"should not be compromised even in a situation where the civil rights of an adult might be at stake."* To a person of Kristin Glen's apparent political propensities, those last nineteen words might be seen as a red flag. (Glen quoted those lines, unemphasized, in the decision, as evidence of Siegler's advocacy position.) In court, Glen had questioned Siegler quite pointedly about what Glen termed as Siegler's "prejudice"—and Siegler, indeed, had set herself up for that charge by volunteering her eagerness to testify, as well as to speak on television, in a child-advocatory capacity.* Yet Siegler had made some serious, at least potentially relevant points: among them, that "hearing or overhearing that the remaining parent, who is now your guardian . . . is perceived as the possible murderer of her mother is [a] catastrophic [position] to place a young child in" and that "[c]hildren love and protect people who are very dangerous to them"; and she had stressed the denial, confusion and late-blooming symptoms of children in trauma.

The judge found that "[al]though on a general level Dr. Siegler's testimony concerning the possible responses of children to charges that a custodial parent had murdered a noncustodial parent† was helpful," Siegler's "interest in the case and her strong advocacy position made her generalized views somewhat less helpful" and her "testimony far less compelling . . . than that of Dr. Green and most particularly Dr. Kalogerakis" especially

---

*No one in court raised the issue of bias when Dr. Arthur Green testified, despite the fact that he is known as an expert witness on behalf of fathers in abuse cases. In a 1991 custody case, State Supreme Court Justice Jacqueline Silbermann termed the testimony of Green and that of a second doctor that of "the worst hired guns" for the father. Testimony by Green and two other therapists in several cases led to the introduction, in 1989 and 1991, of a New York State Assembly bill for the regulation of expert witnesses in abuse-related custody cases.

†Diane Pikul was a "noncustodial" parent only after—and because—she was murdered; and, according to the court transcript, nowhere in the questioning of Ava Siegler was any question or answer phrased in these terms.

"since she had not observed the children or the interaction between them and their father."

Glen's ready identification of Siegler's bias is matched by her perception of Sharon Space. The judge saw Diane Pikul's AA sponsor as "clearly hostile to Respondent and extremely interested in the outcome of the proceeding, a fact which may well have colored her testimony." As for Malcolm Rattner, she identified him as an "extremely angry and emotional witness . . . clearly prone to exaggeration [who] misstated material facts, overdramatized everything he said and expressed extreme hostility towards Respondent." She referred to the pistol-wielding by Pikul, as described by Rattner, as an episode of some "middle level of unpleasantness" and termed it, by virtue of its length of time in the past and the fact that Pikul then was drinking and now was not, "as only a minimal factor in assessing his dangerousness or lack of dangerousness toward the children."

By contrast, Glen highly credited the testimony of Bernetta Seegars, calling her "an extremely competent, solid, no-nonsense person . . . who has the best opportunity to observe [the father-child] relationship over a long period of time," and she stressed Seegar's repeatedly stated lack of fear for herself or for the Pikul children. Yet, while these points may indeed have been well taken, the fact that Seegars "was rehired and is now again their full-time baby-sitter" was noted by Glen with no pause to consider the possibility—suggested by Felder—that a nonunionized, unprotected employee might have a vested interest in saying only good things about the person from whom she receives her full salary—a person who can fire her for any reason at any time.

Glen called Mary Bain a "competent, accomplished and convincing witness" whose "parental feelings were strong, towards her own child . . . and toward the Pikul children." She tangentially acknowledged that Claudia called Bain "Mommy" and that "when Ms. Baines [sic] first testified she offered her and her husband's home as an alternate resource for custody of the children should Mr. Pikul be convicted. Subsequently, for reasons which have not been specified, that offer was withdrawn." These observations would appear to beg some questions. For example, why was a child who was suffering from the death of her own mother being encouraged to use (or at least not being gently *dis*couraged from using) the word "Mommy" for a woman whom she'd known well for less than one month?* Further, Glen's opinion didn't raise the possibility that Mary Bain's early—eventually abandoned—offer of adoption might have affected her interest in the outcome of the case. "Even though this was peripheral to her decision," Bob Wayburn says, "I was surprised that Glen credited Mary Bain's testimony so highly."

With her assessments of Joseph Pikul, however, Glen's critical acumen was once again in evidence—initially, at least. She found him to be "combative," "sparring," "sarcastic," exhibiting signs of "anger," and "not always entirely credible." She said, "Dr. Kalogerakis's characterization of Respondent as a 'troubled' individual seemed apt. However," she went on, "when he spoke about his children and his relationship to them, Respondent appeared as an entirely different person."

As for this "entirely different person," Glen quoted Pikul's remarks about his own "flexibil[ity]" and, despite her assertion that Malcolm Rattner's testimony had "demonstrated that the Respondent is not always truthful," she appeared to accept at face value Pikul's claim that Claudia had said, "[G]oing to a total stranger would be devastating to me." Glen wrote, "I credit that his love and concern for the children is genuine and strong"; that his "main concern seemed to be to provide stability for the children after the death of their mother."

A practical matter Glen had to deal with was the custody of the children during Pikul's murder trial, during which time his presence in Orange County would make it, she ruled, impossible to be a full-time parent. During this period, Glen ruled, the children would go to live with the O'Guins.

This "phony consolation prize" tacked on to the decision infuriated Raoul Felder, as did the decision itself. What the state needed now, Felder said, was "laws to protect children from judges like Kristin Glen." Joe's lawyers, of course, were delighted with the outcome. Be-

*It was determined that Claudia was calling Mary Bain "Mommy" on January 28.

koff was now representing a murder defendant who had been certified a loving and responsible father, and Kurland had won a victory made all the more exceptional by the hostile public climate. He hailed Glen's decision as one of "great integrity." As for Bob Wayburn, he felt the decision was correct, based on Glen's reading of *Bennett* (with which he had long disagreed) and that, on those terms, he and Felder had not met their heavy burden of proof.

Joe Pikul's landlord had given him until June 15 to vacate the Sixth Avenue duplex for nonpayment of $18,000 back rent. No one except Joe's probation officer now had a right to know where he would be taking the children. Joe took advantage of his new prerogative by calling Diane's father. "He told me I would never see my grandchildren again," Don Whitmore says.

As for the transfer of the children to the O'Guins in the fall, Joe Pikul and the new woman in his life were working on a way to circumvent that. Joe knew he'd have a good shot at keeping the children in his custody during the trial if he kept the O'Guins away from the children all summer and if he had a new wife, who could take over child rearing. This latter had to be accomplished quickly, but in New York State divorce is customarily drawn out. There are, however, little-known exceptions. According to Mary, Joe came to her one day with the news that she could get, within twenty-four hours, a divorce from Steven, on the condition that certain concessions be made. In Mary's case, she could have her immediate freedom to marry Joe Pikul if she gave residential custody of Jennifer to her ex-husband.

Again according to Mary, who today attributes the entire decision to Joe: "Joe deceived me into thinking the custody decision was reversible. He said, 'You know how brilliant Paul [Kurland] is—you saw what he did for me; he'll be able to reverse the decision between you and Steven in September.' " (Kurland says he had no part in Mary's divorce nor was privy to Pikul's claim.) That was enough reassurance for Mary, who reasoned that Jennifer would be away at camp most of the summer anyway; for the period between June and September the issue of which parent had residential custody was moot.

* * *

One Sunday at the beginning of July, Joe appeared at his usual strategy session with Ron Bekoff. This time Mary was with him. Bekoff had never met the woman before and was instantly wary of the affection the two displayed. He was on the brink of what he thought would be key pretrial victories in terms of the admissibility of his client's statements to the various interrogating and arresting police officers; he didn't want anything screwing things up. So when Joe asked him, point-blank, "I'm thinking of getting married; what do you think?" Bekoff lost no time in giving his opinion. "Look," he remembers saying, "you're going to trial for killing your wife in a small, close-knit, conservative community. If you trot into court with a new wife on your arm, you might antagonize people. They'll think, Didn't he have the decency to wait until he was cleared of the charge? Some of them may even think she was your motive for murdering Diane."

"I see your point," Joe said. "That's why I hired you—you're a terrific lawyer." Bekoff felt relieved as he and Mary stood up. Then Pikul said: "Now we're going off to get married."

The wedding, on July 2, took place upstate near the apartment Joe and Mary had rented in the Ulster County town of Lanesville. They were married hours after Mary's divorce with Steven was filed. Claudia and Blake were the only attendants. The wedding was to be kept secret, most particularly from Felder, Wayburn and Diane's friends. Mary Bain denies that Jennifer, away at camp during the wedding, experienced her mother's actions as the "transfer of affection" the Grace Church parents saw it to be. She says that her daughter did not feel rejected and that to this day she and Jennifer "are very close; we talk about every possible feeling."*

---

*In several later appearances on the tabloid television show *A Current Affair,* Mary Bain Pikul spoke about how much she loved Blake and Claudia, of how she, Joe and the Pikul children were "a family." When asked why Jennifer was absent from this televised testimonial seen by so many Grace Church families, Mary replied that her daughter "wanted it that way—she was very embarrassed that her father and I had gotten divorced."

Mary became the linchpin of the family. She took a brief paid leave of absence from her job, and began a life of household chores: She awoke at five A.M. to do the family laundry, make breakfast and clean the house. Since Joe hadn't worked since the murder, and since all his money was going to his lawyers (he had paid Bekoff a retainer of $75,000, as well as paying Vinnie Federico $15,000; he also paid fees to Sam Dawson), Mary's paycheck supported the family. Even though she admits breaking one IRA account for Joe, and even though her salary was more substantial than Steven's, she denies that her taking on one grown and two further child dependents cut into Jennifer's lifestyle or security at all. As for the sacrifices of time, labor and money that went into her new marriage to the murder defendant twenty years her senior, she dismisses them as "the things you do when you love someone. It was such a special feeling. I couldn't walk away from love. I was so in love with Joe and with the children."

Kathy and Michael O'Guin made repeated attempts to see the children alone, as Justice Glen's decision had stipulated, but Glen's order was only paper; without the involvement of an agency to enforce it, Joe Pikul's will continued to hold sway. Only three visits between the O'Guins and the children took place all summer—lunches during which Joe and Mary were present. The children called Mary "Mommy" throughout, and the visits were awkward. The O'Guins got the distinct impression that the children were instructed to talk to them as little as possible. Furthermore, when the O'Guins attempted to register the children in Yonkers schools in anticipation of the forthcoming custody change, their lack of guardianship papers stood in their way. It was futile, the O'Guins finally decided. "Their sad conclusion," Felder reported in a letter to Glen, Kurland and Wayburn dated July 27, "is that it would be absolutely cruel and irresponsible to wrest these children away from yet another maternal figure whom they call 'Mommy' and to whom they have bonded. Therefore the O'Guins do not wish to press further in the custody situation and at this juncture [will] step out of the children's lives. To say that this decision has been made with regret and sadness is an understatement. Literally their hearts have been broken. But impelled by that same original concern that they had for the children, they feel that they can take no other course." Like the natural mother in the King Solomon legend, the O'Guins, rather than to tear the children in two, stepped aside.

On August 4, Mary Bain Pikul revealed her secret marriage in an affidavit she filed, requesting, "along with their natural father," the custody of Blake and Claudia "through the conclusion of Mr. Pikul's criminal trial." She added, "It is my intention to seek to adopt Claudia and Blake Pikul irrespective of the outcome of the criminal trial." Having already moved Steven and Jennifer around in her life for her romantic rescue mission, Mary now added to the list her parents, Rudolph and Elizabeth Eik, who owned a home in Brooklyn but who, Mary stated in her petition, rather conveniently resided "in Florida for almost the entire year" and who had just given Mary their permission to move her new family into the Brooklyn house. Claudia and Blake could be reenrolled in Grace Church School. And, the petition stated, "Jennifer . . . will spend part of the week with me and part of the week with my former husband." In fact, the only part of the week Jennifer would spend with her mother were weekends.

Exactly one week later, on August 11, Judge Thomas J. Byrne, who would be conducting Pikul's criminal trial, handed down good news to Joe, Mary and Bekoff: In his review of the pretrial papers filed by both the prosecution and the defense, the judge had decided that Joe Pikul's most damaging words—his serial confession to Investigators Tripodo, Jr., Venezia and Tripodo, Sr., at the Troop F barracks in the hours between his arrest and arraignment—had been elicited "in violation of the defendant's rights." They would be admissible in court only if Pikul took the stand himself, something that Bekoff, despite going over Pikul's story with him for literally months of Sundays, was still uncertain he wanted Pikul to do.

Unfortunately for Bekoff, Joe's statement to Investigator Jim Probst—"I did it; she was such a bitch"—on the ride from Manhattan to Newburgh was deemed admissible by Byrne. "If only *that* last one was thrown out, I'd have a real whodunit," Bekoff would lament. Then he could keep his client where most defense attorneys want their clients to be: *off* the stand. Still, Bekoff felt his chances were good. His adversary, Alan Joseph, had lost the right to use the incriminating admissions Joe had made to Venezia and the Tripodos. More important, Joseph had no eyewitness. And Judge Byrne was known as a cautious, prodefense judge, exceedingly reluctant to have his trials scrutinized for improprieties in appeal.

By the end of the summer, things looked quite positive for Joe. So much so that Mary didn't want to complain about certain things in her life with her new husband that frightened her. She had been married to Joe Pikul for less than two months, but his reaction to her going on business trips, for example, was extremely negative. His counting the minutes she was out grocery shopping, his anger when she was away "too long," and the way he got angry if she wore a dress he didn't like or wasn't losing weight as fast as she promised . . . Mary realized she needed to talk to someone, but no one—not Joe, not any of the authorities—could find out.

In mid-August, Mary drove to the counseling facility at the Ulster County Medical Center and signed in under her maiden name, Mary Eik. She hadn't used that name in fourteen years. There she talked, confidentially, to a counselor named Dale Schumacher. As more things happened with Joe that she needed to talk about, she went back to Ms. Schumacher again. After she returned from a business trip on August 27, her need to pour her heart out to Ms. Schumacher was particularly acute.

The O'Guins, angered at the secret marriage and Mary's adoption bid, decided to renew their custody application, but they held few illusions about their chances. Last spring, Joe had told Mike O'Guin, "I had a plan for everything except you." Now he had a plan for them, too: He requested a hearing to block the O'Guins' reinstated custody bid; on Wednesday, September 14, all the familiar parties—the O'Guins, Felder, Wayburn, Joe and Mary, Kurland—were back in Kristin Glen's courtroom.

Even before the hearing was convened, Joe and Mary posed for victory photographs on the courtroom steps outside. Diane's friends noticed that Joe seemed a little awkward in the role of the triumphant newlywed; but

Mary, bubbly in her answers to reporters, was clearly at ease.

"We don't have a prayer," Mike O'Guin admitted to a reporter as he and Kathy slid into the wooden bench-style seats. Kathy said: "Until he beats the kids, they're his." Even Felder was resigned and subdued. "It looks like a joke, huh?" was the best he could muster.

Indeed, the morning and much of the afternoon enfolded as a wrap-up proceeding by which the way seemed to be paved for the Pikuls' assumption of permanent custody. Joe and Mary presented a hard-to-shake picture of family happiness. Kurland felt he was on his way to the final stage of victory.

Indeed, for Diane's friends and supporters of the O'Guins, everything that could have gone wrong over those months did. A staunch constitutional- and defendant's-rights judge had been drawn. Hearsay was ruled inadmissible. Witnesses for the petitioners had included a man who had been hauled off an airfield in a straightjacket, a psychologist who naïvely advanced her child-advocatory bias, and a former limousine driver who almost stormed off the witness stand. There was also a court-appointed psychiatrist who had very little recent experience with children and a child psychiatrist known for his defense of accused men. Then wife-killer James Lutgen's Illinois custody triumph came just in time to provide a precedent for Pikul. Finally, the summer had gone by with Mary and Joe effectively shutting the O'Guins out of the children's lives.

As the proceedings were rolling to a smooth finish, the phone suddenly rang in the courtroom. A phone ringing in a courtroom is not a usual occurrence. The phone was handed to Bob Wayburn. For a lawyer to receive an emergency call in the middle of a hearing is an even more unusual occurrence. The caller was SSC social worker Barbara Ditman, who had just spent the last few minutes calling around frantically for the courtroom's phone number. Barbara said this: She had just gotten a report from a counseling center worker in Ulster County who, on a hunch, had checked the married name of a patient who had come to her several days before. The reason the counselor had checked the married name— and then placed an emergency call to the SSC when she found it—was that the incident of abuse the patient had detailed had taken place in front of children, and that fact merited a breaking of the condition of confidentiality.

Wayburn listened hard. Then he asked for a recess while he conferred with Glen.

"Everything was different after the recess—the whole atmosphere changed," Paul Kurland remembers. "The judge's attitude told me something was very wrong—and there was suddenly a massing of court officers in the vicinity of my client." Wayburn could barely conceal his look of triumph from Kathy O'Guin. He recalls: " 'Is it good?' she asked me. When I said, 'Yes,' her whole face lit up."

Mary Bain Pikul was called back on the stand. Purposefully, Wayburn approached her.

"Mrs. Pikul, are you aware of what it means to take an oath?" he asked.

"Yes, of course," the witness said quickly.

"Are you aware of the possible prosecution for perjury?" Wayburn paused. "With possible imprisonment?"

"No," the witness said shakily. "I wasn't aware of that."

After explaining the legal concept of perjury to Mary, and ascertaining that she understood the importance of her testimony as "it affects the lives of two children," Wayburn picked up on a prior admission of Mary's that, at the time, had gone nowhere. "You stated earlier that Mr. Pikul raised his voice to you four times. Did he do anything else whatsoever that threatened your physical safety?"

By now, Mary was blinking and sitting up diffidently. "Well, I think it depends on how you construe it," was her answer. From the corner of his eye, Wayburn could see Kurland and Pikul huddled together, whispering furiously. Kurland then rose to his feet to object to the questioning. Glen overruled him.

With coaxing from Wayburn, Mary continued: "There was an incident, but I don't know if you can consider it to be a threat to my well-being."

Glen leaned down from her bench, fixed her gaze at the woman she had called, in her decision, a "competent, accomplished and convincing witness," and firmly ordered: *"Tell us."*

The whole courtroom became electric. Mary was tense. Joe was tense. Kurland was tense. Felder and the O'Guins felt affirmed and expectant.

"I view it as a domestic altercation. We were arguing and I tried to pacify him and he didn't let me pacify him. He kind of stood there," Mary said, "and he pushed me."

Wayburn himself now pushed—against Mary's wall of protestations that the "incidents" she had discussed with Dale Schumacher were "confidential"; that they were "domestic altercations" that had nothing to do with the children; that "Joe and I don't fight in front of the children"; and that "I had always stressed what a wonderful and loving father he's been."

Finally, he led her to the events of an evening shortly before Labor Day when Mary returned from grocery shopping. "I went home and went upstairs and the children were in bed and they came to me and said, 'You were gone over an hour; Daddy is looking for you and he is angry at you.' "

"What transpired after they went back into the bedroom and closed the door?" Wayburn asked.

"Joe was angry at me. And he was questioning me. He was angry and we had a fight."

"Can you describe the fight?"

"He tore my dress."

"How did he tear your dress?"

"I was wearing a two-piece dress, a blouse and a skirt."

"How did he tear it?" Wayburn was unswerving. His placidity could match her reluctance, moment for moment, stall for stall. If necessary he would prod her through each syllable. "Did he use a hunting knife?"

After a pause: "Yes."

"Where did he cut it?"

"On the bodice and on the top."

"Two locations?"

"Yes."

"How long was the cut on the bodice?"

Another pause. "Six to eight inches."

"And how long was the other cut?"

"Approximately the same."

"And what were you doing when he cut the dress?"

"Sitting down on the couch."

"Did there ever come a time that he held the knife to your throat?"

Mary stiffened. "Not in my recollection."

"That evening when Mr. Pikul cut your skirt bodice, did you leave the household?"

"Yes, I did." After coaxing: "I was obviously very upset. I was angry, I was disillusioned. I ran to the neighbor's house."

Repeatedly now Wayburn asked Mary if, as she ran to the neighbors, she saw Joe; after denying it, she finally qualified: "No, I didn't see him . . . but I knew he was there."

"Did you see a flashlight?"

"Yes," Mary conceded. "That's how I knew he was there. I was running toward the neighbor's house and there was a flashlight behind me. . . . The neighbors weren't there, so I stayed in the garden until they came home."

Wayburn now elicited from her the fact that she'd slipped in a marshy area and had gotten wet, that she'd told the neighbors she did not want to go back to her house that night and that she "didn't want Joe to know I was talking to them." After spending the night at a second neighbor's house, she woke up early and only returned to her own home after the neighbor had spoken to Joe and determined that he was no longer angry.

"Then I walked down the road and back to the house and Joe wouldn't let me come in and wouldn't let me get a change of clothes." Mary conceded that Joe had pushed her away from the door, and after first denying it, she admitted that, hours later, she called the police to help her get her car keys and pocketbook out of the house.

"No further questions," Wayburn said.

Within moments, the house of cards that had been constructed over ten months fell: Pikul withdrew his custody petition. Kurland resigned as Pikul's attorney. Glen gave the O'Guins immediate custody and placed them, Mary Bain Pikul and all the lawyers under protective order from any acts Joe Pikul might attempt against them. "It was amazing," Kathy O'Guin sums up. "Once the truth was on the table in a way that no one could overlook anymore, everyone stopped playacting and got down to business."

Kathy and Mike O'Guin left the courtroom to make the two hour drive upstate to get the children from the neighbor's house where Mary and Joe had left them, but Wayburn was still not satisfied. "Hold Pikul here until the children are actually obtained," he demanded of the judge when the proceedings were finally over at nine P.M. Glen refused that final measure. Sure enough, as Wayburn suspected, Joe and Mary were soon in a car, racing the O'Guins upstate. Wayburn rushed over to nearby police headquarters at One Police Plaza, then to a local precinct, where he worked until midnight putting together a team to effect removal of the children from the neighbor's house into protective custody until the O'Guins could reach them.

Kathy and Mike took the children, with just the clothes on their backs, into their arms and into their car, and made the hour and a half drive back to Yonkers. The next day, Kathy would report, "We're scrambling to do everything—get clothes and toys and enroll them in school. Their dislocation last night was hard. But it wasn't their first horror. What they need now—even more than therapy, which they'll have—is stability. That's something we know we can give them."

"I just want to be alone with my children in the country; that's the only time I feel peaceful," Diane had tearfully said to Ann Stern, days before her murder. "My fantasy is not another man but tranquility and an ordered existence," she had written to Pat Jaudon, when Claudia was an infant.

What Diane had so wanted for her children and had been unable to give them herself would now be given them by her cousin.

PART VI

JUSTICE AND DEATH

Chapter 12

"A murder trial is like an Aretha Franklin song. 'Who's zoomin' who?' "

Michael Schwartz, law clerk to People v. Joseph Pikul *judge Thomas J. Byrne*

Joseph Pikul did not take the loss of his children easily.

Two days after the decision, the O'Guins discovered that Joe told Blake, in the one nightly phone call Justice Glen had ruled he could make to his children: "Tonight I am going to come through the window and take you away." Blake Pikul nervously asked his father, "Is that okay with the court?" Private detective Bo Deitl had a security assistant, Louis Fretti, assigned to the O'Guin house at the time. "My instructions to Louis after that were," Deitl recalls, " 'If this maniac comes through the window, do what you gotta do, because if he has an opportunity, he'll kill you.' I drank a gallon of coffee and didn't sleep that night."

But Pikul's kidnapping of the children was thwarted by his own self-destructiveness soon after it began. On Saturday, September 17, at four P.M., Pikul's Lanesville neighbor Richard Roberti rushed out the door of his house when he heard the sound of a car crashing nearby. Roberti recognized the driver as Pikul. "He was very drunk and very demanding," Roberti later told police. "He demanded that I change his tire, which was flat. After he opened his trunk, I saw a twelve-gauge pump shotgun and what appeared to be an automatic hand-gun." Pikul moved these around so the spare tire could be extricated, and Roberti did as he was told.

Later, at Pikul's house to collect money he'd been

promised for his service, Roberti could see that Pikul was "very erratic: at times crying, at times pacing back and forth," bemoaning his having been "set up" to lose his kids. "He kept repeating that he was 'dead,' " Roberti told police. "He kept saying he would go to the border—Canada or Mexico. He said he was 'on a mission,' " that he was going down to a bar, with his shotgun, to " 'relieve my frustrations.' " He muttered ruefully that his first wife was bad, his second wife was dead, and his third wife was good. Then, according to Roberti, he said, "Well, you can't kill them all. . . ."

The next day, the fearful O'Guins left their home and took Blake and Claudia into hiding at a friend's house. The children had no toys and only the clothes they were wearing at the time. That evening they made a call to their father. Mike O'Guin listened in. He heard Joe asking the children how long the drive was from the old house to the new one, and told them to look at the names of adjacent streets. He asked Claudia to look for the street name and get the house number without telling Mike and Kathy and told them to give him the information in their next night's allotted phone call. "This will take some real planning," he said. "The O'Guins are a complication." Later in the conversation he described them as "assholes," "jerks" and "terrible people."

The O'Guins promptly told Felder and Wayburn, and custodial interference was charged. By Tuesday, September 20, the key parties were acting in character: Felder angrily pled for the children's protection from the "homicidal lunatic"; Kristin Glen suspended Joe's phone call privileges, her censure of the demonstrably threatening defendant typically minimal; Alan Joseph was pushing against Judge Byrne's prodefense inclination, trying without any real optimism to use Pikul's statements about fleeing the country, as well as the knife attack against his new wife, and the fact that much of his bond money was put up by others, as grounds for revocation of bail.

And, widening her locus of notoriety from the Grace Church community to all of New York, Mary Bain Pikul had arranged for her husband and herself to plead their case on the television show *A Current Affair*. Playing handily into the oily curiosity of Maury Povich, the show's host, Mary blamed herself for impetuously seeking out counseling instead of quietly living through the "period of adjustment" in her marriage. Joe sat by his voluble bride's side, looking desperate, sleepless and drunk. Diane's friends couldn't believe how the story had gone from brute tragedy to social injustice to this lowest of farce. Their friend had virtually, and pitifully, bartered her life for an assemblage of decadent ironies; now she had wound up the nonperson in a tacky melodrama.

Glen barred Joe from the Yonkers city limit; Judge Byrne denied Alan Joseph's request for bail remand*; the O'Guins enrolled Blake and Claudia in a Yonkers public school. Twice in October, Joe was apprehended by the local upstate police—once for drunk driving (for which he spent a night in jail), the second time for speeding—both times driving with a suspended license. The Orange County newspapers, hard put for juicy news, played up the stories. Citing insufficient change of circumstance, Judge Byrne continued to rule that Pikul stay free on bail. Police at airports and borders had his picture and profile. Predictably, Dr. Arthur Green, now the children's therapist, deemed father-children visitation advisable. So, every Sunday, the O'Guins would drive the children to the nearby White Plains Hilton, where they would meet with their father. Louis Fretti always frisked Joe before he was allowed to enter the room.

Joe would come to this meeting after his earlier one with Ron Bekoff. By now, Bekoff's junior partner, Steven Worth, handsome and corporate-smooth, was assuming an increasing role in the defense sessions. Worth was less goading and demanding than was Bekoff. He became the good cop to Bekoff's bad; and, in one of those odd transferences that such tense intimacy can produce, the fifty-four-year-old defendant came to think of his thirty-seven-year-old attorney as an idealized father. "You're like my daddy," Joe once told Worth.

---

*Judge Byrne's reasons for not revoking Pikul's bail included his agreement with Pikul's attorneys' contention that restoration of a half- to one-million-dollar yearly salary was sufficient incentive to stay and stand trial, as well as the judge's acknowledgment of the defendant's perfect attendance record at all court hearings thus far. Furthermore, Byrne said he did not believe Pikul's utterances about going to Canada were to be taken seriously.

For his part, Worth saw in Joe Pikul "a passionate, bright, volatile guy who had thought he was a Master of the Universe"—the attorney borrows the term Tom Wolfe, in *The Bonfire of the Vanities,* made famous as a synonym for Wall Streeters' hubris—"who had thought he could do and get whatever he wanted. And he expressed every possible emotion about Diane. Her taking the job at *Harper's* and her ability to stand up to him were clearly catalysts of his anger at her."

Joe's fury at women and his lack of even one positive romantic relationship in his lifetime were apparent to Bekoff as well. But Joe's ambivalent feelings about his parents were what he most mused about, especially since his mother, Bobchi, had died the previous winter in the nursing home to which she'd long been confined. "He had bittersweet feelings about both his parents," recalls Bekoff. "He wanted to love them but he was too angry, especially at his father. That his father once broke his arm"—he told Kurland it was his jaw; perhaps it was both—"was particularly hard to erase from his mind." For Joe Pikul, the aberrantly pure love that he had for his children—the sight of which had so impressed Kurland, Bekoff, Kalogerakis and Glen—was probably the only thing that made him feel like the human being he wanted to be. No wonder he'd told Bekoff when he'd retained him that he wanted to fight for custody, even if that meant jeopardizing the outcome of the criminal trial.

Now, Bekoff saw, his client had been true to his word. For the events of September and October had made Joe known throughout the trial jurisdiction as a gun-keeper, a wife-stabber, a dangerous driver, a prospective bail-jumper and a drunk. The advantage the attorney had tallied through his statement-admissibility victories and his drawing of a defense-friendly judge was now diminished, if not destroyed. To make matters worse, delays on Judge Byrne's calendar had pushed the start of the trial date back to the first week of January 1989, so that its opening would probably dovetail with the end of the Joel Steinberg trial in Manhattan. For the first eight months of his prepping of Pikul, Bekoff had hoped to get *his* client's trial over and done with before that huge shadow-caster began. But the Steinberg trial had opened in Manhattan in November, just as Bekoff was attempting damage control of his volatile client. The timing couldn't have been worse. Public attention to that trial was almost unprecedented—Hedda Nussbaum's six days of testimony in early December were televised live on the networks, preempting the game shows and soap operas. The public's wish for vengeance against the defendant was strong. A Steinberg verdict was now almost sure to come in during the opening weeks of the Pikul trial; if that verdict was less than Murder Two (as seemed, from the circumstantial case, likely), the public outcry could well spill over to conservative, law-abiding Orange County. Bekoff says, "I was scared to death about that."

During the pretrial months, both Bekoff and Alan Joseph were keeping each other guessing in key regards. The biggest two secrets Bekoff was keeping from Joseph were what the defense would be and whether or not Pikul would take the stand. Joseph knew the defense would not be insanity, because no psychiatric examinations of Pikul had been conducted, but he had no idea that Bekoff and Worth had been preparing Pikul to testify for over a full year now. Nor did the prosecutor know Pikul was going to claim self-defense. "I wanted," Bekoff says, "to stay in the high weeds with my defense and then spring it on him." His reason for keeping Pikul's planned testimony secret was also clear: Prosecutors are notoriously bad at cross-examination because they get so little practice at it. Bekoff had driven up to Orange County and slipped into a courtroom while his future adversary was trying a case; he judged Alan Joseph to be no exception to that rule, "a pragmatic, tenacious but not very personable prosecutor, a man more comfortable with evidence than with people." Why give this diffident questioner reason to think he'd better start sharpening his skills?

But if Bekoff was planning to ambush Joseph with the justification defense and with Pikul's presence on the witness stand, Bekoff was also bracing for Joseph to ambush him first. The defense attorney knew Sandra Jarvinen had testified before the grand jury but, since Sandra was not a codefendant, this testimony did not qualify under the rules of discovery. So for a year now, Bekoff had been shadowboxing with this most important witness; Sandra's words about the phone calls and meetings from August to October and, most damningly, about the visit Joe had made to her house in the early hours of October 25 could now only be guessed at; and no information he'd gathered to impugn her credibility as a witness was more than a very poor second to the record of those words themselves.

This yearlong lack of discoverability of Sandra's testimony was Alan Joseph's biggest pretrial advantage; she was thus not only his star witness, but his secret witness as well. Nondiscoverable testimony is made available to a defense attorney in the twelve-hour sliver of time between the end of jury selection and the start of opening statements (usually concluded in a day)—such testimony, called Rosario material, must be handed over to the defense. Hence, a D.A. looking to ambush his opponent will put that star, secret witness on the stand first, even if her testimony is out of order with his presentation, and will get her testimony over quickly—thus cutting the time the defense lawyer has to prepare his cross to two all-nighters, at best. "Just watch. . . . He's gonna catch me off guard," Bekoff kept saying to Worth as the two of them arrived with their suitcases at a rented condominium apartment in the Orange County seat, Goshen, on January 8. "Sandra Jarvinen's going to be the first witness he'll call." Nineteen days later, when the witness list was handed out in Justice Byrne's courtroom after the eleven-man, one-woman jury* was finally impaneled, Bekoff turned to Worth and murmured, "What did I tell you?" Jarvinen's name was at the head of Joseph's list.

While Bekoff hastily obtained the Rosario material on Jarvinen's testimony, crossing his fingers for no mean surprises, Joseph surveyed the almost completely male jury and hoped for the best. Then defense and prosecution bid each other good luck and repaired for a weekend of final preparation. On Monday, they would be back in this dramatically modern courtroom of high, raw concrete walls cut by vertical panels of orange fabric, doing battle in earnest at last.

---

*Bekoff tried for an all-male jury, but had to settle for one woman when he ran out of peremptory challenges.

*   *   *

"The People will prove to you that the defendant, Joseph Pikul, and his wife, Diane Pikul, were on the verge of divorce," Alan Joseph began, launching into his opening statement on Monday morning, January 31. The young prosecutor strode around in front of the jury box with his jut-elbowed, headlong gait, shocks of sleek dark hair falling into his eyes. He could be taken for an impatient assistant professor racing to get to a seminar on time. "They left New York City for Long Island in separate cars on Friday, October 23, 1987. The defendant arrived earlier with their two children. Diane Pikul arrived at approximately 1:00 to 1:30 in the morning on Saturday, October 24, 1987. You'll also hear that they had a verbal slight argument and that was the last time that anyone saw her alive." Hearing these words, Joseph Pikul, seated between Bekoff and Worth at the defense table, was emotionless. Mary Bain Pikul, facing her husband from her seat in the spectators section of the sparsely-peopled courtroom, appeared dramatically grave.

"The evidence will show you that after running some errands around Amagansett in his Mazda, the defendant then drives his two children in his 1986 Buick station wagon to the town of New Windsor to the home of an old college friend, Henry Sawoska . . ." As Joseph went on to detail the chronology and highlights of his case, Don and Gretchen Whitmore, Barbara Martin and Pat Bartholomew listened intently from the back of the courtroom. Barbara and Pat were the only two of Diane's friends who could both afford time for the four-hour round-trip drive to Orange County and who were allowed as court spectators. (Maggie Gari, Ann Stern, Carina Jacobsson, Inga Davidsson and Linda McNamera were to be called as witnesses and, as such, were barred from watching the trial.) Both had been stunned when, before the court was called to session, Joe had said an unself-conscious hello to the Whitmores as he strode down the aisle to the defense table, and Mary had waxed effusively cheerful, as if she were greeting the elderly couple at a wedding reception instead of her husband's trial. Between these odd felicitations and a group of senior citizens ensconced in the second row, watching the trial for diversion, there seemed, to Pat and Barbara, an appalling and heartbreaking lack of solemnity and memory in the room. They realized that they alone were bearing witness to the horror that had befallen their friend.

"Various witnesses," Alan Joseph concluded, "will leave *no* reasonable doubt in your minds as to the guilt of Joseph Pikul for the crime of murder in the second degree."

Now Ron Bekoff stood up and strolled slowly over to the panel. In contrast to the brusque, guileless, slightly built prosecutor, the defense attorney was a large, lumbering, theatrically deliberate man who embodied a uniquely urban combination of authority and jive. He mulled over his words before speaking them, the look on his face often hinting that he was either on the brink of a wry revelation or a stinging comeback line. "During the jury selection we agreed to put this case under a microscope, to look for a reasonable doubt, and that's what I'm asking you to do now," he began.

"I'm asking you to pay attention to the witnesses, to hear what happened or didn't happen and make him prove the who, the how, and the where and the *why*.

"I'm asking you to be fair—to give us the good honest shot, the feeling that this is America and we can get a fair trial, regardless of what you might have heard or seen in the newspapers. I particularly want you to keep an eye on the tenor and the focus of the police investigation. Were they trying to find out what really happened? Was it a search for truth, or were they looking for an easy arrest of an eccentric individual?"

Clearly, by focusing the jury on the tactics of the investigation and hinting that the police may have arrested the wrong man, Bekoff had not yet decided to plead justification. He was hedging his bets—keeping one defense tucked in his pocket while brandishing the other now. The weeds in which he was laying in wait were not only high, they were dangerous, for such "shotgun" defenses often backfire. But he seemed willing to gamble on the combination of the great number of the witnesses and his skill as a cross-examiner; if he poked enough holes in his adversary's meticulously connected scenario, maybe those holes, and not the connections, were what the jury would see. Maybe he wouldn't need to put his unpredictable and sometimes uncontrollable client on the stand.

* * *

"The People call Sandra Jarvinen."

Heads turned as a large woman in a blond Dutch-boy haircut and a muttonchop-sleeved flowered dress entered the courtroom and mounted the witness stand. Her head was bent decorously; she avoided the eyes of her ex-husband, who sat, discomfited, at the defense table ten feet away. She raised her right hand and swore to tell the truth.

"Do you know an individual named Joseph Pikul?" Alan Joseph asked his star witness.

"Yes, sir," she whispered. "I was married to Joseph. We met in 1955, we married in 1959, and we were divorced in 1974."

"Do you see Joseph Pikul in the courtroom today?"

"Yes, sir." Sandra's *sir*s had the ring of stagy, almost patronizing deference.

"Point him out, please."

Her eyes still lowered, Sandra pointed to Joe. As Joseph led his witness through her early years with the defendant, Bekoff sat poised to spring up if any hint of Joe's violence toward her was raised. In Sandra's grand jury testimony, Bekoff had read with annoyance and dismay, she had mentioned her fear of Joe every chance she got. With the Joel Steinberg jury out six days and about to come back with a probably reduced verdict any minute now—putting the most famous wife-batterer in America at the top of the news right in the middle of Sandra's testimony—Bekoff had demanded from Byrne that a tight lid be kept on Sandra's past with Joe.

Joseph ascertained that Joe owed Sandra $28,000 in back alimony. Then he asked, "Did there come a time in late summer 1987 when you received any contact from the defendant?"

"Yes. I received a phone call from him in August 1987." Under the prosecutor's further questioning, she went on to say: "He kept calling me regularly. He wanted to meet with me. I didn't see any particular reason for it. I kept putting him off until finally I agreed that if he wanted to fly into Hyannis Airport, not thinking that he would do it, he could. But he said okay, and he did come up on a Sunday."

"Now, before he came up, did he ever discuss with you anything regarding his wife, Diane Pikul?"

"Yes. He was getting a divorce and he was very unhappy. He claimed that she wasn't taking proper care of the children and he didn't know who was with them when he was out of town, that she was blackmailing him. He was just very generally upset." During the Hyannis meeting, Sandra went on, "he didn't feel that his wife would take good care of the children. He did not want her to have custody of the children. He had asked me if I would be their guardian and trustee, and I explained to him that I could not be their guardian, that his wife was the guardian of the children if he passed away, and he made the statement that she'd have to have an accident."

"What was your response?"

"I just said, 'Don't be ridiculous.' " Sandra then detailed Joe's phone calls to her from Amsterdam and Zurich in August. "There was no conversation. I would pick up the phone and he would say, 'She's out again. I don't know where the children are. She's been out five nights now, different baby-sitters every night.' And then he'd hang up the phone."

"Now," Joseph said, "directing your attention to Saturday, October 24, 1987, did you have occasion to hear from Joseph Pikul that day?"

"Yes," she said. The courtroom was entirely still. "In the early evening, I received a phone call from Joe, who said he had something to hide and could he hide it with me." She then admitted that she invited him to her house, and that she drove to the Hitchcock Store, across from the phone booth he was calling from, to lead him there.

"Were you able to see anything else in the station wagon when you pulled up beside Joseph Pikul?" he asked.

"When I pulled up alongside him he had his back turned toward me. In the back of the car there was . . . it was just a big pile"—lifting her hands three to four feet apart—"sort of surrounded, and there were little things around the side that I couldn't distinguish, sort of brown like an old blanket or something.

"He said to me, 'Where can I bury it?' I was very confused at this point. I said, 'Bury what?' And he said,

'Where can I bury it?' And I said, 'Joe, you're going to have to tell me what it is you want to bury.' I suggested him getting a safe deposit box . . . and I finally became just a little short with him and I went around to the library area and sat on the floor and said to him, 'You know, you're really going to have to tell me what it is you want to bury,' and he was pacing back and forth and came over and sat down in the wing chair in the library and slumped down in the chair and put his chin on his hands and said, 'I had to eliminate her.' " Sandra paused, then rushed forth with the forbidden words: "I was very frightened."

Bekoff: "*Objection,* judge!"

"Sustained."

Joseph didn't care that Byrne had struck Sandra's assertion of fear. He wanted to highlight the defendant's damning words. "He said, 'I had to eliminate her'?"

"Yes, sir."

"Those were his words?"

"Yes, sir."

"What, if anything, did you say?"

Sandra took a deep breath to prepare for what she and the prosecutor knew would sound absurdist and self-damaging. "I said it wasn't a good place to bury anybody on my property, because of the high water table. I just had to get him out of the house."

The jury sat, unruffled and inscrutable. The lone woman juror, teacher's aide Maxine Cuciti, would later report that her reaction to Jarvinen's words was: "Only a woman who's scared to death of a man would say something as pathetically placating as that."

"During the conversations you had with Mr. Pikul [after his visit to the house], did he ever ask you what you thought he should do?" This was a question designed to set Sandra up as a law-abiding person with a conscience, after all.

"Yes," she was quick to respond. "I think the phone call from Ware—he was very confused and he didn't know what he was going to do and I said, 'Why don't you turn yourself in?' There was silence on the phone and then he hung up."

"Did you have any further conversations with Joseph Pikul on Sunday, October 25?"

"I received two calls," she said, explaining that she found them on her answering machine after she came home from work. "One was that the package was down and the other was that he had the children and he was going back to New York."

"Did he use those words, 'The package is down'?"

"Yes, sir."

The next morning, Bekoff walked over to the witness stand where Sandra Jarvinen sat, tense and prim. He had a clear goal in mind—"to wear her down, to shake her up, to show the kind of woman she really was." He started by challenging Sandra's humble description of herself as "a self-employed secretary." "Actually, what you do is, you manage money for wealthy people, don't you? So you're not just a secretary, are you? Isn't it a fact that during your marriage to the defendant, you ran his securities, met with limited partners and helped raise funds?" When Sandra demurred, he continued hitting hard. "Are you saying, *ma'am*, that you *didn't* run his securities?"

"Objection!" shouted Joseph at Bekoff's contemptuous voice.

"Sustained."

Bekoff rephrased. "Do you remember testifying in front of a grand jury? Do you remember taking an oath and swearing to tell the truth?"

"Yes." Sandra now admitted: "Eventually, he opened his own business, and I helped him with his securities portfolios."

Next, Bekoff got Sandra to admit that in early 1980, during a phone call in which they "talked and chatted about old times," Sandra got Joe to send her five hundred dollars. "Isn't it a fact, ma'am, that the reason you talked Joe Pikul into giving you that five hundred dollars was so you could sue him? Isn't it a fact, ma'am, that after Joseph Pikul sent you that money, you sued him for the alimony payments? You learned that the statute of limitations on your alimony lawsuit had already expired and by getting Joe to send you that money, you got the statute of limitations to stop? You went and hired an attorney shortly thereafter and won the case based on the fact that Joe paid you five hundred dollars to rekindle the debt?"

"I was told that I won, but the case is still not settled, to my knowledge," she said, her soft voice showing as much distaste for the attorney as he was showing to her.

Now Bekoff asked Sandra, "The defendant told you, did he not, that he was considering changing his will?" With this opening, Bekoff could proceed to imply that Sandra had a monetary motive for wanting Diane dead. Alan Joseph, who had been prohibited from bringing up the proposed change of will (to prove Diane was excluded from it) leapt to his feet. "May we approach?" Joseph asked the judge. Joseph protested that he was being "sandbagged" by the defense. Judge Byrne finally dissuaded Bekoff from pressing for mention of the will with the reminder that bringing in the will would mean bringing in Pikul's AIDS test, something Bekoff strenuously wanted to keep out.

But the striking of any mention of the will was the least important thing the bench conference produced. For, while the attorneys were busy arguing with each other, Joe Pikul walked over to the table near the witness stand to get a glass of water. "Don't let him near me!" Sandra Jarvinen whispered to the guard. The jurors seated near her heard this, and saw the look that crossed her face. Now *there's* a frightened lady, foreman Rick Temple, an engineer, remembers thinking. Juror Jack Rader, a postmaster, realized: She's *petrified* of him.

Thus, while Bekoff had his back turned, Sandra told the jury everything she wanted them to know about her relationship with Joe.

Bringing up the August to October 1987 phone calls, Bekoff next extrapolated from Jarvinen's conversations with Joe evidence of his concern for his children and his claim that Diane was sleeping with someone else. This hairpin turn from impugning a witness's credibility to suddenly using that same credibility to support his own defendant's motives was inconsistent, but Bekoff was attempting to embed Diane's alleged bad mothering and her phantom boyfriend in the jurors' minds. (In one instance this certainly was achieved. In the middle of deliberations, one juror said to another, "Let's face it; she was nothing but a pig and a whore.")

As Bekoff paced around, boring in on small point after small point, Sandra became flustered and testy. She seemed to be trying to respond with the dignity of a highborn witness in a British courtroom drama, but she couldn't keep it up. Finally, she started breathing heavily and clutching her chest. The judge and attorneys grew concerned. Joe Pikul sat, stoic. Alan Joseph rushed over. She told him that her heart was pounding—she had a slight cardiac condition—and that she thought she would faint. Judge Byrne called a recess while the star witness composed herself.

Bekoff now wanted to close his cross by establishing that she was really more complicit in the crime than she wanted anyone to think—and, by extension, perhaps Pikul was less. Through Alan Joseph's objections, sustained by Judge Byrne, Bekoff hammered away at Jarvinen's erasure of Joe's messages on her answering machine. Then he seized on her critique of Joe's proposed disposal of the body, as set forth in the grand jury testimony he had only four days ago been permitted to look at. "Didn't you say he couldn't use either of those [Berkshires] parks?"

Softly she conceded: "Yes."

"That it was a long walk from where he'd have to park his car, and that his New York license plates would be noticed?" Bekoff seemed pleased at how well he exposed the high degree of coverup thinking that seemed to have been on her mind.

The witness said, "Yes," again.

"I have no further questions," the defense attorney said.

"The People call Maggie Gari."

As Maggie approached the witness stand the same afternoon as conclusion of Jarvinen's cross-examination, all she could think about was the telephone call she'd received from Diane in late September 1987. "Joe says he's going to have me killed, and then he'll have my body disposed of where no one can find it," Diane had carefully whispered, so Maggie would hear every word. Why, Maggie berated herself, hadn't she lied and told Alan Joseph that Diane had sounded hysterical? That way, Maggie would be allowed to repeat the conversation on the stand, Diane's "excitable voice" giving her words a legal "higher reliability" than ordinary hearsay. But Maggie had told Joseph the truth, and now Joe's threats to Diane would never reach the jury's ears—unless, Maggie hoped against hope, Alan Joseph found some way to elicit them despite Bekoff's anticipated objections and get them on the record, after all.

"What was your relationship to Diane Pikul?" Joseph asked.

"She was my best friend," Maggie answered. "I never met anyone I had so much in common with. We looked at the world in the same way. We were buddies." She smiled sadly as she repeated: "We were buddies."

Joseph asked Maggie how much Diane had confided in her.

"She told me everything," Maggie said.

Joseph's several attempts to pursue this line of questioning brought objection after objection from Bekoff. A bench conference was called. It lasted fifteen minutes—excruciatingly long for Maggie, who sat still on the witness stand, aware that by turning her head to the right, she would risk eye contact with Joe. Finally, Judge Byrne ruled that Maggie's knowledge of Diane's fear of Joe, the threats he had made, and the fact that Diane did not have a boyfriend was information that could not be revealed to the jury. Alan Joseph was hardly surprised; he had really given up on getting that information in long ago, but his knowledge of its value compelled him to keep trying anyway.

Next, the D.A. pulled three Brazilian beach towels out of his rumpled brown paper evidence bag. In what was to be his final question, Joseph asked his witness if she could identify them. Maggie said she recognized them from the Pikuls' Amagansett house.

Fifteen months of sleepless nights about testifying, . . . Maggie thought bitterly, as she walked out of the courtroom, and "Yes, I recognize those towels" was all they let me say.

His attempt to flesh out Diane's fears thus stunted, Alan Joseph moved quickly through a chronology of Joe's movements after the crime. The delicatessen man, Tony Lupo, testified about the bags of ice Pikul had bought.

Barbara Weingarden testified about her phone call with Diane late in the afternoon of Friday, October 23, during which they planned an activity with the children for the next morning, and Marshall Weingarden testified about his call to Joe the next morning, during which Joe asserted that Diane had "disappeared."

When Judge Byrne called a lunch recess, the Weingardens, emotionally drained from reliving the days of Diane's murder and from avoiding her murderer, the man with whom they'd played Trivial Pursuit for several happy years, repaired to the local coffee shop for lunch. Only after they had placed their orders did they notice that Joe was in a booth with Bekoff and Worth just a few feet away. After tense whispering, they decided that it would be better to stay than risk calling attention to themselves by having the waitress cancel an order already under way. But when they saw Don and Gretchen Whitmore entering the diner with Maggie Gari and Barbara Martin, Marshall sprang up to warn them that Joe was there. The Whitmores, Maggie and Barbara found a booth as far away from Joe as they could, but their meal was impossible to enjoy, much less digest. Across the room, the Weingardens were having the most awkward lunch of their life. But Joe seemed to get through it okay, eating a hearty meal redolent of his Polish working-class origins. "I gotta hand it to you," Steve Worth remembers saying to his client. "You're the only guy I know who can stand trial for murder in the morning and still have the stomach to finish a plate of stuffed peppers for lunch."

Over the next several weeks, Alan Joseph put over two dozen witnesses on the stand, knowing he was risking overtrying his case in order to drive home the point that Joe Pikul had elaborately covered his tracks and eluded or deceived the authorities from the very beginning. The East Hampton dentist's office manager, Patricia Sarlo, described the strange message Pikul had left—about his wife's abandonment and his finding of condoms—on the dental office's answering machine. The hardware store merchant testified to the rope and shovels Pikul had purchased. Henry Sawoska spoke of Joe's bringing the children to his house and asserting he had a "terminal illness." Ann Stern picked up the story from the *Harper's* end. Five separate witnesses described Pikul's erratic behavior at the car wash. Detective John Smith of the Newburgh Police Department described his conversation with Pikul following the finding of the credit cards, and the tape recording Smith made of the phone call was played, with Pikul's nervous voice audible to all; Investigator Don Delaney and Detective Bill Glynn testified about their original Missing Persons interview with Pikul at the duplex; Detective Richie Composto told how he and Ron Finelli had come to Pikul's apartment in the early morning hours and asked him to come down to the Sixth Precinct for additional questioning; and Detective Sergeant Ken Bowen, on Bekoff's cross, admitted that the word "motherfucker" was a standard part of police slang.

Bekoff's tactic, during his cross-examinations of all the officers, was to characterize the police investigation as underhanded, cavalier and prejudicial. The jurors would later reveal that these efforts were largely successful, at least among the men.* But the physical evidence told a different story. Parading a series of minor liaison officers onto the stand (legally obliged to show a chain of custody, Alan Joseph says he "had to put every person who sneezed on the evidence on"), the prosecution established an important reverse sequence, tracing the towels, the tarpaulin and the glitter from the body to the station wagon to the Amagansett house. Bekoff's claims that the police were just looking for an easy arrest by going after Pikul would have a hard time surviving this succinct trail of evidence. Still, he and Worth rigorously relied on the classic defense accusation of sloppy and incomplete forensic work. One prime example, they stressed, was the Newburgh lab officers' failure, for technical reasons, to attempt to take fingerprints on a knife found near the car-wash dumpster.

That knife, which matched a set in the Amagansett house kitchen, was shown to the jury. At this point in

---

*Typical was the reaction of juror Doug Wade, an accountant, who, listening to Composto talk of rousing Joe Pikul, indignantly said to himself: "If a policeman came to *my* door at four in the morning, I wouldn't tell him scratch!" Only juror Maxine Cuciti admired the detectives' clever tenacity; in her view, the investigators were getting to the bottom of a vulnerable woman's disappearance, not deviously threatening a man's privacy rights.

the trial, the prosecutor's case was circumstantial, Pikul's plea was not guilty, and there had been no hint of a forthcoming tale of self-defense. As Bekoff and Worth watched each juror carefully look over the handle, blade and bent tip of this innocuous-looking item that would later be the centerpiece of their client's surprise testimony, only they and their client knew how significant this evidence would soon become.

But if Bekoff had a crucial card up his sleeve in Joe's imminent story and change of defense, Alan Joseph had a card hidden, too. Since the May pretrial hearings, he had been able to keep Bekoff from knowing that Investigator Steve Oates had *not* heard Joe Pikul's confession in the car as he and his partner drove him from Newburgh to Manhattan over a year ago. Bekoff knew that Investigator Jim Probst, sitting with Pikul in the back of the car, had heard Pikul's damning admission, "That's why I did it." This was the only one of Pikul's three confessions to police that Judge Byrne had allowed, and the statement had deprived Bekoff of his whodunit. The lawyer had lamented his hairbreadth loss of a total admissibility victory throughout the pretrial months. But Bekoff's preoccupation with what Probst *had* heard had made him forget to question what Probst's partner might *not* have heard. When Alan Joseph failed to call Oates to testify during the May pretrials, Bekoff had not been alarmed; he assumed he'd get a chance to question Oates at the trial.

When the witness list was issued, however, and Oates's name was still absent, Bekoff grew suspicious of his adversary. "I knew Joseph was hiding something from me but I didn't know what it was." Toward the end of Joseph's witness presentation, Bekoff went to Judge Byrne and demanded to know about Oates. Byrne stopped the trial while Bekoff and Joseph each privately questioned the investigator whose persistence at the Barbizon Hotel had led to Pikul's capture. When Oates said that he had *not* heard Pikul say "I did it," Bekoff became furious. He contended that Oates's testimony was Brady material, information culled by a prosecutor that is advantageous to the defense and which the prosecution is then obliged to turn over to the defense. Bekoff won the right to question Oates. But then, as he had with Sandra Jarvinen, Joseph pulled a fast one: *He* called Oates as the *prosecution's* witness before Bekoff could call him for the defense; furthermore, an incensed Bekoff realized, Joseph was intending to put Oates on the stand *before* Probst. That way, Oates's inevitable admission that he did not hear Pikul's confession would lose its punch entirely; he would merely be the prosecution's warm-up act for Probst's delivery of the key Pikul confession.

"Wait a minute, Judge—he's *my* witness, not *his* witness!" Bekoff shouted in court, just after Joseph called Oates to the stand. During a bench conference with the jury within earshot—as the burly, balding investigator sat embarrassed on the witness stand—Bekoff and Joseph had a verbal battle royale.

After sustaining so many of the defense's objections over the past month, after keeping Pikul's cross-dressing pictures, his AIDS diagnosis, his threats to Diane, his violence against Sandra, and all photographs of Diane's body out of the trial, Byrne ruled for Joseph this one significant time. He let the prosecutor put Oates on the stand. As Probst spoke Pikul's words "She was such a bitch; that's why I did it," now effectively irrefutable by Oates, Bekoff knew he could only win the case by putting Pikul on the stand. Bekoff was betting on the male jurors' belief in the existence of hysterical anger in women; and on the jurors' desire to generously respect the notion of reasonable doubt.

The most important player in Bekoff's game plan, next to Pikul himself, was Dr. Mark Taff, the forensic pathologist who had examined Diane's body. Dr. Taff had no idea how crucial he was to the defense, and it was essential to Bekoff that the pathologist not know that Pikul was going to take the stand. "A major part of my strategy," Bekoff explains, "was to present Taff with a hypothetical situation that only Steve and I knew Joe was going to testify to, and to get Taff to say 'I can't rule it out.' If Taff had *known* or even suspected the story Joe was going to tell, he would have said the scenario we presented was impossible."

Taff, a swarthy, mustached man, indeed did not know what was in Bekoff's mind when he took the stand on February 15 and 16 to answer Alan Joseph's questions.

The doctor presented a comprehensive account of how forensic clues from many organs of Diane's body led to his interpretation of her death: The bruises inside her head were consistent with blunt force trauma; the build-up of fluid in her lungs was consistent both with blunt force trauma and asphyxiation; the pinpoint hemorrhages on the surfaces of the lungs, the congestion on the surface of her voice box, the location of blood in her tongue all indicated asphyxiation; and the sequence of fractures and breaks of the different "anatomical compartments" of her neck (a chart was provided for the jury) showed "severe force" applied to the left side of the neck, in a squeezing motion, front to back.

Taff summarized: "It was my opinion that Diane Pikul sustained traumatic hemorrhages of the brain as a result of multiple—at least ten—blunt force impacts to her head. Simply said, she sustained a beating to the head area." But a beating isn't the *only* way she could have sustained those head wounds, Bekoff and Worth were thinking. Listening to Taff's conventional conclusion, the attorneys scanned the jury and tried to guess how effectively the pathologist and prosecutor were making the case that Pikul had beaten his wife to death. The jurors' impassive faces gave away little, but many of them were impressed. Using his thirty years' volunteer work as an ambulance medic to help him visualize Diane's injuries, juror Jack Rader said to himself, "Boy, Pikul really whoomped her, and he didn't stop." Doug Wade had a similar feeling, noting that "there were bruises three hundred and sixty degrees around her head."

Moving on to what would prove the most significant injuries, Taff said: "In addition, there was evidence that Diane Pikul also sustained neck injuries from being strangled, causing the injuries in her neck and in her eyes as well as the lungs." The strangulation, the doctor said, was "both manual and from a ligature." Manual strangulation was indicated by the presence of Diane's fingernail marks on her own neck (most such victims, Taff said, try to pry away their killer's hands) and by the hemorrhages on both sides of the neck. Ligature (rope or cord) strangulation was evidenced as well, in three different ways. The first: Diane's body was found with a cord tied around her neck. (That same long cord extended down to join with other cords in binding her wrists, then her ankles. "She was wrapped like a golf-club case; Joe even made a little carrying handle," Alan Joseph later remarked.) The second: Dr. Taff had found a mark on the back of Diane's neck consistent with the width of that pink plastic cord.

But there was an important difference, Taff said, between the skin under the neck binding and the skin under the ankle and wrist bindings, and this is where the third sign of ligature strangulation came in: Under the neck binding, a bruise was present; under the ankle and wrist bindings, there were no bruises. Bruises indicate that hemorrhaging has occurred, and hemorrhaging can only occur in a body that is still alive. The reason the ligatures left no marks on Diane's wrists and ankles, Dr. Taff postulated, was that Diane's wrists and ankles weren't bound until *after* her death—and probably then in an effort to contain and transport the body, whereas the bruised neck of Diane told a different story: She'd been cord-bound while alive—strangled. Hearing the explanation stop there, Bekoff and Worth felt a surge of relief and secret excitement, for they'd found a way to make that strangling not an intentional strangling—to account for the telltale bruises on Diane's neck in a different, forensically plausible way, and Joseph and Taff had just left the way clear for them to do so.

Either the head injuries alone or the strangulation alone could have caused Diane's death, Dr. Taff said. "Which death came first?" Alan Joseph asked.

Diane was probably beaten before she was strangled, the doctor replied, but the strangulation is what first caused her death because, as he explained it, "blunt force impacts do not cause a rapid death. [But] if there is sustained or even an intermittent force applied to an individual's neck, which contains very vital structures in the human body, death can be precipitated in a very rapid fashion, within seconds to minutes."

Even more than Sandra Jarvinen's " 'I had to eliminate her' " and Probst's " 'That's why I did it,' " Mark Taff's seemingly minor qualifying phrase "or even an intermittent force" would constitute the five most important words uttered by anyone throughout the entire trial.

Chapter 13

"Sometimes God runs the fastest appeals court."

Raoul Felder, June 2, 1989

When Steven Worth walked up to the witness stand to cross-examine Mark Taff, only he and Bekoff knew how critical his performance would be. The entire defense depended on his success in making the complex and interconnected forensic evidence tell an entirely different story than the one the prosecutor and pathologist agreed on.

Bekoff and Worth had worked a full year for this moment. They were about to rewrite Diane's death, but to do so, they needed first to discredit Dr. Taff, then to obtain at least his grudging assent for each separate component of their counter-scenario.

Striding in front of the jury box, his dignified corporate mein softening his pugnacity, Worth approached his first task: casting doubt on Taff's thoroughness, the police's honesty *and* the charge of ligature strangulation, whose nonspontaneous quality would not fit into a self-defense scenario.

"Now, doctor," Worth said, displaying the plastic utility cord that was found on Diane's neck. "I believe you told us that this pink ligature was found *loosely* around the neck of Diane Pikul, is that correct?" When Taff assented, Worth continued: "Now, did you determine whether or not that ligature had been loosened by any of the police?"

Taff said he thought it had been.

"Doctor," Worth asked, "this ligature has a knot in it, does it not?"

"Yes."

346

"Is it a slipknot?"

"I do not recall," Taff responded. "The analysis of knots is not usually made by me. I'm not going to pretend to be an expert in knots."

"I don't want you to be," Worth said soothingly. "You know what a slipknot is, though. We all put on ties every day. They loosen and they slip and they get tighter, right?" Worth gave Taff the ligature to inspect.

"I think this was the basic circumference at which I found the cord," Taff confirmed.

"And *this* knot was in front of the ligature?"

"Yes."

"Doctor, would you examine the knot and see if that knot will move or slip, as we know a slipknot to do?"

Leaning over the witness stand, Taff pushed one end of the cord into the knot to try to make it slip and loosen, to no avail. He shifted in his seat, took the other end of the cord and did the same. The knot did not budge. He looked diffident and slightly flustered.

"*So*, Doctor," Worth said now, pacing around a bit in measured triumph, his voice taking on an edge of innuendo, "if that knot or that ligature was loosened at the scene by any of the police, it certainly wasn't loosened by them slipping it down like that, right?"

"Objection!" called Alan Joseph to Worth's implications of evidence tampering. "The witness would have no knowledge."

"Overruled," Byrne said. "I'll allow it."

"I don't know if this was loosened," Taff said, slightly annoyed to have been cornered like this. "I don't know what the police did at the scene to loosen this ligature; I can't answer that question. I don't know."

Worth pressed down hard. "Doctor, you're in the business of reconstructing things, aren't you? Isn't that what you do for a living?" After Taff affirmed, he went on: "You examined this slipknot when you did the autopsy and you're examining it here today and *you've tried it and you can't slip this to make a bigger circumference*, can you?"

Taff took a breath, his patience clearly stretched. "No," he responded.

"And therefore we don't have to be geniuses to see that the police *couldn't* slip it to make it a bigger circumference, either. That's the circumference they *found* it at, isn't it?" Worth let the weighty inferences of police impropriety and Taff's own investigative lapse hang in the courtroom air.

"I don't know; I can't answer that question; I don't know what they found at the crime scene," Taff said, now defensive.

Satisfied that he had left doubt in the jury's mind that the ligature had ever been tight enough to strangle Diane—and that he had planted the possibility that the police had misled the inadequately curious Dr. Taff— Worth moved on to more pointedly impugn his witness. "As a medical examiner," he asked, "are you required to accurately fill out a death certificate when you perform an autopsy like you did in this case?"

"Yes."

"Did you list both manual strangulation and ligature strangulation as the cause of death in this case?"

"No, I did not."

"You listed *just* ligature strangulation, right?" Worth scanned the jury with an eyebrow cocked. In other words, the only "cause of death" listed was the one Worth had just rendered dubious?

Taff admitted this. "There was an oversight when I wrote this document."

Now that Worth had proved the forensic pathologist capable of both relying on sloppy statements from the police and of sloppiness in writing the death certificate, he was ready to move on to his counterinterpretation of the forensic evidence. The first unlikelihood to be made plausible was the matter of Diane's hemorrhaging *after* her death.

Taff had previously testified that dead bodies can't bleed. But in order to explain away the hemorrhage-caused neck bruise on Diane's neck, Bekoff and Worth now had to prove that under certain conditions bodies *can* bleed after death.

"Doctor," Worth began, "are you familiar with the term *'para mortem* period'? That means the 'period around death,' right? At the moment of death, everything doesn't absolutely at that minute shut off in the body, does it? Things continue to happen for a period of minutes, don't they?"

Taff assented.

"Doctor, would you agree with me there's a *para mortem* period involved in the death of *anyone,* is that correct? Some could be longer, some can be shorter—right?"

Taff assented.

"Doctor, isn't it possible that in this case, *immediately* after the asphyxiation occurred, the ligature was placed on the neck to use as a handle to carry the body and that *that* is what caused the abrasive mark on the neck and the hemorrhage?"

"In the immediate *para mortem* period, it's possible; however, if the scenario that you're—"

"That's what I asked you," Worth said, cutting him off. "It's *possible* isn't it?" Worth didn't want any qualifications in the transcript; if it came to a readback, he wanted those "possibles" to stand as virtual certainties.

"It's possible right after death, within seconds." But, Taff demurred, "if she's being carried like baggage, then there should be marks all around her neck. There aren't."

Worth had an answer for this. "But if the ligature was around the neck to move the body just for *a matter of seconds,* you would *not* get ligature marks everywhere—isn't that right? That's *possible,* isn't it?"

"In that scenario, it is possible," Taff conceded.

Worth addressed an easel board that had been set up next to the witness stand where an illustration of a woman's neck and shoulder area was displayed. Pointing to the bone of Diane's that had been fractured, the left superior horn of the thyroid cartilage, Worth asked Taff: "Because it sticks up all by itself, this bone lends itself easily to fracture, doesn't it?"

Taff said, "That's correct."

"Now, doctor," Worth continued, "cartilage which is pliable when we're younger ossifies and gets more brittle when we get older, right? More likely to break? That includes thyroid cartilage on the superior horn, right? And that would be true of Diane Pikul, who you agree was the stated age of forty-four?"

Taff agreed. He even added, "There was some ossification, some change with aging in her voice box."

Worth appeared grateful for this bonus.

Now it was becoming clear what the defense was doing: having cast doubt on the prosecution's ligature-strangulation theory through the use of the slipknot, Bekoff and Worth had set up parts two and three of an alternative scenario. But they still needed to use the same forensic evidence in order to establish what kind of violation to Diane's neck area had felled her so that her body would be in the position to be moved, during the very brief *para mortem* period of seconds, by way of the ligature-rigging. Worth again returned to the arena of blunt force trauma. Taff, again, was having none of it.

The two men poised for a showdown. Worth paced; Taff steadied himself in the witness stand. Worth rephrased his crucial question: "In the case of Diane Pikul, *isn't there no way to rule out* that the fracture of the superior horn was caused by a blunt force type of trauma?"

Taff sat tall. "Yes, I *can* rule that out." With blunt force trauma, he explained, there would be much more hemorrhage than had been evident. Also, "tremendous force" would be needed, evidenced by "injuries about the skin surface."

But there *had* been an injury to Diane's skin surface, Worth reminded Taff. A three-centimeter hemorrhage had appeared over Diane's carotid artery. Wouldn't the presence of this hemorrhage, Worth asked, "tend to support that there was some injury in that particular area?"

Taff had to say, "Yes," appearing to affirm the patchwork logic of the defense's scenario.

Buoyed by this key capitulation, Worth now expanded the notion of blunt force trauma to mean "either that some object hits the person *or that person hits the object* . . . right?"

"Yes."

This was Worth's crucial green light. Here came the defense's scenario: "Doctor, the finding concerning the fracture . . . isn't it consistent with Diane Pikul having come forward rapidly, being straight-armed in the neck at that location? Couldn't that—her momentum moving forward, then stopped by a straight arm with significant force—have caused a fracture of her superior horn?"

Bekoff sat very still at the defense table. Beside him, Joe Pikul looked dour and bored. Worth stood and looked at Taff, expectantly confident. At the prosecution table, Alan Joseph affected calm, but his hunched shoulders registered tension. The jurors were typically inscrutable.

Taff said, "Absolutely inconsistent."

Worth girded himself. Bekoff pursed his lips in an almost imperceptible pout.

The thyroid cartilage, Taff explained, is too far back to be the main recipient of damage.

"But," Worth said, "that's *only* if the head, at the time it makes contact with the straight arm, is perfectly dead-on"—facing the other person—"right?"

"Yes," Taff had to concede.

"But if the head was turned to the side, wouldn't that be another story?" Worth asked. He bolstered his supposition by opening and reading from a forensic source book. "Would you agree with this statement: 'With fist and karate blows to the neck, there may be severe destruction of the superior horn of the thyroid cartilage with vertical fracturing of the main portion of the cartilage'?"

Taff agreed, with qualifications.

"Are you saying to this jury that you can categorically rule that [scenario] out?"

Taff protested: "This isn't the pattern of injury to Diane Pikul."

"*Please* answer my question," Worth said, militantly.

After a decided pause, Taff said, annoyed, "I'm trying to."

"Are you saying to this jury you can *categorically* rule out that fact?"

"Yes, I can." Calmly now. "Categorically."

"Categorically?"

"Absolutely."

When Worth rephrased the question in a more qualified way, stressing that blunt force may not have been the only kind of force applied to the neck, Taff finally gave him the answer he needed. "Yes, it's possible that something like that could happen."

The attorney then got Taff to admit it was impossible for anyone to know at what point a person goes from unconsciousness to death. Now Worth had a springboard for the recitation of what would be Pikul's defense on

the matter of the ten head injuries. "Assume that someone quickly moves the body, believing it to be dead.
They pick the body up by the feet, move it over the
metal track of a sliding glass door, down several wood
steps. The body is placed in a station wagon with metal
sides, metal edges." Pointing to the medical illustration
of Diane's head injuries now positioned on the easel next
to Taff, he asked, "These injuries on the back of the
head are blunt-force trauma injuries, right?"

Taff looked at the injuries in question and assented.

"Particularly those three on the back of the head?"
Worth asked eagerly.

"Yes."

Worth pointed to another injury on the chart. "Same
with this one on the left parietal? The head turns, you
can't rule it out—is that a fair statement?"

Taff demurred at the barrage from Worth, but the defense attorney would not let up. Finally, once Worth had
rephrased the question in so qualified a manner Taff
could not say otherwise, the pathologist admitted. "I
can't rule it out within the scenario that you've painted,
but I think it's highly unlikely."

"But you *wouldn't* rule it out."

"I think it's unlikely."

Good—Taff had deleted "highly." After exchanging
looks with Bekoff, an exhausted Worth told the judge:
"This is a good place to stop."

After a year in the high weeds, Worth and Bekoff had
just successfully staged the first phase of their ambush.
They had shown that it was not necessarily beyond reasonable doubt for Diane Pikul to have sustained her neck
asphyxia and all her head injuries through a complex
and specific series of events different from the intentional
beating and strangulation claimed by Alan Joseph and
originally supported by Taff.

Returning to the defense table, Bekoff gave Worth a
quick nod of congratulation. They had done *their* work.
Now it was up to their client to save his own life.

Joe arrived at the courtroom on Monday, February 27,
"drunk," according to Bekoff, "and on tranquilizers. It
was a nightmare for Steve and me. We worried about his
condition all morning and, during lunch, poured as much

coffee into him as we could." Then, after the lunch recess, at 2:05 P.M., Steve Worth stood up in front of the jury and announced, "Your Honor, at this time the defendant will testify on his own behalf."

The courtroom was jolted. "It was a whole new trial now," juror Joe Dineen, a public relations writer for West Point, remembers. Judge Byrne's clerk Michael Schwartz says, "It sure shocked the shit out of me."

As Joseph Pikul walked to the stand, the whispers in the chamber abruptly ceased. All eyes were fixed on the defendant's broad, grim, defiant face as he swore to tell the whole truth and only the truth.

Worth, Joe's "good daddy," strode to the stand. "Joe, take your time," he instructed. "Speak nice and loud and slowly so that everybody can hear you, okay?" Bekoff, at the defense table, tried to calm himself by vowing to pin Mary Bain Pikul down to keeping Joe off the bottle between now and tomorrow, even if it meant her locking him in his room.

"Joe, did you cause the death of Diane Pikul?" Worth asked.

Joe replied, "Yes."

"Are you guilty of murdering Diane Pikul?"

"No."

"Objection!" Alan Joseph sprang to his feet. "That's a leading question!"

"Overruled," decreed Byrne.

Worth led Joe into the Story. Joe predictably assaulted Diane's hiring of baby-sitters while she worked at *Harper's*. The reasons he stated for suspecting she had a boyfriend—that she had cosmetic eye surgery, had provoked "senseless arguments" with him, and had once used the word "we" without specific reference—were feeble at best. Worth spent some time running Joe through his relationship with Sandra, stressing every incident that mocked her alleged fear of him: her back-alimony suit, their recent time together in Hyannis and Manhattan.

"I enjoyed putting the children to sleep myself," Joe contended. "*Diane didn't* enjoy doing that." He spoke of Diane's anger at him the night of Thursday, October 22, when he sent off the baby-sitter, but failed to mention that he had kept Diane from her writing class. "She became abusive and aggressive, she called me some names, and then she attempted to do something she did a lot, which was to scratch my face so I'd be embarrassed at my firm. She chased me, trying to scratch me."

Worth ran his client through his trip from Manhattan to Amagansett, trying to build sympathy for Joe's anger by grilling him on Diane's promised 10:30 arrival. ("Did she arrive at 10:30?" "No." "Did she arrive at 11:00?" "No." "How about 11:30?" "No." "Twelve . . . ?") Several members of the jury wondered why Diane's late arrival was an issue at all, especially since Joe had testified that they now slept in separate rooms, hadn't had sex since early July and were putting the house up for sale in preparation for their divorce.

Joe testified that when he brought the children to their beds from the car, Claudia, until recently asleep, suddenly "said that she had lost one of her shoes and would I help her find it." This, Joe claimed, led to a search under the bed in the master bedroom and the discovery of several GoldTex condoms, which Joe said he had never seen before in his life. The jurors appeared rapt and credulous; but many were hearing dubious elements in the defendant's story as he spoke. To juror Jack Rader, for example, the pretext for the finding of the condoms seemed clearly trumped-up; children, he knew from his own three, don't think of lost articles of clothing in the middle of the night.

"I was devastated," Joe explained of his reaction to finding the strange condoms. "I was just hurt and devastated and angry. I realized not only was Diane having affairs, but she was also bringing them back to my bedroom, which is right next to the children's room."

Joe testified that when Diane entered the house at about 1:15, "I couldn't hold it back any longer—I confronted her about the condoms. I waved them at her and I said, 'Who do these belong to? What does this mean?'"

This was a frustrating moment for Alan Joseph, who had been unable to document his hunch that, far from being an unknown brand to him, GoldTex had actually been one of the condoms Joe had been researching for Bleichroeder. To establish that link, Joseph needed Jean-Jacques, Joe's protégé at the firm. But Jean-Jacques, a worker at Bleichroeder had informed one of Joseph's assistants, was currently "somewhere in South Africa."

"What did she say?" Worth asked.

"She said, 'None of your business' and became abusive and angry."

"And did you say something to her?"

"Yes. I said, 'This means I'm going to fight you in this divorce. This is not going to be an amicable divorce. I'm going to get these children under my control. They'll live with me. I'm going to leave you broke.' " Joe said he was "very angry" and "very hurt" when he said those words and that Diane was "abusive with her language. She called me a faggot and a creep, and then she left the bedroom in a kind of rush and went to the kitchen area." Joe presented himself as passive and sanguine despite Diane's alleged heatedness and provocation: "There was nothing else to say; I was tired; I got ready for bed. I was taking my shirt off."

"What's the next thing that happened, Joe?"

"She came back in the master bedroom and I felt a pain in my back and my side towards the back and I turned and I saw that I had been cut and that she was coming at me with a knife. She had a knife up like this—" He made a fist with his right hand and held it above his shoulder. To those on the jury who had experience with knives in hunting, combat or labor, this clichéd knife-attack position seemed inauthentic.

"I moved to stop her," Joe went on. "I put my hands out and grabbed her by the neck to push her away, and I tried to struggle to get the knife away from her."

"Now Joe, when you put out your arm, what part of her did you grab?"

"I grabbed her throat and I started to squeeze her throat as I struggled for the knife."

"What did the other hand do?"

"The other hand was trying to get the knife."

"What happened during that struggle?"

"She brought the knife down. I deflected it and the handle hit my mouth and knocked out a tooth."

"Did you sustain an injury to your side as a result of where the knife had first cut you?"

"Yes, there was a long cut there."

"Joe, how long did you struggle for?"

"It seemed like seconds."

"Did she still have the knife?"

"Yes."

Bekoff, tensely observing from his seat, glanced at the men on the jury. They seemed to be going for it. But law clerk Michael Schwartz had a different assessment, based on contrasts he'd observed from working first in New York City and now upstate: the more conservative and rural the community, the less likely men are to believe that women are capable of aggressive behavior.

"Did you still have your hand on her throat?"

"Yes, I did."

"Were you squeezing?"

"As hard as I could."

"Why, Joe?"

"Because I was going to be killed."

"What happened next?"

"Well, very quickly her body went limp. The knife dropped." Joe then said he stopped squeezing her neck.

"When she went limp did you notice anything about her?"

"Yes. Her bowels let go and she vomited." Barbara Martin, sitting in the back of the courtroom, burst into tears.

"Joe, when that happened, did you think she was alive or dead?"

"Dead."

"Did you know for a fact whether she was dead?"

"No."

Worth now elicited Joe's denial that he ever punched Diane or hit her head against the wall or the floor, or that he had strangled her with the ligature. So they're going with the follow-the-dots they constructed with Taff, Alan Joseph remembers thinking. But . . . *self-defense*? Out of the blue like this? Joseph was shocked and delighted at what he considered a major defense mistake.

From the minute he realized Joe would have to take the stand, Joseph was sure the defense would be "extreme emotional disturbance": that is, when Diane admitted she had a boyfriend, Joe flew off in a murderous rage. Joe himself had set up this future defense shortly after the murder by telling the boyfriend-and-condoms story to almost everyone he encountered, eleven of whom eventually became prosecution witnesses. For Bekoff to contradict all these witnesses would put Joe's story on the defensive throughout direct testimony, not to mention cross-examination. Why, Joseph wondered, was Bekoff risking that?

Joe testified that he put Diane's body, which he thought was dead, on the bed. "I realized I was bleeding so I went into the bathroom to get a towel to wipe my wound. Then I panicked. I thought I should get the body out of the house as quickly as possible so that if my children heard anything and came in to see us, which they would, they wouldn't see Diane dead and me bleeding. I went out to the sports car and took the tarp from the back, and brought it in and put Diane's body in the tarp." Mindful that the dragging of Diane's body would have to have occurred within the short *para mortem* period in order to account for the cord bruises on her neck, Worth had Joe explain that he rushed to wrap Diane's body only because "I was fearful that my children would see this horrible scene."

When Worth earnestly prodded his client into specifying that he and no one else assembled the towels, bathrobe and belt with which he wrapped Diane, Alan Joseph felt the bitter irony of the defense's hairpin turn. He recalls wanting to shout to Bekoff, Then why the hell did you spend all that time fighting my introduction of every piece of this same evidence you're *pushing* to tie him to now?

The now well-known pink ligature, Joe said, came from under the Mazda, where it normally served as the car's tarp-steadier. Joe claimed to have "quickly" gotten the various other ropes from the utility closet because "I wanted to get the body out of the possible vision of the children." He claimed not to remember how he tied every one because "I was in shock."

This is more preposterous than any of the statements he made to the police! Alan Joseph remembers thinking. "Here he's said the whole thing happened in seconds and he's too shocked to know what he's doing. But he's got to make all these extremely calculated trips to the car, to the utility closet, all over the place. . . ." The contradiction of a dazed state of mind on the one hand and the complex, methodical body-wrapping on the other was inconceivable to the prosecutor.

Following the outline set forth with Taff, Joe now explained that he "pulled Diane by the legs down the hallway to a sliding door on the side of the house." While doing so, the metal track connecting the sliding door to the floor and outdoor steps made of railroad ties had come in contact with Diane's head. "I went down the deck stairs and then went down another flight of stairs and I put Diane's body in the station wagon. I came back in the house and took some cleaning material from the utility closet and cleaned up the blood and the vomit."

"What's the next thing you did?" Worth asked Joe.

"I wrote a note to Claudia and left the panic button by the note and told her I was going out for a short while."

"Joe, when this incident happened with Diane, why didn't you press the panic button yourself?"

"I was afraid that the police would come and wake the kids and they'd see all this disaster, their mother dead and me bleeding, and be terrified."

Joe said that he put Diane's body in the back of the station wagon and drove to Little Albert's Landing. "I took a raft from the car to the water's edge and I took Diane's body to the water's edge." He put a five-pound barbell on the raft with "the idea of leaving her in the water with the weight weighing her down."

"Did you put Diane's body in the water?" Worth asked.

"No."

"Why not, Joe?"

"I couldn't let go of Diane."

Joe explained that, when the children awoke, he told them their mother "had gone out to see one of her friends." He admitted throwing away "incriminating" items at the town dump to cover his tracks, and as Worth led Joe through his recitation of the next twenty-four hours, lawyer and defendant paused over every witness to whom he'd told the disappearance story. Joe claimed he lied "to cover his tracks" so his children wouldn't be taken away from him.

To counter the prosecution theory that Joe had the body of Diane in the car with the kids when he set out on his odyssey, Worth elicited from Joe that he went back to Little Albert's Landing to try once again to bury Diane in the sand but that "I couldn't let her go, because it would break up the family." Several jurors later reported working hard to keep their faces impassive at this remark.

Joe claimed that, after leaving the body buried in the sand at the beach, he drove off with the children, first to the Sawoskas', then to Sandra Jarvinen's. He denied ever using the words "I had to eliminate her" to Sandra, claiming, instead, that he told her, "I had to kill Diane because she was trying to kill me." He described a visit to the grave of his father and grandmother, going on at some length about his respect and love for these people and the insights he derived from meditating at their graves.

Bekoff and Worth needed to frame Joe's disposal of Diane's body in a positive light. Joe had gotten rid of the body out of fatherly concern—"I didn't want Diane's body to be in the car when I picked up the children." An element of hopefulness was also brought in when Joe said, "The work week was beginning, the school week was beginning, I had decided to live. I wanted to take care of my children. I love them so much."

When news of these words got back to Diane's friends, they were aghast and wildly frustrated. "Joe had portrayed himself as the good father during the custody hearings," recalled Ann Stern, "but this was much worse. The jury was almost all men, and none of Joe's craziness and violence, which did get into the custody hearings, was told to them." "Can juries believe self-serving statements like this?" Maggie Gari asked Mary O'Donoghue. "Juries," Mary replied, unconsolingly, "can believe anything." Most upset of all was Linda McNamera. One night, responding to buzzing on her apartment doorbell, she found a process server who handed her a subpoena. Diane's final confidences would now be wrested for Joe's purposes. Linda had just been called as a hostile witness for the defense.

When, on the third day of his questioning of Pikul, Steve Worth moved to put two photographs Investigators Venezia and Tripodo had taken of Joe on the night of his arrest into evidence, the jury and spectators were sharply attentive. Throughout the trial, Judge Byrne had barred from evidence emotionally charged photographs that would have aided the prosecution. The jury was not allowed to see any pictures of Diane's body, for example—although Alan Joseph once left one on the jury ledge, "accidentally," he claimed, until the judge admonished him to remove it. But Judge Byrne apparently felt the pictures of Joseph Pikul which revealed a gash mark to the side of his back were crucial to the defense's case, so he allowed them to be admitted. Bekoff and Worth seemed both tense and confident as each juror silently studied the photographs, their faces betraying nothing. This was the defense's best shot.

Right after the day's adjournment, Alan Joseph called Joe Tripodo. "What about this slash on his body?" he asked the senior investigator. "Did you ask him where he got it?"

"Of course I asked him where he got it, you think I wanted him to be able to claim *we* did it?" Tripodo answered. "He said, 'Playing ball.' " Tripodo and Joseph agreed that that's what it looked like from the picture: a healed-over scratch from chasing a ball into a rosebush. Now Joseph just had to hope that the jury would come to the same conclusion.

Opening his cross on Thursday morning, Alan Joseph hit the ground running—determined, before anything else, to set the record straight on Joseph Pikul as the "devastated" father and loyal husband. Neatly twisting Joe's statement that he "didn't want to let go of her" from a family man's lament to a motive for murder ("Isn't it a fact that *that's* why you killed her, because you didn't want to let go of her?"), the prosecutor fired off a volley of accusations:

"Isn't it a fact that you told her if she left you, you would have her killed, dispose of her body so it would never be found?"

"No."

"Isn't it a fact that most of the verbal abuse in the marriage came from *your* end *to* her?"

"No."

Bekoff: "Objection, Judge!"

Byrne: "Sustained."

"Isn't it a fact that the 'senseless arguments' were the result of things *you* started?"

"No."

"Isn't it a fact Diane Pikul never disappeared on numerous occasions, that *you* would disappear with the children without her knowledge?"

"No."

"Isn't it a fact that you felt threatened by her because she was asserting her independence?"

"No."

"Isn't it a fact that you were jealous of Diane over the years? You even accused a mutual friend of yours of being her boyfriend nine years before the homicide?"

"No."

"Isn't it a fact that you even went so far as to hire a private detective because you believed she had a boyfriend?"

"I did that one or two days."

"Isn't it a fact that as a result of that investigation you knew she didn't have a boyfriend?"

Bekoff: "Objection, Your Honor!"

Byrne: "Sustained."

"Isn't it a fact Diane Pikul didn't take forty thousand dollars out of your account?" (Joe had testified to this on direct.) "It was fifteen thousand dollars for expenses, not forty thousand?"

"*Forty* thousand, Mr. Joseph," Joe said, in a deep, firm voice. Now that Mary—on Bekoff's stern orders— was keeping Joe sober, some of his previous authority had returned. Then Alan Joseph switched gears. Suddenly the combative prosecutor seemed almost obsequious, dangerously lost in meaningless detail as he walked a clearly impatient and arrogant Joe Pikul through every pace of the homicide and its immediate aftermath: closet by closet, gesture by gesture, ligature by ligature.

Diane's friends were concerned. Where was the bombast of Raoul Felder now that they needed it? "Joe is having Alan Joseph for breakfast . . ." was the tense refrain making its way from *Harper's* to Grace Church School during the weekend that followed the first two days of Alan Joseph's cross-examination.

But there was method to the prosecutor's new tone, as would be proved on the last day of the cross-examina-

tion. Intent on getting Joe to explain every motion he
made, Joseph took care to elicit from Joe that he had
"cradled" Diane's dead body from the bed onto the tarpaulin—that detail would have significance soon. And
Joseph was culling signs from Pikul that the self-defense
story was concocted long after the crime; chief among
these was Joe's telltale zeal every time he came to a place
in his story where "proof" of a knife wound could be
worked in.

The most specific Joe got about the results of his alleged knifing was that blood was "coming out of" his
wound and that, because of this, he had wrapped a towel
around his waist. But why hadn't that towel come unfast-
ened while he was attending to Diane's body? And
wouldn't such a wound have severely limited the defendant's mobility? These unanswered questions hung pointedly over the proceedings.

Having said, on direct, that he'd thrown all "incriminating" items away at the town dump, Joe was now so
eager to prove that the bloody towel existed that when
Joseph asked him what else he had thrown away he said,
"and the towel, and the towel, and the towel, yes."
When Joseph asked him about the whereabouts of the
knife (whose later presence in the car-wash garbage did
not bolster his story), Pikul sidestepped the question by
responding, "There wasn't a lot of rhyme or reason to
the things I was doing, Mr. Joseph." And despite remembering little else about rope placement, Joe repeatedly stressed that the ligature he'd placed around Diane's
neck had been a "loose" one.

The defendant was becoming testily self-righteous
under the prosecutor's detailed questioning. At one
point, when the issue of Diane's skirt buckle was introduced, Joe said sarcastically, "I was struggling for my
life, Mr. Joseph. I wasn't about to make observations
about whether something was buckled or not."

Here was the perfect moment for Joseph's long-pre-
pared, full-scale attack on Joe's version of events. "Isn't
it a fact that you tied a knot around Diane's shirt so you
could pick her up by the knot and the waistband to take
her out of the house? And by doing so the clips on her
waistband spread apart?"

The spectators snapped to attention; this was certainly new information.

Joe said, "No. I didn't do it that way."

"Are you telling us you never hit, punched or struck Diane Pikul on Saturday, October 24, 1987?"

"Absolutely."

"Isn't it a fact that you punched her in the rib area?"

"No."

"You heard Dr. Taff testify that there was a ten-centimeter hemorrhage on the muscles of the eighth, ninth, tenth and eleventh ribs—do you remember that?"

"I don't recall that, no."

Now Joseph turned on his heels dramatically, ready to nail Joe with his own testimony. "Isn't it a fact that Diane Pikul's body was wrapped, as you described it— her hands tied, her arms down to her side protecting the rib area so that *there's no way that a bruise could have occurred unless you punched her or struck her?*"

"I did not punch or strike her. I don't know how that got there."

"Isn't it a fact that you struck her in the left cheek area?"

"Mr. Joseph, I didn't touch my wife."

"Isn't it a fact that you struck her twice above the left eye?"

"I didn't hit her at all."

"Isn't it a fact that you struck her twice on the right temple area?"

"No."

"Isn't it a fact that you struck her once on the left temple area?"

"I didn't strike her once, Mr. Joseph."

"Isn't it a fact that you repeatedly struck her, eight to ten times?"

"Objection, Judge!" Bekoff rose to his feet. "How many times does he have to answer the question the same way?!"

"Overruled," said Byrne. "I'll allow it."

"I didn't touch Diane once, Mr. Joseph," Joe said.

But the prosecutor wasn't about to let up. "Isn't it a fact that you struck her head against objects to cause those back three hemorrhages?"

"No. I didn't intentionally do that. It happened when I was dragging her."

"It didn't happen when you were strangling her?"

"I didn't strangle her. What do you mean?"

"When you had your hands around her neck? Did you strike her head?"

"No."

"Isn't it a fact that you argued, you punched her about the face and head, you banged her head and then you choked her with both hands, thereby strangling her and asphyxiating her?"

Worth: "Objection!"

Byrne (after a brief bench conference): "Overruled."

"Isn't it a fact that you took that pink cord and, just to make sure she was dead, you wrapped it around her neck and squeezed and pulled?"

Worth: "Move to strike that, Judge!"

Byrne so ruled, but Joseph pressed on: "Mr. Pikul, isn't it a fact that Diane Pikul never had in her possession the knife on October 24, 1987?"

"No."

"Never came at you with the knife, as you testified?"

"No."

"Isn't it a fact that you're covering your tracks, just as you did with the condoms?"

"No."

"You're telling us you had no conception as to what self-defense was on October 24, 1987?"

"Not in my moment of panic, no."

"How old are you, sir?"

"Fifty-four."

"Fairly well educated? Went to college? Graduate school? Traveled the world?"

"Yes."

Joseph left the inference to dangle as he then walked Joe through his sleepless and labyrinthine drive to shelter the children, cover his tracks and dispose of the body. In this version, Joe claimed to have left Diane's body in the sand of Little Albert's Landing before driving the children to the Sawoskas; then going back to Long Island and digging her up between his trip to Sandra Jarvinen's and his return to New York City. Under Joseph's questioning, Pikul's newest tale seemed a bizarre string of round-the-clock snacks and track-covering pay-booth phone calls.

After tracing Joe's contacts over four days with the string of police officers, Joseph paused to ask Joe if he'd "ever told any police officer that your wife had cut you, had attacked you with a knife: Detective Glynn, Investigator Delaney, Detective Sergeant Bowen, Detective Composto, Detective Finelli, the East Hampton police, Investigator Oates, Investigator Probst, Investigator Tripodo or Investigator Venezia?"

"No," Joe answered.

He explained away his statement to Tripodo Jr.—"My wife tried to kill me *not physically but mentally*"—by saying: "The first part of the statement, that she tried to kill me, was true. I was going to tell the truth and I was crying and I turned and saw Joe Tripodo, Jr., waving to somebody and I realized that he was not my friend but a detective doing his job so I followed it with that other statement."

In the very last moments of the three-day-long cross-examination, two important things happened. First, Joe attempted to deal with the prosecutor's assertion that Diane's rib injuries could not have happened through dragging, as he had claimed earlier. Now, at zero hour, Joe tendered an alternative explanation for the ripped and knotted garments in evidence. Instead of having "cradled" her dead body off the bed and onto the tarpaulin, "on further recollection, Mr. Joseph, I thought that lifting her by her skirt and blouse was probably how it happened."

"I see," Joseph noted, playing strongly to the jury. "*Days later,* you now recall you didn't cradle the body. . . ."

Beyond these last-minute issues, Alan Joseph had another seed of doubt to plant with the jury. To this end, his very last question to Joe seemed, on the face of it, arbitrary and curiously irrelevant. Displaying a picture of the Amagansett house guest room—within which was a tall and commodious armoire previously acknowledged in court—he asked Joe: "And that picture does in fact depict, in fair and accurate fashion, the guest room that you were staying in?"

Seeing the picture of the room again, several members of the jury later reported they instantly understood the message Joseph had been telegraphing: "Joe had that *armoire* to keep his clothes in," as foreman Rick Temple later put it. "So he didn't have any reason to go into the master bedroom to change his clothes that night." And it was while undressing in the master bedroom, Joe had claimed, that he'd been attacked by Diane.

"Yes," was Joe Pikul's final word on the stand. That is precisely how the guest room looked that evening.

Alan Joseph said, "I have no further questions."

There were now just a few important matters left to deal with before the case went to the jury. The first was the prosecution's rebuttal of the defense's claim that Diane had stabbed Joe. To this end, Alan Joseph put a surgeon named Jerome Quint on the stand to testify that the photographed gash on Joe Pikul's side could not have been made from a knife. Worth went after Quint aggressively, citing as suspect his professional work with the police. Would that make the jury deem Quint a noncredible expert witness? Diane's friends were worried.

Linda McNamera, the lithe *Harper's* advertising assistant, had a bigger fear, however: her forced appearance as a witness for the defense. She had honored the subpoena only because the alternative was a court citation for contempt. She mounted the stand, her waist-length hair tied back conservatively. Speaking softly to questions put to her by Ron Bekoff, Linda testified that Diane had said she had gotten angry with Joe the night before her death when he had prevented her from attending her writing workshop, and had run after him down the street. This *proved* Diane's fury and aggressiveness, Bekoff claimed to the jury.

If Joe is found not guilty, Linda thought as she dismounted the witness stand, how will I ever know it wasn't because of what I said?

The last witness called was Joseph Tripodo, Sr. The Troop F senior investigator took the stand on March 10 and testified to Alan Joseph that Pikul confirmed he had strangled his wife the night he was arraigned. "You choked her," Tripodo said he stated to his prisoner, whereupon Joe had nodded yes and, at Tripodo's gentle prodding, had demonstrated the choke with his two hands.

The defense had no intention of letting this devastating testimony stand. When Ron Bekoff stood and began his cross-examination, he pointedly reminded the investigator that Pikul, earlier, had claimed that *Tripodo* was the one who had made the choking motion. The implication of police coercion filled the air.

Tripodo digested this accusation calmly. Over his three decades of police work, he had learned—and now often told his son Joe, Jr.—that the best thing to do when provoked on the witness stand was to avoid getting ruffled, to simply state the truth without rancor, as clearly and briefly as you could. He took his own advice now. In answer to Bekoff's contention, he said, "Mr. Pikul is lying."

On that note, the prosecution rested on rebuttal. So did the defense.

Bekoff approached his summation with a three-part agenda: to characterize the prosecution's case as desperate and empty; to encore the refashioned forensic scenario as the true star witness of the defense; and to implant in the male jurors' minds the strong image of Diane Pikul as a creditable and narrowly thwarted murderess.

Starting with the first item on his agenda, Bekoff scoffed that Alan Joseph's long case was not only "wholly circumstantial" but pointless. Since Pikul had confessed, Bekoff claimed, "*all* this evidence, their four weeks of showing who [committed the act] is irrelevant." Joseph's overwrought case had proved nothing else, he claimed; and Joseph, a "desperate man doing desperate things," had had to resort to an untrustworthy star witness in Sandra Jarvinen and, in rebuttal expert witness Dr. Jerome Taff, a man whose pushy certainty Bekoff likened to "a used car salesman who once sold me a lemon." Bekoff paused and joked, "What I wanted to do to that [car salesman]—*talk* about manual strangulation." With his attitude of condescension and contempt, Bekoff made the point that Joseph's case was pathetic.

What wasn't pathetic—what was the heart of the matter—was the forensics report, reworked through Worth's cross-examination of Taff and Pikul's subsequent testimony. The prosecution's claim of "ligature strangulation just doesn't make sense," Bekoff reiterated. Instead, those ligatures had been applied to Diane's body by Joe solely for the purpose of tying the five-pound weights on her during his aborted attempt to bury her off the shore of Little Albert's Landing. "Dr. Taff went on to say that manual strangulation is the main cause of death; we agree with that," Bekoff said, reasonably. "But it doesn't necessarily mean the classic two-handed wrap around your neck." Leaving that thought for the moment to deal with Diane's head wounds, Bekoff reiterated the defense proposition that all the banging to Diane's head had occurred not from Joe's fists but from his transporting her body from the house to the car.

Reminding the jury that it cannot be known when a person has slipped from unconsciousness to death, Bekoff said:

Diane *could have* been alive when removed by Joe, who because of the body's turning limp and the releasing of the bowels *thought* that she was dead. And even if Diane was dead, that doesn't mean that those marks to the head couldn't have happened—because of *para mortem,* where the body doesn't shut down after death.

You want to know what the key testimony was? Steve Worth got up here and said: Let's assume, Doctor, that Diane Pikul was coming towards Joe Pikul, that he used one hand to straight-arm her, he squeezed her neck hard for a short time with one hand,* he wrapped the body, dragged it out of the bedroom over door tracks down approximately seven steps and forced it into the back of the station wagon. Remember, ladies and gentlemen?! What does Dr. Taff say?

After a dramatic pause, Bekoff repeated the words his colleague had relentlessly coaxed from Dr. Taff: "His exact words: 'It's unlikely, *but I can't rule it out!*'" Bekoff was the picture of confidence. He was standing at a major take-off point in his career. If he won his client an acquittal, or even a conviction on a reduced charge, like Ira London had for Joel Steinberg, then perhaps his creative and sophisticated manipulation of the forensics would be heralded as an effective, controversial defense.

*Neck squeezing was not part of the scenario Worth detailed to Taff.

But to win the case, more than anything else Bekoff had to make the jury view Diane as a woman capable of, and motivated to, homicidal rage.

Bekoff closed his summation by reminding the jury of Linda McNamera's testimony and appealing to what he assumed were these men's contempt for insubordinate women:

> Diane was so physically aggressive the night before. She chased him down the street, physically. I wonder if she was bragging? And this over a baby-sitter leaving early! If she went crazy over a baby-sitter, imagine what happened when Joe hit that raw nerve: "I'll fight you on everything; I'll get the kids; *you'll be alone and broke.*"? When Joe said that, she couldn't take it and he killed her. If Joe didn't do that now, he'd be dead and there'd be a different trial. But he did do it. He protected himself and he saved his life.

From her seat in the back of the courtroom, Maggie Gari scanned one male face after another on the jury as Bekoff spoke these words. Were they believing his story? Had they believed Joe on the stand? To Maggie, who grew up in a small city ringed by farmland, not unlike Goshen and Newburgh and not unlike the South Bend of Diane's youth, these jurors in their 1950s haircuts and short-sleeved button-down shirts looked familiar, decent. One or two of them could have taken her—or Diane—to the high school prom. But Maggie and Diane had rejected those boys and run from those provincial hometowns in pursuit of more glamorous destinies. Would these men on the jury dare to see her best friend's fate objectively—or had they already prejudged Diane as a smart-mouthed pseudo-sophisticate who got what she deserved?

Starting his summation, Alan Joseph reminded the jury: "You don't have to go home and worry about whether you made the wrong decision. If you felt that the evidence spoke the truth, then it *is* the truth. *You* don't convict this man; his actions, his deeds in the early morning hours of Saturday, October 24, 1987—*that's* what convicts him."

From this soothing beginning, Joseph grabbed the of-fense, calling the claimed knife attack "a defense born after hearing and seeing the strength of the People's case, an attempt to tailor the facts to support a version that might aid him in beating the rap."

Shrewdly turning his opponents' stinging cross-examinations to his own purposes, Joseph continued:

> It's not the police who are on trial here, not Sandy Jarvinen, not Diane Pikul; it's the *defendant* who's on trial. I submit to you the police's search for the truth was hampered only by the defendant's actions—by his lies to them, his coverup. His arrest was no easy arrest.
>
> Think about his need to explain away the injuries that Diane Pikul suffered. Think about the fact that the defendant—even when he says he's tired, worn down, isolated—never tells his self-defense version to *one* of the ten or more police officers he speaks to. Not only that, he doesn't show anybody the scratch on his side.

In pointing out other inconsistencies, Joseph said that, despite Joe's repeated claim of having found the unfamiliar condoms of the "lover," "we find nine more of the same brand in the defendant's condom drawer in the bedroom."* Next, Joseph submitted his theory of why Diane was murdered:

> Diane Pikul is now gaining her independence. She's got a job at *Harper's*. She's struggling to get on her feet, to make a life for herself. She's getting ready to sue for divorce and custody of the children. The defendant objected to all this. We told you through

---

*Jury foreman Rick Temple would later say he was relieved to have this point finally cleared up. He'd been waiting throughout the trial for Joseph to indicate whether or not Pikul had been lying when he said he'd never seen GoldTex condoms before, but the prosecutor had never stated this. Alan Joseph had, however, implied that the GoldTex were almost certainly Pikul's since GoldTex was sold only in Europe and since Pikul had gone to Europe for the expressed purpose of researching condoms. Temple anticipated confusion in the jury room as to whether the jurors could infer that Pikul had lied about the condoms being his. "So when Alan Joseph said those words in summation, I could stop worrying about that."

Sandy he did not want Diane Pikul to have custody of those children. Yet remember Diane's ace. She had proof that Joseph Pikul was a transvestite* and that such knowledge might prevent him from gaining custody of his children.

So he makes the decision to eliminate her. With Diane dead and never to be heard from again, he has the children all to himself. The evidence of his cross-dressing remains a secret, locked in Diane's divorce attorney's vault.

I submit to you: That plan might have worked if Diane Pikul's body had never been discovered.

After the homicide, he formulates his plan for disposing of the body, just as he attempts to justify killing Diane by concocting the presence of these condoms under the bed. The boyfriend comes out of thin air.

But in order for his plan to work—in order for his coverup to succeed—he's got to distance himself from Diane's body. He goes to Massachusetts to find a place, yet for whatever reason he doesn't find a suitable location. So he dumps the body off the New York State Thruway. If William Heller had not been out there checking drainage culverts, we probably would not be here today, for by the time Diane Pikul's body was discovered, if at all, it would have been so badly decomposed it would have been nothing but a bag of bones.

From their far-apart seats in the courtroom's spectator section, Mary Bain Pikul was frowning with deep skepticism at Joseph's version of events, while Maggie Gari struggled to hold back tears.

*Although Judge Byrne had ruled that the cross-dressing photographs of Pikul were inadmissible, he allowed mention of cross-dressing to the extent that it applied to Joe's motive for killing Diane, and that line of questioning had been pursued in Alan Joseph's direct examination of Richie Composto. When Joseph here substituted "transvestite" for "cross-dresser," Bekoff objected to what he considered the more negative word. A brief bench conference followed; then Joseph continued his summation.

"The defendant told you he caused Diane's death," Joseph now said, moving to the crux of the Murder Two charge. "The only element you have to determine is: Was that intentional?" In other words, did Joseph Pikul have enough time to know what he was doing when he was manually strangling Diane . . . and, therefore, to decide whether to keep going or to stop? Joseph took a stopwatch and invited the jurors to experience for themselves just how long forty seconds, the length of time required for manual strangulation, really was.

"Objection!" Bekoff called. "He [Taff] never said forty seconds; he said thirty!" So thirty seconds it was. As Joseph held the stopwatch, the courtroom was silent as the seconds ticked slowly by until the full half minute was up.

The next morning, Wednesday, March 15, Judge Byrne charged the jury with deciding if Pikul was guilty or not guilty of either second degree murder, first degree manslaughter, second degree manslaughter or criminally negligent homicide. The eleven men and one woman entered the jury room to deliberate Joseph Pikul's fate. The trial had been long and complex, and juries in recent major murder cases—Chambers, Steinberg and Howard Beach, for example—had taken six to ten days to reach their compromised verdicts, with threatened or (in the Chambers trial's case) actual deadlocking along the way. So Alan Joseph, Ron Bekoff, Steve Worth, Joe and Mary and all of Diane's friends settled in for a long wait.

In the jury room, the eleven men and one woman who had not spoken to each other about the case in six weeks took a virgin vote. Foreman Temple collected the small squares of paper and began to tally them. Guilty, guilty, guilty, guilty, guilty . . . Temple was nervous. We can't decide this thing in ten minutes! he said to himself. He was relieved, however, when two of the jurors voted not guilty. Good—now we can have discussion, he thought.

Discussion yielded an important fact that might have surprised the trial watchers: Not one single juror had believed Pikul's self-defense story. The story had seemed clearly implausible and invented, and several of the jurors who knew weaponry had made up their minds, even before and apart from Dr. Quint's strong assertion, that the knife the defense displayed could not have made that size and kind of cut on Joe's waist. Juror Doug Wade, a seasoned outdoorsman, spoke for the others as well when he said, "Those attorneys didn't know: You can't fool a country boy about a knife."

Thus from the deliberation's outset it was never a question of whether Joseph Pikul was guilty, but *what* charge he was guilty of. The jurors called for the diagrams of Diane's head wounds, the tarpaulin and the ligatures, and took turns playing Joe and Diane in beating, strangling and body-wrapping role-plays, while they considered the absence or presence of Pikul's intention to kill.

Of the two original "not guilties," one was a particularly adamant man who'd had an experience in his youth that haunted him still and had great relevance to the case. As a teenager, he had been in a fight and had nearly killed another boy—by strangulation. "When you've got someone's neck in your grip you just blank out, you get into this blind rage—you *do not* know what you're doing," he said to the other jurors, again and again. Much of the heated talk during the first day of deliberation consisted of the other jurors trying to disabuse the holdout of his views.

The next morning, a read-back of Dr. Taff's direct testimony cleared the point up. Dr. Taff had said that thirty to forty seconds of "even intermittent" pressure on a neck would cause death. Back in the deliberation room, the point was clear: If someone's hands could release from a victim's neck and then resume squeezing, the strangler clearly had the faculties to *decide*.

When Judge Byrne received word, just fifteen minutes after that read-back, that the jury had reached a verdict, Joseph Pikul and Ron Bekoff were in the arbitration room upstairs from the courtroom, playing cards. So soon after that read-back . . . ? Bekoff thought. This cannot be good.

When the jurors marched back out, they were taken aback by how packed the courtroom was—and by the television lights. The local stations and networks, whose cameras were only sporadically present during the weeks of testimony, were in full force to record the event.

"How do you find the defendant on the charge of murder in the second degree?" Judge Byrne asked Rick Temple. "Guilty or not guilty?"

"Guilty," Rick Temple said.

Joseph Pikul, emotionless throughout his trial, leapt to his feet, distraught. Bekoff and Worth looked staunch and grim. Mary Bain Pikul rushed to her husband's side. She would soon, however, regain her composure and, within days, leave for a business trip abroad.

Joe was led away to the jail in handcuffs. He faced an eventual sentence that ranged from fifteen years to life. Alan Joseph broke the good news to a gratified Don Whitmore and told him that he would soon be consulted on his wishes for the sentencing.* When Diane's friends in Manhattan were called minutes later, they were euphoric. Recalls Maggie Gari, "It was as if the world had just turned right side up and and we could finally believe in the system again." Ann Stern put it this way: "After a year and a half of watching one unbelievable legal break after another come Joe's way with a surreal ease, those twelve people cut through the absurdity we were all living through and dared to say that the emperor had no clothes." The women spent the next day, St. Patrick's Day, celebrating. In Yonkers, Mike and Kathy O'Guin gently broke the news to the children, to whom the finality of judgment seemed a relief from the painful ambiguity and wrenchingly torn loyalties they had long endured. Mike O'Guin told Donald Whitmore, "Now we can begin."

The sense of closure and celebration would soon prove premature. As with every prior turn in the case, the right and logical thing would, even when finally legal, not stay fixed for long.

On Tuesday, April 18, as Joe sat again in the Orange

*Whitmore eventually told the Victims' Impact Unit of the Orange County Probation Department that he wanted Joe's prison sentence to last until Blake Pikul was eighteen years old so that both children would be safe from any subsequent custodial claim Joe might make. As is now custom in victim-crime felony cases in many jurisdictions, this request was then tendered to Judge Byrne, who was expected but not bound to take it into consideration in determining sentence.

County courtroom awaiting his sentence, Ron Bekoff announced that there was "new evidence," recently found by Mary Bain, which directly related to Joe's self-defense testimony. Bekoff requested a postponement of sentencing until the evidence could be presented in the form of a petition to set aside the guilty verdict and ask for a new trial; Byrne agreed.

The jurors, having unanimously rejected self-defense from the outset, were stunned; some were appalled. The "new evidence" turned out to be the tape recording Joe had made of the fight he'd provoked with Diane in late August 1987 in Amagansett. In the fight, Diane was vituperative and mocking. "As 'new evidence,' it was pathetic," Alan Joseph said later.

During his trial, Joseph Pikul had appeared to be in good health. Except for the first day of his testimony, when tranquilizers and liquor had dulled his speech, he appeared calmer, hardier and more grounded than during his hyper and ill-kempt appearances at the custody hearings a year before. He read the papers, played cards and chatted with his attorneys with little sign of anxiety. But by the end of May, Joseph Pikul's health was deteriorating rapidly. When Ron Bekoff visited him at the Orange County jail, he was stunned by how wan his client looked, by how much weight he had lost.

On Friday, June 2, in haste and secrecy, Joe Pikul was transferred from the Orange County jail to the nearby Arden Hill Hospital. Mary rushed to his side. She could see her husband fading, but, she later said, "he was still the wonderful Joe I had known, being loving and wonderful, making jokes." It was during this meeting, Mary says, that Joe told her he had AIDS.* Three hours later, he died. There was speculation that Joe, with Mary's help, had committed suicide, but a coroner's examination made clear that the cause of death was AIDS.

After a funeral at St. Joseph's Catholic Church in

---

*Mary denies that this disclosure made her angry. And it did not make her worried because, "after all, we did not plan to have children," she says, alluding to the fact that precautions were taken that would ensure safe sex. Still, taking no chances, Mary got an AIDS test. The results were negative.

Greenwich Village, Joe was buried in the cemetery next to the Amagansett house where he had killed Diane.

Six months later, on December 5, 1989, Joe's conviction was vacated because he died before he had the chance to appeal. Had he lived, Joseph Pikul would have served, Alan Joseph believes, twenty-five years to life. Instead, he died a technically innocent man. Like her life—with its richness, vitality, vanity and grave errors of judgment—Diane's justice was something only the stubborn memory of those who cared about her could insist ever happened at all.

Afterword

Since Joe Pikul's death in June of 1989, these developments have occurred:

The Money

Joe Pikul's destructiveness proved to have been financial as well as emotional and physical. Right after he murdered Diane he began rounding up his assets, and by the time a lawyer was finally brought in to look after Blake and Claudia's interests (in March 1989), he had spent or secreted all that he had. According to that attorney, Diahn McGrath, who has already donated $100,000 worth of legal work in an effort to hunt down and fight for monies for the children:

• Soon after the crime, Joe liquidated by mail his Swiss bank accounts and most of his stock accounts. Indications are that the Swiss accounts held less money than people expected—$100,000 at best. McGrath believes much of this money went to Joe's first attorneys, Dawson and Clayman. The Mexican bank accounts Joe had boasted of apparently did not exist.

• Joe's estate still owes the IRS $150,000 for 1986 alone. He never filed for 1987 or 1988. After murdering Diane, Joe forged her name to several income tax and stock forms.

• The high-premium life insurance policy for which Diane had a physical examination before the Far East/Scandinavia trip in the fall of 1986 has not been found. Either it was never purchased or it has lapsed.

• The children received $46,000 from Diane's *Harper's* life insurance policy.

• The house in Amagansett has not been sold, its notoriety as a murder site having discouraged buyers.

• McGrath is currently pursuing about $20,000 worth of further assets for the children, including closely held stocks and the cemetery plots. And in an effort to recover money for the children, she has been battling the following principals:

Ron Bekoff

Claiming that Joe had paid him only $75,000 up front and promised him the $180,000 left from the bail money as the balance of his defense fee, Bekoff brought suit in Nassau County Supreme Court to have the bail money turned over to him, enlisting the aid of Armand D'Amato, the powerful attorney brother of U.S. senator Alfonse D'Amato. Diahn McGrath fought in two courts to block Bekoff's claim. Finally, the parties negotiated a settlement: McGrath withdrew her claim in return for a guaranteed $30,000 for the children; Bekoff kept the $150,000 balance.

Mary Bain Pikul

Just before Joe's death, Mary befriended Sukhreet Gabel, who, as Judge Hortense Gabel's hapless daughter, had been the hub of the notorious Bess Meyerson alimony-fixing case. To Diane's friends, the bonding of the two (they clutched each other and wept for the news photographers at Joe's funeral) made perfect sense. "It was one of those times," said one of Diane's friends, "when life seems to imitate *Saturday Night Live*."

At the time, Sukhreet was friendly with a conservative securities lawyer named Kenneth H. Chase. In March 1990, however, in a secret ceremony, Mary Bain Pikul married Chase. Sukhreet Gabel angrily bewailed this turn of events to the gossip columnist of the *New York Post*.

Mary filed an election for the one-third of Joe's estate to which she would be entitled as his wife. She offered to drop her claim on Joe's estate when Diahn McGrath dropped her suit against Bekoff. To date, however, according to Diahn McGrath, Mary has not dropped her claim.

Mary Eik Bain Pikul Chase says she and her newest husband are looking forward to starting a family of their own, and that she misses Blake and Claudia very much. Her own daughter, Jennifer, still resides with Stephen Bain.

Paul Kurland

Joseph Pikul's custody lawyer represented both Mary Bain Pikul Chase and Ron Bekoff in their above-described legal claims on Joe's estate.

Sandra Jarvinen

The back-alimony debt that had kept Sandra connected to her first husband for so long continued after his death; like Bekoff and Mary Bain, she threw her legal hat in the ring of claims against Joe's estate: Her attorneys filed a claim for $45,000. In return, she was served with a multimillion-dollar wrongful-death suit by Diahn McGrath on behalf of the Pikul children. Sandra claims she was shocked and upset by the suit. The suit was dismissed in May 1991. Two months later, Sandra relinquished her claim on the Amagansett house, an act that Diahn McGrath terms "commendable."

Sandra considers herself a formerly battered woman and is affiliated with a businesswoman's charity group aiding battered women. She has been in psychotherapy to try to understand the events of her life from the summer of 1987 on.

The Effect of O'Guin v. Pikul on Custody Law

Unfortunately, the lessons learned from this landmark case have not been translated into policy or legislation. A 1988 New York State Assembly bill that simply stated that "domestic violence is contrary to the best interests of children and is evidence of parental unfitness for custody," and which would have thus circumvented the need for a child to have actually *witnessed* an attack by one parent on another before that violence could be considered relevant to custody determination, was defeated by the State Senate. It is being refashioned for reintroduction.

The legislation fashioned by Bob Wayburn, by which the close relatives of a victim of spouse-murder would be able to petition for custody of the children on an equal legal footing with the murderer/parent, did not even receive sufficient city sponsorship to get to Albany. Ironically, some resistance to it came from women's rights advocates who saw it as potentially punitive to those battered women who, after years of being victims of abuse, finally lash back and kill their spouses.

The National Center on Women and Family Law and the Illinois Center on Women and Family Law, two nonprofit feminist legal groups, successfully fought Illinois's *Lutgen* decision all the way up the appellate court system. The U.S. Supreme Court, however, refused to hear the case. Shortly after his release from prison in early January 1989, an Illinois newspaper pictured a smiling James Lutgen adjusting to life as a single father, making breakfast for the little girls who had watched him kill their mother.

Blake and Claudia Pikul

Diane's children have bonded deeply with Mike and Kathy O'Guin and consider them in every way their parents. All parties were joyous when the adoption became final in 1990. In a legal change of appellations that speaks poignantly for the embrace of the new and the honoring of the past, Claudia is now Claudia Diane Whitmore O'Guin and Blake is Blake Joseph Whitmore O'Guin. Their lives are happy and normal.

On August 1, 1991, New York County Surrogate Eve Preminger ruled that the vacating of Joseph Pikul's murder conviction eliminated proof that he intentionally killed Diane, thus paving the way for his estate to be able to inherit from hers. Diane's estate was entitled to pursue a hearing to prove that Joe was indeed guilty as charged and convicted—that his killing of Diane had not been in self-defense. Without such sufficient proof, Joe's creditors would be entitled to claim what little was left in Diane's estate. Diahn McGrath has requested a jury trial in Surrogate Court on the question of Joe's criminal intent.

The dates October 23-24 are quietly commemorated every year by Diane Whitmore Pikul's friends. Maggie Gari believes that if Diane had lived she would now be with her children in a Colorado or Long Island community with good public schools: struggling financially but making strides in her writing. Pat Jaudon imagines the letters, and Ann Stern imagines the conversations, and Allan Gurganus imagines the short stories of this Diane as entertaining as ever, their arch irony replaced by a truer sophistication and the relaxed wisdom that comes from having tried the hard thing and having survived, perhaps to some extent even triumphed.

She is sorely missed for the woman she was—and for the woman she was on her way to becoming.

ACKNOWLEDGMENTS

Maggie Gari was a new friend of mine when her best friend, Diane Pikul, whom I'd met at a party at Maggie's, was murdered by her husband in October 1987. In the midst of her grieving, Maggie encouraged me to write about the tragedy. "Find and tell the whole story," she said. "There's no one else I'd trust with Diane's memory." Maggie gave me her best friend and became one of mine in the process. I'm grateful beyond words for the former—and lucky beyond words for the latter.

Our dear friend Laura Berzofsky was the linchpin of volunteer efforts to protect the Pikul children. She drafted the petition, researched the issues, and organized the demonstrations with her typical heroic refusal to give in, even an inch, to adversity.

Ms. magazine's Mary Thom first saw value in my perspective on the case. She and Gloria Jacobs expertly edited my "Middle Class Murder" (March 1988), through which publisher Anne Summers wished to reach—and warn—other wives of violent husbands.

Ellen Levine did a beautiful job of landing me a book contract. Her ceaseless nurturance of this project—and its often frazzled author—has been simply extraordinary.

Joni Evans and Susan Kamil "got" my idea for the book as perhaps only a female publisher and editor could. Susan's impatience with the melodramatic, the overexplained and the imprecise saved me from my lesser self through all five hundred manuscript pages.

My insistence on making this book about a person, not a crime, led to my great reliance on Diane's friends, present and past. Barbara Martin, Pat Bartholomew, Linda McNamera, Carina Jacobsson, "Gloria Archer," Doug Thompson, Ralph Eric Schnackenberg, Barbara and

Marshall Weingarden, the late Doug Johnston, Mary Beth Whiton and Jamie Kamph had crucial insights and memories. Ann Stern Gollin, a person of sublime quality, was ongoingly helpful. Eleanor Lamperti brought alive the teenaged Diane, and the now farflung members of Diane's South Bend Camp Fire Girl troop led me further back—not just to the girl who no longer exists but to a nostalgic America. Poet Elizabeth Henley and the magnanimous Pat Jaudon gave me what no interviews could match: Diane's own voice, conveyed through her writings.

My many dozens of conversations with everyone who had a hand in the apprehension, prosecution and defense of Joe Pikul, and in the custody hearings, lead to just as many thanks, as well as to great appreciation of their callings. Among the skilled, gallant police team, thanks in particular to Bill Glynn (the West Village's answer to Philip Marlowe), Joe Tripodo, Sr., Bob Venezia, Steve Oates, and especially to Don Delaney, who mentored me on police investigation with generosity and fervor.

My comradeship with Raoul Felder goes back to December 1987. His outrage then and humanity throughout were as authentic as his menschiness. Bob Wayburn patiently gave me a two-year tutorial in American custody law; my debt to him is enormous. Paul Kurland, Ron Bekoff and Steve Worth granted me time and candor in describing their skillful defense tactics. Alan Joseph detailed every inch of his winning prosecution and answered my staggering number of questions. Michael Schwartz, Orange County Criminal Court's raconteur emeritus, walked me through the intricate chess game that is a murder trial. The "Pikul Jury Six" shared the drama, and the humor, of their deliberations.

The Northern Indiana Historical Society, the National Center on Women and Family Law, and the *New York Law Journal* were valuable resources. Sharing their expertise were: Smithers' chief Ann Geller; Mount Holyoke College's head archivist Patricia Albright; Harvard Medical School's Dr. Eli Newberger; Manhattan chief ADA Mary O'Donoghue, Ann Jones, foremost author on battery, and Dr. Penny Grace—three powerful crusaders with senses of humor; Barrister's Dennis Kitchell, attorney Cynthia Schreiber, St. Christopher–Ottilie's Dr. Leonard Gries; and my therapist friends Michael Berzofsky and Sydney Goldenberg. In a different capacity, Sydney—and Jean Furukawa, Barbara Umanov and Michelle Margan—proved the fact that a working mother's biggest lifesaver is something called the playdate. And to my friend dating back to *Coast* magazine: thanks for the favor.

Gratitude to: Steve Sheppard for his elegant legal fighting, Frank Curtis for his supportive counsel, Susan Bell for her deft editing, Patty Meyer for her TV production savvy, Diana Finch for the magazine sale, Karen Rinaldi for her troubleshooting, Beth Pearson and Chris Stamey for their ready red pencils. Special thanks to the immensely astute Lesley Oelsner.

Helen Weller, my mother, and Elizabeth Weller Fiman, my sister, were endlessly supportive, and unstinting with their talents as hardy veteran newspaper reporter and superb contract lawyer. Eileen Stukane, Carol Ardman and Mark Bregman were there for me, as they've always been, over twenty years of irreplaceable friendship. Suzanne Kelly, adored chum and confidante who is also my stepdaughter, was a perceptive reader.

Inexpressable thanks go to Dr. Fred Wolkenfeld.

This book could never have been written without the loving indulgence of the two guys I live with. My husband and best friend, John Kelly, was a wise anchor, a lodestar of professionalism and a tolerant captive audience to my anxiety. He also paid for the errors of my ways—more than figuratively. Our son, Jonathan Daniel Kelly, understood why I was often too distracted to pay attention to his re-creation of Rickey Henderson's latest slide—and shouting for him to lower the sound on Hulk Hogan's tirade so I could finish a paragraph. His forbearance came from his compassion, which I'm so very proud of.

Finally, I wish to thank Diane's family. In March 1989, Don and Gretchen Whitmore took me into their home and, through two days of recounted memories, a generic Florida retirement community gave way to the innocence and moxie of the Midwest in the twenties, thirties and forties. It was a bit like *It's a Wonderful Life,* with pelicans. Then Don put me on the plane back to New York with a scrapbookful of every single picture, report card and lock of hair he had left of his only child. Trust like that disappeared with the Studebaker.

Thanks, too, to Kathy and Mike O'Guin—and their indefatigable attorney, Diahn McGrath—for allowing me to quote from Diane's short stories, in whose images of the late sixties in downtown New York I found more than a little of my own history.

Over the past four years, my mind has often gone back to the woman who wrote those stories, whom I met at Maggie Gari's afternoon party in July 1987. She looked strained and preoccupied during the hours she chatted with me and the other women seated around that metal table with the umbrella in the middle while our children played around us. There was little trace in her face of the former beauty I would later discover in so many pictures. She seemed to be impatiently wondering what she was doing there, the way people do when some obsessed-over condition makes every foray a secret escape-attempt that is ultimately futile. She said things about her husband—"He doesn't like that I work"—that seemed entirely too private to share with brand-new acquaintances. Odd, I thought, interpreting that phrase as a gaffe, not an SOS. In fact, Maggie had been telling me how this best friend of hers had a husband who had threatened to kill her if she left him; but I didn't realize Maggie's best friend was the woman I was making small talk with that day, nor did I believe that those threats were more than hyperbole. Husbands don't kill their wives, I assured myself. Not the people that *we* would know.

"My friends, who are women, tell me stories, which cannot be believed and which are true. They are horror stories and they have not happened to me. . . . Such things cannot happen to us, it is afternoon and these things do not happen in the afternoon," Margaret Atwood wrote, in the poem whose title I have taken for this book, precisely expressing my distance, that balmy afternoon, from the condition of the woman sitting next to me.

Now that that distance has been closed, I think back to what Diane said when Maggie introduced us. They were five unremarkable words, referring to how our mutual friend had described me, but they've since acquired a second, haunting meaning.

"Oh yes," Diane said. "You're the writer."

Neither of us had any idea how true that would turn out to be, and in what sadly different context.

New York City, October 1991

Index